FRENCH PRESIDENTIALISM AND THE ELECTION OF 1995

French Presidentialism and the Election of 1995

Edited by
JOHN GAFFNEY
LORNA MILNE

Ashgate

Aldershot • Brookfield USA • Singapore • Sydney

Published by
Ashgate Publishing Limited
Gower House
Croft Road
Aldershot
Hants GU11 3HR
England

Ashgate Publishing Company
Old Post Road
Brookfield
Vermont 05036
USA

British Library Cataloguing in Publication Data
French presidentialism and the election of 1995
   1.Presidents - France - Election - 1995 2.France - Politics
   and government - 1981-
   I.Gaffney, John, 1950- II.Milne, Lorna
   324.9'44'09049

Library of Congress Cataloging-in-Publication Data
French presidentialism and the election of 1995 / edited by John
   Gaffney, Lorna Milne.
      p.   cm.
   Includes bibliographical references and index.
   ISBN 1-85521-567-5 (hardbound)
   1. France–Politics and government–1981-1995–Public opinion.
2. Public opinion–France. 3. Mass media and public opinion-
-France. 4. Presidents–France–Election–1995. 5. France–Social
conditions–1945- 6. Presidential candidates–France–Attitudes.
I. Gaffney, John, 1950-   . II. Milne, Lorna.
DC423.F745   1997
324.944'0839–dc21   97-22278
                                    CIP

ISBN 1 85521 567 5 (Hbk)
ISBN 1 84014 086 0 (Pbk)

Printed and bound by Athenaeum Press, Ltd.,
Gateshead, Tyne & Wear.

In Memoriam
Peter Morris, 2.9.46 – 1.2.97

CONTENTS

ACKNOWLEDGEMENTS

We are indebted to a number of people and organisations who have helped to fund, research, organise and prepare this project for publication. In particular, we would like to thank the Nuffield Foundation whose grant allowed members of the research group to assemble documents and to travel to France. In addition, we are grateful to the Aston Modern Languages Research Foundation for grants and support which allowed contributors to meet to discuss the project; and to the Association for the Study of Modern and Contemporary France, which helped to fund a one-day conference on the presidential election in May 1995. Aston University's Institute for the Study of Language and Society provided an ideal environment in which to pursue our research. Of the many individuals who contributed to the project, we especially wish to thank Julie Ramsden, Administrative Assistant to the Institute; Christophe Texier for work during his tenure as the Institute's Research Assistant; Wendy Firmin of the Department of Languages and European Studies, Aston University, for collecting and cataloguing our audio-visual resources; Ian Henderson for his help in preparing the manuscript; and Dartmouth Publishers for general encouragement and assistance. Finally, it is the editors' privilege to thank our colleagues and contributors for their positive cooperation in preparing this volume.

John Gaffney and Lorna Milne

LIST OF PRINCIPAL ABBREVIATIONS

ANPE	Agence Nationale pour l'Emploi
AREV	Alternative Rouge et Verte
CDS	Centre des Démocrates Sociaux
CES	Convergence Ecologie Solidarité
CFDT	Confédération Française Démocratique du Travail
CFTC	Confédération Française des Travailleurs Chrétiens
CGC	Confédération Générale des Cadres
CGPME	Confédération Générale des Petites et Moyennes Entreprises
CGT	Confédération Générale du Travail
CIE	Contrat Initiative Emploi
CNCL	Commission Nationale de la Communication et des Libertés
CNI	Centre National des Indépendants
CNPF	Conseil National du Patronat Français
CSA	Conseil Supérieur de l'Audiovisuel
CSG	Constitution Sociale Généralisée
EC	European Community
EMS	European Monetary System
EMU	Economic and Monetary Union
ENA	Ecole Nationale d'Administration
EU	European Union
FEN	Fédération de l'Education Nationale
FLN	Front de Libération Nationale
FN	Front National
FNS	Fédération pour une Nouvelle Solidarité
FO	Force Ouvrière
GATT	General Agreement on Tariffs and Trade
GDP	Gross Domestic Product
LO	Lutte Ouvrière
MDC	Mouvement des Citoyens
MEI	Mouvement des Ecologistes Indépendants
MEP	Member of the European Parliament
MPF	Mouvement pour la France
MRG	Mouvement des Radicaux de Gauche
NATO	North Atlantic Treaty Organisation
NSM	New Social Movement
PCF	Parti Communiste Français
PR	Parti Républicain
PS	Parti Socialiste

PSU	Parti Socialiste Unifié
PUE	Parti Ouvrier Européen
RPF	Rassemblement du Peuple Français
RPR	Rassemblement pour la République
SFIO	Section Française de l'Internationale Ouvrière
UDF	Union pour la Démocratie Française
UDR	Union des Démocrates pour la République
UIMM	Union des Industries Metallurgiques et Minières
UNR	Union pour la Nouvelle République
USSR	Union of Soviet Socialist Republics

1. INTRODUCTION

JOHN GAFFNEY AND LORNA MILNE

In 1995, and for the second time in the course of the Fifth Republic, a presidential election took place during a period of 'cohabitation' between the Socialist President François Mitterrand and a right-wing coalition government, installed after the legislative elections of 1993. For a range of reasons, however, the 1995 election was fundamentally different from the last such occasion in 1988. Most importantly, it was clear that the President would not seek re-election, and the general sense of Mitterrand's failing health and declining power raised public expectations that 1995, by closing the Mitterrand era, would also bring about some sort of renewal of the political scene. Such hopeful predictions of a political watershed were heightened by mass-produced media clichés which stereotyped as *fin de siècle* decay the very real problems facing the political community and society at large: evident fractures within practically all of the political parties and alliances; France's continuing economic difficulties; the 'exclusion' from full economic and social participation of those on the margins of society – the unemployed, the homeless, immigrants, Aids sufferers; and the poor reputation of the political classes following a series of corruption scandals. In addition, the profile of certain potential candidates in the early build-up to the election seemed to promise a highly creative – or else viciously destructive – contest of unprecedented vigour: Jacques Delors, returning from a triumphant period of office in the European Commission, looked for a time as though he might secure the renaissance of a weakened left; the rivalry between Jacques Chirac and Edouard Balladur – close friends for the previous thirty years according to the prevailing view – threatened to bring about an irreparable split on the right. Long before the nine candidates who actually ran for office were declared, the columnists, speculators and commentators looked forward – as their vocation demands – to a glorious fight. In the event, the battle was judged by many to be less spectacular and less bloody than anticipated – partly because this very anticipation so raised the stakes for both right and left that much of the real contest took place away from the public gaze, in corridor conspiracies and back-room betrayals. But the man who won, Jacques Chirac, had, from the beginning, announced himself to be the candidate of 'reform' and 'hope and, therefore, change'. Undoubtedly, Chirac's electoral programme proposed economic, social and political reform: however, the question remains as to whether the election of 1995, its progress and its outcome really altered the shape of politics and the presidency in the Fifth Republic in the radical way which the early media build-up implied.

Any assessment of the extent of 'renewal' in 1995 requires an understanding of the essence of the regime as a whole. In 1958, de Gaulle was brought back into French politics as the saviour of the nation, to resolve the Algerian crisis and re-establish the authority of the French state. The emphasis upon his exemplary status and authority to act at this time was extraordinarily strong. His election by the electoral college of 80,000

MPs, Senators and councillors was a formality, but such restricted suffrage was an inadequate provision for the future stability of a regime which was so personalised – not only in the sense that its foundation relied heavily on the personality of one individual, but also in that its constitution now afforded the potential for the President to assert a high degree of personal authority and power over the legislative and executive bodies. Yet despite his usual boldness, de Gaulle had, in 1958, shrunk from introducing into his new regime the hallmark of Bonapartism, the direct election of the President by universal suffrage. By 1962, with the resolution of the Algerian crisis, the regime was just stable enough for him to risk introducing such a measure. The new constitutional amendment was put into practice in 1965 with the first direct election of the President in a contest between de Gaulle and François Mitterrand. With this, the election of the President became the central event of the institutional process in France, the 'presidentialisation' of daily politics being the inevitable result, for it suddenly became imperative that all political families, organisations, parties and factions identify and promote their potential 'présidentiable' in order to cultivate political ambition and credibility. In this way, and aided significantly by the media, especially the new medium of television, the personalisation of the regime's politics flowed through every level of political life, and the election of the President became – and remains – an event which parties, politicians, voters and commentators all acknowledge (consciously or unconsciously) as a constant influence over choices and activities throughout French politics. Presidentialism is, of course, both reflected in and affected by electoral campaigns and the election itself: any modifications to the central institution of the Fifth Republic inflect developments throughout the polity and are therefore of fundamental significance to French party politics in general and to the country as a whole. It is against this background that our study locates the presidential election of 1995.

The research project which gave rise to this book thus grew out of two essential principles: first, that an understanding of French presidentialism is crucial to a sound grasp not only of what happened in 1995 but of French politics and society in general; and second, that if such an understanding is to be widely achieved, it is important to provide reflective academic analyses to counterbalance the great quantities of instantaneous journalistic comment which are offered by the mass media on the occasion of an election.

The resulting volume will, we hope, have uses for all those students and colleagues who are interested in French politics and society. It is composed of a series of essays by political scientists, historians and other specialists on France, and it treats some of the most important aspects of the election in 1995 in the context of France's presidentialism. The range of topics covered is not exhaustive, nor is there a concerted attempt to impose a uniform style on the various chapters in order to give the impression of a 'single voice' narrative of the election. Nevertheless, close contact and discussion amongst contributors has allowed for the development of complementary contributions which, though distinctively individual in their style and approach, arise out of the same essential desire to study aspects of the 1995 election with a view to broader and more lasting analysis. It is hoped that the reader will enjoy the variety of approaches adopted and that the juxtaposition of different methodologies will be appreciated as an advantage of this inter-disciplinary project. At the same time, there is of course a need for a factual and narrative framework in a volume of this kind; this imperative informs each of the chapters, and a chronology is provided as a summary of the key dates and incidents of the election which are analysed in depth elsewhere.

Chapters 2 to 4 of the book address the context of the 1995 election by explaining how presidentialism emerged in the Fifth Republic, and by examining the legacies of history, of previous leaders, and of France's constitutional arrangements. The second part of the volume focuses on the events of 1995. An exhaustive analysis of the vote provides an appraisal of 1995 and of its significance in relation to previous presidential elections. Chapters on the polls, on television coverage of the election and on the funding of campaigns describe and evaluate the constraints and opportunities created for the candidates by legal regulation and publicity of various kinds. These chapters also give an idea of the extent to which the atmosphere in which French voters went to the ballot box was dominated by the media. The authors of individual studies of the candidates record the key themes and incidents of each campaign and assess the effects of the campaign on the political constituencies represented by the candidates. In addition, the specialist interests of external affairs, business and the trade unions are considered in separate chapters documenting the influence of the election beyond the political classes to diplomatic and socio-economic actors. By studying the moment of the presidential election in this way, the matrix of inquiries, each focusing upon a different aspect of the presidential phenomenon, offers a comprehensive view of the central feature and organising principle of politics in the Fifth Republic.

2. PRESIDENTIALISM IN FRANCE: A HISTORICAL OVERVIEW

PETER MORRIS

Introduction

The importance of the Presidency to an understanding of contemporary French politics is obvious. Ever since 1958, when General de Gaulle and Michel Debré assumed the role of Founding Fathers of the Fifth French Republic, the office has dominated the national political landscape.[1] Each of the five Presidents – Charles de Gaulle (1959-69), Georges Pompidou (1969-74), Valéry Giscard d'Estaing (1974-81), François Mitterrand (1981-95), and Jacques Chirac (1995-) – has been able to decide the main themes in France's domestic and foreign policy agenda. The presidency has become the institution around which national political life is organised and is the supreme prize in party competition. It is true that between 1986-88 and 1993-95 the powers of the then President were curtailed by the existence within the National Assembly of a majority made up of his political opponents. Yet even in these two periods of what has become known as 'cohabitation', the President's adversaries did not try to deprive the incumbent Mitterrand of all his influence, particularly in the foreign policy sphere; still less did they risk damaging the status of the office by forcing him to resign. Such restraint demonstrates the legitimacy which the office of President has acquired in the Fifth Republic. The ambition of de Gaulle and Debré to make the presidency the 'cornerstone' ('clé de voûte') of the French political system has been largely realised. To the question 'who rules in France?' the conventional – and, except in the circumstances of cohabitation, correct – answer is 'the President of the Republic'.

The reasons for the emergence in the Fifth Republic of a strong presidency are complex and cannot be limited to an enumeration of the formal powers granted it by the 1958 constitution. We shall see in this chapter that the contributions of historical traditions, individuals and circumstances are also important, and so too is the constitutional amendment of 1962 establishing the direct election of the President. In words that have acquired near canonical status, Maurice Duverger wrote of the 1962 amendment that 'it gave the President no new powers, but it gave him power'.[2] Henceforth the President possessed the political authority which derives from a national mandate. In voting for their President, the French are choosing the man (the gender qualification is, so far, unavoidable) who will govern France. At a time when public confidence in the integrity and competence of politicians is very low, opinion polls – and the high turnout at presidential elections – demonstrate strong levels of approval for the proposition that the presidency should be a powerful institution.[3] None of France's major political parties, with the exception of the fast declining Communists, seeks to weaken the authority which the presidency derives both from the powers granted it in the 1958 constitution, and from the democratic mandate it possesses.

Thus the directly elected presidency has become a central element in France's claim to be a democracy. In France, as elsewhere, the theory and the practice of democracy have a long history, several meanings and many critics. In the nineteenth century, conservatives denounced democracy as synonymous with mob rule, while liberals feared its consequences for individual liberty. Marxists have argued that universal suffrage, unless accompanied by common ownership of the means of production, is no more than a weapon with which the bourgeoisie can assure its domination of the exploited classes. In our own day, when liberal democracy is regarded by many commentators as the only viable form of political organisation, its claims have as much to do with the protection of the individual's rights against the power of government as with the People's right to choose its governors. Yet all definitions of democracy include the free choice by the adult citizens of a polity of their lawmakers and governors; and in this respect France became a (masculine) democracy much earlier than was the case in other European states. In 1789, the French Revolution proclaimed that political sovereignty rested with the People and that laws and governments were only legitimate if they derived from popular choice. The French did not achieve full electoral democracy overnight: the road from the formal assertion of popular sovereignty to universal suffrage was a long one, not reached – so far as women were concerned – until 1945. But by the mid-nineteenth century (far earlier than in the United Kingdom) the principle of universal male suffrage, and thus of the democratic basis of government, was established. In 1848, the new Second Republic established universal male suffrage for elections to the National Assembly and for the Head of State; the Second Empire of Napoleon III (1852-70) based its authority on a series of national plebiscites; and the constitutional laws of the Third Republic (1875) confirmed that all males over 21 could vote in elections to the Chamber of Deputies, which was one of the two houses of the French Parliament.

France's history as a political democracy includes, however, a problem which is central to any discussion of the contemporary presidency. In the United States, the idea that the President, as head of the Executive power, should be elected by universal suffrage was accepted very early as an integral part of the model of political democracy created by the American Revolution. In France, by contrast, the nineteenth century champions of the democratic principles of the 1789 Revolution came to regard a powerful Head of State, and in particular one elected by universal suffrage, as incompatible with political liberty and the sovereignty of the people. It is true that in 1848, the constitution of the Second Republic introduced direct elections for the Presidency as well as the National Assembly. They did so, however, out of fear of social turmoil rather than out of a belief in the ability of the presidency to represent the national will; and we shall see that the experience of the next few years placed an insuperable ideological barrier between a powerful, directly elected President and the theory of Republican democracy. The constitution makers of the Third (1875-1940) and Fourth (1946-58) Republics refused to countenance not only a presidency based on the ballot box, but one possessing the sort of independent powers available to the American President.

Given that hostility to a strong presidency had become an entrenched part of the political culture of French democracy, it follows that a radical transformation in the constitutional and democratic status of the office must have taken place since 1958. An institution which was for long regarded as a standing threat to the safety of French democracy is now celebrated as its principal instrument. The purpose of this chapter is to describe, and explain, the transformation. The first section examines why the defenders of democracy came to fear a strong President, and analyses the 'Republican model' of the presidency which resulted. The second considers the attempts made before 1958 to increase presidential authority and the reasons for their failure. The third explains how the Fifth Republic was able to overcome the prejudice against a powerful, and directly elected, President and to construct the presidential model which exists today.

Republican democracy and the rejection of a strong presidency

The enduring tension between a powerful Head of State and a democratic polity began with the rejection by the makers of the French Revolution of the historic claim of the French kings to embody State sovereignty in their person. To this extent, 1789 mirrors the rejection of the monarchic absolutism of James II by the English Parliament a century earlier. But the ambitions of 1789 were much greater than those of the Glorious Revolution. Whereas the architects of the latter had sought merely to affirm the parliamentary basis of certain acts carried out by the Crown, and claimed, in so doing, that they were restoring the traditions of the balanced constitution, in Revolutionary France the goal was to replace the Divine Right monarchy of Louis XVI with a new political order founded on the Rights of Man and the sovereignty of the Nation. In the words of the revolutionary leader quoted in Claude Nicolet's study of French Republicanism: 'Our history should not be the basis of our political order'.[4] From the outset, the office of Head of State was regarded with suspicion as a potential threat to the aims of the Revolution. The constitution voted by the National Assembly in 1791 preserved the monarchy as head of the Executive but deprived it of its law making powers.[5] Less than two years later the monarchy was abolished and the king executed; and the 1793 constitution establishing a Republic declared that the only political institution with the authority to represent the sovereign Nation was the Legislature. Herein lay the beginnings of what in the nineteenth and twentieth centuries became the aversion felt by democratic Republicanism to a powerful Head of State, an aversion which in time would give rise to an Assembly dominated regime (the 'régime d'Assemblée').

In the decades of constitutional instability which followed the Revolution, and which saw France experiment with a variety of regime forms, the model of politics identified with a Republic and the sovereignty of the Legislature was frequently challenged. Groups on both the extreme right and the extreme left rejected the model, the former calling for a return to the Divine Right monarchy of the Ancien Regime, the latter advocating one version or other of a proletarian regime. Neither of these alternatives was ever put into practice, although the restored Bourbon king Charles X (1824-30) made efforts to revive the claims of the pre-1789 monarchy, and the Paris Commune of 1871 provided Europe with its first, short-lived, example of a workers' state.

Two other challenges to the Republican model did, by contrast, have a strong impact on French constitutional and political life. One was the Liberal model of mixed government known as Orleanism, after Louis Philippe, king of the French (rather than of France) between 1830-48. In accordance with the principles of nineteenth century constitutional liberalism, the Orleanist system acknowledged that Parliament was the law maker and that the monarch could not veto its decisions. But Orleanism did not accept the Republican thesis that Parliament should be elected by universal suffrage – regarded as synonymous with mob rule – and it firmly believed that the monarch had a role to play in the governing of the country. Louis Philippe saw himself as supreme arbiter, appointing ministers on whom he could rely to respect his political judgement and regarding them as responsible to him at least as much as to Parliament. In this respect, Orleanism differed from the nineteenth century British model of parliamentary government in which ministerial responsibility was to the Legislature rather than to the Crown. There was thus an inherent tension within the Orleanist regime between the rights of Parliament and those of the Crown. Louis Philippe was overthrown in 1848; but the Orleanist model of mixed government did not disappear with him and would play an influential role in the constitutions of the Third and Fifth Republics.

The second challenge to the Republican model of Assembly democracy came from the plebiscitary government of Napoleon I (1799-1814) and, above all, his nephew Napoleon III (1851-70), who was elected President of the Second Republic in 1848, as we have seen, and who seized power by a military coup in 1851. What came to be known as Bonapartism insisted that only a powerful Head of State could provide France with the strong government it needed and that in consequence the role of the Legislature needed to be severely controlled. Yet there was a basic difference between the Bonapartist theory of power and that of traditional monarchies in that the Head of State's legitimacy depended not on an inherent, or ascribed, right to rule, but on the approval of the nation expressed via plebiscite. It was thus possible to regard Bonapartism, as the nineteenth century English constitutional expert Walter Bagehot acknowledged, as a democratic creed.[6] This view was, however, unacceptable to the champions of the Republican model of French democracy. They condemned its rejection of the parliamentary basis of law; its disregard for civil liberties and the rights of political opposition; its recourse to the anti-Republican imagery of Cæsarism (both Napoleons were crowned emperor); and, above all, its denial of the claim of the National Assembly to be the instrument through which national sovereignty was expressed. French Republicans never forgave Louis Napoleon for the coup d'état of 1851 in which he overthrew the Second Republic. They drew from it the lesson that a directly elected President was a permanent threat to Republican democracy.

Napoleon III was no more successful than Louis Philippe in putting an end to France's constitutional instability. His regime collapsed in ignominy in 1870, after its armies were defeated by Bismarck's Prussians at the Battle of Sedan. There followed the brief, but bloody, civil war known as the Commune and a four year period of constitutional limbo during which a monarchist-dominated National Assembly, elected by universal male suffrage in February 1871, laboured to establish a new regime. The result was the series of constitutional Laws voted in 1875 which created the Third Republic.

It was during the Third Republic that a 'Republican' model of the constitution was constructed, whose major characteristic was a presidency lacking the power to control France's policy agenda and the authority to challenge the political pre-eminence of the Legislature. The Third Republic has always, and correctly, been regarded as an Assembly regime in which the President was reduced to the position of constitutional figurehead. Between 1875-1940 there were thirteen Presidents of the Republic. None of them features in lists of France's great men or acts as a role model for today's political leaders, and some of them, notably Paul Deschanel (1920) and Albert Lebrun (1932-40) have become caricatures of presidential incompetence. The remark of the Radical politician Georges Clemenceau (1841-1929) that the presidency was as useless as the prostate gland is one of the most ubiquitous clichés in analyses of the political system of the Third Republic. We will see below that there were ways in which Third Republic Presidents could influence policy and political outcomes. But the conventional analysis of a Presidency subordinate to the Legislature cannot be challenged.

To understand why this should be so, it is necessary to look beyond the constitutional laws of 1875. For the point about those laws is that they were voted by a National Assembly, the majority of whose members were conservative gentlemen appalled by the social upheaval of the 1871 Commune and much more fearful of Republican democracy than of Executive authoritarianism. 1875 was thus a compromise between conservatives who had hoped to establish a constitutional monarchy (and still believed that one might be possible) and Progressives who believed that the constitutional laws, for all their democratic shortcomings, did at least establish a Republican form of government. The two groups were separated by social class and political conviction. Yet they shared a fear of the revival of plebiscitary Bonapartism and of social radicalism. The former led them to reject a Head of State elected by universal suffrage; the latter produced a set of constitutional laws which certainly did not aim to render the President powerless. The 1875 laws established a bicameral legislature in which the Upper House (known as the Senate) was chosen by a highly restricted electoral college dominated by rural conservatives and was intended to act as a brake on the democratically elected Chamber of Deputies. The same desire to constrain the excesses of electoral democracy can be seen in the institution of a presidency possessing a raft of powers. The President was Head of the Armed Forces; he had the right to negotiate and ratify treaties; he appointed the government and all military and civil offices; he had the right to initiate laws; and he was empowered, with the consent of the Senate, to dissolve the Chamber of Deputies and call fresh elections.

Thus the key point about the 1875 laws, and their conception of the presidency, is that they embody, much more than those of the Assembly democracy identified with the Republican tradition, the principles of mixed government in which no one branch of government has a monopoly of political authority. Their inspiration has been variously located in Orleanism, in the British system of parliamentary government and in the United States. None of these is compatible with the absolute sovereignty of the Chamber of Deputies which the French Revolution had proclaimed, and the Orleanist and American references emphasise the political authority of the Head of State. To a leading left-wing opponent of the constitutional laws, the President of the Republic had all the characteristics of a monarch, apart from his lack of hereditary status.[7] His constitutional right to dissolve the elected Chamber was a challenge to the Republican model of Assembly sovereignty.

Why then did the mixed government of 1875 give way to an Assembly dominated regime in which the President of the Republic lost the powers, and status, accorded him by the constitution makers? Part of the answer to this question resides in the weight of historical memory. The traumatic events of 1851, when a directly elected President overthrew the Republic he was supposed to protect, produced a deep-seated fear among Republicans of a military adventurer – the term frequently used to describe Napoleon III is 'the man on horseback' – destroying parliamentary institutions. The fear of plebiscitary Cæsarism, which was shared, albeit for different reasons, by French monarchists, explains the constitutional provision that the President should be elected by the two houses of Parliament rather than by the electorate. With hindsight, this provision, together with the constitutional requirement for a ministerial countersignature for presidential acts, can be seen to have done great damage to the authority of the presidency. Yet it is on its own inadequate as an explanation of presidential weakness. The constitution makers of 1875 assumed that the powers granted to the President would allow him to influence policy and politics.

A second reason for the decline in the authority of the presidency relates to the political developments of the late 1870s and in particular to the constitutional crisis of 1877. The first President of the Third Republic was Marshal MacMahon who had been voted into office by the National Assembly in 1873, that is to say before the constitutional laws of 1875 were voted. Although a committed monarchist, MacMahon remained President after 1875 and rapidly came into conflict with the Republican majority elected to the Chamber of Deputies in 1876. On 16 May 1877 he provoked the resignation of the incumbent government and appointed a Conservative ministry which did not have the support of the Chamber; five weeks later he used his constitutional right to dissolve the Chamber of Deputies. The legislative elections which followed became the occasion for a thoroughgoing clash between two opposing readings of the regime established in 1875. MacMahon's supporters claimed that 'the President of the Republic in our constitution possesses an independent political authority. He is not the passive and blind servant of the will of the majority of the Chamber of Deputies. He has his own powers'.[8] The Republican majority in the outgoing Chamber of Deputies argued by contrast that Parliament alone possessed political authority since only it represented the sovereign nation. After a bitter campaign, in which MacMahon's ministers used all the administrative resources of government to harass their Republican opponents, the election produced a Chamber majority similar to that of 1876. MacMahon's attempt to appeal to the electorate over the heads of its elected representatives had failed. Faced with the blunt alternative that he must submit or quit ('se soumettre ou se démettre'), MacMahon in rapid succession did both. He first acknowledged that he would no longer challenge decisions made by ministers who had the confidence of the Chamber of Deputies and then, eighteenth months later, resigned office rather than accept military appointments made by the government of which he disapproved.

For all that MacMahon's actions in 1877 did not breach the constitutional laws, they provoked enormous controversy at the time and have done so ever since. Historians still use the word 'coup' to describe what happened. Thus the 16 May 1877 has great importance in explaining the decline of the political authority of the presidency in the Third Republic. It consummated the divorce between the principles of Republican democracy and the existence of a strong Presidency; it demonstrated that the political survival of governments depended on the Chamber which voted for them and not on the President who appointed them; and it showed that the electorate was not prepared to defend presidential authority against the claim of the Legislature to represent the Nation. MacMahon's successor was Jules Grévy, a veteran Republican who in 1848 had argued that the office of President was incompatible with a true Republic and who promised on taking office that he would never use his constitutional position to challenge the supremacy of Parliament. In the words of Marcel Prelot, a noted constitutional expert, 'the Grévy presidency was not simply the election of a new Head of State, it was a new constitution'.[9]

By the early 1880s the victory of the 'Republican' interpretation of the 1875 constitutional laws looked complete – Presidency and Senate, as well as the Chamber of Deputies, were all in the hands of Republicans. It is true that at the end of the decade, a populist, anti-parliamentary movement led by General Boulanger achieved great success by denouncing the inadequacies of the existing parliamentary leadership, including President Grévy, who was forced to resign in 1887 after a corruption scandal. What became known as Boulangism revived the spectre of a plebiscitary dictatorship overthrowing Republican institutions and confirmed, if confirmation was necessary, that Republican democracy was only safe when the Executive was subordinate to the Legislature. One sign of the taming of the presidency was the paucity of the administrative and material resources which it possessed; another was that its abolition ceased to be demanded by radical Republicans. But the clearest evidence of the determination of the French Parliament to constrain the presidency was its refusal to elect to it high profile political leaders. With the exception of Raymond Poincaré (1913-20) and Alexandre Millerand (1920-24) none of the Third Republic's leading statesmen succeeded in being elected. Jules Ferry (1887), Georges Clemenceau (1920), Paul Painlevé (1924) and Aristide Briand (1931) all failed in their bid. Successful candidates were usually regime dignitaries, presidents of the Senate or Chamber, who could be relied on to defend the interests of the Parliament from which they came. Writing in the early

1930s, W. L. Middleton observed that presidential contests impacted very little on the intense world of French party politics and that the popular press made virtually no reference to them until a week or so before they took place.[10] Critics of the political system of the Third Republic referred derisively to the 'flower show opening' nature of the presidency.

It would be wrong to underestimate the influence of the Republican presidency which emerged after 1877. Some Presidents (Grévy, Loubet, Poincaré, Millerand) played an interventionist role in foreign policy and many more were able, through their right to nominate the Prime Minister, to influence the kaleidoscopic parliamentary politics of the Third Republic. Grévy was able to blight the ministerial career of Léon Gambetta, the most prominent politician of the early years of the Third Republic, and in the 1920s President Doumergue made and unmade governments with conspicuous skill. Although French Presidents never became, as the British monarchy did, the focus of patriotism or apex of the social order, some of them did succeed in personifying a national unity which transcended political divisions. In the late 1880s and early 1890s President Carnot used his endless provincial tours to blunt Boulanger's assault on the parliamentary Republic and his assassination on one such visit in 1894 brought him much posthumous respect.[11] Faure (1895-99) and Fallières (1906-13) were widely popular figureheads; Poincaré worked unsparingly during the First World War to maintain national morale; and Doumergue (1924-31) became the best liked personality of his day. Thus the paradoxical fact is that, for all its apparent weakness, the presidency did have a part to play in the consolidation of the Republican model of democratic politics. W. L. Middleton's conclusion about the Third Republic President was that 'the ornamental in him is so visible that it hides the useful'. He does not only, in Bagehot's phrase, 'act as a disguise for the government which really governs; he is a disguise for himself'.[12] The skilful regime dignitary using his office to moderate the excesses of ministerial instability without threatening the pre-eminence of Assembly democracy became an important asset to the Third Republic.

The crisis of the Republican presidency

The Third Republic was France's longest lasting regime since the Revolution and managed to acquire the elusive quality of legitimacy. De Gaulle himself recognised that the 'Third Republic was able to rebuild France and its armies, to create a vast Empire, to construct a solid alliance system, to introduce valuable social reforms and to put in place an educational system'.[13] Having overcome many crises, its triumph appeared assured when it was able to regain Alsace-Lorraine from Germany after the First World War. Yet for all its resilience, the Republic failed to provide France with the image, and the reality, of stable government which were such a feature of the British parliamentary system. With rare exceptions, governments came and went with great frequency – there were over a hundred between 1875 and 1940. To the champions of the Republican model of Assembly democracy, such instability was no more than the proper tribute paid by government to the sovereignty of the People expressed through its elected representatives. Political observers noted that the frequent changes *in* government were more than counterbalanced by the stability of the personnel *of* government – individual ministers sometimes spent years in the same department. Many public figures, however, did regard ministerial instability as a threat to France's ability to survive the international tensions of the modern world, and in particular the rising threat posed by Germany. The support of the late nineteenth century nationalist Paul Déroulède for a directly elected President could be expected, given his hostility to the political system of the Third Republic. More interesting were the plans to strengthen the Executive, and the presidency, put forward by politicians from inside the Republican Establishment in an attempt to end ministerial instability. In his successful 1913 campaign for the presidency, Poincaré challenged existing orthodoxies by arguing for a more active presidential role in foreign policy and for the rehabilitation of the presidential power to dissolve the Chamber of Deputies.[14] After the First World War, Millerand (1920-24) extended the parameters of the debate. As well as asserting the right to intervene in domestic as well as foreign policy choices, he sought to revalorise the political authority of the office by arguing that the President should be 'France's representative to the world' and by making public his dissatisfaction with governmental decisions of which he disapproved. He also argued that the Electoral College for the presidency should be expanded to include representatives of local government, business groups and intellectuals and intervened in the 1924 elections on behalf of the existing right-wing majority.

Millerand's interventions show the existence of a movement for strengthening the Executive before the crisis years of the 1930s to which we shall shortly turn. Yet at this stage the Republican model of French democracy remained strong even among mainstream conservative parties. As President, Poincaré made no attempt to challenge existing constitutional conventions and Millerand never regarded an extended presidential electoral college as paving the way to a presidency based on universal suffrage. He wanted the presidency to reflect the status of France's industrial and intellectual élites, not to be the voice of the democratic will. Even so, Millerand paid a heavy price for his outspokenness, being compelled to resign in 1924 when the left won control of the Chamber of Deputies. His successor, Doumergue, was, as we have seen, a good example of how the surreptitious exercise of presidential influence could coincide with respect for the Republican model.

In the 1932 elections, constitutional issues were virtually absent from the campaign. They were, however, soon to re-emerge at the forefront of political debate as France's international and domestic situation worsened under the twin pressures of a revived German threat and economic depression. The inability of French governments to respond to the economic and foreign policy crises of the 1930s fuelled a violent debate about the inadequacies, and the corruption, of the political system which led, in February 1934, to what many interpreted as an assault on the regime led by ex-servicemen's leagues and extreme right militias. If the controversy reflected in part the European wide challenge to liberal democracy posed by Fascism and Communism, it also derived from domestic preoccupations with the perceived inability of the Republican model to provide strong government. Thus the question of constitutional reform was now linked to France's survival as a great power. From outside the political establishment, the monarchist Action Française movement run by Charles Maurras was one of a number of extreme right movements which denounced the principles, as well as the shortcomings, of Republican democracy. Yet more revealing of the decline of confidence in the Republican model were the attacks launched on it by prominent regime politicians. André Tardieu, a former Prime Minister and Poincaré's successor as leader of the conservative Republicans, launched a root and branch denunciation of the parliamentary system; and former President Doumergue, who was briefly Prime Minister in 1934, tried unsuccessfully to strengthen the authority of government by giving it the power to dissolve the Chamber of Deputies.[15]

The presidency failed to benefit from the disillusionment with the existing political system. It featured little in reform proposals and the parties of the left mounted a successful 'defence of the Republic' in the parliamentary elections of 1936. The terms of the defence show the continuing power of the Republican model. Doumergue's proposal to revive the right of dissolution of the Chamber was denounced by the leader of the Socialist Party, Léon Blum, as an assault on the foundations of parliamentary democracy, a legalised coup d'état. The attitudes of French democrats towards the comparative legitimacy of the presidency and Parliament can be summed up by the declaration of a prominent Radical politician, Campinchini, that 'so long as MacMahon remains in his grave the Chamber will never be dissolved'.[16] When, in the traumatic circumstances of France's invasion by Nazi Germany in 1940, the authority of Parliament itself collapsed, the presidency was nowhere to be seen. Power passed to Marshal Pétain, a veteran military hero of the First World War, who first signed an armistice with Germany and then embarked on a radical programme of constitutional revision based on the abolition, rather than the reform, of the institutions of the Republic. Pétain established an authoritarian political order known as the French State ('Etat français'), generally known as the Vichy regime. Given that Pétain believed that the principles of the French Revolution were responsible for the national decadence which had led to the 1940 disaster, the ideology of the Vichy regime was explicitly anti-Republican and anti-democratic. Order, authority and hierarchy replaced liberty, equality and fraternity as the guiding principles of politics.

Vichy was unable to prevent the emergence of a Resistance movement inside and outside France which opposed not only the Nazi Occupier but also, and increasingly, the anti-democratic values of Pétain and his supporters. By the time the Allied armies landed in France in summer 1944, the legitimacy of the Vichy regime was in tatters. During the Occupation, the groups and individuals who participated in an intense debate about how to guarantee France's post-war existence as an efficiently functioning democracy were in near unanimous agreement that the governmental instability of the 1930s could not be allowed to continue after the Liberation and that the process of national reconstruction required a new constitutional order. That this view was shared by the electorate was shown by the 96% who voted against returning to the Third Republic in the October 1945 referendum on the country's political institutions. How then was stable, democratic government to be ensured? One of the most melancholy features of the 1940 disaster had been the inability of the President of the Republic, Albert Lebrun, to prevent, or even to try to prevent, the accelerating military and political collapse. The fact that the presidency appeared irrelevant to the supreme crisis of France's existence as an independent country led some commentators to argue for a strengthening of its constitutional powers. Even Léon Blum, the 1930s defender of the Republican model, suggested from his prison cell that the French President should be, like his United States equivalent, the effective head of the Executive.[17]

Nothing came of these recommendations. The constitutional debates which followed the 1945 referendum and culminated in the Fourth Republic produced a system in which the presidency obtained no new authority, and even lost some of the powers it had been granted in 1875. The constitution of the Fourth Republic, finally approved by a referendum in November 1946, deprived the President of his title of Head of the Armed Forces and of his right to appoint to civil and military offices and to communicate by message with the National Assembly. Even his power to nominate the Prime Minister was constrained by the need for the latter to obtain the prior approval of the National Assembly. It was clear that for the political parties who sought to reshape French democracy a strong presidency, let alone one based on universal suffrage, was still a threat: their hopes for governmental stability resided instead in a strengthened Prime Minister and a disciplined party system. That this should be so reflects not only the enduring sway of the Republican tradition, but also two other influences. One was the deeply discredited model of authoritarian rule identified with Marshal Pétain. The other was the threat posed by General de Gaulle who soon, on leaving office in January 1946, revealed his hostility to the party system of post-war France and to the institutional framework of the Fourth Republic which protected it. De Gaulle's belief that France's future could only be assured by a powerful Head of State able to decide policy was a direct challenge to the Republican model of Assembly democracy and one that went beyond the aspiration of Third Republic reformers like Poincaré. Once de Gaulle's intentions became clear, Léon Blum abandoned his brief flirtation with an activist presidency in favour of the orthodoxies of the Third Republic. He spoke for the cross-party Republican Establishment when he insisted that de Gaulle's personality made a directly elected presidency impossible and that there could be no compromise around the basic Republican principle that 'the first and last word must belong to the Assembly elected by universal suffrage'.[18]

Thus the Republican model continued to shape constitutional principle and practice. This did not mean, any more than it had done in the Third Republic, that the presidency was invisible. Neither of the two Fourth Republic Presidents, Vincent Auriol (1947-54) and René Coty (1954-58) was a ceremonial figurehead. Both men strove to use their representational role to cement national unity, and Coty acquired, like Doumergue before him, considerable personal popularity. Auriol's influence went further. The late 1940s were a period of great political tension in France as two mass anti-system parties, the Communists and de Gaulle's Rassemblement du Peuple Français (RPF), sought – for very different reasons – to bring down the Fourth Republic. De Gaulle in particular evoked memories of the anti-Republican politics of Napoleon III and General Boulanger. By using the remaining presidential role in the nomination of governments, Auriol was able to play an important role in shoring up the authority of the pro-system parties. For a brief period in the early 1950s it even looked as if the assault from the anti-system parties might be contained. The Communist Party abandoned its plans (if such they were) to provoke revolution and the RPF failed in its bid to force the regime to abdicate. De Gaulle withdrew from public life in 1954 and began to write his memoirs, an activity which in politics often signals the end of ambition. Opinion polls indicated that he was no longer regarded as having a future in French politics.

This constitutional calm, if such it can be called, was short-lived. By 1956, many of the Fourth Republic's senior politicians – including Pierre Mendès France, the most respected champion of the Republican model of Assembly democracy – were convinced that the chronic government instability produced by fragmented multi-partyism threatened France's existence. The circumstances of Coty's election in 1953 – it took thirteen ballots before he was elected – contributed to the image of the presidency as the plaything of the parties. The authority of the Prime Minister was no greater: divisions within the National Assembly meant that France was without a government for one day in every four in 1957-58. We have seen that in the past the Republican model had been able to withstand a divided party system. In 1958, however, a crisis in civil-military relations made its position untenable. Since 1954 a brutal war had been waged in Algeria between the Front de Libération Nationale (FLN) independence movement and the French settlers who were only too willing to believe that the existing regime lacked the energy to defend them. What sealed the fate of the Fourth Republic was that by 1958 sections of the French Army had come to agree with this assessment and that the existing political leadership lacked the popular support which would have allowed it to launch, as it had done in 1936, an appeal to the 'defence of the Republic'. Faced with the prospect of military insurrection (and almost equally fearful of a possible Communist coup), President Coty and the bulk of France's party leaders turned, as their predecessors had turned in 1940, to a military leader who stood outside the political establishment. On 1 June 1958, de Gaulle became, as Pétain had done eighteen years earlier, Prime Minister of a Republic which he was determined to overthrow. Compared with his predecessor Lebrun in 1940, President Coty played an active role in the management of the crisis. Yet the fact that his decisive intervention took the form of a threat to resign unless the

National Assembly accepted de Gaulle's return shows that the regime had lost the confidence even of the man who, as Head of State, could have been expected to defend it.

The construction of a new presidency

The inability of Fourth Republic governments to resolve, by military victory or diplomatic negotiation, the conflict in Algeria sounded the death knell of the Republican presidency which had emerged after 1877. General de Gaulle made his return to power conditional on the power to draw up a new constitution which would revalorise the office of Head of State. After a short period of constitution drafting (from which the existing Parliament, in contrast with Republican tradition, was excluded), a constitution establishing a Fifth Republic was submitted to a referendum of the entire French nation. On 21 December 1958, 79% of the electorate voted their approval.

De Gaulle's theory of government had been set out in his 1946 Bayeux speech attacking the constitutional principles which underpinned the emerging Fourth Republic. He believed that France's existence as a nation depended on the existence of a strong Head of State with the authority to take decisions. He was convinced that an Assembly dominated regime like the Fourth Republic inevitably handed over power to the political parties which were incapable of subordinating their sectional interests to the cause of stable government. Thus for de Gaulle the Fourth Republic combination of a fragmented party system and uncontrolled Assembly power posed a permanent threat to the ability of the State to promote the national interest. He regarded a new constitution as essential if the authority of government was to be protected from parliamentary interference; and in that protection the Head of State had a central role to play. Shortly before the 1958 crisis exploded, the penultimate government of the Fourth Republic had introduced measures to strengthen the Executive; but its plans still excluded the presidency. From now on, things were to be very different. De Gaulle had briefly been a government minister in 1940 and was haunted by the inability of the then President of the Republic, Lebrun, to exercise leadership in a time of supreme national crisis. The Lebrun presidency thus became the anti-model against which the Fifth Republic presidency was designed. The constitution set out from the beginning to make the presidency a powerful – and independent – institution. Far from being a figurehead, the President is defined as the protector of national independence and the guardian of the constitutional, and judicial, order. The constitution emphasised his independence from Parliament by creating an electoral college for the presidency and by restoring his power (which existed in the 1875, but not the 1946, constitution) to appoint the government. It also provided him with a series of powers to enable him to counterbalance the power of Parliament and the parties. Henceforth the President could, on his own prerogative authority, declare a state of emergency and govern by decree (article 16); call a referendum on any proposal affecting the organisation of public powers (article 11); and dissolve the Chamber of Deputies and hold a general election. The latter provision demonstrates de Gaulle's determination to break the Republican orthodoxy, entrenched since 1877, that the presidency was subordinate to the Parliament and that the latter was the sole repository of political authority. To downgrade Parliament's claims to a monopoly of democratic power was one of the central ambitions of the new Republic. By emphasising the independence and the authority of the presidency, the 1958 constitution goes beyond the Republican theory of Assembly democracy to the mixed government model, described earlier, of Orleanism and the constitutional laws of 1875.

It is, however, important to emphasise that the 1958 text did not establish a presidential regime, or base the presidency on universal suffrage. Alongside the clauses strengthening the power of the President there are others which resemble the model of responsible parliamentary government identified with Great Britain, a model which many reformers, including de Gaulle's Justice Minister, Michel Debré, greatly admired. The law making – and constitution amending – function belongs to Parliament. Policy making and policy execution are the responsibility of the government; the government is headed by a Prime Minister; the Prime Minister is responsible for national defence. The President shares with the government the power to make military and civil appointments, and all his actions, with the exception of the prerogative powers listed above, must be countersigned by a minister. The constitution lays down that the President does not have the power to dismiss a government but only to accept its resignation; a government, by contrast, must resign if it loses the confidence of the National Assembly. All these constitutional provisions show the persistence of the core Republican principle that French democracy is only safe when ministers are responsible to a National Assembly elected by universal suffrage.

1958 should be regarded, therefore, not as the inauguration of a presidential regime but as an amalgam of – or compromise between – de Gaulle's belief that a strong State needed a strong President and the Republican model of Assembly democracy. De Gaulle was only able to return to power in a (more or less) constitutional way because he persuaded the political Establishment of his acceptance of the principles of parliamentary government. The 1958 constitution evades the problem of the extent of presidential power and does not link presidential authority to universal suffrage. One way of analysing the 1958 constitutional settlement would be to say that it overcame the Republican fear, incarnated by the MacMahon dissolution of 1877, of a President challenging Parliament, but that it did not attempt to exorcise the nightmare of 1851 when a directly elected President overthrew the Republic.

Thus the final issue in our analysis of the presidency becomes that of explaining how it moved in the Fifth Republic from being an important, but ill-defined, office based on the personal authority of one man to being the accepted instrument of French democratic politics. Part of the answer resides in the use de Gaulle made of the presidency in the early years of the Fifth Republic. From the outset, he saw himself not just as guardian of the new institutional order but as national leader. He used the word 'guide' rather than 'arbiter' (which appears in the constitution) to describe his role, and embarked on a programme of constitutional pedagogy designed to emphasise the pre-eminence of the presidency and to contrast the effect of government it provided with the damage allegedly caused to French interests by the chaos of the Fourth Republic. He also employed all the constitutional powers he possessed to their full extent. In 1961, after an attempted putsch in Algeria, he invoked Article 16 of the constitution which enabled him to rule by decree; he used national referendums to obtain support for his Algerian policy; and in Spring 1962 he obtained the resignation of his government, despite the fact that it still possessed the confidence of the National Assembly. Opinion polls and referendums showed that a large majority of the French supported de Gaulle's progressive acceptance of the inevitability of Algeria's independence and welcomed the image of strong government provided by the President.

The long term basis of presidential power, however, remained unclear. De Gaulle's political authority derived less from the constitution, or from the Electoral College which had chosen him, than from the widespread recognition that he alone was capable of solving the Algerian crisis. What he himself called his 'personal factor' ('équation personnelle') set him apart from other political leaders, based as it was on the 'special relationship' with the French nation which originated in his assumption in 1940 of a historic mission to guide its destinies. It was as national saviour that de Gaulle had been summoned back to power in 1958 to prevent France from collapsing into civil war. Four years later, the signature of the Evian Agreements ending the Algerian war and their subsequent massive approval by referendum ended the crisis. For de Gaulle, the achievement of peace in Algeria had always been less important than the victory of his ambition to make the presidency the guiding force of a reinvigorated France. The irony of the new situation was that the former might compromise the latter. The political parties, with the exception of de Gaulle's Union pour la Nouvelle République (UNR), had never been happy with what they regarded as the creeping, or indeed galloping, increase in the powers of the new presidency. They resented de Gaulle's contempt for the rights of Parliament and other manifestations of authoritarianism such as the frequent prosecutions for insulting the Head of State.[19] So long as the Algerian war continued, they were reluctantly willing to accept de Gaulle's predominance. Once peace broke out, however, they tried to reassert their own authority by emphasising the parliamentary, as opposed to the presidential, basis of government. In the summer of 1962, the 1958 compromise between de Gaulle and the parties broke down. A struggle began for the future shape of constitutional government in the Fifth Republic.

Following an attempt on his life by a supporter of the lost cause of French Algeria, de Gaulle announced in September 1962 a referendum on the introduction of universal suffrage for the election of the President. The decision was less self-evident than it might seem. De Gaulle did not have an elevated belief in the political wisdom of his fellow citizens and we have seen that he regarded his own right to rule as transcending electoral mandates. He was also concerned that linking the presidency to elections would deprive it of its independence by making it the plaything of the parties, a concern which led to his extraordinary flirtation with the idea that the pretender to the French throne, the Comte de Paris, might be his successor. Yet de Gaulle also recognised that in the modern world elections were the only source of political legitimacy and that his own 'heroic' authority could not, by definition, be transferred to the ordinary mortal who would one day succeed him. Even before the assassination attempt had demonstrated the dangerous identification between his own survival and that of the regime, he had stated that 'the direct agreement between the People and the man who has the responsibility to lead it has become in today's world essential to the Republic. We will need, when the time is ripe, to ensure that, whoever is in charge, the Republic can remain strong and stable'.[20] In his judgement, the time was indeed ripe: the presidency he had created could only survive if it was based on the People's vote.

To his opponents in the political parties, the proposal for a directly elected President threatened the existence of the Republican model of French democracy. As early as 1946, Léon Blum had forecast that de Gaulle's concept of the presidency must inevitably lead to his election by universal suffrage. It was to prevent such an assault on the Republican tradition that all the parties, with the exception of de Gaulle's supporters in the UNR, rose in protest against what they regarded as an undemocratic measure introduced by the unconstitutional means of a referendum. The anti-de Gaulle coalition included the political heirs of Poincaré's conservative Republicans as well as the Socialists and Communists. In a highly charged atmosphere, the National Assembly responded to de Gaulle's referendum proposal by exercising its constitutional right to vote a motion of censure on the recently formed government of Georges Pompidou, which was thereby compelled to resign. De Gaulle retaliated by using his constitutional power to dissolve the National Assembly – and to keep the government in office until the result of the referendum, and the parliamentary elections, was known. On 28 October the referendum proposing a directly elected President was approved by 62% of the electorate. Shortly after, the parties which had opposed it went down to crushing defeat in the elections for a new National Assembly.

These two votes constitute a turning point in the history of democratic politics in France. A coherent and disciplined majority now controlled the National Assembly; that majority was elected to support the government appointed by the President of the Republic; that government acknowledged the right of the President to determine the main contours of national policy and to determine how long it should remain in office. The non-Gaullist as well as the Gaullist groups within French conservatism henceforth accepted the legitimacy of presidential power which the 1962 referendum had confirmed. Yet as important as the victory of de Gaulle and his supporters was the lesson taught by the referendum to the defenders of the Republican model that a presidency based on universal suffrage could no longer be challenged on democratic grounds. Without doubt, many of those who voted 'yes' in the referendum did so principally out of fear of the instability which a 'no' vote, and the inevitable consequence of de Gaulle's resignation, would have produced. The result could not, however, be explained away as the politics of panic. In the Fourth Republic, opinion polls had shown a large majority in favour of a directly elected President with the power to lead, and during the 1962 referendum campaign, the Opposition was compelled to concentrate its power on the way in which the proposal was introduced rather than on its merits.

Conclusion

Shortly before his government was defeated by the 1962 censure vote, Georges Pompidou, de Gaulle's second Prime Minister, told a meeting of the Council of Ministers that 'twenty-two years of Gaullism have wiped out the stain of Bonapartism'.[21] By this he meant that a powerful President, and one elected by universal suffrage, would no longer be contaminated by association with the rape of the Second Republic by Louis Bonaparte in 1851. In the very short run, the defeat of Pompidou's government by the National Assembly suggested that such confidence was misplaced. The 1962 referendum result, however, revealed the extent of popular support for de Gaulle's proposal. Three years later, in December 1965, the first presidential election by universal suffrage since 1848 showed the impact of the new system on the politics of French democracy. With over 24 million people voting in each of the two rounds, the participation rate was 85%, the highest percentage in French electoral history, and one that compares favourably with the turnout in American presidential elections. De Gaulle gained a comfortable second round victory (55% of the vote) a result which consolidated the acceptance by the French right of this new form of democratic politics.

The real significance of 1965, however, lay with the left-wing parties which had hitherto identified with the Republican model of Assembly democracy. De Gaulle's principal opponent in the election was François Mitterrand, an independent anti-Gaullist who made himself the head of a coalition of the parties of the left. Mitterrand was one of the relatively few non-Communist Fourth Republican politicians who had opposed de Gaulle's return to power in 1958, and in 1964 had published *The Permanent Coup d'Etat* (*Le coup d'état permanent*), a denunciation of the political system of the Fifth Republic which was steeped in the traditions of the Republican model. In 1965, Mitterrand presented himself as the 'candidate of the Republicans' and as the enemy of personal power. His manifesto, however, did not include the repeal of the 1962 amendment establishing the direct election of the presidency. More important, the success of Mitterrand's campaign – he was able to force a second round in which he won 45% of the vote, including a majority of male voters – showed that the new system could benefit opponents as well as supporters of de Gaulle. 1965 was thus an important moment in the creation of a cross-party coalition around the new concept of the presidency as the instrument of democratic politics in France.

Over the next sixteen years, presidential elections became the means for the orderly transfer of power from one political majority to another as the parties of both right and left formed disciplined coalitions for presidential and parliamentary elections. It is true that the massive protest demonstrations in May 1968 appeared to challenge not only de Gaulle's concept of presidential power but also the relevance of electoral democracy to tensions within French society. At the height of the demonstrations, commentators rushed to the conclusion that the Fifth Republic had proved no more successful than its predecessors in closing the gap between democratic freedom and stable government which David Thomson had described as the problem of French politics.[22] Yet the real lesson of 1968 was that the politics of street protest was no substitute for the winning of power through elections. In the June 1968 parliamentary elections, the Gaullist party obtained a massive majority, and in 1969 the resignation of de Gaulle did not lead, as many had feared (and some hoped), to the disintegration of the regime, but to the easy victory of his former Prime Minister, Pompidou, at the head of a political coalition of Gaullist and non-Gaullist conservatives. The failure of the parties of the left to construct an equivalent alliance around a credible candidate led to their humiliating failure even to get to the second ballot. François Mitterrand spent the next decade constructing a union of the left capable of winning the presidency. In 1974 he narrowly lost the presidential election which followed Pompidou's death; seven years later he succeeded. In office, Mitterrand made no attempt to reduce the presidential powers contained in the constitution or to deny their democratic legitimacy. We have seen that in 1986 and 1993, the election of a right-wing majority to the National Assembly did lead to a reduction in the President's power to determine policy; in so doing it confirmed the lesson of 1962 that the full exercise of presidential power depended on the existence of a supportive parliamentary majority. The real significance of 'cohabitation' lies, however, in the unwillingness of both right and left to use it to attempt to dismantle the institutional system introduced between 1958 and 1962.

It is therefore possible to conclude that a consensus now exists in France around the democratic legitimacy of a powerful, and directly elected, presidency. The presidency has given France strong leadership and has created the link, which did not exist in the fragmented parliamentary coalitions of the Third and Fourth Republics, between election results and government policies. There are, of course, many complaints about the shortcomings of French democracy and in particular about the way in which the Fifth Republic presidency has become a form of elective dictatorship. All of the Fifth Republic Presidents have been denounced for their allegedly authoritarian exercise of power. The inability, or unwillingness, of the National Assembly to exercise its function of controlling government has been much criticised. It is certain that de Gaulle would deplore the way in which the presidency has become the first prize in inter-party competition and has thereby lost its ability to represent a purely national interest which transcends political divisions. As early as 1965, de Gaulle regarded the parties' enthusiasm for the presidential election as evidence that 'the Devil has got into the confessional'. Yet this vision of a directly elected presidency replacing party conflict was always unrealistic. Democratic politics depends by its nature on the legitimacy of political disagreement, on the ability of parties to put forward rival visions of the national interest, and on the rights of a democratically elected majority to exercise power while respecting the rights of minorities. By these criteria, the Fifth Republic is a democracy and the presidency is indeed its 'clé de voûte'.

Notes

[1] Charles de Gaulle (1890-1970) was Prime Minister and Michel Debré (1912-1996) Justice Minister when the Constitution of the Fifth Republic was drawn up.

[2] Maurice Duverger is one of the most prominent analysts, and critics, of the constitutional settlement of the Fifth Republic. See notably his *Le Système Politique Français. Droit constitutionnel et Institutions politiques* (Paris, Presses Universitaires de France, 19th edition 1986), pp.178-181.

[3] A SOFRES poll taken shortly before the 1995 presidential election showed that 64% of the French hoped for 'a real leader who can establish order and take decisions'. *Le Monde*, 11 April 1995.

[4] C. Nicolet, *L'Idée républicaine en France (1789-1924)* (Paris, Gallimard, 1994), pp.290-291.

[5] P. Rosanvallon, *L'Etat en France de 1789 à nos jours* (Paris, Seuil, 1990), p.53.

[6] W. Bagehot, *Caesareanism as it now exists* (1865), in N. St. John Stevas (ed.), *The Collected Works of Walter Bagehot, Vol 4, Historical Essays* (London, The Economist, 1968).

[7] M. Marabito, *Le chef de l'Etat en France* (Paris, Montchrestien, 1995), p.93; Nicolet (1994), p.155ff.

[8] J. Gicquel, *Président de la République (IIIe, IVe et Ve République)*, in J.-F. Sirinelli (ed.), *Dictionnaire historique de la vie politique Française au XXe siècle* (Paris, Presses Universitaires de France, 1995), p.840.

[9] J. Gicquel, *Essai sur la pratique de la Ve République* (Paris, Librairie générale de droit et de jurisprudence, 1968), p.33.

[10] W. L. Middleton, *The French Political System* (London, Ernest Benn, 1932), pp.187-188.

[11] For a literary portrayal of the popular appeal of Carnot see Anatole France's novel *L'Orme du Mail* (Paris, Calmann-Lévy, 1927), pp.61-62. Carnot's photo became one of the most frequently portrayed images in French town halls after his assassination in 1894.

[12] Middleton (1932), p.183.

[13] Quoted in J. Charlot, *Le gaullisme*, in J.-F. Sirinelli (ed.), *Histoire des droites en France, Tome 1: Politique* (Paris, Gallimard, 1992), p.662.

[14] R. Poincaré, *How France is Governed* (London, T. Fisher Unwin, 1915), p.179.

[15] See F. Monnet, *Refaire la République. André Tardieu, une dérive réactionnaire (1876-1945)* (Paris, Fayard, 1993), part 3; and N. Rousselier, 'La contestation du modèle républicain dans les années 30: la réforme de l'Etat', in S. Berstein and O. Rudelle (eds.), *Le modèle républicain* (Paris, Presses Universitaires de France, 1992), pp.319-335.

[16] Gicquel (1968), p.34.

[17] On the debates about post-war reconstruction, see A. Shennan, *Rethinking France: Plans for Renewal* (Oxford, Oxford University Press, 1989).

[18] Quoted in F. Goguel, *Les liens entre le Président de la République et le peuple*, in *De Gaulle en son siècle, Tome 2: La République* (Paris, Plon/La Documentation Française, 1992), p.197.

[19] On prosecutions for insulting the President see D. Frémy, *Quid des Présidents de la République... et des candidats*, (Paris, Robert Laffont, 1987), p.84.

[20] Marabito (1994), p.134.

[21] J. Hayward, 'From Republican Sovereign to Partisan Statesman', in J. Hayward (ed.), *De Gaulle to Mitterrand: Presidential Power in France* (London, Hurst & Co., 1993), p.53.

[22] D. Thomson, *Democracy in France* (Oxford, Oxford University Press, 1969), p.36.

Indicative Bibliography

Berstein, S., *The Republic of de Gaulle* (Cambridge, Cambridge University Press, 1993).

Bury, J. P. T., *Gambetta and the Making of the Third Republic* (London, Longman, 1973).

Duhamel, O., *La Gauche et la Ve République* (Paris, Presses Universitaires de France, 1980).

Frémy, D., *Quid des Présidents de la République...et des candidats* (Paris, Robert Laffont, 1987).

Gaffney, J. (ed.), *The French Presidential Elections of 1988* (Aldershot, Dartmouth, 1989).

Hayward, J. (ed.), *De Gaulle to Mitterrand: Presidential Power in France* (London, Hurst & Co., 1993).

Morabito, M., *Le Chef de l'état en France* (Paris, Montchrestien, 1995).

Monnet, F., *Refaire la République. André Tardieu: une dérive réactionnaire (1876-1945)* (Paris, Fayard, 1993).

Nicolet, C., *L'Idée républicaine en France* (Paris, Gallimard, 2nd edition 1994).

Noël, L., *De Gaulle et les débuts de la Ve République* (Paris, Plon, Collection Espoir, 1976).

Quermonne, J.-L., *Le Gouvernement de la France sous la Ve République* (Paris, Presses Universitaires de France, 3rd edition 1987).

Sirinelli, J.-F. (ed.), *Dictionnaire historique de la vie politique au XXe Siècle* (Paris, Presses Universitaires de France, 1995).

Thomson, D., *Democracy in France since 1870* (Oxford, Oxford University Press, 5th edition 1969).

3. The Myth of the President in French Political Culture

Lorna Milne

Introduction

The President of the French Fifth Republic fulfils functions and an office which have been created and consolidated by historical precedents and constitutional arrangements. His centrality, authority and influence over the political landscape also derive from a complex of less tangible qualities, foremost amongst which is the mythology surrounding his office and person.

The term 'myth' has come to be used in a variety of ways. Many apply it in its widely used meaning of a popular but misleading fiction; others take it to designate the semiological accumulation surrounding individuals and objects and explored in the 'mythologies' of Roland Barthes.[1] The myth of the President, however, must be seen as a more profound – indeed primordial – phenomenon than these, as a modern variant of the great traditional myths and legends which structure societies and influence consciousness. In this chapter, therefore, we shall draw on the definition offered by the anthropologist Edmund Leach, for whom a myth is 'a sacred tale about past events which is used to justify social action in the present'.[2]

The person and office of the French President of the Fifth Republic are the subject of just such a sacred tale. It is an epic narrative which draws on traditions in French thought and politics, and which has become supported by a system of codified ceremonies, icons, gestures and language which have grown up around the presidency and become imbued, in the French national understanding, with ritual or symbolic significance as well as (or occasionally instead of) any practical or literal meaning.

But for all its appearance of authenticity based on long tradition, the myth of the President is particular to the relatively young Fifth Republic and was in fact largely 'invented' by its first President, Charles de Gaulle. The functions of the myth and symbolism surrounding the President are thus similar to those described by the historian Eric Hobsbawm in his discussion of invented traditions. These ritualised or symbolic practices are performed as if they had existed in the same form for many years, even though they are in fact relatively new. Hobsbawm advances the theory that they fall into three overlapping categories:

a) those establishing or symbolizing social cohesion or the membership of groups, real or artificial communities, b) those establishing or legitimizing institutions, status or relations of authority, and c) those whose main purpose was socialization, the inculcation of beliefs, value systems and conventions of behaviour.[3]

The myth of the President in the Fifth Republic, however intangible it may be as an influence in politics, is nevertheless an active one, and may be said to correspond simultaneously to each of these three types of tradition. It provides a focus for social and political cohesion of the nation which concurs – consciously or unconsciously – in acknowledging the legendary status of the President; and it contributes both to the legitimation of the institution of the presidency, and to the inculcation of a certain set of political values and conventions.

Complementing other contributors' discussion of the 'real' events which have shaped the presidency, this chapter will show the particular ways in which the myth of the President manifests itself, and will address the effects of the phenomenon on the conduct of candidates. The first two sections will examine the invention of the presidential myth and show something of its specific nature. The second part will present the 'text' – the presence and formulation – of the myth as it emerged in the campaigns of the candidates during the 1995 election. The third will offer some conclusions about the relationship between this text and the changing social, cultural and political configurations for which it was adapted in 1995.

Morphology of the myth

Like many great myths in which the protagonist is represented as an ambiguous, liminal personage (for example as an androgyne, or as both man and god), the myth of the President in the Fifth Republic is structured by a paradox. That is to say that the President has to occupy two contradictory positions which can be seen as situated on a vertical axis, one far above the other.

The higher of the two positions derives, quite naturally, from the President's function as Head of State, a title which itself indicates the President's metaphorical superiority over others. This emphasis on supremacy is important to the extraordinary authority of his position which colours all presidential activity. His superiority is both supported and emphasised by certain quite tangible physical and constitutional symbols of his supreme responsibility and high status: for example, he appoints and accepts resignations from Prime Ministers; he is entitled to invoke article 16 of the Constitution; he lives in an especially grandiose dwelling, the Elysée Palace; he travels in special presidential transport; he has his own staff; he is always addressed by his title. Further, according to article 5 of the Constitution – itself a highly symbolic document, being the 'holy writ' of the political and institutional sphere – the President is 'arbitre' of the nation, which implies that he must transcend base factional squabbles to protect the morally and metaphorically superior domain of the national interest.

At the same time, the President's duties also situate him at a lower level on the vertical axis. Under the Constitution of the Fifth Republic as amended in 1962, not only are the French people – not the President – 'sovereign', but the President is directly elected by the people, to be directly representative of them. What is more, he is not simply a figurehead as previous Presidents were, but is immediately and actively involved in politics, and is therefore obliged to engage in debate (and deceit) like any other mortal.

The French leader thus embodies the representation of two overlapping Frances: the legal, geographical and sentimental entity which protocol has always required the President to symbolise; and the France composed of the French people in all the diversity of their political interests. The President of the Fifth Republic has, therefore, at one and the same time, to satisfy two opposing conditions of his office: transcendence – the superiority of a leader who is above the rest of the polity and in particular above the party political fray; and representativeness – the ability to understand the electorate on its own level and to engage in politics on its behalf. A rich array of rhetorical and symbolic devices has been deployed in order to express and sustain this paradox from the early Fifth Republic onwards.

At first sight, the paradoxical situation of the French President is not in itself very different from that of most leaders, political or otherwise, who seek to demonstrate that they are capable of being both ordinary and extraordinary as occasion demands. And, generally, a figure such as the President is susceptible to a certain 'mythification', simply because of the symbiotic relationship which exists between myth and the symbolism of office. A Head of State occupies a role which has always been openly recognised as partially, or even completely, symbolic and, as symbol of the French nation, the President necessarily takes part in a great number of overtly symbolic and ritualised state ceremonies, from the welcoming of foreign dignitaries to Bastille Day celebrations. It was always possible that the ceremonial reiteration of symbols of presidential power and authority would ensure that those symbols became signifiers of almost religious meaning, through which the President and the system which legitimates him would somehow come to be seen as sacred. This effect of ritual has been noted by the historian of religions, Mircea Eliade, who observes: 'ritual forces man to transcend his own limits; it obliges him to place himself on the same plane as the gods and mythical heroes in order to reproduce their acts. Directly or indirectly, myth brings about an "elevation" in man'.[4]

Seen in specific and detailed terms, however, the myth of the President in the Fifth Republic also has its own particular qualities which are dependent on the manner of its invention. In order to define and understand these qualities, therefore, we must examine the crucial contribution of General de Gaulle, authoritative 'father' of the Constitution, founder of the presidential lineage in the Fifth Republic and therefore, as it were, the archetype against which subsequent Presidents are measured. It was de Gaulle who, by his discourse and behaviour, inflected the presidential paradox in the modern period so as to give it its specific contours, and who was principally responsible for elevating the powerful 'tale' of the President into a sacred one.[5]

It is less important here to attach our study to specific moments of de Gaulle's political and presidential leadership than to recognise that the 'légende dorée'[6] of de Gaulle's history forms – in retrospect, and doubtless aided by de Gaulle's own mythographers – a mythical whole which now constitutes the equivalent of the 'temps fort'[7] or sacred Beginning of the present tale. We shall therefore draw our examples not only from his tenure as President or as a candidate, but from his entire career, that is to say from the 'legendary life' that informs the republic he created.

De Gaulle and the invention of the myth

It is clear from the enormous amount of writing about the life of de Gaulle that both as heir to the presidency and occupant of the office, he was able to fulfil both aspects – the transcendent and the representative – of the presidential paradox. François Goguel, tracing the development of de Gaulle's view of the presidency, points out that between 1958 and 1960 de Gaulle had already moved from depicting the new President of the Fifth Republic as a 'national arbiter' who would be 'above political struggles' and guided only by the national interest, to intervening himself in politics (for example over the matter of self determination in Algeria), and finally speaking of the presidency as a 'power' while truly beginning to 'govern' rather than to practise 'arbitrage'.[8] Equally, other writers have analysed the demeanour and activities of de Gaulle[9] which clearly influenced the myth he generated. However, since all political activity is essentially communicative activity – that is to say that the description, discussion and (re)interpretation of political events and activities can be as decisive and influential as the events and activities themselves – we shall concentrate in this chapter on de Gaulle's discourse and the way in which he created a mythical climate around the figure of the President through his speeches and writings. To see how this operates we need to examine, first, de Gaulle's portrayal of the country over which the President presides.

In de Gaulle's discourse, France is presented not in merely anthropomorphic but in theomorphic terms, that is, she (and the attribution of the female gender by de Gaulle could not be clearer) is personified and portrayed as a great goddess. This is hinted at in the famous opening paragraphs of de Gaulle's *Mémoires de guerre* in which he reveals that his 'certain idea of France' is always essentially associated (however vaguely) with greatness.[10] More particularly, though, de Gaulle's France shares the divine qualities of a variety of mythical figures. In the following quotation, for example, she evokes both Catholic representations of the Virgin Mary and pagan Earth Mother deities who cradle the dead in their womb-like depths:

> To France, to Our Lady France, we have only one thing to say: that nothing matters to us, nothing occupies our thoughts, except serving her. [...] We have nothing to ask of her except perhaps that, when the day of freedom comes, she will hold us in her mother's embrace that we might cry for joy in her arms; and that on the day when death strikes us, she will enfold us gently in her good, her sacred earth.[11]

A similar mixture of pagan and Christian references occurs in another wartime quotation which casts France in the role of a Venus emerging from a sea of adversity to confer a gesture of Christian benediction upon the sons whose successes in battle are turning the tide:

> ...invincibly, Fighting France is emerging from the Ocean. When, at Bir-Hakeim, a golden ray of her reawakening glory kissed the blood-stained brows of her soldiers, the world knew that this was France.[12]

We shall look in a moment at examples of other archetypal representations of France in the discourse of de Gaulle's later years. But it is clear that the unashamed hyperbole, sentimentality and reverence of the two quotations above typify the great majority of de Gaulle's portrayals of France, serving each time to underline France's elevation to the status of a benign and ancient deity.[13]

In many ways, of course, this myth of France was not radically new. It has direct antecedents in the work of French writers such as the Romantic historian, Jules Michelet, and the proponents of Christian renewal and Catholic nationalism whose works influenced the young de Gaulle – Barrès, Bergson and Péguy being perhaps the most important.[14] And since the myth of a sacred and feminine France already existed and was reinforced regularly in French public life – by association, for example, with the republican symbolism of Marianne or the nationalist and Christian iconography of St. Joan of Arc as an embodiment of French virtues – we may assume that de Gaulle's version of the myth would have met with an acceptance favoured by familiarity in a great number of French men and women: that it was, in short, one of those intangible points of consensus which help bind a culture or society together, indeed all the more so because it so obviously invoked the unifying power of patriotism. The important feature of de Gaulle's discourse – and his genius, in rhetorical and political terms – was that he created, in his speeches and behaviour, a new relationship between the goddess France and himself as a Frenchman, a devotee of 'Our Lady France', an active leader and, ultimately, the archetypal President of the Fifth Republic. Whereas most other leaders and writers who exploited or subscribed to the myth of France identified their relation to their country almost exclusively in terms of suffering or servitude (where they created a privileged relationship between themselves and France at all), de Gaulle was able – partly because of his extraordinary personality and wartime record – audaciously to cast himself in a relationship to France which allowed him to share the same supernatural status as the Motherland herself, while still anchoring the relationship in the republican tradition.

Other commentators have suggested that de Gaulle's special relationship with his country arose from a conception of personal greatness which made him the equal of France. Jean Lacouture points out de Gaulle's fondness for the formulae 'I was France', 'I am France' and, developing an observation of Mauriac's, Lacouture notes that in de Gaulle's discourse:

> De Gaulle can watch de Gaulle, because de Gaulle is France and her leader at one and the same time. Now embodying France, now guiding her, he is double and yet unchanging. Which allows him to indulge in that mixture of distance and admiration, that play of mirrors which makes him say, by turns, 'me' and 'de Gaulle', and allows him to slip easily from 'I' to 'he' in a single sentence....[15]

De Gaulle's portrayal of himself as the protagonist of an epic tale in which he periodically becomes not merely the equal or symbol but the avatar of 'Our Lady France' herself, places him on a plane which lies beyond the heroic and touches upon the supernatural.

But de Gaulle's mythical status is underpinned and defined by a much more intricate complex of associations than this straightforward dual postulate of personal and national greatness. Scrutiny of his writings and speeches shows that he portrayed himself in a variety of roles in relation to France, each of which contributed to his legend in important ways. Amongst these roles, that of the Favoured Son is implicit in the portrayal of France as a mother goddess. The Favoured Son is, for de Gaulle, characterised by the overtones of fervent devotion, readiness for sacrifice, and heroism in the service of the Mother which we have already noted. More than this, as the Favoured Son of France, he also becomes the Chosen one, singled out as the only true heir to the fabulous qualities of the Motherland.

This complex of associations is taken even further in de Gaulle's portrayal of himself in the role of Guide. In his years as President, de Gaulle frequently referred to himself as 'the Guide of France and the Head of State',[16] but it is once again his Memoirs which best reveal his interpretation of his relation to France. As the Chosen Son of France during the war years, he depicts his mission via the metaphor of a guide lighting a path out of the abyss:

> Leaning over the deep chasm into which our country has tumbled, I am her son, calling her, lighting her way, showing her the road to salvation....Now I hear France replying to me. At the bottom of the abyss, she picks herself up, she moves, she climbs up the bank. Ah! Mother, such as we are, here we are to serve you.[17]

This striking image of de Gaulle standing high above his country and successfully drawing her out of danger could almost serve as an emblem of the relationship his discourse creates between himself and France. He is cast as the immutable, steadying force who stands firm on the high ground, his unique and unwavering vision forever trained on the right path forward; she appears as vulnerable despite her greatness, a goddess who can be dashed from her pedestal and who relies on the strength of her solicitous son to bring her back to her natural position of superiority.

Variants of this theme and image also emerge repeatedly in de Gaulle's obsession, throughout his career, with the notion that France should 'be herself'.[18] Constant references to this idea in his texts imply that France, as he sees her, has both a true, steadfast identity and a tendency to drift away or be distracted from it under adverse influences (usually the fickleness, foolishness or factional bickering of the French). De Gaulle's discourse implies that only he, de Gaulle, is in a position to rise above the 'propensity of the French to be divided amongst themselves'[19] in such a manner as to return France to a position worthy of her true self. His insistence that France must 'be France' is, however, far more than a tautology. It bespeaks the dread of relativity and the nostalgic yearning for a mystical absolute[20] which characterises many mythological systems, including certain strands of the Catholic one in which de Gaulle was raised. In de Gaulle's 'sacred tale' of his relationship with his country, he pursues an unceasing – and in many ways regressive – quest to re-create France as a metaphysical ideal, an entity whose name and nature, superficial form and profound identity are one, and whose sacred status derives partly from that very absoluteness. In claiming the unique ability not only to perceive France's true identity but to ensure that she embodies it, de Gaulle arrogates to himself a greatness and a knowledge of France which exceeds even that of the deity whom, at other moments, he so fervently serves.

To the almost messianic archetypes of son and guide, we may also add the role of Consort, which develops the myth of de Gaulle even further. Once again, the archetype may be expressed in different ways: on the one hand, France and de Gaulle may be cast as an elderly couple, familiar and fond, leaning on one another for support, an image which posits perfect intimacy and equality:

> I am speaking to France. Well, my dear old country, here we are together again, facing a difficult challenge.[21]

At the same time, this intimation of companionship is lent a further mythical dimension by the word 'old', one of de Gaulle's favoured adjectives in emotive rhetoric. The suggestive impact of the quotation is that France, as old as the world spinning on its axis, is outside time, and that by association, de Gaulle, as her consort, is timeless or immortal too.

On the other hand, the figures of Consort and Creator may become mingled when France is portrayed more as a youthful bride, the Beloved, or even as an Eve remodelled by the hand of her leader, as when the President declares that 'We must transform our ancient France into a new country and match her to her time' [in French, literally, 'marry her to her time'].[22] Here, the speaker seems to fulfil the implied role of bridegroom (as a modern President, he is the man of the times to which France must be 'matched'). But perhaps even more forcefully, he is also understood as the Father of the 'bride', who not only marries her off, but who will first (re-)create, or 'transform', her. In this quotation, the President again takes on an authority and significance which transcend even that of France, who is here reduced to a passive dependence on her Pygmalion. Clearly, as a leader who twice saved his country from catastrophe, the second time, in 1958, by renewing the Republic itself, de Gaulle was in a position to impart some authenticity to the image of the President not only guiding France but effectively re-creating her as her true self. As we shall see below, this gift of re-creation remains a powerful characteristic of the myth of the President today.

The notion that de Gaulle, in his personal and official capacities, united in one individual the favoured son, the 'creator', the consort and the avatar of the 'patrie' confers upon him the superhuman status which makes of him a myth in the proper sense. As avatar of France, he seems able not only to embody a deity, but to take on the attributes of a female divinity despite his own virile form. This implied androgyny – a *coïncidentia oppositorum* highly symbolic of divine status in most mythological systems[23] – is reinforced by echoes at other moments of de Gaulle's discourse as, for example, when he (humorously?) represents himself in his administrative duties as a motherly figure, tidying up France and running an orderly household: 'The housewife wants progress but she doesn't want a mess. Well! It's the same for France. We need progress, we don't need mess'.[24] In addition, and related to the ambiguity of androgyny, the fact that de Gaulle could seem to embody such a variety of personae contributes to his aura of divinity by suggesting the supernatural quality of ubiquity. Once again, this attribute of the divine finds resonances elsewhere in de Gaulle's speech, this time in his propensity, mentioned above, to slide from one personal pronoun to another ('I', 'he') when speaking about himself.

The whole enterprise of 'mythification' is of course supported by the strongly religious overtones of de Gaulle's vocabulary in speaking not only of France, as we have already seen, but of his own experience and office. Perhaps the most striking portrayal of this occurs in a press conference speech of 31 January 1964, in which the President of the Republic appears as a sort of Alpha and Omega, both origin and repository of power, despite the fact that this power proceeds from the people:

> ...the spirit of the new constitution consists [...] in making power proceed directly from the people, which implies that the head of state, elected by the nation, is both its source and its keeper....[25]

No doubt, de Gaulle meant here that the President, as distinct from political factions or even the parliament, is guardian of the sovereign power of the people. Nevertheless, the formulation of this thought is suggestive of the opposite interpretation, that is, that de Gaulle seems ultimately, without a hint of conscious blasphemy, to reinvent the President as a sort of god after the Christian model and the 'peuple souverain' as communicants who share in the presidential power by virtue of direct universal suffrage.[26]

However, despite the large number of portrayals of the President as a superior being which our analysis has so far emphasised, it is important to note that de Gaulle did not neglect the representative nature of presidential office: after all, the 1962 constitutional amendment which introduced the direct election of the President was specifically his. The following quotation, in which we might note once again the quasi-religious and incantatory repetition of 'la France', is typical:

> France is everything at once, it's all French people. The left isn't France! The right isn't France! [...] To claim to see all of France in a single faction is a serious mistake, and to claim to represent France in the name of a faction is an unpardonable error on a national scale. I'm not on one side, I'm not on the other, I'm on the side of France.[27]

Here de Gaulle demonstrates his mastery of the paradox which has become central to the presidential myth. In setting the political in-fighting which he so despised in opposition to the superior and all-embracing nature of the deity France, and by clearly identifying both himself and 'all French people' with the latter (an identification once again made easier by the appeal to nationalism, an inclusive, unifying and representative rhetorical device), he implies that it is the President's very transcendence – his ability to rise above factional politics – which ensures his capacity to represent the whole French population. It is this type of discourse – even if such affirmations as the above ultimately were highly debatable in practical terms[28] – which laid the foundations of the myth of the President in the Fifth Republic.

The myth embodied by de Gaulle, then, has a number of particular characteristics. It not only defines the President as both transcendent (divine, superior, aloof) and representative (elected by, and speaking for, all French people): it also, in its creation of a mythical France, provides a point of equilibrium between these two paradoxical poles of transcendence and representativeness which structure the presidential myth. Furthermore, in inventing the sacred relationship between the President and the country, de Gaulle's myth endows the President himself with specific qualities: uniquely clear vision and perfect understanding of the country; the ability to draw France out of the abyss and to renew her strength; the capacity to reunite France with her one, true, original identity. Finally, as each of these aspects of the myth was established and reiterated, the myth itself contributed powerfully to the legitimation of the role of the President in the new Fifth Republic and provided a focus for social and political cohesion within the new regime.

The myth has been handed down through consecutive presidencies, as a central point of reference, an ideal which Presidents attempt to embody and to which contenders for the office are compared at election time. Much of such comparison is conducted by candidates themselves who lay claim to presidential status in order to establish their credibility and fitness for office; and most of their claims are expressed in the candidates' presidential campaigns. These exploit the highly symbolic channel of direct communication from candidate to electorate which has existed since the first election was fought after the constitutional amendment of 1962, and which so clearly evokes the representativeness of the presidential office sought by the candidate. It is not within the scope of this study to catalogue the extent to which each successive President has acknowledged, flouted, embodied or reshaped his difficult heritage. We need simply note here that de Gaulle's 'blueprint' for the presidency has remained an unavoidable model for Presidents and candidates throughout the life of the Fifth Republic.[29] Even for President Mitterrand, life-long opponent of de Gaulle, who, as the first Socialist President, might have appeared to promise a radical reinterpretation of the presidency, de Gaulle was an essential point of reference: Dominique Labbé's quantitative analyses of Mitterrand's language during his first term of office show, for example, that the proper noun 'de Gaulle' is the most frequently-quoted name of a person in the whole corpus of speeches and interviews studied.[30] The same study further demonstrates the continuing almost numinous importance of presidential office by crunching through a statistical analysis of lemmas, lexical fields and interchangeable expressions to conclude that President Mitterrand's most frequently repeated message can be distilled into the sentence 'I am the President of the Republic'.[31] This constantly reiterated appeal to authority and legitimacy by simple affirmation suggests something of the continued very powerful mythical status of the office of President two decades into the Fifth Republic.

In the next section of our study, we shall look at how the myth manifested itself in the election of 1995. In order to communicate something of the tone of the campaign, and to examine candidates' self-projections in relation to the myth, our analysis is based upon the set of electoral communications composed of campaign literature, broadcasts, interviews and public meetings.

The 1995 Election

As in all French elections and much non-electoral political communication, all the candidates and many of the commentators in 1995 drew heavily on metaphors and models from mythology, legend and folklore in the course of the campaign.[32] There is nothing new or surprising about this: on the contrary, the exploitation of a collectively-held body of universal narratives as referents for persuasive, elucidatory or illustrative political rhetoric is very common, if not commonplace (indeed, we have already seen how de Gaulle used both Christian and pagan mythology in this way). Our concern here, however, is to show the survival and development of a myth which, although akin in *type* to the great traditional myths, is nevertheless a modern, 'invented' myth in its *content*; it is not universal but particular to the French Fifth Republic, and contributes to the organisation of the political system in a much more specific way than do rhetorical references to the great myths and legends which now belong to a general western cultural heritage.

Let us, then, describe briefly the representation of the myth of the President in the communication of the nine candidates for the presidency in 1995. They can, for the purposes of this analysis, be divided into three groups uniting individuals who may not otherwise have much in common. Thus there are two groups of minority candidates: those who minimise explicit reference to the presidential myth, and those who maximise such references; the mainstream candidates form the third group.

The first group is composed of the minority candidates Jacques Cheminade, Arlette Laguiller, Robert Hue and Dominique Voynet who, from their 'alternative' basis in anti-establishment politics, scarcely make explicit reference to the presidency (and indeed to the election) in their campaigns at all. Still less do they project themselves into the presidential myth. In proposing programmes, all four prefer to use such impersonal phrases as 'one must', 'France needs to', 'people should', 'it's possible if...'[33] rather than the more presidential 'I' ('je') which would hint both at the candidate's predicted success and at a strong, active and authoritative ego: the representative half of the presidential equation is here privileged to the exclusion of the transcendent half. These candidates (particularly the three more established ones) thus make no secret of the fact that they are, in traditional fashion, using the first round of the election as a referendum on their policies, seeking to give these a legitimacy derived from popular support which can be 'stored up' and used after the first round of the election to influence the round two candidates and, eventually, the winner of the contest. Arlette Laguiller is the candidate who expresses this in the plainest terms:

...It is a programme of this kind that I ask you to endorse by your vote. If there are millions of us who approve it, then we shall have the means to force the person who is elected, whoever he is, to apply it.[34]

By contrast with the above group of candidates, those in the second category – Jean-Marie Le Pen and Philippe de Villiers, candidates of the far right – experience no such coyness about casting themselves in the role of possible future Presidents. The language of both campaigns makes much use of the first person and of promises of action ('I myself'; 'I propose...'; 'Vote for me'[35]) and both employ the classic televisual style of the serious 'présidentiable', dressed in a dark suit and directly addressing the viewer-elector from behind an important-looking desk. De Villiers carries forward the image of the 'présidentiable' by beginning all his broadcasts with the salutation 'Françaises, Français' so famously favoured by the first President of the Fifth Republic and employing, at the start of each television appearance, a lengthy filmed montage in which shots of the candidate strolling through the French countryside alternate with clips of 'ordinary people' going about their work. This attempted synthesis – the candidate as both ordinary and extraordinary – is made even plainer by Le Pen in a slogan from his electoral tract which is perhaps the campaign's crudest in its appropriation of the presidential paradox of representativeness and transcendence: 'Jean-Marie Le Pen, a man of the people, a statesman'.[36]

The two candidates seem able to carry off this self-projection with different degrees of success. In the case of de Villiers, unaided by his portrayal in popular satire as something of a clown,[37] and representing only a tiny political movement and a poorly delineated electoral platform,[38] the effect of his claim to occupy the myth of the presidency seems, from a stylistic point of view alone, so presumptuous as to be largely bathetic.

Le Pen is altogether different. Because of his larger-than-life personality, his evident personal conviction, his party backing, previous notable electoral scores and proven influence on the national political agenda, it is much easier for him credibly to occupy a mythical plane, even if his natural role there is, for many, that of a mythical monster or 'anti-President'. His campaign blatantly juxtaposes a projection of Le Pen as President of the Republic with language recalling sacred tradition as, for example, when his campaign tract expounds the 'Ten Commandments for the return of France to the French',[39] which show a remarkable degree of overlap with the 'Five Qualities of a Good President of the Republic',[40] and the (supposed) personal qualities of Jean-Marie Le Pen. In this exercise, Le Pen is careful to dress up his usual contradictory mixture of populism and bombast as a felicitous union of opposites, worthy of the sacred status of President of the Fifth Republic who both represents the people, and rises above them. Perhaps even more influential in his portrayal of himself as a serious presidential candidate is Le Pen's exploitation of 'la France'. His nationalism, drawn partially from similar influences to de Gaulle's, parasitises Gaullist notions of French 'grandeur' and the traditional – not to say old-fashioned – myth of France which was so powerful a feature of de Gaulle's presidential discourse.[41] Le Pen implies his own adequacy for office partly by suggesting a vision of France in which 'France' and 'the French' should be – and could, under his presidency, become – one, evoking the nostalgia for mythical unity which has characterised the myth of the President since the beginning of the Fifth Republic. It should be stressed that it is not our aim here to compare Le Pen's policies or politics with de Gaulle's, but rather to point out that the form of Le Pen's rhetoric owes much to the myth of the President whose sacred vocation is to 'see' the true path for France and to re-create her in a form fit to return to it. Contrary to the effect on de Villiers, and for the reasons outlined above, Le Pen's claim to the presidency, couched in these terms, aligns him with the heavyweight contenders and confers on him a certain seriousness, however sinister many sections of the polity may find this.

The third group is comprised of the three principal candidates of 1995: Jacques Chirac, Edouard Balladur and Lionel Jospin. All three major candidates established a powerful 'presidential' identity in their campaigns, on the one hand developing a strong relationship with their readers or viewers in their texts and broadcasts and insisting on the credibility of the partnership between President and people which would be established if they won; and on the other, projecting themselves clearly into the role of presider, leader and judge through the authoritative and self-assured use of electoral promises and personal pronouns. All three also extensively used references to the identity of France in ways which awakened echoes of the myth of the President.

Balladur, for example, who commands the most 'gaullien' literary style of the three, evokes in his campaign brochure a France in which the French population and France herself mysteriously overlap:

France, in the deeper recesses of her self, commands reserves of intelligence, generosity and enthusiasm which have in the past made our republican motherland a reference point, a beacon of hope and an example, and will do so again. It is this cause which I intend to serve, together with all French men and women.[42]

The message of this short passage is at one and the same time inclusive, egalitarian, representative ('serve...with all French men and women') and yet autocratic ('I intend'), grandiose, transcendent: the candidate lays claim to superior status through his special knowledge of what France contains 'in the deeper recesses of her self' and on the basis of his capacity (the capacity of the Guide and Chosen Son) to restore her to her former – and proper – glory ('resources...which have in the past...and will do so again').

The extended Jospin and Chirac campaigns made approximately equal reference to the myth of the President, but in different ways. Chirac, as the Gaullist candidate in the second round, was of course able to call openly on the spirit of de Gaulle to preside over his candidacy and to confer on Chirac the sacred legitimacy of the true inheritor of the Gaullist tradition. In his tract for the first round, for instance, Chirac used a formulation highly reminiscent of de Gaulle's own words, which he also repeated on other occasions:

France is truly herself only when she rallies around the values of the Republic. That is the great lesson of General de Gaulle. It is my highest ambition.[43]

Jospin, on the other hand, clearly felt less able to invoke the name and reputation of his predecessor, Mitterrand, as part of a claim to presidential status and legitimacy. When he did so, it tended to be slightly sheepishly and in 'private' (that is, to thousands of PS supporters during rallies[44]) rather than on television or in his campaign literature to a wider public. Jospin seemed also to find it more difficult to embody the notion of presidential transcendence, in part because his campaign was promoting the idea of the 'président-citoyen' and a reformed model of executive and legislative power based more on lateral negotiation and less on a traditional vertical hierarchy. Nevertheless, Jospin's insistence on the need for 'a President who is close to the French people and who is guarantor of Republican values',[45] and on the concept of the Citizen-President as 'a President who listens to the country, a President who takes decisions',[46] although somewhat lacking rhetorical colour, is a clear attempt to express and appropriate the paradox of representativeness and transcendence. In addition, in contrast to Chirac whose television campaign in particular was somewhat static, Jospin gave his second round campaign a dynamic, narrative effect by altering its format daily. Both candidates relied heavily on the mediation of their ideas through other people who figured in their broadcasts: Chirac frequently had senior RPR colleagues speaking in his place, and both men responded to 'interviewer' figures, who asked questions and supposedly directed the discussion.[47] But whereas Chirac's campaign never deviated from the same striking but repetitive formulae even in the second round, Jospin devoted a steadily increasing proportion of each broadcast to direct addresses to the viewer or listener, thus gradually claiming as his own the channel of immediate communication from President to people legitimated by the 1962 constitutional amendment. Jospin thereby progressively 'became' a President of all the French, gradually appropriating the President's position as unique and authoritative speaker to, and spokesman for, the nation. This strategy of developing a presidential voice reached its culmination when, on the last day of the campaign, Jospin began his short final broadcast with the presidential 'Françaises, Français' and ended with 'Vive la France, vive la République!'

Most important, perhaps, for the myth particular to the Fifth Republic, is Jospin and Chirac's acknowledgement of the presidential responsibility to see that France is in crisis, and to guide her out of it as the first President did in the Beginning of the Fifth Republic. This imperative to 'save' the country of course shares in the dynamics of the universal myth of Paradise Lost and Regained which is a favourite point of reference with all politicians promising a better future. Nevertheless, it has in the French Fifth Republic the particularity of a peculiar vocabulary and national resonance which is the specific legacy of the way in which the presidency was shaped by de Gaulle. The President of the Fifth Republic possesses, exclusively, the almost supernatural vision which enables him to identify France's departure from her real nature, to guide her back to the true path and to forge her anew, restoring her to her one profound and indivisible self. Chirac, as we have seen above, was able to use de Gaulle's own vocabulary to refer to this aspect of the myth ('France is truly herself only when...'), but he also referred to it implicitly when he declared his intention to (re)-create and preside over a 'new' France which would play the historic role which is rightfully hers.[48] Jospin also communicated the same message by inference, promising a re-creation of historical grandeur by claiming that: 'If I am President, I can guarantee that our country will be worthy of her history', and hinting at a re-birth of French values in the statement: 'Because of our history, we are the heirs of a democratic and republican culture. I want to make that culture live today'.[49]

The style in which the 'text' of the myth is rewritten by each candidate and at each election is, of course, subject to a great variety of influences. In 1995 as in other years, in addition to the personal and party political influences over each candidate's reinterpretation of the myth, aspects of contemporary culture could be detected in many aspects of the campaign. For instance, references to the televisual medium itself continued to dominate many of the candidates' television broadcasts, which mimicked the format of the (unscripted) political interview or documentary programme in order to imply the supposed importance, individuality, spontaneity and impartiality of the candidate.[50] The effect of consumerism and commercial advertising was also notable: a prime example of this was to be found in the smart postmodern montages of the Chirac broadcasts, highly reminiscent of contemporary advertising campaigns for hi-tech computer systems. However, our short survey of the nine campaigns indicates that whatever the influences of the cultural climate, personality and party, the French presidential elections do indeed, even thirty-seven years into the Fifth Republic, and even given a field of candidates chiefly composed of less than charismatic orators, invoke the myth of the President. More interestingly, the text of the myth and its different versions in 1995 also reveal some of the principal political preoccupations in the Fifth Republic of the 1990s. These will be examined in our conclusions.

Conclusion

We have already noted that candidates position themselves in relation to the myth of the President in different ways, depending on the purposes for which elections are exploited by various individuals or groups. We have seen, for instance, that minority candidates who do not seek to 'become' a mythical President in their campaign use the first round of the election for a wide variety of motives: as a means to establish themselves at the head of a political grouping; to gain wider recognition of their views; to establish the credibility of their party; to influence the agenda of the mainstream candidates and their parties. Some minority candidates, on the other hand, notably on the extreme right, seek to acquire legitimacy and broader acceptance by projecting themselves as claimants to a myth which is, by its very nature, generally shared and approved of in France.

The mainstream candidates of both right and left are positively obliged to affirm their fitness for office by asserting, in addition to serious and detailed policy programmes, their right and capacity to occupy the mythical, liminal region, above yet within the Republic and France, which is the domain of the President. This positioning of such candidates confirms the extraordinary influence which the myth exercises over campaign discourse, dominating and structuring the language of any candidate, left or right, who wishes to be taken as a serious contender.

This is not to say that all presidential candidates speak a single language, but rather that each one has to measure his or her rhetoric against the myth of the President in much the same way as one would refer to a compass when mapping out a journey. Nor would it be sensible to suggest that there is such a thing as a 'good' or 'bad' evocation of the myth of the President and that a 'good' campaign alone will necessarily lead to electoral success. The great majority of the electorate of course give no conscious thought at all to the mythological mechanisms at work beneath the surface of campaign discourse. Indeed, many are likely to see the various textual strands of the myth of the President as just so many monotonous electoral clichés. Yet this in itself can be taken to indicate the extent to which the myth of the President has become a given of the Fifth Republic: that parts of its text have apparently become commonplace within the polity signals its success as an 'invented tradition', demonstrating a generalised acceptance of presidentialist politics and the cohesion of the Fifth Republic as a social and political 'family' or identity group.[51]

In 1995, a strand of campaign language which to some extent united all the candidates was the theme of 'real change', this last slogan becoming a strong rhetorical focus of differentiation between Chirac and Jospin during the second round. Calls for change are of course a staple of electoral discourse: the difference in a French presidential election, as we have seen, is that they are couched in a vocabulary which alludes to the specific myth of the Fifth Republic. Calls for change which invoke the myth of the President – as in the 1995 election – are therefore closely bound with the notion that France is in a crisis which disfigures and splits her true identity, the (prospective) President alone being in a position to restore her to absolute integrity. In other words, the candidate has, in his or her discourse, to 'invent' a France in crisis, and to present his or her policy proposals as a way of recreating the true France.

It is apparent from this emphasis on change that the aspect of the myth which most particularly asserted itself in 1995 was the theme of recreation or rebirth. Indeed, it imposed itself so strongly in the discourse of the candidates that it became something of a cliché, with each major player alluding to the 'crisis' and presenting every possible policy as a guarantee of 'renewal'. The dominance of the theme was reinforced by the highly active French media, nourished by a large number of political polls, which peddled the notion of change as a central electoral issue, making it an unavoidable point of reference for every candidate. It is interesting to suggest why this strand of the presidential myth, rather than any other, gained such prominence in 1995.

The crisis alluded to by the candidates on this occasion was based on the emergence of real divisions within French society. A popular characterisation of 1990s politics amongst journalists and academics at the time of the election was the theory that the traditional division between left and right had been superseded by the division between pro- and anti-Europeanism.[52] More pressing for the candidates, however, was the fact that domestic questions such as wages, unemployment, homelessness and immigration were being seen less in traditional party political or ideological terms than as socio-economic puzzles, with the issue of 'exclusion' figuring as a major focus of the campaign. The preferred metaphors used by both commentators and candidates to describe the real social and economic distress of many French voters called on images of fragmentation, fracture and division: Chirac, in particular, made much in his campaign of the 'social fracture', but other candidates were also compelled to use the same type of vocabulary.[53] The split between those members of society who were living in at least reasonably secure economic conditions and those who were not was, after all, highly visible: magazines sold by the homeless were available on every street corner; demonstrations on behalf of the 'excluded' were organised by pressure groups in the run-up to the elections; and the candidates Hue, Voynet and Laguiller in particular used the elections to keep up high profile pressure on this issue on the mainstream candidates and the government.

In the hyperbolic rhetoric of the campaigns, structured by the myth of the President, these divisions within French society became characterised as a near-mythological descent into generalised fragmentation and chaos which threatened also to split France and the French identity, and which required (presidential) leadership and change to reunite the nation. Such portrayals of descent into disorder followed by harmony and synthesis draw on classical patterns also found in alchemical and initiatory myths from civilisations all over the world: both types of imagery project scenarios of chaos followed by order, fragmentation followed by wholeness, dark followed by light, and trials or even death followed by serene rebirth. But in each case, the metamorphosis is effected by the guide, alchemist or shaman who alone holds the secret of successful transformation.

The most striking slogans of 1995 participate in this dynamic of renewal and naturally enough attribute to the candidate the role of presidential guide or re-creator. Chirac's 'A France for everyone'[54] acknowledges that divisions exist by making an implicit comparison with the corollary 'a France for some', and openly hints at healing and oneness; Jospin's word-play 'With Lionel Jospin, it's clear' slightly more subtly implies that the present chaos can be seen as darkness and the future (under Jospin) as clarity and light[55]; while Voynet's 'Dare to vote Voynet, it'll change everything'[56] also calls forth the promise of total transformation. Such slogans are seductive, partly because, by association with initiatory and presidential myths, they pledge so much: the scholar Walter Kaelber notes in a discussion of initiation in the religious and anthropological spheres that, upon emerging from such profound metamorphosis as that hinted at here, 'One is not simply changed; one is made new'.[57] The 'renewal' or 'rebirth' of the nation offered by candidates at the 1995 French election was, therefore, not only imperative in the light of the real fragmentations being perceived or experienced by society at the time. It was also a particularly powerful strand of the campaign in the circumstances, for it seemed to offer more than simply a set of new policies or legislative reforms. Proffered in the terms of the myth of the President, and overlapping with those of universal initiatory ritual and mythology, the promise of renewal invoked wholesale transformation on an historic, indeed almost cosmic, scale, from a fragmented, chaotic state into a whole, re-ordered one. On closer analysis, it also reveals the underlying fear of divisions and the general social and economic unease which stalked the pre-election and election period in 1995.

In Jacques Chirac's acceptance speech, made barely an hour after learning that victory was his, he referred directly to this whole complex of ideas and images in terms which evoke the myth of the President very clearly. On the subject of unemployment, he said:

> Every initiative will be supported. All our energies will be mobilised. Every success will be encouraged. The same will be true for the fight against exclusion.
> When we have beaten back these scourges, then France will be herself again....[58]

On this occasion, those phrases which might previously have been viewed by many as rather tired clichés are somehow transformed, 'resacralised' by the knowledge that Chirac now speaks as the next President of the Republic: the victor in the contest, whatever we may think of his politics and his campaign, steps into a mythical role, simply by virtue of his having won the presidency. When Chirac declares, in the same speech, that he will be a President of all the French, that he wishes a State which does not isolate those who govern from the people who elected them, that he wishes that France may become herself again, his words assume a new dignity aided by the protocol and symbolic circumstances of the declaration.

As with all great myths, perhaps the most significant quality of the myth of the President is this very elasticity, the ability of the myth to take different shapes according to circumstances and personalities. It can contract into near-imperceptible references and shadowy mechanisms driving forward or structuring a campaign; or it can expand into full-blooded declarations of presidential authority and legitimacy. It is this versatility and ambiguity which assure the myth's resilience and guarantee its vital role in French political culture.

Notes

1 R. Barthes, *Mythologies* (Paris, Seuil, 1957).
2 E. Leach, 'Approaches to the Study of the Bible,' in Edmund Leach and D. Alan Aycock, *Structuralist Interpretations of Biblical Myth* (Cambridge, Cambridge University Press, 1983), p.8.
3 E. Hobsbawm, 'Inventing Traditions,' in E. Hobsbawm and T. Ranger (eds.), *The Invention of Tradition* (Cambridge, Cambridge University Press, 1983), pp.1-14: p.9. Hobsbawm also notes that: 'Indeed, most of the occasions when people become conscious of citizenship as such remain associated with symbols and semi-ritual practices (for instance, elections), most of which are historically novel and largely invented: flags, images, ceremonies and music' (Hobsbawm, p.12).
4 '...le rite force l'homme à transcender ses limites, l'oblige à se situer auprès des Dieux et des héros mythiques, afin de pouvoir accomplir leurs actes. Directement ou indirectement, le mythe opère une "élévation" de l'homme'. Mircea Eliade, *Aspects du mythe* (Paris, Gallimard, 1963), p.173.
5 See John Gaffney, 'Introduction,' *The French Presidential Elections of 1988*, pp.11-12. For an analysis of de Gaulle's leadership discourse, see H. Drake and J. Gaffney, 'Introduction,' in H. Drake and J. Gaffney (eds.), *The Language of Leadership in Contemporary France*, (Aldershot, Dartmouth, 1996), pp.11-33.
6 Jean Lacouture, *Citations du Général de Gaulle* (Paris, Seuil, 1968), p.57.
7 Mircea Eliade, *Aspects du mythe*, p.48. Eliade and other specialists in the study of myths agree on the particular numinous power surrounding stories of the Beginning which show strong isomorphism from one culture and mythology to another. See also Erich Neumann, *The Origins and History of Consciousness*, trans. R. F. C. Hull (1949; trans. 1970; reprinted Princeton, Princeton University Press, 1973).
8 François Goguel, 'Les Circonstances du référendum d'octobre 1962' *Le Référendum d'octobre et les élections de novembre 1962*, Cahiers de la Fondation Nationale des Sciences Politiques no. 142 (Paris, Presses Nationales de la Fondation Nationale des Sciences Politiques, 1965), pp.9-36.
9 See Institut Charles de Gaulle, *Bibliographie internationale sur Charles de Gaulle* (Paris, Plon, 1981).
10 Charles de Gaulle, *Mémoires de guerre. L'Appel (1940-1942)* (Paris, Plon, 1954), p.1.
11 'A la France, à notre dame la France, nous n'avons à dire qu'une seule chose, c'est que rien ne nous importe ni ne nous occupe, excepté de la servir. [...] Nous n'avons rien à lui demander, excepté peut-être, qu'au jour de la liberté, elle veuille bien nous ouvrir maternellement ses bras pour que nous y pleurions de joie et qu'au jour où la mort sera venue nous saisir, elle nous ensevelisse doucement dans sa bonne et sainte terre.'

Charles de Gaulle, Speech in Tunis, 27 June 1943 *Discours et messages 1940-1946* (Paris, Berger-Levrault, 1946), pp.334-335.

[12] '...invinciblement, la France Combattante émerge de l'Océan. Quand, à Bir-Hakeìm, un rayon de sa gloire renaissante est venu caresser le front sanglant de ses soldats, le monde a reconnu la France'. Charles de Gaulle, speech in the Albert Hall, London, 18 June 1942; *Discours et messages 1940-1946*, pp.212-220.

[13] De Gaulle's France has nothing of the powerful malignity which accompanies the benign powers of traditional goddesses, most of which have counterparts in, or simultaneously embody, Terrible Mother archetypes. See Erich Neumann, *The Great Mother*, (trans. Ralph Mannheim; Princeton, Princeton/Bollingen, 2nd edition 1972).

[14] See Jean Lacouture, *De Gaulle*, vol. 1, trans. Patrick O'Brien (London, Harvill/Harper Collins, 1993), pp.26-28. Indeed, de Gaulle cites Péguy at the end of the 1942 speech quoted above: 'Mother, behold thy sons who have fought so long and hard!' ('Mère, voyez vos fils qui se sont tant battus!').

[15] 'De Gaulle peut regarder de Gaulle, puisque de Gaulle est la France, et son chef à la fois. Tour à tour incarnant et guidant, il est double et constant. Ce qui lui permet ce mélange de distance et d'admiration, ce jeu de miroirs qui lui fait voir et dire tour à tour "moi" et "de Gaulle," qui lui permet de passer tranquillement du "je" au "il" dans les mêmes phrases..'.. Jean Lacouture, *Citations du président de Gaulle*, p.177. Mauriac's book on de Gaulle remains an interesting analysis of de Gaulle's language and persona by a major French intellectual who himself contributed something to the myth of de Gaulle by writing about him. See François Mauriac, *De Gaulle* (Paris, Grasset, 1964).

[16] 'Guide de la France et chef de l'Etat'. See, for example, radio and television address, 28 December 1958 in *Discours et messages. Avec le renouveau 1958-1962* (Paris, Plon, 1970), pp.64-67; and radio and television address, 20 September 1962, in *Discours et messages. Pour l'effort 1962-1965* (Paris, Plon, 1970), pp.19-24.

[17] 'Penché sur le gouffre où la patrie a roulé, je suis son fils, qui l'appelle, lui tient la lumière, lui montre la voie du salut.... Maintenant, j'entends la France me répondre. Au fond de l'abîme, elle se relève, elle marche, elle gravit la pente. Ah! mère, tels que nous sommes, nous voici pour vous servir'. *Mémoires de guerre (1940-1942)*, p.216.

[18] See, for example, de Gaulle's speech at Strasbourg, 23 November 1961, in *Discours et messages. Avec le renouveau*, pp.367-371: 'En aucun temps, la France n'eut à ce point le droit et le devoir d'être elle-même...'.

[19] 'la propension des Français à se diviser'. *Mémoires de guerre. L'Appel*, p.225.

[20] See Mircea Eliade, *La Nostalgie des origines* (Paris, Gallimard, 1971).

[21] 'Je m'adresse à la France. Eh bien! Mon cher et vieux pays, nous voici donc ensemble, encore une fois face à une lourde épreuve'. Charles de Gaulle, radio and television address, 29 January1960, in *Discours et messages. Avec le renouveau.*

[22] '[...] il s'agit de transformer notre vieille France en un pays neuf et de lui faire épouser son temps. Il s'agit qu'elle en tire la prospérité, la puissance et le rayonnement. Il s'agit que ce changement soit notre grande ambition nationale'. Charles de Gaulle, radio and television address, 14 June 1960, in *Discours et messages. Avec le renouveau*, pp.224-229.

[23] See for example June Singer, *Androgyny* (New York, Anchor/Doubleday, 1977).

[24] 'La ménagère veut le progrès mais elle ne veut pas la pagaille, eh bien! c'est vrai aussi pour la France. Il faut le progrès, il ne faut pas la pagaille'. Radio and television interview with Michel Droit, 15 December 1965, in *Discours et messages. Pour l'effort*, pp.432-440.

25 '...l'esprit de la Constitution nouvelle consiste [...] à faire en sorte que le pouvoir [...] procède directement du peuple, ce qui implique que le chef de l'Etat, élu par la nation, en soit *la source et le détenteur'*. Charles de Gaulle, press conference of 31 January 1964, in *Discours et messages. Pour l'effort*, pp.162-182. My italics.

26 For a discussion of the 'sacred' nature of universal sovereignty in the democratic process, see Helen Drake and John Gaffney, 'Introduction' in *The Language of Leadership in Contemporary France*.

27 'La France, c'est tout à la fois, c'est tous les Français. C'est pas la gauche, la France! C'est pas la droite, la France! [...] Prétendre faire la France avec une fraction, c'est une erreur grave, et prétendre représenter la France au nom d'une fraction, cela c'est une erreur nationale impardonnable. [...] Je ne suis pas d'un côté, je ne suis pas de l'autre, je suis pour la France'. Charles de Gaulle, radio and television interview, 15 December 1965, *op. cit.*

28 In March 1967, for example, only 17% of French people thought that de Gaulle, as President, had behaved as an independent arbiter; nearly two-thirds of those polled thought that he had conducted himself rather as the leader of the Gaullist party.

29 This does not mean that others have tried to emulate him in a simplistic way, but rather that his 'légende dorée' has become an integral and formative part of French political – and presidential – culture. This point has of course already been made elsewhere: see for example Helen Drake and John Gaffney, 'Introduction', *The Language of Leadership in Contemporary France*. For a discussion of some aspects of successors' comportment as related to de Gaulle, see also John Gaffney, 'Introduction: French Political Culture and Modernisation' in J. Gaffney (ed.), *France and Modernisation* (Aldershot, Avebury, 1988), pp.1-7.

30 Dominique Labbé, *Le Vocabulaire de François Mitterrand* (Paris, Presses de la Fondation Nationale des Sciences Politiques, 1990), pp.315-316. This review of Mitterrand's vocabulary in 68 public speeches and interviews from 14 July 1981 to 4 March 1988 shows that 'De Gaulle' appears 42 times in total, the next most frequent individual's name being Reagan (26 times), followed by Fabius (22 times). The most frequently-used proper nouns are of course 'France' (1,1219 citations) and 'Français' (425).

31 'Je suis le Président de la République'.

32 See for example Emmanuel Souchier and Yves Jeanneret, 'L'Election présidentielle, ou la quête du Graal,' *Le Monde diplomatique*, July 1995, pp.18-19.

33 'il faut', 'la France doit, 'on devrait', 'c'est possible si...'.

34 '...C'est un tel programme que je vous demande d'approuver par votre vote. Si nous sommes des millions à l'approuver, nous aurons alors les moyens de contraindre celui qui sera élu, quel qu'il soit, à le réaliser'. Formula repeated in many of Laguiller's campaign broadcasts, e.g. France 2, 12 April 1995, 13.30h.

35 'moi, je...'; 'je vous propose...'; 'Votez pour moi'.

36 'Jean-Marie Le Pen, un homme du peuple, un homme d'état'.

37 The popular programmme *Les Guignols de l'info* regularly referred to him as 'le neuneuh' ('the twit'), representing him as a fool dressed in his smart dark suit and a jester's bonnet. For a discussion of the role of satire in the elections, Chapter 12.

38 See Chapter 9.

39 Giving work to every French citizen; reducing the number of immigrants; priority for French people; giving French people the fruits of their labours (fiscal reform); pursuing the triumph of values; re-establishing justice and security for decent people; guaranteeing the public health service; ensuring the greatness of France; reclaiming

French sovereignty. We need hardly draw attention here to the use of grandiose and religious imagery to attach Le Pen's programme to notions of mythical transcendence and inevitability.

[40] Foresight; courage; experience; patriotism; decency. The text continues: 'These qualities are those of Jean-Marie Le Pen' ('Ces qualités sont celles de Jean-Marie Le Pen').

[41] For a detailed analysis of Le Pen's discourse as leader of the Front National, see Catherine Fieschi, 'Jean-Marie Le Pen and the Discourse of Ambiguity', in Helen Drake and John Gaffney (eds.), *The Language of Leadership in Contemporary France*, pp.107-132.

[42] 'La France dispose au fond d'elle-même des ressources d'intelligence, de générosité et d'enthousiasme qui ont fait et qui feront à nouveau de notre patrie républicaine une référence, un espoir et un exemple. C'est cette cause que j'entends servir, avec toutes les Françaises et tous les Français'.

[43] 'La France n'est elle-même que lorsqu'elle se rassemble autour des valeurs de la République. C'est la grande leçon du général de Gaulle. C'est mon ambition la plus haute'.

[44] See for example his only reference to President Mitterrand during the 20,000-strong rally at Bercy in Paris on 3 May 1995, which took the form of a qualified allusion to Mitterrand's 1988 campaign slogan 'La force tranquille'. Enumerating the qualities and energies which were driving his campaign, Jospin included – to the approval of the crowd – 'cette force tranquille, oui, pourquoi pas' ('this quiet strength, yes, why not').

[45] 'un président proche des Français, garant des valeurs républicaines' Jospin, campaign brochure, second round.

[46] 'un président à l'écoute du pays, un président qui *décide*'. Jospin, election broadcast, France 2, 3 May 1995, 13.30h.

[47] Chirac's campaign favoured a smart, *7 Sur 7*-style studio decor with black background for these discussions, while Jospin was seen in rather less glamorous surroundings, answering questions from young people in informal and 'spontaneous' seminar style. For a tactical reading of Chirac's TV campaign, see Chapter 12 in this volume.

[48] 'Cette nouvelle France qui...pourra jouer le rôle historique qui est le sien'. Chirac, campaign brochure, first round.

[49] 'Si je suis président, je peux garantir que notre pays sera à la hauteur de son histoire... Par notre histoire nous sommes héritiers d'une culture démocratique et républicaine. Je veux la faire vivre aujourd'hui'. Jospin, campaign brochure, first round.

[50] See in particular the longer Balladur broadcast (France 2, 11 April 1995), the first section of which brilliantly simulates a biographical documentary about a Great Man.

[51] See Murray Edelman, *Politics as Symbolic Action* (Chicago, Marham, 1971), especially pp.73-74.

[52] See, for example, Etienne Schweisguth (ed.), *Droite-Gauche: un clivage dépassé?* Special Number of *Problèmes politiques et sociaux* , no. 719, 14 January 1994.

[53] Some moments of the televised debate between the two final contenders were devoted to the question of the vocabulary itself, Chirac using 'Social fracture' ('fracture sociale'), Jospin preferring 'social fault line' ('faille sociale').

[54] 'La France pour tous'.

[55] 'Avec Lionel Jospin, c'est clair'. The slogan also, of course, implies a lack of clarity in the activities and utterances of Jospin's opponents.

[56] 'Osez Dominique Voynet, ça change tout'.

[57] Walter Kaelber, 'Men's Initiation', in M. Eliade (ed.), *The Encyclopedia of Religion* (New York, Macmillan, 1987).
[58] Jacques Chirac, Hôtel de ville de Paris, 7 May, 1995, 21.00h. (Reprinted, e.g. in *Libération*, 8 May 1995). 'Toutes les initiatives seront soutenues. Toutes les énergies seront mobilisées. Toutes les réussites seront encouragées. Il sera de même pour la lutte contre l'exclusion.
    'Lorsque nous aurons fait reculer ces fléaux, alors la France redeviendra elle-même....'

Indicative Bibliography

Drake, Helen and John Gaffney (eds.), *The Language of Leadership in Contemporary France* (Aldershot, Dartmouth, 1996).
de Gaulle, Charles, *Mémoires de guerre* (Paris, Plon, 3 volumes: 1954, 1956, 1959).
de Gaulle, Charles, *Mémoires d'espoir* (Paris, Plon, 2 volumes: 1970, 1971).
de Gaulle, Charles, *Discours et messages* (Paris, Plon, 5 volumes: 1970).
Edelman, Murray, *Politics as Symbolic Action* (Chicago, Marham, 1971).
Eliade, Mircea, *Aspects du mythe* (Paris, Gallimard, 1963).
Eliade, Mircea, *La Nostalgie des origines* (Paris, Gallimard, 1971).
Gaffney, John, *The French Presidential Elections of 1988* (Aldershot, Dartmouth, 1989).
Hobsbawm, E. and T. Ranger (eds.), *The Invention of Tradition* (Cambridge, Cambridge University Press, 1983).
Labbé, Dominique, *Le Vocabulaire de François Mitterrand* (Paris, Presses de la Fondation Nationale des Sciences Politiques, 1990).

4. THE MITTERRAND LEGACY

ALISTAIR COLE

Introduction

Elected President in 1981, triumphantly re-elected in 1988, François Mitterrand was largely absent from the 1995 presidential campaign. Aged physically, weakened by prostate cancer, politically immobilised after the Socialists' electoral defeat in the National Assembly elections of March 1993, and morally subdued by new revelations of his wartime record, the incumbent President was little more than an observer throughout the second period of 'cohabitation' (1993-95). Notwithstanding the melancholy decline of the *fin de règne*, however, François Mitterrand will be remembered as one of the key statespersons of his century, having survived at the helm for 14 years, longer than any other French political leader in the twentieth century.

The *fin de règne* was accompanied by an explosion of books on various aspects of Mitterrand's life and political career. The French literature on Mitterrand is so abundant as to preclude any attempt at exhaustive listing here. Along with the usual journalistic diet of scandal (Montaldo) and the personal memoirs of former advisors (Attali, Laure), there have been several serious attempts to evaluate the consequences of the Mitterrand presidency (Favier and Martin-Roland, Colombani and Portelli, and Schneider), a major work consecrated to Mitterrand's early years (Péan), and an attempt by Mitterrand to give his own version of his personal and political legacy (Mitterrand and Wiesel).

Péan's book in particular sparked a storm of controversy both in relation to Mitterrand's activities during the wartime Vichy regime, and his dubious acquaintances thereafter. The 'revelations' in relation to Vichy were scarcely new: Mitterrand's service as a minor agent of the Vichy regime had been a regular subject of polemic since the 1965 presidential election campaign. But solid documentary and photographic evidence forced out into the open the ambiguous role performed by Mitterrand during the Second World War (first as an agent of the wartime Pétain regime, later as a resistance fighter). The intensity of the debate revealed France as a nation still to come to terms with its Vichy past. The ambiguities of Mitterrand's behaviour were real enough: Péan's book revealed that Mitterrand had remained in the service of the Vichy regime longer than had originally been thought, though it did not refute the argument that the Vichy regime contained numerous genuine (and undercover) *résistants* and French patriots serving alongside extreme-right elements. In his defence, it might be pointed out that Mitterrand's trajectory was shared by other wartime figures who went on to perform key roles in the post-war Fourth Republic. Indeed, many anti-German French patriots initially considered Pétain's Vichy to be a patriotic, anti-German regime. Such a view was progressively less feasible, however, as the anti-Semitic, pro-Nazi activities of the regime became apparent, especially after 1942. In the appreciation of one otherwise critical observer:

> Mitterrand was sincerely and successively a Pétainist, then a Giraudist, then a Gaullist, succeeding by his remarkable courage in countering the bad initial choice he had made. His trajectory was a classical one, one that does not justify prolonged scrutiny.[1]

At least Mitterrand ended up on the right side. But while his wartime ambiguities were understandable, the fact that the President had maintained friendly relations with René Bousquet – a leading police chief of the Vichy state – for decades after the war for many simply unpardonable. The Bousquet episode illustrates the dangers of one key feature of Mitterrand's political style: the cultivation of personal networks in all walks of life, and amongst all types of politician, with loyalty to friends and to clients playing an important role. The President's televised self-defence in relation to Bousquet lacked conviction. It was also notable that, in accordance with Gaullist tradition, Mitterrand refused to apologise for the crimes of the Vichy state 'in the name of the Republic': the President stuck to the argument that, because the Vichy state had 'killed' the Republic in 1940, it was not for the Republic to apologise for the acts of an illegal regime. This argument was not new: it had been used by former Presidents de Gaulle, Pompidou and Giscard d'Estaing. But it increased a general sense of disquiet with the President, even amongst the ranks of Socialist politicians. By contrast, President Chirac's unambiguous apology to French Jews in July 1995 drew support from certain leading Socialists (such as Rocard and Jospin) who had not appreciated Mitterrand's hesitations on this issue.

The controversy occasioned by the Péan 'revelations', along with the hopeless balance of political power after the March 1993 elections, combined to reduce Mitterrand's policy input during the second period of 'cohabitation', a period during which the Fourth President of the Fifth Republic attempted to prepare an honourable exit. In accordance with the theme of this book, an attempt will be made in the ensuing chapter to tie in the personal contribution of François Mitterrand to French politics with the systemic and policy evolution of the French Fifth Republic during the period 1981-1995.

The Mitterrand presidency 1981-95: an overview

Mitterrand was elected as President in 1981 committed to a break with capitalism. He was re-elected in 1988 advocating the merits of consensus, national unity, and the modernisation of capitalism. The victorious Socialist candidate of 1981 was forced to water down, or to abandon, the key precepts of his presidential platform within two or three years. But the first two years of Mitterrand's presidency stand out as a period of reformist effort unprecedented in scope, at least since the post-war tripartite government of 1946-47. The reforms undertaken by Pierre Mauroy's government combined 'classical' quantitative left-wing policies in the sphere of social, economic and industrial policy with qualitative reforms in other areas, notably decentralisation, enhanced workers rights, the creation of a ministry for Women's affairs and various liberal civil rights measures. The main reforms enacted included the nationalisation of leading industrial groups and banks, the decentralisation measures, and the accomplishment of wide-ranging welfare reforms (partly financed by redistributive taxation measures). Certain reforms were transient; the effects of others only became slowly apparent. The decentralisation reforms of 1982-3 belong to the latter category. The transfer of major policy responsibilities to the ninety-six departmental councils, and the direct election of the twenty-two regional Assemblies had a major long-term impact whose effects are only becoming clear today.[2] Other measures had unintended consequences, notably in the sphere of industrial policy and economic management.[3]

Mitterrand came to office as a champion of the people of the left. In the French context this meant alliance with the Communist Party (PCF), Keynesian reflationist economic policies, nationalisation, and support for traditional industrial sectors. By 1984, a complete reversal had taken place: a definite abandonment of reflation in March 1983 for the strong franc policy; a drastic industrial modernisation programme which virtually shut down the coal and shipbuilding industries; the beginnings of a partial privatisation programme; and the expulsion of the PCF from government. These policy reversals indicated that governments do not act in isolation, especially in the economic sphere: the combined pressures of the international economy, spiralling trade and budget deficits, a sharp increase in inflation and diplomatic pressures from European Community partners all constrained the French Socialists to change course. Mitterrand's salvation lay in the fact that the fourth President was sufficiently adaptable as a political leader to make a virtue out of necessity. Under President Mitterrand's second premier, Laurent Fabius (1984-86), the theme of 'modernisation' became the key ideological justification for a range of disparate policies.

From 1984 onwards, Mitterrand's attentions were increasingly focused on issues of foreign policy, defence, and, above all, Europe. In appraising Mitterrand's foreign policy, Stanley Hoffmann concluded that it was 'Gaullism by any other name'.[4] In key areas of foreign policy, Mitterrand was more faithful to the model of national independence promoted by General de Gaulle than his immediate predecessor had been: his acceptance of the strategic doctrines underpinning the French independent nuclear deterrent was a case in point. The importance placed by Mitterrand on bilateral Franco-German relations also recalled that of de Gaulle some twenty years earlier. The parallel with de Gaulle should not be overstated, however. The Euromissile crisis of 1982-83 revealed Mitterrand as a stauncher supporter of the Atlantic cause than past French Presidents, less prone to idealism in relation to the Soviet Bloc countries. In European Community policy, in both symbolic and substantive terms, Mitterrand's Europe was far more integrationist than that espoused by de Gaulle.[5] From 1984 onwards, Mitterrand concentrated upon portraying himself as a great European statesman, with a coherent vision of Europe's future. Mitterrand was more genuinely convinced of the merits of a unified Europe than any of his predecessors, and proved more willing to sacrifice elements of national sovereignty in the interests of European integration than any of his forerunners as President had been.

As the Mitterrand presidency progressed, the fourth President withdrew from the intricacies of domestic policy. We shall examine the reasons for this in more detail below. The process preceded the 1986-88 'cohabitation', but expressed itself most fully during this episode. By calling upon Jacques Chirac, the leader of the victorious RPR-UDF coalition, to form a government in March 1986, President Mitterrand respected the democratic logic that the clear victors of the most recent general election should be given the responsibility for governing the nation. Any other outcome would have been undemocratic, although there was wide speculation over Mitterrand's possible choices at the time. Presidential primacy disappeared once the President was faced by a determined Prime Minister armed with a parliamentary majority. During the 1986-88 cohabitation, Mitterrand discovered a new role: that of 'arbiter-president'. The government was to be encouraged to govern, but as the arbiter of the nation, according to article 5 of the 1958 constitution, Mitterrand reserved for himself the right to criticise government policies by speaking in the name of the 'French people'. Mitterrand was comfortably re-elected against a divided right-wing challenge in the 1988 presidential election.

Mitterrand was elected in 1988 because he attracted the support of a vital fraction of the centre-right electorate alienated by Chirac and not attracted to the other conservative challenger Raymond Barre. And yet why Mitterrand stood was more difficult to discern.

His 1988 presidential platform, the *Letter to the French*, contained no firm proposals in the sphere of domestic policy, limiting itself to justifications of past presidential actions. Mitterrand was more ambitious in respect of Europe, which the incumbent President made a leitmotif of his second presidential mandate. Mitterrand's European mission, which appeared to triumph with the adoption of the Maastricht Treaty in December 1991, consisted of a steadfast vision of closer European integration, for which the French President deserved much credit or blame, depending upon one's viewpoint. Notwithstanding, the political and diplomatic weight of the French President was diminished after the historic event of German unification in 1990, which altered the balance of European power in favour of Germany.

The pattern of presidential interventionism during Mitterrand's first mandate was curiously reversed during his second term. Whereas he had been highly active after his election as President in 1981, he was content – or at least constrained – to allow his fourth premier, Michel Rocard, a relatively free hand in domestic policy-making from 1988 to 1991. Rocard's enforced resignation in May 1991 temporarily recalled Mitterrand's pre-eminence as President, but it was a move from which he never fully recovered, not least because his move was misunderstood by public opinion. Indeed, under the premiership of Rocard's successor, Edith Cresson, President Mitterrand was forced to intervene more than he would ideally have liked, both in order to support publicly his beleaguered Prime Minister, and to ensure that her policy choices were not adopted. In response to criticisms, Mitterrand protested that the major error of his second presidential term was not his nomination of Cresson in 1991, but that of his historic rival Rocard in 1988.[6]

The succession of Prime Ministers during Mitterrand's second term (Michel Rocard from 1988 to 1991; Edith Cresson from 1991 to 1992; Pierre Bérégovoy from 1992 to 1993) increased public disquiet with the Socialist governments' apparent lack of a sense of purpose. The economic policy of the strong franc, pursued vigorously by Socialist and centre-right administrations since 1983, appeared to deprive governments of much leeway in conducting policy elsewhere, especially if this involved raising public expenditure. And in spite of their credible economic performance in most spheres, the inability of Mitterrand's governments to control unemployment in particular had a devastating effect upon the Socialist Party's electoral fortunes. This was revealed in the 1993 National Assembly election, at which the ruling Socialists were reduced to under 20% and 67 seats. In addition to their perceived inability to master the economy, the Socialists suffered from a series of damaging corruption scandals which did much to demolish their prior claim to moral superiority over the right. There was no incident as serious as the Bokassa diamonds affair (which did so much damage to President Giscard d'Estaing's image in the 1970s) to implicate Mitterrand personally, but the belief was widespread that men close to the President had been engaged in dubious activities that were not censured. The suicide in May 1993 of Pierre Bérégovoy, Mitterrand's sixth Prime Minister, appeared to many to symbolise the moral bankruptcy of a Socialist Party destined for an extended period in the desert.

The appraisal or measurement of an individual political leadership cannot be isolated from the cultural and political environment within which this leadership is exercised. Any such appraisal should be based on a consideration of the interactions between the resources at the disposal of the leader, and the constraints limiting his or her margins of manœuvre.[7] Of particular importance, we should appraise a leader's personal characteristics, the strengths and weaknesses of his institutional position, and the impact of the environmental constraints and opportunities he faces. There *was* a Mitterrand style which was recognisably different from that of other French Presidents and European political leaders. And, however constrained the policy-making environment, the policy choices adopted by Mitterrand as President were different in important respects from those that other individuals would have made. In spite of this, in most spheres Mitterrand's leadership was of a reactive variety; throughout his presidency, he was forced to address agendas he had not selected, and react to events he had not predicted. To some extent, his style of reactive, adaptable leadership might be contrasted with a more innovatory and voluntaristic brand of affirmative leadership, of the type associated with Margaret Thatcher, and – possibly – Jacques Chirac.[8] At the beginning of his first presidential term, Mitterrand exercised a degree of mastery over key resources rare even for a French President. These included: a direct electoral mandate; a seven year term in office; an established constitutional precedent in favour of a strong presidency as the pinnacle of systemic legitimacy; a precedent also of presidential initiative in policy formulation and personnel selection; a strong presidential bargaining position in relation to other essential institutions (bureaucracy, government, parliament, parties, interest groups); an absolute majority for the President's supporters in parliament; and sympathetic public opinion. But Mitterrand's early political credit was rapidly dissipated: within one year, public opinion had become wary of 'la vie en rose', and the full force of constraints facing the new government became apparent. The loss of a sympathetic parliamentary majority to support the President in 1986 accelerated a process of presidential withdrawal from domestic politics which had been gathering pace since 1983. The arbitral interpretation of the presidency (forcibly) espoused by Mitterrand during the 1986-88 'cohabitation' was carried over in a modified form to his second presidential term after 1988, when the Socialists disposed of only a relative majority within the National Assembly. Despite being re-elected in 1988, the lack of a sense of clear purpose permeated Mitterrand's second presidential term in office. After 1988, Mitterrand too often gave the impression of vacillation, of vindictiveness, and of being unconvinced of the measures propounded by his governments. Indeed, there emerged a certain nostalgia for the period prior to 1982-83, which called into question Mitterrand's commitment to the fundamental choices made in the first term: this was one interpretation behind Mitterrand's nomination of Cresson as premier in May 1991. It was increasingly difficult to discern any agenda motivating presidential activity, except in the field of European affairs. The Socialists' shattering defeat in the National Assembly elections of 1993 removed Mitterrand's last remaining source of political legitimacy and virtually reduced the President to bystander status. Mitterrand's presidency was thus subject to a law of diminishing returns. As well as the wearing-down effects of power, Mitterrand had to cope with the effects of the ageing process, and the public disclosure of his illness in 1992. In fact, all French Presidents have been subjected to a tendency for diminishing political returns as their presidencies have progressed; this suggests a natural threshold (variable for each incumbent, but not exceeding 10 years) beyond which the effectiveness of presidential political leadership is seriously impaired.

The constraints on foreign policy-making are, if anything, more imposing than in the sphere of domestic politics, although their domestic effects are different. They include the consequences of past foreign policy decisions, the need to respect existing alliance structures, the pressures of foreign governments, and an important bureaucratic input into foreign policy-making. Initially pledged to implement a pro-Third World 'Socialist' foreign policy, President Mitterrand gradually reverted to a more Gaullist approach. The Gaullist foreign policy legacy was clearly visible in a number of spheres during Mitterrand's presidency. This was the case with respect to the affirmation of maximum national independence in foreign policy-making and defence; the assertion that France remained a first-rank power; the observance of the canons of Gaullist nuclear doctrine; the refusal to return to the military command structure of NATO; the preservation of a priority relationship with Germany within Europe; the maintenance of neo-colonial relations with francophone African states (until 1990 at least), and the concentration of foreign policy making within the presidential sphere. In several respects, however, Mitterrand went beyond the Gaullist foreign policy model. This occurred notably in relation to his European policy (the promotion of closer European integration); his closer co-operation with NATO; his difficult relationship with the USSR and the countries of Eastern Europe; and his belated attempt to promote a democratic evolution in francophone states of sub-Saharan Africa. While Mitterrand managed to surpass the Gaullist legacy in certain respects, French foreign policy remained predominantly shaped by key policy choices taken by his predecessors.

Mitterrand and the changing norms of presidential politics

Mitterrand's personal contribution to the development of French politics in the Fifth Republic might be analysed in terms of four criteria: as a catalyst, as a legitimator of new policy directions, as a consensus builder, and as a reluctant moderniser.

Mitterrand acted as a *catalyst* for a series of developments which would probably have occurred anyway, but whose particular form was unmistakably shaped by his personality. This aspect of Mitterrand can be charted most pertinently in relation to his activity as a political opponent of Gaullism in the 1960s and 1970s. During this period, Mitterrand was strongly associated with the rejuvenation of the Socialist Party in the 1970s, and the strategy of the union of the left between Socialists and Communists; had Mitterrand not been the catalyst for these sentiments, there is a strong argument that someone else would have done so. The real tribute to Mitterrand's political skills derives from the fact that he came to embody the aspirations of the French left, in spite of his past as a Fourth Republican centrist politician, and his reputation for being an unprincipled, Florentine leader. The consistency with which Mitterrand held to his strategic objectives after 1958, throughout difficult political circumstances, contrasted strongly with the portrait sometimes painted of him as a political dilettante.

Mitterrand also acted as a *legitimator* and a *facilitator* of important policy evolutions throughout the course of his presidency. By his active support as President for policies he had previously eschewed, or underplayed, Mitterrand legitimised new policy directions. This role was especially important in relation to economic policy, to European integration, and in his acceptance of important aspects of the *gaullien* legacy in foreign policy. Let us illustrate this in relation to economic policy. As the left's first President in the Fifth Republic, Mitterrand was closely associated with support for the Keynesian, reflationary policies of the first Socialist government under Pierre Mauroy. By mid-1982, most economists agreed that these policies had failed: the attempted economic relaunch had virtually no effect on unemployment (on an underlying upward curve), but had extremely damaging and negative effects in relation to a whole range of other economic indicators: especially inflation, the trade balance, and the budget deficit. The crucial turning point in Mitterrand's first presidential term occurred in March 1983, when the President was called upon to arbitrate between two opposing economic policies in a move which set the course for the rest of his presidency. The choice lay between whether to remain within the European Monetary System (EMS), devalue the franc for the third time and accept a deflationary economic package (the choice adopted); or else to withdraw from the EMS, adopt protectionist measures for French industry and continue on the reflationary path traced since May 1981. After much hesitation and various indications to the contrary, Mitterrand chose the former course of action. He confirmed thereby that France could neither isolate itself through protectionism, nor indefinitely pursue radically different economic policies from those of its main trading partners, especially those within the EC (and in particular the Federal Republic of Germany, France's closest trading partner).

It is clear that the credibility of the new economic direction decided upon in 1983 depended upon explicit, repeated support from Mitterrand, as the ultimate symbol of the left in power. Mitterrand performed this legitimising role throughout the 1983-84 period, in spite of his past enthusiastic endorsement of the previous economic policy. This ability to rectify past errors, and to legitimise new directions was performed credibly by Mitterrand, on account of an adaptable or flexible political style which facilitated such evolutions. Mitterrand's style of reactive, adaptable leadership had its positive and its negative facets. Adaptability was a practical virtue of Mitterrand's political leadership, almost a price for survival (as with other Social-democratic leaderships elsewhere). Adaptability is a form of leadership style well suited to reformist Social-democratic governments, forced to come to terms with the constraints represented by existing society, and by the external economic and international environment. Mitterrand's adaptable style enabled him to face the consequences of policy reversals with some degree of conviction, as revealed above in relation to economic policy. In fact, adaptability could not be celebrated as an end in itself, since it always involved a retreat from a previously held position and therefore a measure of at least implicit failure. But Mitterrand's adaptability was rarely synonymous with crass opportunism. The conviction articulated by Mitterrand in relation to new directions taken during his first term helped to legitimise these directions, once the President appeared genuinely convinced of their merits. This was the case notably for the economy and the drive to closer European integration after 1983.

As a *consensus-builder*, Mitterrand aspired to create agreement on several issues that had previously polarised French opinion. These included the economy, Europe, foreign policy and to some extent constitutional issues. Mitterrand's critical economic arbitrations of 1982-84 set the course for a broader (although by no means unanimous) acceptance of the economic policy known as the 'franc fort', and reconciled the left in government with the realities of economic management. Such a consensual approach also characterised European policy under Mitterrand. In his foreign policy activity, Mitterrand left office in many senses a more 'gaullien' figure than his predecessor Giscard d'Estaing. In relation to constitutional consensus building, finally, the manner in which Mitterrand presided over the 1986-88 'cohabitation', by scrupulously respecting constitutional rules and regulating procedures, ensured that the experience proceeded without undue crisis. Taking the period 1981-93 as a whole, it is clear that Mitterrand reverted to a more arbitral interpretation of the presidency than that practised by his two predecessors.

There was a diminution of Mitterrand's power during his second presidential term; Mitterrand suffered renewed contention in each of the above spheres after 1988, suggesting that his achievements as a consensus builder were imperfect. This was evident in relation to the economy. In strictly statistical terms, the economic policy promoted since 1983 could claim a large measure of success ten years later: with the notable exception of unemployment, the main economic indicators (inflation, balance of trade, budget deficit as a proportion of GNP, growth) were sound, at least by comparison with France's European partners.[9] From this perspective, the electorate's harsh punishment of the Socialists in the 1993 elections appeared rather unjustified. The very real achievements of economic management since 1983 were overshadowed by the fact that the economy tended to exclude any other social or political perspectives. The social costs of economic rigour exacted a political price, in particular a demotivating effect upon those once considered as the left's natural constituency, especially since former Socialist voters were amongst those most likely to suffer from the reality or the prospect of unemployment.

Mitterrand's achievements with respect to Europe were widely recognised. Critical to Mitterrand's decision to remain within the EMS in 1983, the European constraint became progressively more important throughout the course of his presidency. At the same time, Europe developed into a source of considerable domestic benefit for Mitterrand. It was undoubtedly the case that Mitterrand's proactive European policy facilitated his re-election in 1988, as well as enabling French governments to play a leading role in moves towards closer European political and economic integration. Indeed, Mitterrand transformed the art of consensus-building in this sphere into a powerful political weapon. His mastery of this reached its height during the 1988 presidential campaign, when he forced other serious candidates to fight upon consensual grounds he had himself defined as President. Mitterrand's European achievements continued into the second presidential term. The Maastricht Treaty of 1992 was a diplomatic triumph for Mitterrand: moves towards monetary union were foisted upon a reluctant Chancellor Kohl. His political misjudgement in calling a referendum on French ratification of the Treaty in 1992 was thrown into relief in part because of his former reputation for political and diplomatic astuteness. The consensus carefully cultivated around the issue of the European Union was seriously endangered by the 1992 referendum, although, in the event, leading politicians from all mainstream parties pledged their support for the Treaty, which was narrowly ratified by the electorate.

In respect of constitutional issues, finally, it was indicative of Mitterrand's style that proposals for constitutional reform had to wait until the end of his presidency, when there was the least prospect of their being enacted. The impression that Mitterrand had resisted any constitutional reform which might have weakened his power base was an irresistible one, widely shared by public opinion. Whatever his motivations in calling for constitutional reform in 1992-93, Mitterrand stood accused of concocting diabolic political schemes in order to divide his enemies. Nor was this impression restricted to the issue of constitutional reform. For if anything detracted from Mitterrand's activity as a consensus builder, it was the widespread perception of him as an unprincipled manœuvrer.

Closely linked with his role as a legitimator, Mitterrand was, however reluctantly, a *moderniser* and *liberaliser* of the French economy. This was one of the most surprising of Mitterrand's achievements, given his economic empiricism, and his faith in the cardinal virtues of the State. But the modernisation of the French economy during the Mitterrand presidency was manifest in several key spheres, most especially those linked with the application of measures to implement the Single European Act of 1986 and prepare the single market of 1993. This included the ending of exchange controls, an effort aimed at fiscal harmonisation with other EC countries, a return of the nationalised industries to the private sector in a situation of profit and, more generally, a commitment to 'competitive deflation' as the cornerstone of economic policy, in order to compete efficiently in the single market. Other measures symbolised the Socialists' new spirit of managerial competence, and reconciliation with the world of business. These included the de-indexation of prices and salaries, and the deregulation of the Paris Stock exchange. There was some evidence that Mitterrand was unhappy about certain of the measures contained in the Single European Act, fearing an excessively liberal interpretation of the Act along the lines of that espoused by Margaret Thatcher. But in the interests of his wider European mission, he accepted the consequences of his pro-European choices. Indeed, in spite of his rather interventionist vision of the future European Union, Mitterrand accepted that the Maastricht Treaty both implied limited national economic sovereignty and presupposed a liberal, capitalist economy.

While Mitterrand made a major contribution towards the liberalisation of the French economy, his belief in the state remained a powerful one: the President defined his own economic philosophy as that of the mixed economy, and continued to advocate a broad measure of state interventionism, especially where national prestige was at stake, or else where the private sector proved unwilling or incapable of investment. The key architect of the technical details of economic and industrial policies was Finance Minister Pierre Bérégovoy (1984-86, 1988-92). Mitterrand deserves credit, however, for the critical economic arbitrations made during the period from 1982-84, and for his role as an artisan of closer European union.

Set against these qualities, most observers discerned powerful negative features of Mitterrand's leadership, reputedly responsible for inciting an unprecedented degree of political dissatisfaction amongst the French electorate. These included a political style which promoted cynicism, an excessive taste for personal settling of scores, and a weakness in the elaboration of long-term perspectives.

The counterpart to Mitterrand's promotion of consensus politics was a *demobilisation* of political activity. The predominance of the economic perspective reduced the activity of politics to a supplementary, and subordinate concern. One recent work even evokes the Death of Politics under Mitterrand.[10] In order to win in 1981, the left had to promise the earth. Then they had to face the harsh realities of governing. The Socialists were therefore victims of their idealistic but unrealistic pre-1981 discourse, and of their early reformist programme of 1981-82.[11] Neither bore much relationship to the core of routine economic management which Socialist governments had to concentrate upon after 1982. The predominance of the economic perspective thus led to a demobilisation not only of the electorate, but also of many of the Socialist movement's own activists. The proliferation of corruption scandals throughout the course of the second presidential term led to a pervasive cynicism. The belief was widespread that the President was insufficiently in control of his entourage, and too bound by ties of personal loyalty to apprehend the corrupt practices of those around him.

There were also negative consequences of Mitterrand's style. The Machiavellian manœuvrer was only one face of Mitterrand but it would be futile to deny that it formed a powerful part of the public's impression of him. Widespread cynicism in relation to politics was aggravated by Mitterrand's rather cynical political style, notably his rather obvious divide and rule tactics which appeared to many to lie beneath the dignity of a statesperson. On occasion, this was unfortunate for Mitterrand himself, since it fuelled suspicions that the President was engaged in base political manœuvres even when his motives were noble. One of the most criticised acts of Mitterrand's presidency was his introduction in 1985 of proportional representation for the 1986 National Assembly election. Although this was a campaign commitment in 1981, critics contended that the introduction of PR occurred uniquely for partisan political reasons: to divide the parties of the mainstream right (UDF and RPR), and to ensure that the far-right Front National secured enough deputies to prevent the orthodox right from obtaining an overall majority.[12]

Throughout his political career, Mitterrand had attracted animosity and distrust from political rivals within his own camp, as well as amongst declared adversaries. His liking for personal score-settling was a consistent feature of his long political career. This desire to take revenge on political opponents was particularly acute in his complex relationship with Michel Rocard. It would scarcely be an exaggeration to declare that a principal objective of Mitterrand's career was to prevent the successful fruition of Rocard's career. The same sentiment was repeated to a lesser degree in relation to other politicians who had been unwise enough to offend Mitterrand. This ultimately rebounded against him, leaving him an isolated and lonely figure at the end of his presidency, his normally sound political judgement appearing increasingly open to doubt. The manner in which Mitterrand set leading PS tenors against each other also proved ultimately highly damaging to the Socialist Party, the vehicle for his conquest of power in 1981. Towards the end of his presidency, the appearance of Mitterrand as a base manœuvrer came more starkly to the forefront, since his ideological and policy achievements lay in the past.

I argued above that the perspective of European integration and the need for sound economic management provided the main policy justifications for Mitterrand's governments. Outside of these interrelated sectors, there further appeared to be a paucity of long-term perspectives bequeathed by Mitterrand. This was the counterpart to his reactive style of leadership analysed above. Mitterrand's principles were illustrative of a certain political style, rather than predictive of any particular political policies. After the initial reformist period, it was easier to decipher what Mitterrand was against than what he stood for: this was symbolised by his 'Neither nationalisation, nor privatisation' pledge in the 1988 campaign. The generality of the propositions contained in Mitterrand's 1988 'Lettre à tous les Français' revealed an arbitral conception of the presidency which reflected Mitterrand's presidential practice since 1984. This represented a shift from the ultra-interventionism of the 1981 campaign's '110 Propositions'. And yet to some extent this declaration of arbitral intent trapped Mitterrand, since it made it more difficult to intervene later on. When Mitterrand did attempt to redescend into the domestic arena, notably by calling for a 'nouvel élan' in 1990 and 1991, it appeared as if the President was intent on destabilising Premier Rocard's reformist effort for purely personal motives. The manner in which Mitterrand actively sought to minimise the impact of the important reforms enacted during Rocard's premiership not only reflected poorly on his statesmanship, but also called into question his political judgement, since public opinion perceived Mitterrand and Rocard as a couple whose fortunes were intricately linked.

The policies of the Socialist governments drew their inspiration from Social-democratic incrementalism, notwithstanding the radical tone of the 1981-82 period and the boldness of certain reforms. In economic policy, for instance, after the initial attempt to reflate the economy (itself hardly revolutionary), the left-wing government resorted to a conservative deflationary economic policy largely indistinguishable from those administered elsewhere in Europe. Once the initial reformist enthusiasm had withered away, there remained little other motivation for Socialist governments except to prove managerial competence in the execution of public policy. To believe one close observer, one of Mitterrand's key motivations was precisely to prove that the left could govern as effectively as past conservative administrations.

Conclusion

The advent of the Balladur government in March 1993 confirmed the diminishing political returns of Mitterrand's extended period in office. In the final period of his presidency (1993-95), Mitterrand's bargaining power appeared far weaker than at any other time of his tenure, including during the first 'cohabitation' of 1986-88. This was partly because he was an obvious non-contender for a third presidential term; partly because the Socialists' electoral humiliation of March 1993 removed any real illusions of grandeur.

Any attempt to disentangle important themes running throughout Mitterrand's career encounters the difficulty of a vocation lasting almost fifty years, spanning the entire political and historical spectrum of post-war France. The search for consistency in a politician's beliefs over such a period is likely to prove vain. The difficulties in relating Mitterrand's attitudes and his behaviour are likely to be even more formidable: a leader's self-justifications should not generally be taken as a reliable guide to his actions. Mitterrand performed a variety of different leadership roles at different stages of his career, requiring varied skills and responses. For these reasons amongst others, any attempt to discern the 'real' Mitterrand through charting his expressed beliefs is a difficult, subjective, exercise. I have argued elsewhere that Mitterrand should be situated within the classical traditions of Radical republicanism of the Third Republic, transposed to the political conditions of the Fifth.[13] The apparent paradoxes and contradictions of Mitterrand's beliefs were themselves typical of a particular type of republican tradition. In accordance with the Radical tradition, there were two facets to Mitterrand. A firm belief in values such as the Republic, the nation, social justice or the rule of law and a highly developed sense of politics as an autonomous activity (or game), with its own rules and rites. The most common image of Mitterrand was that of 'the Prince of equivocation', a man for whom the means of politics became an end in itself. In fact, the ambiguity surrounding Mitterrand stemmed partly from the psychological characteristics of his personality. But it also reflected the fact that his – genuine – principles were vague and general, and were not necessarily predictive of a particular type of political behaviour.

Mitterrand shaped the Fifth Republic more than any other President since de Gaulle. In key respects, the legacy of Mitterrand involved the deconstruction of the 'French exception', both domestically and on the international stage: France was a country rather less different from its European neighbours in 1995 than in 1981. His major achievements were in those spheres where his action had been least expected: he promoted European integration beyond the limits conceded by former French Presidents: he contributed, under pressure, towards the modernisation of French industry and financial capitalism; he de-ideologised the left and reconciled it to the market economy. The fact that these real achievements bore only a tenuous relationship to his presidential platform of 1981 bears testament to the limited margins of manœuvre for national political leaderships in an increasingly interdependent and global age.

Notes

[1] G. Martinet, 'Le crépuscule du mitterrandisme', *Le Monde*, 10 September 1994.

[2] D. Lorrain, 'Après la décentralisation: l'action publique flexible', *Sociologie du Travail*, 3, 1993, pp.285-307.

[3] H. Machin and V. Wright (eds.), *Economic Policy and Policy-Making under the Mitterrand Presidency: 1981-84* (London, Pinter, 1985); G. Ross, S. Hoffmann and S. Malzacher, *The Mitterrand Experiment* (Oxford, Polity Press, 1987).

[4] S. Hoffmann, 'Gaullism by any other name', in Ross *et al.*, pp.294-305.

[5] G. Lemaire-Prosche, *Le PS et l'Europe* (Paris, Editions universitaires, 1990); H. Drake, 'François Mitterrand, France and European Integration', in G. Raymond (ed.), *France during the Socialist Years* (Aldershot, Dartmouth, 1994), pp.32-63.

[6] F. Mitterrand and E. Wiesel, *Mémoire à deux voix* (Paris, Odile Jacob, 1995).

[7] A. Cole, *François Mitterrand: a Study in Political Leadership* (London, Routledge, 1994).

[8] On Thatcher see J. Moon, 'Innovatory Leadership and Policy Change: Lessons from Thatcher', *Governance*, 8, 1 January 1995, pp.2-25.

[9] A. Geledan, *Le Bilan économique des années Mitterrand* (Paris, Le Monde editions, 1993).

[10] J. Laughland, *The Death of Politics: France under Mitterrand* (London, Joseph, 1994).

[11] J. Gaffney, *The French Left and the Fifth Republic* (London, Macmillan, 1989).

[12] See in particular E. Faux, T. Legrand and G. Perez (eds.), *La Main droite de Dieu* (Paris, Seuil, 1994).

[13] See Cole, *François Mitterrand*.

Indicative Bibliography

Adler, L., *L'Année des adieux* (Paris, Flammarion, 1995).

Attali, J., *Verbatim I, 1981-86* and *Verbatim II, 1986-88* (Paris, Fayard, 1994, 1995).

Cole, A., 'Studying political leadership: the case of François Mitterrand', *Political Studies*, 42, 3, September 1994, pp.454-468.

Cole, A., 'The Presidential Party and the Fifth Republic', *West European Politics*, 16, 2, April 1993, pp.49-66.

Cole, A., *François Mitterrand: a Study in Political Leadership* (London, Routledge, 1994).

Colombani, J.-M. and H. Portelli, *Le Double septennat de François Mitterrand* (Paris, Grasset, 1995).

Drake, H., 'François Mitterrand, France and European Integration', in Raymond, G. (ed.), *France during the Socialist Years* (Aldershot, Dartmouth, 1994), pp.32-63.

Faux, E., T. Legrand and G. Perez, *La Main droite de Dieu* (Paris, Seuil, 1994).

Favier, P. and M. Martin-Roland, *La Décennie Mitterrand. 1. Les ruptures* and *2. Les épreuves* (Paris, Seuil, 1990, 1991).

French Politics and Society 'A Symposium on Mitterrand's past', 13, 1, Winter 1995, pp.4-35.

Friend, J.-W., *Seven Years in France: François Mitterrand and the Unintended Revolution* (Boulder Colorado, Westview Press, 1989).

Gaffney, J. (ed.), *The French Presidential Election of 1988: Ideology and Leadership in Contemporary France* (Aldershot, Dartmouth, 1989).

Gaffney, J., *The French Left and the Fifth Republic* (London, Macmillan, 1989).

Geledan, A., *Le Bilan économique des années Mitterrand* (Paris, Le Monde editions, 1993).

Laughland, J., *The Death of Politics: France under Mitterrand* (London, Joseph, 1994).

Le Monde editions, *François Mitterrand: 14 ans de pouvoir* (Paris, Le Monde dossiers et documents, April 1995).

Lemaire-Prosche, G., *Le PS et l'Europe* (Paris, Editions universitiares, 1990).

Lorrain, D., 'Après la décentralisation: l'action publique flexible', *Sociologie du Travail*, 3, 1993, pp.285-307.

Machin H., and V. Wright (eds.), *Economic Policy and Policy-Making under the Mitterrand Presidency: 1981-84* (London, Pinter, 1985).

Martinet, G., 'Le crépuscule du mitterrandisme', *Le Monde*, 10 September 1994.

Mitterrand, F., and E. Wiesel, *Mémoire à deux voix* (Paris, Odile Jacob, 1995).

Mitterrand, F., J.-F. Beau and C. Ulmer (eds.), *Discours 1981-1995* (Paris, Europolis, 1995).

Montaldo, J., *Mitterrand et les quarante voleurs* (Paris, Grasset, 1994).

Moon, J., 'Innovatory Leadership and Policy Change: Lessons from Thatcher', *Governance*, 8, 1, January 1995, pp.2-25.

Northcutt, W., *Mitterrand: a Political Biography* (New York, Holmes and Meier, 1992).

Péan, P., *Une jeunesse française* (Paris, Fayard, 1994).

Rondeau, D., *Mitterrand et nous* (Paris, Grasset, 1994).

Ross, G., S. Hoffmann and S. Malzacher (eds.), *The Mitterrand Experiment* (Oxford, Polity Press, 1987).

Schmidt, V., *Democratising France* (Cambridge, CUP, 1990).

Schneider, E., *Les dernières années* (Paris, Seuil, 1994).

Stasse, F., *La Morale de l'histoire: Mitterrand – MendèsFrance, 1943-1982* (Paris, Seuil, 1994).

Tiersky, R., 'Mitterrand's legacies', *Foreign Affairs*, 74, 1, January-February 1995, pp.112-121.

5. ANALYSIS OF THE ELECTION RESULTS

DAVID B. GOLDEY

Introduction

General de Gaulle's successful assault on, and (unanticipated) reconstruction of, the detested traditional French multi-party system, depended primarily on his potent plebiscitary appeal in the great crisis accompanying Algerian decolonisation (1958-62). In these charged circumstances, the 1958 reintroduction of the Third Republic's single-member, two-ballot, majority electoral system (unlike its operation before 1940) encouraged the formation of disciplined majorities on – and partly thanks to – the second ballot. This remarkable transformation of a system of shifting, multi-party parliamentary coalitions to one of stable, majoritarian alliances, confirmed in elections and continued in office, was powerfully reinforced by provision for the direct election of the President of the Republic (also on two ballots) in a 1962 referendum. Given the metamorphosis of the party system already underway, and the profound legitimising effect in France of popular election, this constitutional amendment induced further presidentialisation and bi-polarisation of the parties, spurring citizens to vote from the first round for the most likely left or right victor on the run-off. The bi-polar constraints of the second ballot thus seeped through to the first, a tendency attenuated since 1978 by intra-coalition enmity and – particularly since the 1993 parliamentary poll – by growing public dissatisfaction with the major parties of government of both left (the PS) and right (the RPR-UDF coalition). Elections have thus been marked by the rise of the National Front (FN) and, intermittently, the Ecologists, and by dissidence in both major camps (Philippe de Villiers on the right with his Combat pour les Valeurs and his anti-Maastricht campaign; and the equally anti-Maastricht Jean-Pierre Chevènement with his Mouvement des Citoyens on the left).[1] 12.05% of the register on the first ballot (over 20% of the vote if abstentions run at 30%) is the legal threshold for a candidate from the first ballot to be able to stand at the second in a parliamentary contest; only the top two candidates (after withdrawals, if any) are entitled to stand in the presidential run-off. For many left-wing voters in 1995, however, the anxiety was whether there would be any left candidate at all at the second round, or whether the left would suffer the humiliation of 1969, when two conservatives, Centrist Alain Poher and Gaullist Georges Pompidou, came ahead on the first ballot and were therefore the only two candidates entitled to contest the second, decisive ballot. On both left and right these fundamental choices helped squeeze candidates whom the polls, the media and 'le bons sens populaire' marginalised. But whereas there was a choice of two potential second-ballot contenders on the right (Balladur and Chirac), on the left, only one, Socialist (PS), candidate could plausibly pretend to figure, making 'voting usefully' a peculiarly pertinent issue on the left. Even so, in the presidential arena where every vote counts, they are distributed territorially, a counter to the more intense institutional pressure to vote 'usefully' for a major presidential candidate is the incentive for isolated minority party voters in safe parliamentary constituencies to show the flag.

This recurring feature of the presidential poll, combined with the more recent lessening of the major parties' control over their putative electorates, and in 1995 with the sense of assured victory for the right and certain defeat for the left on the second ballot, made people uncertain as to how best to express their conflicting political impulses. Left voters were thus cross-pressured by their contradictory desires to vote usefully from the first round, and the impulse to show their exasperation with the PS and RPR-UDF for their common inability to resolve the problem of unemployment and its attendant miseries and insecurities. Conservative voters hesitated between two serious candidates who were too similar to one another, and the temptation to vote for populist mavericks on the first ballot without fear for the second. The difficulty in discerning any substantial difference between Balladur and Chirac (though not for a crucial portion of the young popular electorate); the disrepute attaching to all politicians, thanks partly to a series of scandals which were given maximum publicity during the campaign; and the general scepticism that any of the candidates was capable of resolving what was overwhelmingly regarded as the outstanding problem, unemployment, explain the want of enthusiasm for any of the candidates. Many voters found the campaign – effectively dragging on for eight months – tedious, enlivened only somewhat by two popular satirical television programmes: the *Bébête Show* on TF1 and the *Guignols de l'info* on Canal Plus (see chapter 12).[2]

The first round

The importance to the French of electing a President for a seven-year term of office in fact heightened the disappointment of the electorate with what they were offered by politicians, leaving voters disillusioned, irritated, uncertain, and cross-pressured. The consequence was an abnormally high level of voter indecision as the election approached: the ballot itself attracted the highest proportion of spoiled papers ('blancs et nuls') since 1965, and of abstentions (with the exception of 1969). 30% of the electorate were still telling pollsters the Friday before the poll that they might change their minds.[3] Over a quarter of the voters questioned in the CSA first ballot exit poll said they had decided how they would vote only in the previous few days or on polling day itself. The largest number of the undecided were torn between Chirac and Balladur, but bulked larger as a proportion of those who finally voted for Laguiller, Voynet and de Villiers (over 40% for the first two, over a third for the latter, and 25% of Le Pen's voters, 16% of them deciding on polling day itself according to SOFRES).[4] As Table 1 suggests, hesitation amongst candidates was not random, but generally followed the traditional left/right divide which, however eroded, still structures French electoral politics.

More Ecologists wavered longer, perhaps not surprisingly given the blood-letting attendant on the hotly contested nomination of Dominique Voynet; and over a fifth of Socialist and UDF sympathisers decided late. By region, last minute waverers were most numerous in the west (Balladur and de Villiers country) and the east (where Balladur and particularly Le Pen improved on the 1988 UDF and FN scores). Indeed, the pattern amongst waverers suggests a repetition of a phenomenon noted by Jean Charlot in 1988: the late rallying to Jean-Marie Le Pen of working class, often jobless, voters, most concerned by unemployment, both in the east and north and to the east and west of Ile-de-France. In 1995 these provided perhaps a quarter of his final tally (as against a third in 1988).[5]

While disillusion and exasperation profited protest candidates it also fed abstention, many of those most severely cross-pressured spoiling their ballots or staying at home. Abstention is characteristically under-reported in opinion surveys, though decreasingly so. In France (as in other countries), it is particularly concentrated amongst the youngest cohort of voters, many of whom are also unregistered in the larger towns (up from 3.5% in 1981 to 5.5% in 1988 and 7% in 1995) and amongst the ill-educated, and the unemployed, who make up a large number of those with very little or no interest in politics and no party identification. In 1995, abstention also included the cross-pressured or those without a suitable candidate: a much higher proportion than usual of managers and intellectual professions, more employees and workers than usual, more of the 25-34 year-old cohort (the 'génération Mitterrand') and of the 35-49 year olds (the lycée and university generation of May '68). Not surprisingly, amongst abstainers with a partisan preference, Ecologists were most numerous, followed by disabused Communists and Socialists (the 'déçus du mitterrandisme') and those who expressed their alienation from the political system – or their existential despair – by identifying with the Front National.[6]

Table 1: Which other candidate did you consider voting for?*

Other candidate considered	Laguiller	Hue	Jospin	Voynet	Balladur	Chirac	de Villiers	Le Pen
Arlette Laguiller	-	16	9	16	3	2	3	3
Robert Hue	14	-	17	8	-	2	1	4
Lionel Jospin	18	25	-	27	5	6	5	4
Dominique Voynet	8	4	9	-	2	1	2	1
Edouard Balladur	4	1	4	4	-	22	16	9
Jacques Chirac	11	3	7	9	33	-	28	19
Philippe de Villiers	1	-	1	2	8	7	-	11
Jean-Marie Le Pen	3	2	2	2	5	9	14	-
Did not consider another candidate	32	34	38	21	30	41	19	36
No answer	9	15	13	10	14	10	12	13

* IFOP Exit Poll 23 April 1995. The table reads: of those who voted for Arlette Laguiller, 14% thought of voting for Robert Hue, 18% for Lionel Jospin, etc.

The same factors that contributed to the very high rates of abstention and spoiled ballots on the first round of a presidential election also contributed to a greater dispersion of support amongst minor candidates than ever before. As Table 2 shows, the number of candidates by itself does not explain the dispersion of the vote. It is generally acknowledged that no candidate with less than 20% of the vote on the first round is likely to win, even if he or she qualifies for the second ballot: too much too disparate support would need to be accumulated in the two-week gap between ballots. Similarly, no candidate with less than 15% of the vote has to date got through to the second round. In five of the six direct presidential elections of the Fifth Republic, the two candidates entitled to pass to the second ballot have represented the left and right. The top two candidates together had never won less than half the total first ballot vote until 1995; and the candidates with no hope had never shared even a fifth of the vote, until this election.

The initial cause of the dispersion of the vote from 1981 has been intra-alliance first ballot competition (RPR v UDF, PCF v PS). In 1995, the bulk of the RPR rallied to Chirac. Although formally RPR, Balladur's cautious style, Orleanist and centrist inclinations, and his success in capturing the support, spatially and sociologically, from (most of) the UDF made it reasonable to see him as the UDF standard-bearer on the first ballot (and to classify him as UDF in the tables). There has, moreover, been a growing disillusion of the electorate in the 1990s with both governmental alternatives: 20% of Chirac's supporters, a quarter of Jospin's and Balladur's, a third of de Villiers' and Hue's electors, nearly half of Le Pen's, and a striking 69% of Laguiller's voters voted primarily to reject other candidates.[7]

Table 2: Number of Candidates by Percentage First Ballot Vote*

	1965		1969		1974		1981		1988		1995	
Candidates with:	No.	%	No.	%	No.	%	No.	%	No.	%	No.	%
20%+ of vote	2	76	3	89	2	76	2	54	2	54	2	44
15-19% of vote	1	16	-	-	1	15	2	33.5	2	31	2	34
Under 15% of vote	3	8	4	11	8	9	6	12	5	15	5	23

* % vote rounded to nearest integer.

The last published polls, the week before the ballot, registered Chirac at 25-27.5%; Jospin at 19-20.5%; Balladur at 16-20%; Le Pen at 11-14%; Hue at 8-10%; de Villiers at 5-7% and Laguiller at 3.5-6%. In the week before the first ballot, voters were moving to confirm their choices without the benefit of polls, though candidates had access to them and structured their campaigns accordingly – Balladur stomping round the country; Chirac playing the statesman; Jospin pleading for a place for the left on the second round; Hue arguing that his Socialist competitor was safely there and that, besides, the PS was so right-wing that it hardly mattered even if he were not. Le Pen urged 'villiéristes' to vote 'usefully' to bring the FN leader to the second ballot, while de Villiers himself responded that the best way to advance truly right-wing ideas was to vote for him. Laguiller had the hardest-hitting last-minute slogan, characteristically illegally postered after the end of the official campaign: 'The only vote that will shake them up! The only vote that will make them take notice!' The unpublished surveys indeed showed Laguiller consolidating her support in the last few days before the poll at some 5%; Hue was steady at about 9%; Le Pen was up marginally at around 14.5%; Jospin (around 20%) seemed to be edging out Balladur (around 18%, except for BVA) and Chirac was down a little but apparently stable at 24%.[8]

Jospin lost support to Hue and Laguiller from those on the left who felt he was not radical enough and those in the centre who felt he was not yet presidential timber, but won back PS supporters late in the campaign, often on polling day itself, for fear that no Socialist – and so no left candidate – would figure on the second ballot.[9] The polls were also looked to by more conservative voters who, convinced Chirac was comfortably ahead (by mid-April 70% of probable voters thought he was most likely to be elected), were tempted to exclude the left from the run-off by voting Balladur (especially if they lacked confidence in the notoriously volatile Chirac), or to abandon a 'useful' for an expressive vote for de Villiers or particularly Le Pen. The latter appeared to promise more radical change, especially for those mobilised by the 'social issue'[10] (see Table 1, above).

Jospin's unexpected 23% at the first round allowed the Socialists to turn defeat into apparent victory; it embarrassed the Communists, who had hoped to be able to avoid endorsing him on the second ballot; it exposed the divisions amongst the Balladurians; left the Gaullists stunned; and encouraged Jean-Marie Le Pen, with his 15%, to pose as the arbiter of the second ballot, and demand the appropriate tribute for his support from either side. Most politicians (though not the former Minister of Culture, Jack Lang) were careful not to step towards that slippery slope, although the temptation remained throughout the second round (see Table 3).

Abstentions were higher than in any presidential election except 1969 when the old Socialist Party (SFIO) was in terminal decline and fielding an implausible candidate; spoiled papers were more numerous than ever in a presidential contest, twice the average. More of the small number of Ecologist sympathisers or previous voters for Ecologist candidates abstained, but the largest group of abstainers in 1995 came from Socialist sympathisers and those previously voting PS. In Ile-de-France, the increase in abstention was double the increase in the national average over 1988 (2.5%), probably partly due to the school holidays and the difficulty (not reproduced in the provinces) of getting proxy voting forms from the local police stations (absentee ballots have been abolished to combat electoral fraud, particularly in Corsica). Abstention increased by twice the national average in Var, where local leaders of the dominant conservative component of the UDF, the Republicans (PR), were deeply implicated in scandals; and by almost three times in Alpes-Maritimes, where PR local worthies were in trouble (and the Médecin machine in Nice was in its scandal-ridden death throes). It rose by half as much again as the national average in Marseille, where the local hero-villain, Bernard Tapie, was out of action, Le Pen was no longer standing locally, and the once dominant Socialist machine was in tatters; in Nord and Pas-de-Calais, rust-belt departments with worn Socialist and Communist machines, touched by scandals; in relatively rural Meuse, deprived by yet another financial scandal of its conservative strong-man, the Balladurian Gérard Longuet (PR); and in Meurthe-et-Moselle, another rust-belt department, with an old but diminishing Catholic centrist tradition, and a newer Socialist one, undermined by the previous Socialist governments' closing of the mines and steel mills. Otherwise, the increase in abstention in the east was below the national average, as it was in the inner west' (often up by less than half the national increase) where de Villiers had a 'favourite son' vote, and in Limousin and the southern rim of the Auvergne, where Chirac had his favourite son support.

Despite the 'divine surprise' of 23% on the first round, the PS was obviously the great loser compared with 1981 and 1988, for the 3.3 million PS votes lost between 1988 (Mitterrand) and 1995 (Jospin) could hardly be compensated for by the 900,000 gained by the Communists and extreme left on 1988 (see Table 3). Jospin could take the credit for stopping the rot: there had been a total of only 17% for the PS at the 1994 European elections (Rocard + Chevènement), and 19% for the PS in the 1993 general election. With 23% Jospin was back to the Socialist score in the 1989 European elections, one point better than the non-Communist left's tally in 1973, but still 3 points down on Mitterrand's 26% in 1981. Relative to 1988, the PS vote was down least in Ile-de-France and Languedoc; and down most in the line from Haute-Normandie across to Alsace and to their north, and in the Centre and in Burgundy – regions where Le Pen gained most on 1988.[11]

The shrinking of the Socialists' geographical influence reflected a change in their electorate already evident in 1993 (see Table 4). Their advantage amongst (mostly younger) women was sustained, but not their appeal to younger men. In 1988, Mitterrand had taken 36% of the ballots of first-time presidential voters (18-24): 7 years later, only 28% of the same age group (now the bulk of the 25-34s) chose Jospin, 23% of first-time 1995 voters making the same choice. The attitude of 21-24 year olds had changed most from 1988 to 1995, no doubt as a consequence of youth unemployment, more acute in

Table 3: Six Presidential Elections (Metropolitan France only) 1965, 1969, 1974, 1981, 1988, 1995

First Ballot		Vote (Millions)						% of Vote						% of Register					
		1965	1969	1974	1981	1988	1995	1965	1969	1974	1981	1988	1995	1965	1969	1974	1981	1988	1995
	Registered	28.2	28.8	29.8	35.5	36.95	38.55												
	Abstain	4.2	6.3	4.5	6.5	6.6	7.9							15.0	21.8	15.1	18.3	17.9	20.6
	Spoiled	0.2	0.3	0.2	0.5	0.6	0.85							0.9	1.0	0.8	1.3	1.6	2.8
	Valid Votes	28.8	22.2	25.1	28.5	29.7	29.8							84.2	77.2	84.1	80.4	80.4	77.2
Extreme Rt. (FN) (Royalist)	Tixier	1.3						5.3						4.4					
	Le Pen			0.2						0.8						0.6			
	Renouvin			0.04						0.2						0.1			
	Le Pen					4.3						14.6						11.7	
	Le Pen						4.5						15.3						11.8
Right	Royer			0.8						3.2						2.7			
	Debré				0.5						1.6						1.3		
	Garaud				0.4						1.33						1.1		
	de Villiers						1.4						4.8						3.7
Gaullist	De Gaulle	10.4						43.7						36.8					
	Pompidou		9.8						43.9						33.9				
	Chaban			3.6						14.6						12.2			
	Chirac				5.1						18.0						14.5		
	Chirac					5.9						19.75						15.9	
	Chirac						6.1						20.5						15.8
Centre/UDF	Lecanuet	3.8						15.8						13.3					
	Marcilhacy	0.4						1.7						1.5					
	Poher		5.2						23.4						18.1				
	Giscard			8.3						32.9						27.7			
	Muller			0.2						0.7						0.6			
	Giscard				7.9						27.8						22.3		
	Barre					4.9						16.5						13.2	
	Balladur						5.5						18.5						14.3

Party	Candidate																
Ecologist	Dumont		0.3														
	Lalonde			1.1				1.3	3.9					1.1	3.2	3.1	
	Waechter									3.8							2.6
	Voynet					0.9					3.35						
Socialist	Mitterrand	7.7					32.2										
	Defferre	1.1					5.1					27.1	3.9				
	Mitterrand		10.9											36.5			
	Mitterrand			7.4				43.4	26.1								
(MRG)	Crépeau			0.6					2.2						1.8		
	Mitterrand				10.1					33.9	23.2					27.25	
	Jospin					6.9											17.9
PSU	Rocard	0.8		0.3			3.7						2.8				
	Bouchardeau				0.6			1.1							0.9		
	Juquin								1.1	2.1						1.7	
Communist	Duclos	4.8					21.5						16.6				
	Marchais			4.4					15.5						12.4		
	Lajoinie				2.0				6.9							5.5	
	Hue					2.6	1.1				8.7						6.7
Trotskyite	Krivine	0.2	0.09					0.4					0.8	0.3			
	Krivine		0.6					2.4									
	Laguiller			0.7					2.3						1.8		
	Laguiller				0.6					2.0						1.6	
	Boussel				0.1				2.0	0.4						0.3	
	Laguiller					1.6					5.4						4.15
Misc.	Barbu	0.3					1.2					1.1					
	Ducatel		0.06					1.3					1.0				
	Sebag/Héraud							0.2						0.2			
	Cheminade					0.08			0.3		0.3						0.2

Table 3: Six Presidential Elections (Metropolitan France only) 1965, 1969, 1974, 1981, 1988, 1995

Second Ballot	Vote (Millions)						% of Vote						% of Register					
	1965	1969	1974	1981	1988	1995	1965	1969	1974	1981	1988	1995	1965	1969	1974	1981	1988	1995
Registered	28.2	28.8	29.8	35.5	37.2	38.55												
Abstained	4.4	8.9	3.6	4.8	5.75	7.5							15.5	30.9	12.1	13.6	15.4	19.5
Spoiled	0.6	1.3	0.3	0.9	1.1	1.9							2.3	4.5	1.2	2.5	3.05	4.8
Valid Votes	23.2	18.6	28.5	29.8	30.3	29.2							82.2	64.5	86.7	83.9	81.5	75.7
De Gaulle	12.6						54.5						44.8					
Pompidou		10.7						57.6						37.2				
Giscard			13.1						50.7						43.9			
Giscard				14.2						47.8						40.1		
Chirac					13.9						46.1						37.5	
Chirac						15.4						52.7						39.9
Mitterrand	10.6						45.5						37.8					
Poher		7.9						42.4						27.3				
Mitterrand			12.7						49.3						42.8			
Mitterrand				15.5						52.2						43.8		
Mitterrand					16.35						53.9						43.9	
Jospin						13.8						47.3						35.8

France than elsewhere in Europe: only a little more than half as many in this age group voted for Jospin compared with Mitterrand.

The proportion of those who thought of themselves as working people voting for Hue (17%) was almost double his share of the poll, but more of them (19%) voted for Le Pen, while Jospin's share of this popular electorate (23%) was only just over his share of the poll. Moreover, continuing unemployment under Balladur meant a whole third of those who classified themselves as underprivileged ('défavorisés') voted for Le Pen in 1995 (20% in 1993), as against only 19% for the PS. Jospin thus took less than his share of the underprivileged, Hue (13% of 'défavorisés') almost half as many again as his percentage of the vote and Le Pen more than twice his share. (It required the bi-polar choice of the second ballot to restore something closer to the anticipated pattern: see Table 5.) The FN, which had been exploited by Mitterrand to confound the right, was now making serious inroads into the disabused electorate of the left.

Jospin kept the vote of the educated professional middle classes, but lost lower-middle class shopkeepers and supervisory personnel, employees and especially workers. The PS thus did better in bourgeois Paris than in its council flat, working class, inner suburbs or its lower-middle class outer suburbs. And as those of modest means were driven further from Paris (by the cost of housing) or from the suburban 'petite couronne' around Paris by gentrification or the intensification of social problems linked to unemployment and associated in their minds with immigration, so Le Pen moved to take an above average share of the poll, over 20% in Oise. Some of that popular support which had already abandoned the Socialists in 1992 also went to the mayor of Paris, in the inner and outer ring of departments around the capital. Chirac's best showing was in Paris and its region, and the ring of departments to the south and west of his fief in Corrèze. He also did well in conservative Basse-Normandie, and those traditionally conservative departments of the inner west, east of Ile-de-France, in the Alps and Pyrénées. The areas were much the same as in 1988, as was his proportion of the vote.

However, a change in the composition of his 1988 electorate was essential for Chirac if he was to win in 1995: he had to differentiate himself from Balladur and widen his narrow 1988 social and political base. This he did by force of personality and by accumulating promises that he represented change, in order to convince a generation that could barely remember him as Premier in 1986-8. Revealingly, amongst all the RPR/UDF leaders caricatured on the *Guignols*, only Chirac's effigy was found sympathetic by the relatively apolitical, young, left-leaning audience of the programme. Whereas in 1988 his appeal was largely limited to older voters, regularly or occasionally practising Catholics, farmers, shopkeepers, businessmen and the liberal professions, in 1995 he sacrificed support amongst older voters (attracted to Balladur) to do much better amongst the under 25s, and rather better amongst the 'intermediary' group, with a substantially improved (though still below his average) share of the working class vote – more of which, as we have seen, went to Le Pen than in 1988. Age and religion help explain why Balladur had an advantage amongst female voters, which Chirac had had in 1988 but lost in 1995. If Chirac's vote was concentrated in his 'favourite son' regions, Balladur's was concentrated in the old centrist UDF areas that had voted for Giscard and Barre in 1974, 1981 and 1988, reinforced by the PR bastions of the Côte d'Azur. Unpopular with the young, Balladur took the characteristically elderly, Catholic, rural, shopkeeper, business voters of the right, a base that was, in fact, too narrow, as Chirac's had been in 1988.

De Villiers' vote was heavily concentrated in his own favourite son region of the inner west and nearby departments in Poitou-Charente and Centre, the same conservative areas that had provided most of the support for the 1974 champion of sound morals and small shopkeepers, Jean Royer. De Villiers appealed especially to farmers fearful of external

Table 4: CSA Exit Polls 1st Ballot 27 April 1988 and 23 April 1995 (% vote, rounded up/down)*

	Trotskyite Laguiller (Boussel)		PSU Juquin†	PCF Lajoinie	Hue	PS Mitterrand	Jospin	Ecologist Waechter	Voynet	UDF Barre	Balladur‡	RPR Chirac		Right de Villiers	FN Le Pen	
	1988	1995	1988	1988	1995	1988	1995	1988	1995	1988	1995	1988	1995	1995	1988	1995
Total	2(.4)	5	2	6	9	34	23	4	3	17	19	19	21	5	15	15
Gender																
Male	2	5	2	7	10	33	23	3	3	15	15	18	22	5	19	17
Female	2(1)	5	2	5	8	35	25	5	4	18	21	20	19	4	11	14
Age																
18-20	3	8	2	5	10	34	23	6	6	19	14	12	22	4	19	13
21-24	3	5	2	6	6	38	20	7	8	17	12	12	30	3	16	16
25-34	2(1)	8	4	6	7	41	28	6	4	12	11	14	19	4	15	19
35-49	2(1)	7	2	6	10	33	25	4	5	16	12	18	21	5	18	14
50-64	2	2	1	7	11	33	20	2	2	17	23	24	20	7	14	16
65+	1	2	1	7	5	30	25	1	1	23	34	26	17	3	11	13
Occupation Head of Family:Farmer	1	2	2	7	4	23	21	7	0	22	25	18	26	9	19	13
Occupation Interviewee (Status 95)*																
Shopkeeper/ businessman	0	2	1	3	2	21	14	2	4	20	21	26	35	11	2	10
Liberal professions, Higher Management	1	5	3	2	5	30	30	4	4	24	19	26	27	4	11	6
Intermediary	3(1)	7	3	4	9	33	29	4	6	17	14	17	22	2	18	11
Employee	2(1)	6	2	6	8	38	29	5	4	16	11	15	17	5	14	20
Worker	3	9	2	15	14	40	21	2	3	8	9	8	14	5	21	24
Retired*	1	3	1	7	9	38	22	1	1	15	29	24	18	3	11	15
Unemployed*	6	10	2	11	7	36	23	3	4	8	6	17	16	4	17	30
Non-employed (Student/Housewife)*	2(1)	5	2	4	8	32	17	7	4	20	20	20	24	5	14	16

Education																
Primary	2	5	1	10	12	37	25	3	2	13	17	19	14	5	15	19
Secondary	2	5	2	6	7	33	23	5	3	17	21	17	21	5	17	15
Tech/Comm	2(1)	5	2	7	10	32	20	4	3	14	13	17	17	7	22	25
Higher	2(1)	6	3	2	6	33	28	6	6	21	18	22	26	3	10	7
Religion																
Catholic: Reg. Practice	1(1)	2	1	1	3	16	17	4	2	33	40	34	21	8	12	7
Occ. Practice	1	5	1	2	2	24	15	3	1	22	24	35	34	3	13	16
Non-practising	2	5	1	4	7	35	21	4	3	16	17	19	23	4	19	20
Other (Prot 1995)	1(1)	8(4)	1	6	11(9)	50	36(33)	6	8(4)	10	18(8)	16	10(6)	7(16)	11	2(20)
No religion	3(1)	10	7	15	19	44	36	7	7	9	5	6	12	1	10	10
Partisan Preference																
Ext. Left + PSU 1988	12	37	26	4	12	39	28	5	3	1	0	1	5	0	8	14
PCF	3(1)	5	5	77	77	9	10	0	0	2	1	1	5	1	4	5
PS (MDC 1995§)	2(1)	6(16)	2	2	3(18)	84	78(33)	3	3(5)	2	2(4)	1	3(10)	1(2)	4	4(12)
MRG/Radical 1995	3	18	3	1	9	55	36	6	7	17	11	6	7	3	10	9
Ecologist	2(1)	11	2	1	1	11	16	65	37	11	15	4	10	2	4	8
UDF	0	2	0	0	1	1	1	1	1	75	59	16	23	9	7	4
RPR	0	0	0	0	0	1	1	1	0	11	22	73	61	8	14	8
FN	0	1	0	1	1	2	1	1	0	4	4	2	6	3	90	84
None	3	4	2	4	7	29	19	4	5	20	17	20	23	7	18	17

* In François Platone (ed.), *Les Electorats sous la Vème République: Données d'enquêtes* (2nd edition, Paris, CEVIPOF, Fondation Nationale des Sciences Politiques, 1995).

† Supported by PSU and successors, dissident Communists and left-ecologists.

‡ RPR but supported by major UDF components: PR-Republicans, CDS-Centrists, and Radicals, though Giscard, Madelin and Millon backed Chirac.

§ MDC: Mouvement des Citoyens, Jean-Pierre Chevènement's club/party based on his former left-wing PS faction. See D. B. Goldey and R.W. Johnson, 'The French Presidential Election of 24 April-8 May and the General Election of 5-12 June 1988', *Electoral Studies*, 7, 3, 1988, pp.195-223; and D. B. Goldey, 'The French General Election of 21-28 March 1993', *Electoral Studies*, xii, 4, 1993, pp.291-314.

competition. Royer's appeal had also extended to farmers, as did de Villiers' to shopkeepers, and they both disproportionately attracted regularly practising Catholics. De Villiers probably lost slightly fewer voters to Le Pen than Le Pen did to him, but (as may be seen from Table 1) he took most votes from Chirac (just as Royer in 1974 had done most harm to Chaban).[12]

Expressive voting was only a little more random than instrumental voting. Real 'révoltés', intransigent left voters, voted Laguiller, 73% of whom thought the battle against social inequalities was one of the issues that counted most when voting, with the battle for employment next (47%), and raising wages just behind at 46%. For Voynet's voters the environment logically came first (71%), but they were next most concerned with inequalities (59%) and with unemployment (51%). Hue's supporters were almost equally mobilised by unemployment (62%), inequalities (61%), wage increases (60%, his great campaign cry) and protection of social security (59%), the characteristic concerns of the (usually) employed, masculine, urban working class. Jospin's supporters were most concerned by inequalities (64%), then by social security (52%, reflecting his appeal amongst older voters), only then with unemployment (48%), and then by education (36%, more than any other candidate, reflecting support among teachers and the intellectual professions). Balladur's electorate were most concerned by unemployment but, like their standard bearer, they were moderate (47%) in their concern. 36% were preoccupied by personal security and an equal proportion by social security (his elderly supporters); a quarter were concerned about the development of the French economy and by the construction of Europe (the latter reflecting his Centrist support).

The concerns of Chirac's voters showed the heterogeneity of his 1995 first ballot support, both the cause of his disappointment on the first ballot, and the promise for the second: 48% were mobilised by employment, 38% by inequalities; 36% by insecurity, 35% by social security, 30% by immigration. The priorities of de Villiers' voters reflected their ideological preoccupations – especially his and their hostility to Maastricht and fear of external competition – and their religious convictions, age profile, and class origins: 41% were for the defence of French economic and social gains in Europe; the same proportion were worried by insecurity, 39% by immigration, only 38% by unemployment, but 30% by corruption. The widely shared concern with security and immigration on the right was of course magnified amongst Le Pen's voters: 75% were obsessed with immigration, 53% with security, 49% were worried by unemployment, 28% exasperated by corruption, and 22% hoping for wage increases.

With a higher proportion of working class and unemployed voters than any other candidate in 1995, the self-identification of Le Pen's voters was much more heterogeneous in 1995 (almost a fifth placing themselves on the left) than in 1988, when it had been markedly skewed to the extreme right. Gérard Grunberg's analysis of northern France by canton – from Normandy to Alsace and northwards – confirms that where Jospin lost most on Mitterrand's 1988 score, Le Pen gained most on his showing 7 years earlier (the correlation is .69). Nonetheless, despite the striking decline in the Socialist vote and the rise of the right, there was an underlying stability in geographical concentration of support for most candidates between 1988 and 1995. The correlation, by department, from 1988 to 1995 was: .95 for the PCF, .92 for Chirac, .86 for Barre-Balladur, and .78 for Mitterrand-Jospin.[13]

Towards the second round

Whatever the impact on the candidates and on the public of Jospin's surprising score ahead of Chirac on the first ballot, the total left first ballot score, even counting in Voynet, was a thin 40% to the right's 60% (FN included). That was a ratio that was near

Table 5: Subjective Class & % first ballot vote 1993 General & 1995 Presidential Election (and second ballot 1995 Presidential Election)*

| | Extreme Left | | PCF | | PS & Other Left | | Ecologists | | RPR/UDF | | | FN | |
| | Laguiller | | Hue | | Jospin | | Voynet | | Balladur + Chirac | | de Villiers | Le Pen | |
	1993	1995	1993	1995	1993	1995	1993	1995	1993	1995	1995	1993	1995
Total	1	5	9	9	21	23 (47)	8	3	44	40 (53)	5	13	15
Subjective Social Class													
Privileged	2	5	6	3	21	20 (41)	7	4	55	49 (59)	6	8	13
Well-to-do	2	3	5	4	18	19 (33)	8	2	54	59 (67)	4	10	9
Upper Middle Class	1	3	5	5	22	25 (40)	8	4	50	46 (60)	5	11	12
Lower Middle Class	2	5	10	9	21	23 (49)	8	4	41	38 (51)	6	13	14
Working People†	2	8	18	17	22	25 (68)	7	2	31	24 (32)	4	16	19
Underprivileged	1	4	16	13	14	19 (57)	5	3	41	23 (43)	5	20	33

* See D. B. Goldey, 'The French General Election of 21-28 March 1993', *op. cit.*; IFOP Exit polls, 1995. 'Others' (mostly bogus ecologists, 1993, 4%; Cheminade, 1995, 0.3%) not included.
† 'Classe populaire'.

impossible to reverse, barring an extraordinary second-round campaign. Chirac, for his part, was temporarily destabilised, personally as well as politically, by a first-round result below expectations. His task was to ensure a better transfer of Balladur (and de Villiers) supporters to him on the second round than he himself had been willing to offer Giscard in 1981; he then still needed a margin of Le Pen's voters, but they could not be bid for too obviously. The better the transfer from the traditional right, the safer he would be. Balladur made public his support on the night of the first ballot, but the rallying of his prominent supporters was briefly delayed first by a vain attempt by François Léotard, Nicolas Sarkozy and Simone Veil to organise a Balladurian lobby and bargain their support; and then, with Chirac still stunned, by Alain Juppé's refusal to allow Philippe Séguin to play a mediating role, or to guarantee no future victimisation of Balladur partisans. Partisan and personal calculations on all sides were further complicated in 1995 by the risks, as well as the opportunity for bargaining and reprisals, presented by the municipal elections, originally scheduled for March 1995 but postponed on the recommendation of Interior Minister Charles Pasqua to the second fortnight in June. Precious time was thus lost, until the Balladurians surrendered unconditionally several days into the round two campaign. At Chirac's big meeting on Saturday 29 April, under an enormous tent at the Bagatelle in Paris, enthusiastic supporters, bussed in from the provinces as well as the Paris area, applauded Pasqua, Giscard, Séguin, Juppé, and Madelin, welcomed Balladur ('Dou-Dou avec nous!') and de Villiers ('Le neuneuh avec nous!'), ignored Veil and Bayrou, and hissed Léotard and Sarkozy. The assembled worthies were all seated before the podium, which was occupied by Chirac alone, joined at the end of his speech only by his wife and assorted youngsters ('la jeunesse avec nous!').

Socialist strategists reckoned to take the bulk of PCF support and to win a minimum of 46%, a maximum of 48% on the second ballot. Only if they got to 48% and Chirac made some enormous blunder was there any hope of victory. To preserve that outside chance and to increase their candidate's future clout in his faction-ridden party, they also needed to win over Voynet's support, grudgingly given, and Laguiller's. But the Trotskyites, with over 5% (and thus the reimbursement of their legitimate election expenses for the first time), had every interest in refusing any compromise, and Laguiller opted for the unstated Communist strategy since 1978 by calling for abstention on the second round – with the long-term aim of replacing the PCF itself as the extreme left's most significant force.

The PCF itself was torn between the calculations of, respectively, its elected representatives and the party machine. Part of the party apparatus – backed by the powerful hard-line Pas-de-Calais federation – wished to break the bitter second-ballot embrace with the Socialists, and saw the 1995 presidential contest as an opportunity to do so. That strategy depended, however, on Jospin's coming no better than second, with no more than 20% to Hue's hoped for 10%. Even then, PCF mayors who needed PS support for their election in the forthcoming municipals would have been sorely tempted to break ranks, as had already a number of PCF (and ex-Communist) mayors in the old working class municipalities around Paris, particularly in Seine-St.-Denis, but also in Hauts-de-Seine and Val-de-Marne. With 23% for Jospin to 8.7% for Hue, the party could not refuse to choose or call for abstention, as in 1969. The compromise reached after intense internal debate was a call for the PCF to defeat the right rather than to back Jospin, a distinction tartly recalled by *L'Humanité* before the second round, and explained by Hue as 'neither an appeal nor support for, nor a rallying to, nor a withdrawal for' Jospin. The consequences for the PCF, proud of its national discipline, were local variations that would have done credit to the old SFIO. Federal secretaries by and large echoed the party's call to stop the right; but not in Pas-de-Calais, where Socialists and Communists have been bitter competitors even longer than they have been reluctant allies. That was the only departmental federation not to call for a vote against the right; elsewhere, however, federal secretaries were notable by their absence from the departmental Jospin committees, which had been widened for the second ballot; and the party organisation made no effort to mobilise the Communist vote, but devoted itself instead to preparing the party's traditional sale of lily-of-the-valley for May Day. An exception was Aisne, where the party was desperate to hold St-Quentin, and where the federal secretary came out in support of Jospin, only to depart immediately on vacation. In Sarthe, despite the prudent reserve of his federal secretary, the Communist mayor of a dormitory suburb of Le Mans declared for Jospin; as did the dissident PCF mayors of the Paris red-belt, while the party apparatus there encouraged abstention.[14]

A problem for both of the second-round candidates was how to consolidate the support from their own camps while discreetly trawling for FN votes, for with 15% of the vote on the first round, Le Pen seemed to hold the key to the second, a theme taken up with alacrity and alarm by the media. But Le Pen could no more afford to offend the bulk of his electorate than the Communists could theirs. The influence of the PCF and FN candidates and parties over their voters was thus real but limited; the retiring candidate's message was coded precisely because it cut across the instincts of too many of his voters. The deciphering was not equally easy for all voters, as may be seen from Table 6, where high proportions of Hue and Le Pen voters crossing the left/right watershed to their second ballot choice, appeared to be unaware that they were indeed following such advice. (The relatively high proportion of 'No Answer' for the minority of Hue voters transferring to Chirac and of Le Pen supporters moving to Jospin probably veils the embarrassed reception of the real message).

Table 6: Did you take account of your first ballot candidate's advice on how to vote on the run-off?*

1st Ballot Vote	Laguiller		Hue		Voynet		Balladur		de Villiers		Le Pen		Spoiled		1st Ballot Abstention	
2nd Ballot Vote	JC	LJ	JC	LJ	JC	LJ	JC	LJ	JC	LJ	JC	LJ	JC	LJ	JC	LJ
Yes	10	16	12	42	10	18	52	8	34	25	21	24	3	13	17	16
No	78	75	72	45	72	74	35	85	52	64	65	54	80	69	54	49
No Answer	12	9	16	13	18	8	13	7	14	11	14	22	17	18	29	35

* IFOP Second Ballot Exit Poll, First Ballot Vote as a % of votes cast for Chirac (JC) and Jospin (LJ).

The FN vote which became so important in the second round was a composite of middle class hard-line conservatives with working class and unemployed former or young, potential left-wing voters, united in a common detestation of immigrants (especially from north and sub-Saharan Africa), on whom they blamed all their other woes and those of their country. Middle class Catholic reactionaries had provided the original core of FN support from the mid-1980s; working class, irreligious, poorer voters, disabused by the unfulfilled promises of Mitterrand's Socialist administrations, increased that initial support by half in 1988. This same support came late to Le Pen in 1995, probably in the last week of the campaign, and, as in 1988, much of it was likely to return to the left in the run-off – if it turned out to vote at all – rather than switch to Chirac. Right-wing middle class Le Pen supporters, on the other hand, were anxious to settle hereditary scores with the left. The composite was held together by Le Pen, an experienced politician and accomplished demagogue, and an increasingly well-organised party, whose activists were, however, a motley crew of Catholic fundamentalists and royalists, neo-fascists and anti-Semites, those with a nostalgia for Vichy and 'l'Algérie française', and some in the twilight world between electoral politics, organised football hooliganism and skinhead gangs from the council estates of the urban wastelands around certain major French cities. They hated the system, and particularly Jacques Chirac, from whose RPR they had sometimes come, and which stood as the great barrier to their expansion as the only effectively organised party of the right with popular appeal.

After an initial and politically costly hesitation in the 1980s, Chirac had been convinced that to compromise with the FN would weaken his party and destroy his presidential ambitions. Socialist decline, which allowed the right to win elections without FN support, had made it easier for him to prevent RPR/FN second ballot alliances, at national elections at least. Le Pen and FN activists wanted proportional representation which, as in 1986, would give them parliamentary representation, denied them under the two-ballot majoritarian system. This, in 1995, was on offer from the PS, but as part of a long-standing commitment of the party (though contested within it) as much to attract dissident ecologists and Communists as for anything else. But Jospin was unwilling to be suspected of bidding for the FN votes, and indeed argued forcefully for repealing Pasqua's restrictive reform of French nationality laws, a reform the FN itself denounced as too timid. Because FN voters were characterised by their fixation on immigration, this made it unlikely that Jospin would appeal to any but the working class voters who had strayed to the FN on the first round. Chirac had no trouble with Pasqua's reforms, but no time for proportional representation, and could not afford to stoop to conquer.[15]

In 1988, Le Pen had treated Chirac with disdain, as the 'residual candidate of the right'. In 1995, frustrated at not being able, by and large, to break the right's boycott of the FN, and disappointed at not getting to the second ballot at what was arguably his last shot at the presidency, he, as it were, raised the stakes. First he maximised media attention by insisting he would give no advice on the second ballot for a week, waiting until the FN's usual May Day demonstration in honour of Joan of Arc, to see if either candidate treated FN voters with the respect they deserved rather than as pariahs. On May Day itself, the FN procession, led (as usual) by an imitation Maid of Orleans on a real horse, was even more ill-tempered than usual. The murder of an immigrant by toughs took place at the back of the procession. In the almost full place de l'Opéra, the leader's remarks were interrupted, to the fury of the crowd, by the unfurling of two large banners from the Hôtel de La Paix and the Opéra, denouncing fascism and racism. Le Pen's speech was a sustained, vitriolic attack on Chirac – 'Jospin, only worse' – and contained a long litany of the major towns where the FN had obtained a plurality, to remind the RPR of the coming municipals. It ended with the suggestion that first ballot supporters might 'return to your origins' – an invitation to those so inclined to vote for Jospin – or stay home.

The other significant event between the two rounds was the traditional televised debate between the two remaining candidates. Both sedulously avoided extended discussion of immigration, and indeed connived to spend minimum time on what most preoccupied voters or divided their own supporters: unemployment and Europe. Chirac had every interest in playing it safe; Jospin, less well-known, needed to look responsible and presidential. The result was a courteous contest, so much so it lost much of its audience before it ended.

The second round

The week before the second ballot again saw no published polls, with the usual perverse effects. But the Thursday and Friday before the run-off, Socialists began to believe victory might be in reach; the right began to doubt the rules of arithmetic. This was due to Jospin's increasing assurance, while Chirac worried pro-European UDF voters by suggesting another referendum, this time on European institutions, should these be modified after the European Union Inter-Governmental Conference of 1996. Even though RPR Balladurian deputies had rallied without hesitation to Chirac after the first round, many RPR activists were uneasy, disorientated and not easy to mobilise. Pasqua pretended to have an Interior Ministry 'renseignements généraux' (RG) poll which showed Chirac coasting home with 54% (which the Minister of the Interior himself opined was too optimistic). There were further rumours of another RG poll (also apocryphal) which showed Jospin winning by 50.5%, and further fictitious BVA or SOFRES polls with Jospin ahead by 51% or 52%, picked up by the *Journal de Genève*, which also published a genuine CSA survey on the effect of the televised debate. Rumours of these phoney polls seem to have originated with Pasqua's entourage and from Jean-Louis Debré, the second-in-command at RPR headquarters. They helped boost Socialist hopes, but were designed to mobilise the right and discourage better off conservative supporters from neglecting their civic duty for a long weekend away from town over an election Sunday followed by a Monday bank holiday on 8 May.

Not only did Chirac's potential pool of supporters outnumber Jospin's, but more of them decided earlier, and in order to elect their man rather than to defeat his opponent: 74% of those who voted for Chirac on the run-off had made their choice the night of the first ballot, or before, as compared to 69% for Jospin. 13% for each decided during the course of the second-ballot campaign. The last few days of the campaign (taking in the televised debate and Le Pen's final advice – a plague on both your houses, but particularly Chirac's) saw 7% more decide for Jospin to 4% for Chirac, 10% to 8% finally making up their minds at the last minute. Last minute waverers were most numerous amongst the 25s-34s; managers and the intellectual professions and workers; sympathisers for the ecologists (25%) and for the FN (29%); and amongst Voynet's voters (23%), Le Pen's, (19%), de Villiers's (17%), and Hue's (14%).[16]

Late deciders were often negative voters: 36% of second-ballot participants, but 40% of Jospin's electorate (to 32% of Chirac's). Amongst those who reported voting in both ballots, half of Hue's and of Le Pen's first ballot supporters cast their second-round ballot to block the other candidate, as compared to 41% and 43% respectively who voted positively in favour of their candidate. Similarly, 49% of Voynet's and 59% of Laguiller's supporters voted negatively, as compared with 41% and 35% of positive votes respectively. Amongst the negative voters deciding late were those crossing the left/right boundary, often in pursuit of a kind of spoiling tactic: anti-PS Communists and Laguiller protesters most concerned to cut the PS down to size, and bitter anti-Chirac FN supporters.[17] We have seen the cross-cutting power of the immigration issue. Younger voters, whatever their class origins, also tended to favour Chirac (see Table 7).

With these exceptions, the characteristic religious/class basis of the traditional left/right divide in French politics re-emerged with the constrained bi-polarisation of the second ballot (see Table 8). However, the two decades of effort by the PCF to break the reflex of second ballot 'Republican discipline' – voting against the common right-wing enemy and for the PS – was bearing fruit (see Table 8), despite there being limits as to how far such sabotage could go, for the natural inclination of most PCF voters was to vote left. At the same time, Le Pen was having some success in his attempt to do down the RPR, denying the right support, even if this manœuvre favoured the left. Table 9 shows that Le Pen's

Table 7: Gender and Occupation by Age, Second Ballot % of Vote*

Gender/Occupation	Jospin	Chirac
Male		
18-24	38	62
25-34	47	53
35-49	54	46
50-64	44	56
65 and over	44	56
Female		
18-24	50	50
25-34	50	50
35-49	53	47
50-64	43	57
65 and over	44	56
Farmer		
Under 35	33	67
35 and over	27	73
Artisan, Shopkeeper		
Under 35	16	84
35 and over	23	77
Manager, Liberal Professions		
Under 35	37	63
35 and over	32	68
Intermediary		
Under 35	46	54
35 and over	55	45
Employee		
Under 35	49	51
35 and over	56	44
Worker		
Under 35	61	39
35 and over	69	31
Non-Employed		
Under 35	44	56
35 and over	39	61

* IFOP Second Ballot Exit Poll

hostility to Chirac and the RPR did have some effect on the transfer of his support from the first to the second ballot, but that voters most concerned by immigration – whatever their first round choice – rightly perceived that Chirac and his allies took a tougher line on it than did the Socialists.[18] It also suggests that, at least in the present climate, the problems of race-immigration-insecurity (the so-called 'social issue') can still attract left-wing voters to the FN from their traditional moorings on either or both ballots.

The alchemy of the bi-polar second ballot helped restructure the divided, dispersed electorates of the first ballot along the weakened but still pertinent historical left/right divide in French politics, as may be appreciated by comparing Tables 4 and 5 with Tables 8 and 10. The recomposition was social as well as political: new voters on the second round broke disproportionately for Jospin; more angry FN supporters abstained or spoiled their ballots on the second round than did vengeful Communist voters; part of the popular electorate that had strayed to Le Pen on the first round returned to home ground on the run-off.

Jospin had re-established the PS as the only serious opposition force to the RPR-UDF, but only Mitterrand in his first bid for the presidency in 1965 had won a smaller proportion of the vote for the left on the second round, and that was against the Republic's founding father, General de Gaulle. Jospin carried 26 of the 96 metropolitan departments: 6 in the working class north, but only 2 (Meurthe-et-Moselle and Belfort) in the industrial east, only Isère in the south-east; traditionally left-wing Allier and Nièvre; Sarthe and Côte d'Armor in the west; and 12 departments in the traditionally left-wing south-west (where the PS was generally in decline). He won only one Communist department in Ile-de-France, Seine-St-Denis, where several important PCF mayors were in open, and others in more discreet, contention with the party; but he lost the only other Communist-controlled department, Val-de-Marne. High rates of abstention in Communist municipalities there are part of the explanation for this. In Ivry, a PCF stronghold, abstentions barely declined from the first ballot (down 3 points for the department as a whole), and Jospin took just 29 votes more on the second ballot than he and Hue together had won on the first: 61.7% of the vote on the run-off against 61.3% for himself, Laguiller and Hue (who obtained an implausible 37.56%) and a further 3.33% for Voynet on the first round.

Chirac took a smaller proportion of Le Pen's vote than did Jospin of Hue's (smaller) first ballot vote, but his margin of potential support was substantially greater. He carried the 'beaux quartiers' of Paris with two-thirds of the vote, bourgeois Yvelines and Hauts-de-Seine by three-fifths; and by the same proportions the prosperous seaside retirement resorts of the Atlantic and Mediterranean coasts. In these constituencies, more of Le Pen's older, middle class supporters voted for the mayor of Paris. But by and large spoiled ballots were most numerous where Le Pen had done best on the first round: the Mediterranean littoral, Alsace and northern and eastern France more generally, the north and east of Ile-de-France and the Eure Valley.

Conclusion

Chirac was not the first candidate to have won an election with conflicting promises designed to accumulate maximum electoral support and to hold together divided partisan supporters (and potential successors). The powerful legitimising effect of direct national election in France would give him a breathing space over the summer – after the markets were pacified with the appointment of Alain Juppé as Prime Minister and Alain Madelin at Finance. But the easy promises to keep were not the essential ones. Constitutional amendments extending the parliamentary session to nine months and increasing the possibility of holding referendums would not suffice to accomplish a long list of

Table 8: Second Ballot Electorates, Left & Right 1974, 1981, 1988, 1995*

	Mitterrand			Jospin	Giscard		Chirac	
	1974	1981	1988	1995	1974	1981	1988	1995
% Vote	49	52	54	47	51	48	46	53
Gender								
Men	53	56	53	47	47	44	47	53
Women	46	49	55	47	54	51	45	53
Age								
18-24		63	60	45		37	40	55
21-34	59				41			
25-34		63	63	52		37	37	48
35-49	49	51	51	53	51	49	49	47
50-64	46	47	51	45	54	53	49	55
65+	40	40	47	38	60	60	53	62
Occupation Interviewee:†								
Farmer	28	32	33	36	72	68	67	64
Shopkeeper/Tradesman	33	36	36	22	67	64	64	78
Manager/Liberal Prof.	44	45	31	51	56	55	69	44
Intermediary/Employee	53	62	63	55	47	38	37	45
Intermediary			63	57			38	43
Employee			62	54			37	46
Worker	73	72	70	53	27	28	30	47
Non-employed/Retired	45	45	53	43	55	55	47	57

Sector/Situation								
Interviewee:								
Independent	57		33	30			67	70
Salaried	70	59	62	55			38	45
Private Sector		73	60	47	43	41	40	53
Public Sector			66	67	30	27	34	33
Unemployed				57				43
Non-employed			53	42			47	58
Occupation, Head of Household†								
Farmer	31	33	35	32	69	67	65	68
Shopkeeper/Tradesman	36	40	37	21	64	60	63	79
Manager/Liberal Prof.	34	38	36	50	66	62	64	50
Intermediary/Employee	51	58	61	52	49	42	39	48
Intermediary			59	53			41	47
Employee			64	51			36	49
Worker	68	67	68	57	32	33	32	43
Non-employed/Retired	44	45	52	43	56	55	48	5
Religion‡:								
Catholic								
Reg. practice	23	20	27	29	77	80	73	71
Occ. practice	49	40	44	32	51	60	56	68
Non-practising	74	61	58	49	26	39	42	51
Other Religion	64				36			
No Religion	86	88	75	69	14	12	25	31

Education								
Primary	51	51	58	44	49	49	42	56
Secondary	43	50	51	43	57	50	49	57
Technical/ Commercial	49	58	56	50	51	42	44	50
Higher	49	50	49	53	51	50	51	47
Partisan Pref.								
Ext.Left (+PSU 1974)	93				7			
PCF	95		95	90	5		5	10
PS (+MRG'74)	89		97	94	11		3	6
Ecologists			61	72			39	28
Reformers	15				85			
UDF	5		6	6	95		94	94
(Majority 1974)								
RPR			2	2			98	98
FN			15	49			85	51
None			51	43			49	57
Political Family[9]								
Extreme Left	97	98	100	92	3	2	0	8
Left	89	95	97	92	11	5	3	8
Centre	16	29	42	41	84	71	58	59
Right	4	6	6	6	96	94	94	94
Extreme Right	2	5	3	7	98	95	97	93
Marais	34	42	53	34	66	58	47	52
Left/Right Axis								
Extreme Left			100	92			0	8
Left			97	92			3	8
Centre			45	45			55	55
Right			6	6			94	94
Extreme Right			3	7			97	93

1st Ballot vote[α]		NA	NA/Abs	BN	Abs	NA		BN	Abs	NA	NA/Abs	NA	NA/Abs	BN	Abs	NA	NA/Abs	BN	NA/Abs
Extreme Left[β]	68	8	76	5	0	0	62	14	8	24		19					16		
PCF[χ] (Juquin '88 2%)	92		85 (96)	89	4 (1)	0	82	9	5		2	3 (1)					5		
Mitterrand/ Jospin	96	2	97	0	2	0	94	0	3	2	1	1					3		
Ecologists[δ]	53	21	70	7	5	0	75	3	11		26	18					11		
VGE/Barre/ Balladur	2	2	14				9		97	1	96	79	4	2	1	84	3	4	
Chaban/Chirac	11	16	3				2		83	6	73	94	0	1	1	92	1	5	
Royer/de Villiers	10						13		80	10						74	7	7	
Le Pen			27	7			28				57	57	8	8	0	51	11	10	
Abs/BN/NA[ε]			23	7							12	12		32	26				

* Source: SOFRES post-election presidential second ballot polls in François Platone (ed.), *Les Electorats sous la Veme République* (Paris, CEVIPOF, 2nd edition 1995).

† Category changes: 1974-81, Farmer, farm labourer; Small shopkeeper, artisan; Manufacturer, large merchant, liberal professions, higher management; Middle management, employee; Worker; Inactive. 1988-95, Farmer, Artisan, shopkeeper, manufacturer; Manager, intellectual profession; Intermediary; employee; Worker; Non-employed, retired. 'Intermediary': primary school teachers, nurses, social workers, clergy, executive grade civil servants, middle managers, technicians, supervisors, foremen/women.

‡ 1974: Very practising Catholic – attends Mass at least 1 or 2 times a month; rarely practising – attends Mass from time to time, for major holidays and for ceremonies; non-practising – never attends Mass; from 1981: regularly practising Catholic – attends Mass at least once or twice a month; irregularly practising – attends Mass from time to time for major holidays; non-practising – attends Mass for ceremonies, baptisms, marriages, burials, or never.

§ Based on self-placement on a 7-point scale from Extreme Left to Extreme Right with Centre as mid-point. The Marais includes those unable to place themselves on the scale plus those who *faute de mieux* place themselves in the Centre, but are uninterested in politics, don't read or watch political news (see E. Deutsch, D. Lindon, P. Weill, *Les Familles Politiques* [Paris, Editions de minuit, 1966]).

α From the standard SOFRES polls except for 1988, the larger more detailed SOFRES poll for CEVIPOF.

β 1974-1995, Laguiller + Boussel, 0.4%, 1st Ballot vote 1988.

χ 1981 Marchais; 1988 Lajoinie; 1995 Hue.

δ 1974 Dumont; 1981 Lalonde; 1988 Waechter, 1995 Voynet.

ε Abs = Abstention; BN – *Blancs et Nuls* = Spoiled Ballots; NA = No Answer.

promised improvements: putting the budget into balance while raising expenditure and lowering taxes; sustaining the value of the franc while reducing unemployment; maintaining the welfare state while reducing the deficits of the health and unemployment funds; privatising the public sector while maintaining the powerful Colbertist – and Gaullist – tradition of state enterprise and intervention in the economy, and meeting social needs as well as – or despite – the demands of the market.

The presidential poll, then, still dominates French politics, and the forced bi-polarity of its second ballot helps bolster the eroded but still dominant left/right cleavage in French politics. The presidency has been used by leaders to create or recreate parties: de Gaulle, Giscard d'Estaing, Mitterrand, and Chirac all found it necessary to organise their supporters if they wished to consolidate or win power. Direct election has presidentialised the French party system, so that in the Fifth Republic majorities in parliament tend to confirm the previous presidential majority, and parliamentary majorities tend to change with presidential ones, partly because of the President's right to dissolve the Assembly. The presidency also powerfully affects the balance between coalition partners, the President's own party benefiting from his prestige and patronage often at the expense of its partner, thus creating tensions within the coalitions and encouraging the weaker partner to seek to defeat the stronger, as Marchais and Chirac set out to sabotage the presidential hopes of Mitterrand and Giscard respectively in 1981.[19] Most of the parties have become presidentialised, for potential parties of government need plausible presidential candidates as their electoral locomotives, just as potential candidates need organised support in the country and the Assembly. Both mass and cadre parties have had to adapt to these constraints, becoming catch-all parties in the process. The great exception to the rule is, of course, the PCF: organised and selecting its leader according to other, internal principles, it has been unwilling to adapt, partly because the sacrifices required would not be likely, in the event, to elect a Communist as President. But this refusal has contributed (among other things) to the party's marginalisation in the course of the past two decades.

Presidentialisation has helped the big battalions, but policy failure has nonetheless weakened the hold of the government parties on their electorates, and the presidential campaign has become a priceless sounding board for minorities with messages: the far left from 1969, Ecologists from 1974, and the far right from 1988 all made use of this possibility. With little or no hope of winning themselves, such candidates hope to bear witness, make converts to their cause, or win notoriety for the long march through the institutions, if not (so far) to dictate terms to second ballot candidates in exchange for their support.

By mid-1995, President Chirac, his party and coalition partners controlled the presidency, both houses of parliament, most regional and departmental councils and many large towns, including Paris, Lyon, Marseille, Bordeaux and Toulouse. They owed that supremacy more to the failures of President Mitterrand's second seven-year term than to any great credibility of their own. To keep it, they faced the problem whose solution had eluded successive French governments of differing persuasions since the first oil shock of 1973-4: how to manage sufficient non-inflationary growth in an open economy to absorb and diminish unemployment. That failure entailed serious political consequences: a loss of faith in politicians and to a certain extent in the political system; lower participation rates in elections and higher proportions of spoiled ballots; and on the first ballot of the 1995 presidential election, six candidates, with no hope of winning themselves, polarised to the left and the right of the candidates of the parties of government (PS, RPR-UDF), and who together took 38% of the vote, mostly from the unemployed, workers and employees.[20]

Table 9: Are you hopeful that the ideas of the Front National will be given more consideration by the President elected on 7 May?*

1st Ballot Vote	Laguiller		Hue		Jospin		Voynet		Balladur		Chirac		de Villiers		Le Pen		Spoiled		1st Ballot Abstention		All	
2nd Ballot Vote	JC	LJ	JC	LJ	JC	LJ	JC	LJ	JC	LJ	JC	LJ	JC	LJ	JC	LJ	JC	LJ	JC	LJ	JC	LJ
A Lot	12	5	20	5	4	4	2	-	12	11	10	13	21	18	69	54	10	10	18	11	18	8
Some	20	12	12	11	11	9	20	12	27	24	28	22	38	32	15	21	33	16	22	12	25	11
A Little	25	17	12	12	8	13	14	12	24	18	24	28	16	7	1	4	7	24	18	15	20	14
Not at All	30	57	40	60	69	59	41	68	23	33	26	31	14	22	3	2	37	47	25	45	23	52
No Answer	13	9	16	12	8	15	23	8	14	14	12	6	11	21	12	19	13	3	17	17	14	15

* IFOP Second Ballot Exit Poll, First Ballot Vote as a % of Second Ballots cast for Chirac (JC) and Jospin (LJ).

Table 10: Unemployment & % 1995 Left/Right Vote*

% Vote	1st Ballot					2nd Ballot	1st Ballot					2nd Ballot
	Laguiller	Hue	Jospin	Voynet	Total Left 1st Ballot	Jospin	Balladur	Chirac	de Villiers	Le Pen	Total Right 1st Ballot	Chirac
% Vote	5	9	23	3	41	47	18.5	20.5	5	15	59	53
Presently unemployed	8	10	19	4	41	52	12	19	3	24	58	48
Unemployed at least once	5	11	23	4	43	55	16	18	5	18	57	45
Member of family presently unemployed	6	10	24	3	43	53	16	20	4	17	57	47
Fear of becoming unemployed	6	10	26	4	46	50	15	19	4	15	53	50
None of these situations	4	7	24	3	38	43	22	22	6	12	62	57
No answer	6	8	20	2	36	47	24	19	4	16	63	53

* IFOP First & Second Ballot Polls. The table reads: of 100 voters 'presently unemployed', 8% voted Laguiller, 10% for Hue, etc.

Chirac was elected with the smallest portion of first ballot votes, the smallest proportion of the register (39.9%) on the run-off of any President bar Pompidou (37.2%) (who had faced no left candidate on the second ballot, and where the PCF, then controlling 20% of the vote, had advocated abstention). Chirac's first government represented a limited political base drawn from a large, heterogeneous, uncertain and divided majority in the Assembly. To win, Chirac had raised the expectations of a better future for a crucial component of the young, popular electorate, impatient with unfulfilled promises and hopes too long delayed. The honeymoon period of the right coalition, which ordinarily benefits a new administration, had already been squandered by Balladur in 1993. Elections provide opportunities to exercise power; by themselves they do not guarantee political success in its exercise once in power.

Notes

[1] On the bi-polarising tendencies of the first ballot see D. B. Goldey and P. M. Williams, 'France', in V. Bogdanor and D. Butler (eds.), *Democracy and Elections* (Cambridge, Cambridge University Press, 1983); on their attenuation, see D. B. Goldey, 'The French General Election of 21-28 March 1993', *Electoral Studies*, xii, 4, 1993, pp.291-314; on recent fissiparous voting behaviour, see P. Habert, P. Perrineau and C. Ysmal (eds.), *Le Vote Eclaté* (Paris, Presses de la Fondation Nationale des Sciences Politiques, 1992) and *Le Vote Sanction* (Paris, Presses de la Fondation Nationale des Sciences Politiques, 1993).

[2] On the difference between Balladur and Chirac, see IFOP, 'Election présidentielle, premier tour du 23 avril 1995', exit poll; on the disrepute of politicians and want of enthusiasm for candidates, see Gérard Le Gall, 'Présidentielle 95: une opinion indécise', *Revue politique et parlementaire*, 976, mars-avril 1995, pp.10-17; on scepticism on unemployment, Roland Cayrol, CSA pre-election polls; on lack of interest in campaign and satirical TV programmes, see CSA, 'L'Election présidentielle: Explication du vote et perspectives politiques', first ballot exit poll. A Louis Harris study reckoned 37% of those of voting age habitually (i.e. once a week) viewed *Les Guignols*, 26% the *Bébête Show*, the *Guignols* audience being more masculine, younger (51.5% of audience 18-24 years old, as against 51% over 55 for the *Bébête Show*) and more left-wing. See E. Fraisse, 'Les Politiques et leurs marionnettes à la télévision', *Mediaspouvoirs*, 38, 2, 1995, pp.103-109.

[3] Information courtesy of Jean-Luc Parodi, IFOP pre-election polls.

[4] CSA, exit poll, *op. cit.*; IFOP, 'Election présidentielle, premier tour du 23 avril 1995' and SOFRES, 'L'Election présidentielle de mai 1995 – sondage post-électoral'. BVA first ballot exit poll and commentary in *Le Monde, L'Election présidentielle 23 avril-7 mai 1995* (Paris, Dossiers & Documents du Monde, 1995), pp.47-50.

[5] J. Charlot in P. Habert and C. Ysmal (eds.), *L'Election présidentielle 1988* (Paris, *Le Figaro*: Etudes Politiques, 1988); on 1995 regions, see CSA *op. cit.* and SOFRES for moment of decision.

[6] *Le Monde, L'Election Présidentielle, 23 avril-7 mai 1995*, p. 39; IFOP Exit Poll, *op. cit.*, SOFRES post-electoral, *op. cit.* for analysis of abstainers.

[7] SOFRES post-election poll, *op. cit.* See also IFOP exit poll, *op. cit.*

[8] See tables of published and unpublished first and second ballot polls in Le Gall, *op. cit.*

[9] CSA and BVA exit polls, *op. cit.* CSA undirected interviews regularly registered the fear of former PS voters, angry with their party, that no left candidate might figure on the second ballot. Information courtesy of Roland Cayrol.

[10] SOFRES poll, Le Gall, *op. cit.*, and BVA, *op. cit.*

[11] On geographical distribution of the vote, see the useful (but not always accurate) maps in *Le Monde, L'Election Présidentielle, 23 avril-7 mai 1995, op. cit.* and Colette Ysmal, *Le Figaro*, 25 April 1995.

[12] On gender differences, see the BVA first ballot exit poll, *Le Monde, L'Election Présidentielle, 23 avril-7 mai 1995, op. cit.* p.47; and Janine Mossuz-Lavau, 'Les électrices françaises de 1945 à 1993', *Vingtième Siècle*, 42, April-June 1994, pp.67-75. For 1974, see the polls in François Platone (ed.), *Les Electorats sous la Vème République* (Paris, Centre d'Etude de la Vie Politique Française, 2nd edition 1995); *Le Monde, L'Election Présidentielle de Mai 1974* (Paris, Dossiers & Documents du Monde, 1974), and Alain Lancelot, 'La relève et le sursis', *Projet*, 88, September-October 1974, pp. 942-958.

[13] For issue analysis, see CSA exit poll, *op. cit.*; for interesting analyses of the Le Pen vote, see 'Populaire et inquiet', *Politis*, 336, 4 May 1995; on partisan self-identification amongst Le Pen voters, see SOFRES post-election polls 1988 and 1995, in François Platone, *op. cit.*; on correlations, François Platone, 'La droite et la gauche au regard de l'élection présidentielle de 1995', Maison Française-CNRS Round Table *Le clivage gauche-droite est-il dépassé en France*, Oxford, 23 September 1995.

[14] On abstention, see 'Le cœur des communistes balance', *Libération*, 28 April 1995; for the internal party debate, see *L'Humanité*, 27 and 28 April 1995.

[15] On Chirac's and the RPR's earlier ambivalence to the FN, see A. Knapp, *Gaullism since de Gaulle* (Aldershot, Dartmouth, 1994), pp.84-86, 101-103, 110, 124-125, 129-130.

[16] SOFRES post-election poll *op. cit.*

[17] *ibid.*

[18] On the behaviour of Le Pen voters on the run-off, see Jérôme Jaffré, *Le Monde*, 24 May 1995, and IFOP, second ballot exit poll.

[19] Goldey and Williams, 'France', *op. cit.*

[20] Pascal Perrineau, *Le Monde*, 26 April 1995.

Indicative Bibliography

Bergounioux, A. and G. Grunberg, *Le Long remords du pouvoir: le parti socialiste français 1905-1992* (Paris, Fayard, 1992).

Boy, D. and N. Mayer (eds.), *The French Voter Decides* (Ann Arbor, University of Michigan Press, 1993).

Cole, A. and Peter Campbell, *French Electoral Systems and Elections since 1789* (Aldershot, Gower, 3rd edition 1989).

Frears, J., *Parties and Voters in France* (London, Hurst, 1991).

Gaxie, D. (ed.), *Explication du vote: un bilan des études électorales en France* (Paris, Presses de la Fondation Nationale des Sciences Politiques, 1985).

Habert, P., P. Perrineau and C. Ysmal (eds.), *Le Vote sanction: les élections législatives des 21 et 28 mars 1993* (Paris, Presses de la Fondation Nationale des Sciences Politiques, 1993).

Johnson, R. W., *The Long March of the French Left* (London, Macmillan, 1981).

Knapp, A., *Gaullism since de Gaulle* (Aldershot, Dartmouth, 1994).

Penniman, H. (ed.), *France at the Polls, 1981 and 1986: Three National Elections* (Durham, N.C., Duke University Press, 1988).

Perrineau, P. and C. Ysmal (eds.), *Le Vote de crise: l'élection présidentielle de 1995* (Paris, Presses de la Fondation Nationale des Sciences Politiques, 1995).

Pierce, R., *Choosing the Chief: Presidential Elections in France and the United States* (Ann Arbor, University of Michigan Press, 1995).

Wahl, N. and J.-L. Quermonne (eds.), *La France présidentielle: l'influence du suffrage universel sur la vie politique* (Paris, Presses de la Fondation Nationale des Sciences Politiques, 1995).

6. FINANCING THE PRESIDENTIAL CAMPAIGN

IRÈNE HILL

Introduction: historical background

The Constitution of the Fifth Republic gave the parties complete freedom of action and at the same time enhanced their role in the democratic process of elections:

> The parties and political groups help mobilise voters. They come into being and carry out their functions without constraint. They must abide by the principles of national sovereignty and of democracy.[1]

After 1958, the question immediately arose as to whether the independence of the parties would be sufficiently preserved if they were to be financed, even partially, by public money. This did not, however, become a burning issue until the 1980s. The situation changed essentially because of a new conception of political campaiging, and the belief that experts were necessary to promote a candidate's image and the ever-rising costs this entailed.

Escalating costs

The presidential election has been one of the major causes of the escalation of campaign costs. The first campaign in 1965 had sought to modernise campaigning methods. The translation into French of Theodore White's analysis of John Kennedy's victory in 1960[2] had caused right and left to reflect on how to adapt these innovations to French politics. For the first time in France the Centrist candidate, Jean Lecanuet, had his campaign directed by a political campaign consultant, Michel Bongrand and his agency *Services et méthodes*.[3]

From 1974 onwards, television was the principal source of information used by voters during presidential election campaigns. As the use of television was regulated and given free of charge by the State it had become a source of greater democratisation, since each candidate was given an equal amount of time. Similarly, one of the major innovations that television had brought – the debate before the second ballot between the two remaining candidates – treated them with rigorous equality.[4] In reality, however, some candidates are always more equal than others. They prepare for these programmes with varying degrees of expertise and advice, and they use media-men, sound-bite specialists and campaign consultants (see Table 1).

Table 1: Means of information gathering used by voters in French presidential elections, 1974-88

Presidential election 1974	Presidential election 1988*
television	television
press	press
radio	radio
private conversations	private conversations
the hustings	opinion polls
posters	the hustings
leaflets	leaflets
	posters

* Same list as for the presidential election of 1981.

Sources: Roland Cayrol in: D. Gaxie, ed. (1985), *Explication du vote: bilan des études électorales en France* (Paris, Fondation Nationale des Sciences Politiques, 1985), p.386; and see SOFRES, *L'Etat de l'opinion* (Paris, 1989), p.221.

When Jean Lecanuet decided in 1965 to wage a modern-style campaign it cost four or five times more than the campaign of the major opposition candidate François Mitterrand whose campaign was more traditional.[5] Modern campaigning is not inexpensive and not within equal reach of all candidates, and as time has gone by costs have escalated. In 1988, François Mitterrand in his turn adopted the new methods, including a ninety-second multi-image clip similar to pop videos.[6] And in 1995, Jacques Chirac used images drawn from his programme – much as a commercial advertisement might – to put forward key words and themes.

Table 2: Creation of private institutes of public opinion carrying out political surveys

Founded		Director(s)
1938	IFOP	Jean Luc Parodi, Laurence Parisot
1963	SOFRES	Jérôme Jaffré
1970	BVA	Pierre Giacometti
1975	IPSOS	Jean Marc Lech
1977	Harris France	Philippe Mechet, Jérôme St Marie
1979	IFRES	Dominique Genée
1980	Faits et Opinions[7]	Jean François Tchernia
1985	CSA	Roland Cayrol

Source: Irène Hill.

The amount spent on opinion polling has also increased massively since 1965 when IFOP announced in advance that General de Gaulle would be forced to a second ballot.[8] This gave the polls an increased credibility. The importance of polling is clearly reflected in the growth of the industry (see Table 2).

Potential presidential candidates begin commissioning surveys – which are usually not published – months before the election starts. They test the images of the candidates, the importance of different issues and, more generally, campaign strategy. The influence of published opinion polls was considered so great in France in the 1970s that a law was passed on 19 July 1977 to prevent 'the publication, circulation and commentary' of any opinion poll having a direct or indirect link with the election during the week preceding each ballot and on election day itself.

Presidential campaigns have become more streamlined, better packaged and infinitely more expensive. The information we have before 1988 is hypothetical: but all the estimations go in the same direction, suggesting that a presidential campaign costs more and more.

Funding expenses

The finding of new sources of revenue to match these costs became increasingly difficult in the 1980s. It should be remembered that in France at the time corporate institutions were legally prevented from contributing to political expenses, and there was no public funding of the parties. The situation was unsatisfactory and funders and recipients engaged in dubious practices. Already, according to the journal *Pouvoirs*,[9] there were some twenty-two major scandals between 1979 and 1984 (roughly one every seventy-five days); Yves Mény in his book on political corruption in the Republic[10] puts the figure higher, at thirty-six scandals (thus one every fifty-seven days). In the following period, from July 1984, numerous scandals were revealed concerning false payments, clandestine practices, even personal enrichment. Cases came before the courts whereas formerly such practices had been tolerated. Political corruption could no longer be ignored. These scandals were widely publicised and discussed by the press, and public opinion was duly shocked. In September 1994, for instance, there were 'affairs' involving the Director General of the Saint Gobain group, the Director General of the Sofirad and the Director General of the COGEDIM. Personalities including Michel Noir, Pierre Botton, Michel Nouillot and Patrick Poivre d'Arvor were sent before the courts. The financing of the villa at St. Tropez of Gérard Longuet, Minister for Industry, was under discussion, although the Minister said he would not resign (he later did), and the financing of the Republican Party (PR) was also under investigation. Prime Minister Balladur in the same month announced he would set up a committee to look into how to fight corruption. Philippe de Villiers resigned from the PR on account of the 'affairs' his party was involved in, and Charles Millon presented a bill to forbid the financing of French political life by corporate bodies. Such major scandals called into question the trust the voters had in the parties and the politicians, thus endangering democracy itself.

The legislators intervene

Reaction to the increase in costs of presidential campaigns and to the means used to fund them has led to attempts to regulate the raising and spending of money in campaigns. But change was brought about slowly. In 1971 President Georges Pompidou commented:

> The resources of political parties ... are not what they are thought to be, they are on the whole far from clear, for various reasons which are not in fact necessarily immoral. I'm quite happy to see them controlled – that won't change much.[11]

In 1974, the new President, Valéry Giscard d'Estaing, wanted to draw up legislation concerning the financing of the parties. He declared:

> I have told the Prime Minister that I want him to begin to work on a bill which will regulate the political parties and elections in France. It is not simply a question of control, but also of ensuring resources.[12]

In June 1978, the Head of State again announced in a press conference that the problem of the funding of political parties had not yet been solved:

> I believe that the moment has come for the government to introduce a regular means of funding political parties.

He went on to say that the only just criterion was the 'results of universal suffrage, expressed on the occasion of general elections'.[13]

On 27 April 1978, Prime Minister Raymond Barre sent a letter to the Presidents of the different parliamentary groups asking them their opinions as to the setting up of public funding of political parties. The Prime Minister was not encouraged by the replies of the Gaullists, Socialists and Communists who, for different reasons, were very reticent. Nonetheless, Barre drew up a bill which proposed that the State should contribute to the funding of political groups and parties. A text six articles long stipulated that to benefit from this funding a group must have thirty MPs or Senators. The minor parties reacted immediately, claiming the project 'was a new attempt to limit the freedom of expression of the minorities' (Michel Crépeau, President of the MRG) and 'a scandalous project' (Huguette Bouchardeau, National Secretary of the PSU). The project was dropped after its presentation to the Commission des lois de l'Assemblée Nationale (Legislation Committee of the National Assembly) and never reached the full Parliament.

In 1981, François Mitterrand revived the idea in his presidential manifesto:

> Political life will be made more moral. Candidates will be obliged to declare their revenues and their patrimony at the beginning and the end of their mandates whether they are standing as President of the Republic, Members of Parliament, Senators or Ministers.[14]

There were eleven bills between 1978 and 1988 in connection with the financing of campaigns but only three had provisions related to presidential elections. None of them reached the statute book. The organic law of 11 March 1988 relative to 'financial transparency in political life' and that of 1990 relative 'to the limitation of election expenses and the clarification of the funding of political activities' set up new regulations for election campaigns. Between that time and the 1995 election, other laws were passed: in particular the law of 29 January 1993 concerning the transparency of economic life and state intervention, and the laws of January 1995 (four in all but only two of which related to the election of the President of the Republic). They modified quite substantially the procedures which were to be followed. The modifications were made to outlaw illegal practices and to reassure the electorate prior to the imminent presidential election. In each of the legislative texts, three key aspects of the financing of political life remained of central concern:

1) The need for transparency – all the financial operations of political parties and candidates should be verified and verifiable.
2) The safeguarding of independence – political actors should be able to stand for election with an equal chance. They should not be at the mercy of corporate donors.
3) The necessity for moderation – costs must be lowered.

Transparency

The State – now contributing quite substantially to the financing of candidates via public funding of political parties (Law of 11 March 1988) – imposed in exchange a clarification and total transparency of all sources of revenue and spending during election campaigns (Law of 15 January 1990).

The Law of 15 January 1990 obliged all candidates to submit a campaign account ('compte de campagne') covering the year preceding the election.[15] Unless the candidate is totally self-financing his or her campaign, this account is in the hands of an attorney ('mandataire financier'). For presidential elections, the attorney can collect donations under the same conditions as for other elections: there is no limit to the proportion of expenses that may be paid for by donations, but they must all be accounted for prior to the date of the election. Certain conditions however apply for the type, the payment and the receipt of donations.

Figure 1: Sources of revenue

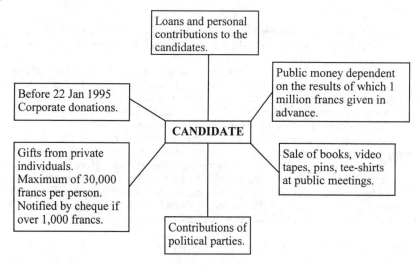

Source: Irène Hill.

As the diagram shows, the candidate can finance a campaign from different sources. First of all, s/he can finance it totally or partially herself or himself. S/he would only benefit from a tax reduction for the first 30,000 francs. During the campaign, public meetings can, through sales of books, tee-shirts etc., contribute to the cost of promotion.

The other sources of revenue are much more binding and sometimes controversial.

Contributions of political parties.

The financing of political parties by public money seemed a necessity especially after the very unpopular amnesty of all offences connected with electoral fraud committed before 15 June 1989, except in the case of personal enrichment.

The political parties can finance the campaign of their candidates wholly or partially, by making a contribution to the financial account or by taking on the burden of certain costs such as the organising of election rallies. They can also settle the account prior to the deposit date. The only requirement yet again is transparency: all payments made by the political party must be listed in a specific section of the account. Study of the 1995 presidential campaign reveals the drawbacks to the public financing of the parties. A public financing of elections rather than parties, with direct payments to the candidates, might have been preferable. However, the Chirac government and the Parliament of the day (1988) favoured an annual public funding of the parties leaving them to decide whether the money should be used to finance a campaign or spent in other ways. In the end, it was agreed that a joint proposal from the Bureaux of the National Assembly and Senate would be budgeted. The sum given is calculated as follows:

- 50% is distributed to the parties according to the percentage of votes obtained by each of them in the first round of the national election.
- the other 50% is distributed according to the number of seats each party holds in the Assembly and the Senate.

The amount of money is substantial. In 1995, the total amount was 526.5 million francs (each fraction thus representing 263.25 million francs). For a breakdown of how this money was divided see Table 3.

The report of the parliamentary commission of inquiry into the financing of political parties and electoral campaigns, presented on 21 November 1991 by Pierre Mazeaud (RPR) and Jean Le Garrec (PS), showed that despite the 1988 and 1990 laws institutionalising the public funding of political parties and introducing regulations to ensure transparency undeclared payments had not disappeared.[16]

The distribution of public financing as shown in Table 3 demonstrates that half the money is fairly shared out and depends on the number of voters actually voting for each party. The distribution of the other half is more questionable as it gives a great advantage to the majority parties over the opposition. The Socialist Party (PS) for instance has only 499,000 fewer votes than the RPR: 19% as against 20.2% of valid votes. But it has 216 fewer seats: 12% as against 42%. So on the second count, the Socialist Party receives 64.7 million francs less. Third and minor parties lose out even more.

Gifts from private individuals and corporate donations

The candidates, as well as the parties, can seek and receive donations from private individuals. These gifts are, however, in line with the transparency aim, controlled. They must be, whether cash or cheque, registered in full by the attorney (amount, date, identity of the donor although his or her name will remain anonymous). No private individual can give more than 30,000 francs, and for any gifts over 1,000 francs a cheque is the only

Table 3: Public financing of political parties

First fraction: 50%

Political party	number of votes (in thousands)	amount (in million francs)
RPR	5,203	58.6
UDF	4,830	54.5
PS, MRG	4,704	52.8
FN	3,153	35.6
PCF	2,253	25.4
Les Verts	1,046	11.7
Génération Ecologie	926	10.4

Second fraction: 50%

Political party	number of members of Parliament	amount (in million francs)
RPR	345	103.4
UDF	337	101
PS, MRG	129	38.7
PCF	36	10.8
Mouvement des réformateurs	12	3.6
CNI	7	2.1
Mouvement des citoyens	4	1.2

Source: Articles 8 and 9 of the Organic Law of 11 March 1988, Statutory Order of 21 March 1995.

mode of payment allowed. The Law of 19 January 1995 also specifies that the candidates may seek donations by advertising in the press. In 1995, several candidates including Balladur and Jospin but not Chirac actually advertised in the major newspapers. In fact, one of the candidates in the 1995 presidential election, Philippe de Villiers, made a financial appeal to his electorate after the results of the first round (23 April 1995). Having obtained less than 5% in the first ballot, he was not eligible for the substantial reimbursement from the State that he had hoped for. He had until the day of the second round to collect money from private individuals to be able to reimburse the loans he had incurred. In the event, his appeal was successful.

Before 22 January 1995, corporate donations were permitted. After that date the Law of 19 January 1995 applied. This stipulated that from then on no corporate donations were allowed. This meant that those candidates who had not declared that they were standing before January 22 were disadvantaged.

Reimbursement from the State

The law of 19 January 1995 compensated for the loss of revenue from corporate donations by extending the system of reimbursing candidates at least partially in all types of elections. This was a system which had until then been reserved for general elections.

Figure 2: Reimbursements from the State

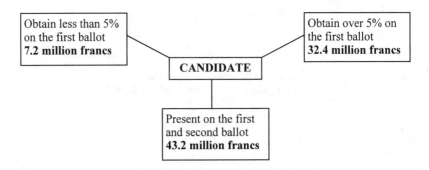

Source: Irène Hill.

As can be seen in Figure 2, the maximum amount of the reimbursements depends on the results obtained by the candidates. If the candidate obtains 5% of the votes the reimbursement is 32.4 million francs; if s/he obtains less it is 7.2. If we take the example of Philippe de Villiers again, all the polls during the campaign showed a result well above the 5% threshold but in fact he obtained only 4.74% and thus failed to obtain the higher reimbursement, hence his subsequent appeal for funds.

Candidates will only be reimbursed under certain conditions. The first condition is the approval of the campaign account by the Constitutional Council. In other elections (general, European), if the financial account is rejected there is no reimbursement by the State, the election is invalidated and the candidate is ineligible for a year following this decision. This in fact does not really apply to the person elected. It would obviously be difficult to invalidate a new President eight months after his election.[17] The Law of 1962 modified in 1995 does not allow the Constitutional Council to invalidate the presidential election for financial reasons but articles L52-15 and L52-17 of the Electoral Code allow its members to refer any breach of the law to the courts. However, the President would not receive any reimbursement from the State and would certainly damage his image if his account was not within the prescribed limits.

The second condition is that the amount reimbursed cannot be greater than the amount spent which may of course be well under the legal limit. Thus it only covers what the candidate has already paid out or what s/he still owes. In addition, since article 17 of the decree of 14 March 1964, the State finances certain general costs such as ballot papers, circular letters and official posters; not to mention the official television campaign.

Despite some allegations during the campaign about the extent to which certain candidates might not have applied the rules, the publication of the financial accounts is there to ensure transparency. It is today possible to identify in detail the financial situation of the candidates and the way they have financed their respective campaigns. In addition, although the law (since 1988) requires all candidates to deposit a sealed official statement of their personal fortune when standing for office, only that of the elected President will be officially published: the other statements will be returned unopened. In fact, during the 1995 campaign, most candidates allowed their statements to be published with a view to clearing allegations of personal enrichment. The exception to this was Jean-Marie Le Pen, for whom journalists produced approximate figures.

Independence

Developing further what the Laws of 1988 had achieved in terms of transparency, the Law of 15 January 1990 permitted corporate donations (except those from public enterprises, gambling institutions and foreign corporations) on condition that they were identified, controlled and limited.[18] The Law of 30 January 1993 tried to tighten previous legislation by requiring that the exhaustive list of all corporate donations should be given (with the exact amount contributed) and made public with the publication of the candidate's financial statement. This new regulation was widely criticised. André Lajoinie (PCF) declared that financing by companies was 'intolerable' and described the limit of 500,000 francs as 'hypocritical' since major companies had 'up to ten or so subsidiaries'.[19] More generally, there was a feeling that candidates would be put under pressure from the corporations that had supported their campaigns. The government, itself under pressure from public opinion, decided to withdraw the possibility of corporate donations. Now the only corporate donors allowed were political parties. Financial, legal and penal sanctions were put in place to see that the law was applied.

For the 1995 presidential candidates, since the new law only came into force on 22 January 1995, all corporate donations given before that date were legal. The financial statements will enable us to see exactly what they gave and to whom.

Moderation

As shown in Table 4, controlling the level of spending by reducing the ceiling allowed, i.e. the amount a candidate is entitled to spend, has been another key aspect of tackling the financing of political life.

This quite substantial reduction had two aims in mind, both related to the problem of corporate donations. First, a reduction in spending meant there was less need to find sources of revenue. It also put candidates on a more equal footing. Second, candidates were thought to have become subject to pressure from their corporate donors. One could also see in this reduction a will to stop the ever-escalating costs mentioned previously.

In conclusion, the three key principles of transparency, independence and moderation, refined through several laws since 1988, are a sign of a desire to move away from past practices and to create a legal framework in which the Constitutional Council (in case of presidential elections) could exercise a specific control over all the different phases of the

Table 4: Ceiling on spending (in million francs)

	first round candidate	second round candidate
ceiling before 1993 (from 1988)	120	160
increase – August 1993 (7%)	128.4	171.2
new ceiling (Organic Law of 1995)	90	120

Source: Constitutional Council.

election process. They could also refer back any illegal practices to the public prosecutor's department. There was thus a move away from corrupt practices towards a more open and egalitarian democracy.

An analysis of the 1995 elections

The 1995 presidential election campaign accounts are more revealing than those of 1988[20] as they are better structured and detailed. Each candidate has to use the same categories, and this of course facilitates comparisons. Transparency meant that a detailed analysis of all the sources of revenue and all expenses could be undertaken.

All the candidates save one presented a balanced account or one that showed slightly more money coming in than going out (L. Jospin, J. Cheminade). Edouard Balladur, however, presented a deficit of over thirty million francs. This should have been covered by a loan or by the candidate himself. In effect, the law of 19 January 1995[21] specifies that the account must not show a deficit nor should it take into account reimbursements by the State. This reimbursement is not a revenue as such since it is not granted automatically, only according to the results and with certain conditions attached. As we have seen, one of the conditions is that the sum must not be greater than the personal contribution of the candidate and the loans s/he may have contracted. Accordingly, most accounts match the loans and personal contributions category[22] with the reimbursement they hope for. Yet Arlette Laguiller and Edouard Balladur do not appear to have fulfilled that condition when they both presented accounts with no record of loans and personal contributions, and yet respectively requested reimbursements of over 10 and 30 million francs. Similarly, Dominique Voynet's contribution was 1 million but she sought 7.2

millions from the State. In the event, the Constitutional Council did not sanction these campaign accounts: to do so would clearly have been politically difficult.

How the money was spent

All candidates were within the authorised limit of spending. Surprisingly only two of them spent over 90% (Balladur 93%, Chirac 97%); one over 70 % (Jospin 73%, but he only campaigned for three and a half months); and one over 50% (Hue 54%). The other five candidates all spent less than half the amount allowed. The real reason for their not reaching the ceiling of expenses lay no doubt in their lack of resources.

The 1995 presidential election also confirmed that advertising was in most cases the primary cost in electioneering. Seven out of nine spent more on advertising than on anything else – 30% or more of the total campaign costs. Three of the first round candidates spent over 50% of their budget on advertising – Le Pen 51%, Laguiller 59% and Hue 60%. While posters and billboards were controlled and direct advertising in the press forbidden, the cost of other forms of advertising had increased: communication consultancy fees, the production of TV party political broadcasts; but mostly that of pamphlets and campaign journals (design and printing costs included). The two candidates who did not put advertising first did so for very different reasons. Edouard Balladur as Prime Minister probably felt that the exercise of his office was in itself sufficient. What he needed was greater personal contact with voters, so he spent more on public meetings than on anything else (30% against 15% for advertising). As for Philippe de Villiers, he had higher general costs than the other candidates – 31% of total spending – mainly because he did not have the infrastructure of the candidates with a party behind them. A very local candidate from the Puy du Fou, he had to install a network of target locations and his money went on hiring halls and equipment. Both he and Balladur also spent 18% of their budgets on postage and telecommunications.

Another interesting expense was the amount spent on personnel. This varied considerably from no budget at all in the case of Laguiller or a small budget of 2-3% for R. Hue and J. Chirac, to higher amounts for Jospin (15%), Cheminade (23%) or Voynet (20%). Although this is quite logical in the case of Cheminade, or even Voynet, one would have expected the Socialist Party to be able to mobilise its activists and furnish its candidate with a sufficient number of voluntary workers.

On the other hand, the amount spent on public meetings was less than in previous campaigns. This was not necessarily a disadvantage. Each of the principal contenders had three or four major meetings that were extremely well covered in the press, on radio and on television. Meetings came second in the hierarchy of Lionel Jospin's expenses (19% after 45% for advertising). They had represented a major cost for Jacques Chirac in his 1988 presidential campaign (second position with 29%). This time the amount spent was reduced to fourth position (13%). But this did not mean that the meetings were not a success, even at the level of expensive technical backup.

All the candidates – except for Jean-Marie Le Pen and Dominique Voynet – spent some proportion of their money on opinion polls, but not very much. It varied from 0.5% for Jacques Cheminade to 4% for Philippe de Villiers. The three major candidates spent 2-3% – Balladur 2%, Chirac 3%, Jospin 2%. It must be said that all the candidates scrutinised closely the results of the polls published in the press.

Who the money came from

All the financial operations were clearly detailed in the campaign accounts. Each candidate sought different ways of financing the campaign. The fact that no corporate donations were allowed after 21 January meant that most candidates could not benefit from any such donations as they entered the race after this deadline. Even for those who were able to receive money from corporate bodies, this added surprisingly little to their total revenue: De Villiers 0.6%, Voynet 0.02%, and Chirac 2%.

What is more striking is that we can draw up a typology of the candidates according to which sources of revenue they relied on most. The first category concerns those candidates who relied principally on reimbursement from the State. They benefited from no corporate donations, their parties helped them little and it was the State which eventually financed a high proportion of their campaigning costs: Hue 66%, Le Pen 78%, Voynet 91%, Laguiller 95% and Cheminade 99%. The State thus contributes very effectively to the campaigns of the minor candidates and ensures that they, too, can take part in the competition.

Into the second category fall those who relied heavily on contributions from their political parties. There is however some ambiguity here. It looks as if Arlette Laguiller, Dominique Voynet and Edouard Balladur borrowed substantially from their respective parties. *Lutte Ouvrière* contributed 86% of the costs of Arlette Laguiller's campaign, Les Verts 75% to Dominique Voynet's campaign, and the UDF 57% to Balladur's costs (although, of course, the UDF was not, strictly speaking, Balladur's party). Since all three candidates asked for a substantial reimbursement from the State and did not declare any loan or personal contribution in the case of Laguiller and Balladur and an insufficient loan in the case of Voynet, we must assume that the party contribution was in fact a loan.

For Lionel Jospin on the other hand, 45% of his campaigning costs came from the Socialist Party. The 49% expected to be reimbursed by the State was to be used to cover bank loans and personal contributions. Similarly for Philippe de Villiers – the party contribution of 51% was independent of the loans and the personal contribution he hoped to have reimbursed by the State.

The third source of revenue was an appeal to the voters, that is to private individuals who support the candidate and who cannot legally give more than 30,000 francs each (and often give much less). The only candidate whose campaign was essentially financed by private individuals was that of Jacques Chirac (60%). In 1988, his financial account showed a low level of revenue from personal gifts from private individuals and corporate donations (regrouped at the time) altogether covering only 22% of his total revenue as opposed to 42% coming from the RPR. Chirac's presidential campaign in 1995 was founded on a grass roots campaign which was also used to fund his election expenses. Most of these gifts were small ones from individuals: only 2% came from corporate donors. The RPR only contributed 1% to his campaign. His loans and personal contributions matched exactly the maximum he could expect from state reimbursement (37%).

Conclusion

From the point of view of the researcher, the accounts of 1995 were significantly more comprehensible and comparable than those of 1988. Transparency had therefore become much greater. It is possible to see from this, however, that great disparities still exist between the ways in which candidates finance their campaigns, depending on their resources and – to some extent – their ideologies. One thing is generally clear, however, and applies to every candidate: a presidential election campaign in France does not come cheap. This is of course not surprising. What is less customary is for the State to finance elections by public money to the extent that it does in France.

Notes

[1] Article 4, Constitution of the Fifth Republic, 4 October 1958.
'Les partis et groupements politiques concourent à l'expression du suffrage. Ils se forment et exercent leur activité librement. Ils doivent respecter les principes de la souveraineté nationale et de la démocratie'.

[2] T. White, *La Victoire de Kennedy ou Comment on fait un président* (Paris, Robert Laffont, 1961).

[3] Since then all the major presidential campaigns have been orchestrated by consultants: Jacques Seguéla – François Mitterrand, 1981 and 1988; Thierry Saussez, Gérard Demuth – Valéry Giscard d'Estaing; Elie Crespi – Jacques Chirac, 1981; Jean Michel Goudard, Bernard Brochand – Jacques Chirac, 1988 and 1995; and Bertrand Delanoy – Lionel Jospin, 1995.

[4] This was first organised on 10 May 1974 between Giscard d'Estaing and Mitterrand and 81% of voters followed it.

[5] See R.G. Schwartzenberg, *La Guerre de succession* (Paris, Presses Universitaires de France, 1969), p.254. He evaluated the cost of Lecanuet's campaign at 400-500m *anciens francs* and Mitterrand's at 80-100m *anciens francs*.

[6] It recalled the history of France and the left since the French Revolution, linking the candidate with French history.

[7] *Faits et Opinions* is now part of IFOP and has a new name, Gallup France. Director: Laurence Parisot.

[8] IFOP predicted that General de Gaulle would only have 43% of the votes cast and not the 50% needed to be re-elected in the first ballot. He obtained 43.7%.

[9] See 'La corruption en France à travers *Le Monde* (January 1980-June 1984)' in: 'La Corruption', *Pouvoirs*, 31, 1984, pp.115-120.

[10] See Mény, Y., *La Corruption de la République* (Paris, Fayard, Série Espace du Politique, 1992).

[11] 'Les ressources des partis politiques ... ne sont pas ce qu'on croit, elles sont peu claires en général, pour des raisons très variées, et pas forcément immorales d'ailleurs – je veux bien qu'on les contrôle, cela ne changera pas grand-chose'. President Georges Pompidou, press conference, 23 September 1971.

[12] 'J'ai indiqué au Premier Ministre que je souhaitais qu'il mette en chantier un projet de loi organisant le financement des partis politiques et des élections en France. Il ne s'agit pas seulement de contrôle, il s'agit d'assurer les ressources'. Réunion de presse at the Elysée, a new style of press conference, 25 July 1974.

[13] Valéry Giscard d'Estaing's Declaration, 4 June 1978.

[14] See François Mitterrand's Manifesto, Proposal number 49.
'La vie politique sera moralisée: déclaration des revenus et du patrimoine des candidats aux fonctions de Président de la République, de députés et sénateurs ainsi que ministres en exercice, avant et après expiration de leur mandat'.

[15] The 'compte de campagne' must cover the year preceding the first day of the month in which the election will take place until the day the election takes place. Thus for the 1995 presidential election from 1 April 1994 (first round: 23 April 1995) until the date of the second round, 7 May 1995.

[16] *Le Monde*, 22 November 1991.

[17] The financial account must be handed in at the most two months after the second round and the Constitutional Council has at the most six months to validate it.

[18] See the journal *Présidentielles Infos*, 1, Editions du Mandarin, April 1995, pp.4-17.

[19] There is a limit of 10% of the allowed spending ceiling (i.e. Organic Law 1995: 90 million francs for candidates in the first round and 120 million francs for candidates in the second round). Also, no donation must exceed 500,000 francs.

[20] *Journal Officiel*, National Assembly, 3rd sitting of 4 October 1989, p.3127.

[21] Law no. 95-65.

[22] Candidates can contract a personal loan directly from a bank or from their political party. They can then seek some reimbursement from the State in order to pay back their loans.

Indicative Bibliography

Carcassonne, G. et al., 'L'Argent des élections', *Pouvoirs*, 70, 1994.

Marmorat, V., P. Cohen-Séat and J.-L. Péru, *Guide du financement électoral* (Paris, Dalloz, 1995).

Mény, Y., *La Corruption de la République* (Paris, Fayard, Série Espace du Politique, 1992).

Uguen, J.-L., *Les Elus et l'argent* (Paris, Syros, 1995).

7. THE MAINSTREAM RIGHT: CHIRAC AND BALLADUR

JOHN GAFFNEY

Introduction

In French politics, a heavy premium is placed upon friendship and loyalty; treachery, therefore, is everywhere. Every political party, party headquarters, even ministry and 'cabinet' strives to appear as noble in public as it is bloodstained off-stage. This is perhaps especially true on the right: Gaullism, and later the Republic it created in 1958, by placing great stress on the cult of the leader and his trusted companions, created a kind of politics in which personal rivalries not just between but within political parties and movements are as imperative as personal allegiances.

The 1995 contest for the presidency between the RPR leader, Jacques Chirac, and his former colleague, Prime Minister Edouard Balladur, offers the most spectacular demonstration of a semi-presidential system in which personal loyalties and antagonism are so central that they have come close to becoming the organising principles of the whole political system. Allegiance to individuals who represent political traditions, and all the virtues and vices which surround such allegiance, have an influence upon politics uncharacteristic of comparable political regimes in comparable societies. The way in which politics is organised in France brings into the heart of the political process an unpredictability and intensity which in fact undermines the institutional machinery constructed expressly to overcome political division and provide effective national leadership beyond the endemic factionalism of French politics. In this chapter we will discuss the right's return to power in the National Assembly elections of 1993 and the circumstances surrounding the nomination of Edouard Balladur rather than Jacques Chirac as Prime Minister. We shall then look at the effects of this upon the relationship between the two men and the fortunes of each as potential candidates for the presidency. We shall comment upon the relational aspect of their status in each of the years 1993, 1994 and 1995 as the campaign for the presidency began, and look at the political context, particularly that of the Socialist Party's candidate selection and its significance for the rivalry between Balladur and Chirac. Finally, we shall examine the campaign itself and draw conclusions regarding the wider significance for presidential politics of the period 1993-1995.

1993: The return of the right

In March 1993, the right-wing coalition of the Rassemblement pour la République (RPR) and the Union pour la Démocratie Française (UDF) won a landslide victory in the legislative elections. The RPR held 244 seats and the UDF 213. The Socialists, having governed for most of the previous decade with over 280 seats, were reduced to less than 70. According to political convention, the premiership should have been offered to the RPR leader, Jacques Chirac. For reasons we shall analyse below, he himself declined the office and encouraged his own close colleague, Edouard Balladur, to form a government, a government which was supposed to play a caretaker role until the right – which held power now at nearly all levels of political activity: local, departmental, regional and national – could claim the ultimate prize in 1995, the presidency of the Republic. Instead of being a caretaker government, this two-year 'interlude' turned into a power struggle between Chirac and Balladur, which divided the right, and for a period even threatened the right's grip on power.

The two-year Chirac-Balladur rivalry has been documented in several books and in the media, with explanatory frameworks which range from gossip to psychoanalysis and to history. There is, however, little emphasis in all the commentary upon the institutional structures which made the rivalry possible, if not inevitable. For the issue is quite straightforward, even though it gives rise to an infinite number of complex political effects: the presidential election takes place every seven years, legislative elections every five. The political parties must play an active role in each election in order to remain politically credible. The parties organise chiefly around two activities: choosing a 'présidentiable' and electing MPs. Normally, moreover, the 'présidentiable' must lead the party in both activities in order to minimise rivalry. However, in cases where the opponents of the sitting President win legislative power in the National Assembly,[1] there will normally be a period of government before the next presidential elections, a period in which the party leader/'présidentiable', now Prime Minister, has ample time to lose his presidential status given the wear and tear of office and the 'normal' unpopularity of governments. This was the case, for example, for Prime Minister Chirac between 1986 and 1988. Indeed, in the French Republic it is almost as if the premiership were designed as an unpopular post in order to protect the 'grandeur' of the President. This assumes that the President and Prime Minister are working in tandem, the latter appointed by the former, and normally a lieutenant of the President from his own political party or family. Where this is not the case, as in 1986-1988 and 1993-1995, the threat to the 'présidentiable'/Prime Minister becomes enormous, witness Prime Minister Chirac's vulnerability to Mitterrand's perpetual assertions of the President's hierachical superiority over the Prime Minister between 1986 and 1988.

An alternative to the presidential challenger's occupying the premiership was the strategy chosen by Chirac in 1993; namely to 'delegate' a lieutenant, who would fall on the sword of government while the 'présidentiable' – Chirac – avoided unpopularity, saving his energies for the battle for the presidency. In this way the unsynchronised rhythms of French political life might be dealt with.[2] The problem, unforeseen by most (although not all) observers, was that this tactic furnished the delegated Prime Minister with a national platform which allowed him to entertain the idea of becoming himself a 'présidentiable'. It also risked marginalising the party leader/'présidentiable' who, by refusing the premiership, could have been seen as hesitant, while his party dealt with the nation's problems and attended to its needs. For presidential aspirants, therefore, one of the difficult problems is to manage the contingencies of the political cycle while trying to maintain credibility within the overarching presidential seven-year cycle (itself also prone to unpredictability as in 1969 and 1974).

In terms of Chirac's own political fortunes, he did virtually everything necessary to take him to the commanding heights of the Fifth Republic: he transformed the old Gaullist Party into the Rassemblement pour la République (RPR) in 1976, whose fundamental task now was to put Jacques Chirac into the presidency. He served as Prime Minister twice (1974-6, 1986-8), had a national profile and experience, could claim to be President Pompidou's protégé, and in spite of the widespread view that perhaps ultimately Chirac did not have the 'weight' of a de Gaulle, Pompidou, Giscard d'Estaing or Mitterrand (a weight Balladur himself *would* subsequently be seen as possessing), it was as if his 'turn' in the presidency had come: he was a candidate in both 1981 and 1988, and was throughout much of the 1970s, 1980s, and 1990s often the only credible, even conceivable, candidate of the right, and only viable candidate of the Gaullist Party.[3]

In the aftermath of the 1993 legislative elections, Jacques Chirac would have been swept into the presidency on the tide of the right's popularity had there been a presidential election. But there was not; it was not due for another two years. For Chirac, the lesson of 1986-8 was clear: at that time, he had taken the premiership, and had seen his popularity and esteem gradually sinking in inverse proportion to President Mitterrand's rise. This time, a lieutenant would play that role while Chirac (symbolically) withdrew into the wilderness to reflect upon France's needs prior to the realisation of his political destiny and his return to fight once more – and successfully – for the ultimate political prize. Which lieutenant?

Friends for thirty years

Chirac joined Prime Minister Georges Pompidou as a 'chargé de mission' in 1962. In 1965, he was elected as a Gaullist local councillor and in 1967 became an MP and junior minister. Balladur, an ENA graduate like Chirac, joined Pompidou's team in 1964. The moment in France's political history that unites Edouard Balladur and Jacques Chirac is 1968. Both were involved in the Matignon Accords with the trade unions which, after near-revolution by the students and an effective general strike by the workers, defused the threat of social upheaval and transformed a regime-threatening uprising into a negotiated settlement. Pompidou's temporary eclipse between 1968 and 1969 saw no diminution in Chirac's thirst for political action; for Balladur, it had the opposite effect. Without the master, and with a patrician disdain for 'la politique politicienne', he withdrew from political life and turned his attention to the world of industry and finance.

When Pompidou won the presidency the following year in 1969, Chirac, still Pompidou's political protégé, gained ministerial office as Minister for Relations with the Parliament (1971), then Minister of Agriculture (1972) and, later, Minister of the Interior (1974). Balladur too was called back, now promoted to deputy General Secretary and, in 1973, General Secretary of the Elysée. Upon Pompidou's sudden death in April 1974, Balladur again withdrew from public life, this time as a kind of semi-official keeper of the late President's memory.[4] Chirac on the other hand organised a Gaullist Party rebellion against the party's official presidential candidate, the former Prime Minister, Jacques Chaban-Delmas (for Chirac, too left-wing), and helped secure the election of the non-Gaullist, Valéry Giscard d'Estaing, to the presidency. His reward was the premiership, but in 1976 Chirac resigned after two difficult years in which personal rivalry between himself and Giscard d'Estaing was compounded by a developing power struggle between the Gaullist and the non-Gaullist right. However, from 1974, he began to create and enjoy a rally of opinion around himself within the Gaullist Party, brushed aside the older 'barons' of Gaullism, becoming General Secretary of the UDR (the immediate predecessor of the RPR) and in 1976 renamed it – with himself as its President – the Rassemblement pour la République, imbuing it with the kind of leadership cult and rally style reminiscent of 1940s Gaullism, and characterising its activists as if they were made in the image of the new leader: young, vigorous, right-wing, populist, 'agité', and prepared to go in every contradictory direction in order to achieve power. The early Chirac, therefore, was highly successful within the confines of 'neo-Gaullism', itself oriented towards the ultra-right by two advisors, Marie-France Garaud and Pierre Juillet, whose influence upon Chirac was enormous. We shall come back to this phenomenon in our conclusion; here we can say that such influence increased the virulence of neo-Gaullism while diminishing its wider popularity. In the 1979 European election, Chirac's party gained a mere 16% of the vote. In the 1981 presidential election, Chirac gained 17.99 %, a vote low enough to help the left's candidate, François Mitterrand, into power. It was as if Gaullism was, thanks to Chirac, losing its influence in the Republic, even though his leadership of the RPR remained unquestioned. By the early 1980s, it was a question for many in the party of first changing Chirac's advisors in order to save the party from decline.

Re-enter Balladur. Circumspect, wise, slightly older, moderate in manner, and more centrist in outlook and policy proposals, Balladur came into Chirac's orbit once again at the time of the 1981 presidential election campaign, now as an advisor rather than a colleague, propelled by friends of Chirac weary of his dependence upon Garaud and Juillet. Once he had replaced Garaud and Juillet, some in the party resented Balladur as they had his predecessors: not only was he considered too circumspect to be a 'true believer', but he was also seen as too fastidious, and as somewhat precious and vain in this world of back-slapping young men. Chirac, however, accepted his advice and treated him almost as one of the new barons of Gaullism, conferring upon him a kind of grand vizir status as the voice of centre-right moderation, further alienating such Gaullist figures as Philippe Séguin on the left of the party and Charles Pasqua on the right. Balladur's more centrist politics and style in fact made him more of a threat to them than the deposed Garaud and Juillet.

Whether Balladur was the architect of the party's subsequent successes or simply accompanied them is open to question, but successes there certainly were, Chirac's party heading the victorious coalition in the 1986 legislative elections. Chirac became Prime Minister; Balladur was made Finance Minister.[5] The President, François Mitterrand, was of course hostile to them, and his authority and growing support in the country were enough to mar the successes of the new team. And although Chirac and not the UDF's candidate, Raymond Barre, faced Mitterrand as challenger in the second round of the presidential elections in 1988, he was beaten. Even though Chirac was the right's main leader, he was seen as being not quite strong enough to lead the right to ultimate victory. This impression of Chirac was to be significant later on and informed the attitudes of many towards him throughout the late 1980s and early 1990s. Upon re-election in May 1988, Mitterrand dissolved the Assembly and the left returned to power. The solidarity between Chirac and Balladur remained, however (again, much to the resentment of those jealous of Balladur's privileged place). For a time, active collaboration was put in abeyance while Chirac considered whether, as twice a loser in the presidential contest, he could ever win. Eventually, he resolved to continue his twenty-year campaign for the presidency, although now he had to counter dissent within the party, particularly from factions led by Charles Pasqua and Philippe Séguin. Opposition to him surfaced in the immediate aftermath of the 1988 elections and again during the referendum campaign for ratification of the Maastricht Treaty in 1992 which Chirac supported. Throughout, Balladur's advice remained decisive; during 1992, for example, it was he who stressed how important it was for Chirac to remain, as he had become, pro-European, and not gain deceptive, cavalier advantage from taking up an anti-Socialist, anti-Mitterrand, anti-

Maastricht, anti-European position. In the legislative elections of 1993, as we have seen, the RPR-UDF alliance swept back into power after five years of Socialist government. The kind of Gaullism and the kind of Chirac that Balladur had helped shape now held – along with the RPR's junior UDF partner – majorities in almost all areas of political power; in the regions, the municipalities, the Assembly and the Senate. In fact, Gaullist influence was greater now even than in its 'Etat-UDR' heyday in the 1960s.[6] Only the presidency remained to be conquered, the political office upon which Chirac had built his political ambition. In the aftermath of the 1993 elections, Balladur was named as Prime Minister. Although officially chosen by the President, he was Jacques Chirac's nominee. Some commentators, while noting both the obvious reason for substituting Balladur for himself (it left Chirac untainted by the unpopularity which normally accrued to a sitting Prime Minister), also referred to the sheer emotional unwillingness of Chirac to face Mitterrand again and the humiliations he had known in 1986-88. Some of Chirac's colleagues were already convinced of Edouard Balladur's duplicity, and his having sensed both his leader's weakness and his own advantage at the moment he stepped forward to offer his services as Prime Minister. Chirac, nevertheless, needed someone who would be competent and not govern badly; yet only someone without a power base of his own, such as those possessed by Séguin and Pasqua, would be Chirac's puppet. He also needed someone who would be acceptable to the (slightly) junior UDF partner to the governing coalition.[7] Balladur had no power base, neither nationally nor in the party (where he was, as we have said, much disliked by the Gaullist barons for his influence upon Chirac); but he had been Jacques Chirac's respected Minister of Finance between 1986 and 1988. In many ways, Balladur was the acceptable face of centrist Gaullism, and in a sense he was the antithesis and therefore political complement of Chirac: Chirac was impetuous, Balladur calm; Chirac populist, Balladur aristocratic; Chirac radical (right or left, depending), Balladur centrist; together they might enable Gaullism under Chirac's leadership to cast its appeal across a wide political spectrum.

The Balladur premiership: sowing the seeds of conflict

1993

Edouard Balladur had learned from some of the mistakes he had made between 1986 and 1988 when, asserting himself as Chirac's deputy, he alienated many of Chirac's closest supporters, as well as many of the UDF ministers. In 1993, as the new Prime Minister, he immediately set about wooing political support. He incessantly studied the opinion polls, courted journalists and leading political figures, especially in the UDF. He had, in fact, at least a year before becoming Prime Minister, had a relatively high profile in the media, had cultivated intellectuals and the cultural élite, and published books on his political views. Before becoming Prime Minister, he also cultivated influential RPR MPs, inviting them to work semi-officially on policy documents and in small working groups. He did the same with several influential members of the UDF (hence, in part, the hostility of Giscard who felt that Balladur was stealing his supporters). He took as his own advisors Nicolas Bazire and Nicolas Sarkozy, highly talented young men whose dynamism and ruthlessness resembled those of the younger Chirac, who became, respectively, directeur de cabinet and government spokesperson. Sarkozy had in fact worked for Chirac until 1993 when, with Chirac's agreement, he joined Balladur's team.

On Balladur's becoming Prime Minister, it was agreed between Chirac and Balladur that a certain distance would have to be set up between them in order that Chirac not be seen as orchestrating the government from the wings and undermining Balladur's authority. Chirac did not anticipate the degree to which Balladur would distance himself.

Balladur formed his government[8] in fact with little reference at all to Chirac, although it inevitably contained many of Chirac's supporters, the most significant being his right-hand man, Alain Juppé, named Foreign Minister. Juppé agreed, along with all the new ministers, to Balladur's ruling that none of them was to speak publicly of the presidential elections. The silence rule was justified by all in order that the government could get on and govern without being distracted by the media ever speculating on the presidential dimension. Balladur's ruling does, however, demonstrate that there was a problem from the start concerning the Prime Minister's position; what had been justified in terms of good management, became a means of controlling Chirac's supporters. In fact, the ruling endowed the remarks that did get through to the media, from both Chirac's and Balladur's supporters, with explosive effect, as we shall see below.

Balladur also controlled the public appearances of all his ministers. All except one. Balladur's greatest catch was Charles Pasqua, a tough, uncompromising Gaullist, now a leader of the hard-right of Gaullist populism, with a strong power base within the party. Pasqua became Interior Minister and early felt he could profit from the association with Balladur (either as a supporter or broker). Pasqua could say what he liked when he liked. Gradually his support became more unequivocally pro-Balladur, compounding the view by 1995 that Balladur would win the presidency. Balladur also included in his government the main party leaders: Juppé (RPR), Méhaignerie (CDS) and Longuet (PR). In this way, Balladur imposed his will upon his government and therefore upon the parliamentary majority (something Chirac had himself been unable to do in 1986, particularly among UDF ministers and MPs), while incorporating each of the political forces of the ruling coalition. Balladur appointed 16 UDF ministers (against 13 RPR). This wooing of the UDF partner to the coalition could not be seen as anti-RPR as Balladur was himself a member of the RPR.

So began Edouard Balladur's 'caretaker' government: reflecting the various elements of the right, managing the economy and nation's affairs until the end of Mitterrand's presidential term in 1995, which would allow the right's main leader, Chirac, having stepped back from public life for a while, to re-enter the political arena and bid for the présidency. Then a strange thing happened.

Balladur – seemingly socially out-of-touch, incapable of the open and dynamic 'one-of-us' warmth that Chirac was renowned for, without a power base, and aptly caricatured in the press as a cardinal or a monarch-like figure in a sedan chair – from May 1993 onwards, saw his opinion poll rating begin to climb and climb. Chirac's rating, on the other hand, began steadily to fall, and this to the point where the Balladur camp could eventually treat Chirac as splitting the right and bring pressure upon him to withdraw from the race, to allow Balladur to run for the presidency.

The irony of this astonishing development was compounded by the fact that one of the reasons put forward for Chirac's fear of taking the premiership in 1993 and its effects upon his image was that the economy was in continuing recession; indeed, the recession and rising unemployment[9] continued as, throughout the year, did Edouard Balladur's popularity. This was in part due to Balladur's public style: reassuring, unpolemical, managerial, thoughtful and competent. In part it was due to his novelty value: compared to the main political leaders, Balladur was perceived as a newcomer and a consensus Prime Minister, yet with the gravitas of age, intellect and personality more reminiscent of a Mitterrand than a Chirac. Immediately upon his taking office 70% of those polled expressed their confidence in him.

Balladur also made great use of television. He appeared frequently on television and his reassuring manner was extremely popular.[10] Over this two-year period as Prime Minister he was to make thirty-five major public interventions, nearly thirty of which involved major television appearances. Using one means of support (media popularity) to compensate for his lack of means within his own party, if the pressure became strong enough he might draw the party towards him. Balladur filled the public space where government was seen by the electorate/viewers. It became difficult to imagine anyone else as Prime Minister, or perhaps even as President.... In such a situation, Chirac was reduced to virtual silence as his own and his party's popularity was still linked to the new government.

Chirac had overlooked a fundamental difference between the 1993-95 'cohabitation' government and the 1986-88 one: President Mitterrand was no longer a major player. It was clear to all that he would not stand again for President, and in fact his physical decline only occasionally abated enough to allow him to influence the political climate – usually by expressing his confidence in the Prime Minister. In such a situation, Balladur was able also, to some extent, to move into the space usually occupied by the President, becoming more and more presidential in his style and image. It seemed as if the two people who had dominated and divided the right for twenty years, Giscard and Chirac, would now be forced to give way to a new political leader of national stature.

The opening shots in retaliation came from Philippe Séguin, now President of the National Assembly, as early as 16 June 1993 when he referred to various French governments' attitude to unemployment as a 'Social Munich' and included the present government in his criticism. Chirac failed to denounce the speech. Then, in the month of July the franc came under pressure. By widening the exchange rate margins in order to maintain the European Monetary System, the government had effectively devalued the franc (in order that no actual devaluation take place). Weakening the franc has always brought political unpopularity in France. Significantly, once again, this setback for Balladur's government drew little solidarity from Chirac.

So, within a matter of months, even by the summer of 1993, such omissions of support, oblique allusions to one another's view, 'significant' absences at RPR meetings by each of the two men, created a public rift between them. And against the background of Balladur's continuing popularity in the opinion polls, the rift became a rivalry; Balladur was transformed into one of the RPR's potential presidential candidates. As supporters with varying degrees of allegiance ranging from devotion to cold calculation began to organise around the two men, the rivalry turned into open conflict.

Much of the duelling was in fact undertaken by their lieutenants in the corridors of the Assembly and the columns of the national press. For Balladur, through intermediaries, the strategy was to woo the UDF so that Balladur became a de facto candidate of the UDF and therefore the most potentially successful candidate of the right as a whole. For Chirac and his lieutenants, and this was especially the task of the deputy leader of the RPR, Jean-Louis Debré, it was a question of maintaining loyalty to Chirac within the RPR, so depriving Balladur of a party base.[11]

On 20 December 1993, and with calculated simultaneity, the two most prominent UDF ministers, Simone Veil and François Léotard, publicly announced their support for Balladur's candidacy for the presidential election, thus drawing the argument around the two contenders into the open. Now Balladur's earlier silence rule was beginning to have strange effects: if a minister spoke in favour of Balladur, it was not seen as scandalous because it did not undermine the government; if he or she spoke in favour of Chirac it was depicted as breaking the collective governmental solidarity. One 'code' was being used to influence an entirely different one.

Chirac's decision in 1993 not to become Prime Minister began to be seen as an enormous miscalculation. He could not criticise the government which he himself supported and had helped create. He also had to hold on to his party machine and ensure that it did not, with the prospect of a resounding Balladur victory, begin to lend its support to Balladur, and then cause a stampede away from Chirac. A further consideration was Charles Pasqua. Pasqua had already demonstrated his independence from Chirac. And from early 1994, Pasqua regularly called for 'primaries' to choose a single presidential candidate within the right, in which it was obvious that Balladur had a strong chance of beating any rival. Far closer to Chirac both personally and ideologically, Pasqua nevertheless acted as Balladur's 'right-wing' to the political benefit of both himself and Balladur; he gradually became more and more pro-Balladur, drawing from Chirac some of his potential populist appeal both within the RPR and the wider electorate, until, on 14 January 1995 he publicly endorsed a Balladur candidacy, hoping to tilt the election in Balladur's favour and perhaps become his Prime Minister in turn.

It has been disputed whether there was a formal pact made between Edouard Balladur and Jacques Chirac over the former's taking the premiership in order to leave the latter to prepare for the presidency. It is, however, beyond dispute that this was the logic of the whole operation. Nevertheless, all the above developments are clear indications that Balladur himself was in a position from the beginning of his premiership to entertain thoughts of his own presidential future.

By the end of 1993, the question of personal image had become a crucial factor. The Balladur camp needed to appeal to the UDF and to the voters by portraying the Prime Minister as highly competent, calm, reassuring and as the steady leader who could take the economy and the country forward into the next century. Chirac, as well as ensuring that the RPR MPs and party members did not begin to go over to Balladur needed to maintain a national profile. As regards image, then, the two essential tasks for Chirac were to try and counter the developing view that he had become irrelevant to both party and country; and to substitute his established reputation as an impetuous 'agité' (a term Mitterrand had exploited in 1988) with an image which could counter Balladur's serious profile. Chirac had simultaneously, therefore (and contradictorily), to maintain *and* replace his established image. So while Balladur cultivated the media with many interviews portraying his fashioned image of wise counsellor (now of the nation), Chirac – having chosen withdrawal from public office – attempted to cultivate the idea that he too was reflecting, reassessing and developing a philosophy for governing France while remaining enough in the public eye not to be totally eclipsed.[12]

1993 thus saw the emergence of two Gaullist leaders, each potentially successful candidates for the presidency; Chirac's support was drawn from France's strongest political party. Balladur's from opinion poll popularity virtually unknown for a political leader in the Fifth Republic, and certainly more sustained and intense than Chirac himself had ever known. On the one hand, given the victory of the right in 1993, it seemed clear that in 1995 any candidate of the mainstream right would win. There was also the view that so strong was the right that it could 'tolerate' two of its own candidates, as both would go through to the round two run-off of the 1995 election. On the other hand, Chirac had always seemed unable to extend his personal support beyond 20% of the electorate at best; this raised questions of the right's vulnerability if a highly popular opposition candidate were to emerge. Given the weak situation of the left, such, however was unlikely. At the end of 1993, only the right – and rivalry – filled the political arena.

1994

Both Chirac and Balladur entertained the idea of leading an RPR or a majority list as the major electoral event of 1994, the European elections of the 12 June, approached.[13] The European election, however, had remained, since its inception in 1979, more a critical referendum on the government than an election about European issues. If Balladur associated too much with a campaign which did not do well, his personal reputation would suffer. Chirac, if the list did well, would only enhance the status of the government – besides, Chirac could not have led an RPR-UDF alliance list, which would have been unacceptable to the UDF, nor were separate lists feasible given the alliance itself. The divisions within the RPR over Europe, moreover, made leading a campaign extremely problematic. The solution in the end was to head a majority list with a compromise candidate (Dominique Baudis, UDF) and for both men to keep as well out of the limelight as possible; the danger of opening up the rivalry between the two such a long time before the 1995 campaign was thus avoided.

There was another reason why the European campaign and elections exacerbated the problems within the mainstream right as regards the choice of presidential candidate. Paradoxically, the reason for this was the defeat of the left. Unlike Balladur and Chirac, Michel Rocard, the leader of the PS, had chosen the opposite strategy and led his party's list – to crashing defeat (14.49%). Rocard's subsequent resignation meant that the left now had no credible presidential candidate at all. Into the vacuum came the Delors phenomenon. Jacques Delors, President of the European Commission and a member of the PS, remained a potential candidate for the presidency until December 1994, and while he did his opinion poll rating began to soar, giving the left renewed hope after repeated defeats at the hands of the right and low esteem in public opinion. Until the end of 1994, this increased the tension dramatically between Chirac and Balladur. Until Delors came on the scene in the summer of 1994, the right had adapted to its difficult situation by portraying itself as a right strong enough to have more than one candidate for the presidency; suddenly it looked divided enough to split the right's vote and allow the left the prospect of yet another presidential victory. From the moment the possibility of a Delors candidacy emerged, the luxury of two RPR hopefuls appeared less affordable. Hitherto, in many opinion polls, although Balladur remained the favourite, Chirac's situation was tolerable because he too would beat any other candidate, except Balladur, in a run-off match. As Delors' star rose throughout the autumn of 1994, the polls predicted that only Balladur could defeat Delors. In some polls, even he was seen as unlikely to triumph. The imperative of a united right therefore became most forceful only weeks before the campaign would begin in earnest from the beginning of 1995. If one of the candidates stood down, a united right would (most probably) avoid the previously unbelievable – but now increasingly believable – prospect of a left victory in 1995.

The Delors 'candidacy' (Delors never in fact became a candidate) raises a further important issue in relation to the divisions within the governing majority. Normally, the right has been represented by two main families: the Gaullists and the centre-right UDF, which each contain elements that are both pro-European and strongly 'social' in the traditions of European Christian Democracy. Chirac could only reasonably expect to represent one of the families, however, given his leadership of one of the parties, and his long history of ambivalence over Europe. Balladur, however, as a Gaullist, could claim to represent the Gaullists but also, as a liberal, as a pragmatist and as 'Pompidolian', more pro-European and less ideological than Chirac, he could be seen as representative of the other family of the right as well – on condition the UDF presented no candidate. Balladur had to show that he was the UDF's candidate while remaining capable of representing his own party. Chirac had to be the Gaullists' true candidate while trying to woo the 'social' centre-right elements of the UDF in the first round, as the pre-requisite to rallying the rest of it in round two. The advantage for Balladur and disadvantage for Chirac was that it was precisely this UDF culture and constituency that Delors so effectively threatened to capture. Not only that, Delors could also lay claim to a more 'statist' and leftist Gaullist tradition as he had once worked for the centre-left government of the Gaullist, Jacques Chaban-Delmas (1969-1972) whose prospects for the presidency in 1974 were to be so effectively undermined by the young Chirac. The right's indulgence in the Balladur-Chirac rivalry was no longer appropriate in this developing complexity – especially given the historical precedent of a divided right which had 'let the left in' in both 1981 and 1988 in part as a result of personal squabbling.

Given the threat from Delors, the fortunes of Balladur and Chirac vis-à-vis one another rested upon the question of a UDF candidacy.[14] For Chirac, the paradoxical conclusion at this stage was that a 'real' UDF first-round challenger on the right was necessary (on condition, of course, that such a candidate would be eliminated in round one). Thus he was to renew his old alliance with his arch-rival, the former President, Giscard d'Estaing, who as overall leader of the UDF confederation was witnessing his own movement slip away from him into Balladur's arms (in fact, Giscard and Chirac had met as early as February 1994 to discuss how they might reassert themselves over Balladur). Giscard's task would be to try to ensure that he himself or another UDF candidate (Raymond Barre or Charles Millon) occupy the platform Balladur was reaching for. Balladur, however, remained ahead of Chirac in the polls.

In order not to be overwhelmed by demands for Balladur's 'unitary' candidacy, Chirac declared his own candidacy on 4 November 1994. Only crushing poll evidence in favour of Balladur could now force Chirac to pull out.

On 11 December, Delors declared that he would not run for the presidency. The effects on the left were, of course, dramatic (see the chapter by David Bell and Byron Criddle in this volume). On the right, it meant that the Chirac-Balladur fight – now envenomed by two years of hostility and the last-minute desperation of the Chirac camp to avoid being completely sidelined – would now be obliged to play itself out. A Balladur-Chirac run-off was now considered a strong possibility, in fact an assumed *probability* given the left's disarray at the beginning of 1995. At the beginning of the home straight, Balladur still seemed set to win with Chirac trailing him as a poor second with only around 20% of the ratings in the polls to Balladur's 30% (see the chapter by Jean and Monica Charlot). In fact, although Balladur's positive ratings in the polls had declined gradually since 1993, around 60% of those polled still regarded him as a good Prime Minister and/or potential President at the beginning of 1995. Balladur declared his candidacy on 18 January 1995.

1995: The campaign

A first and major point to note concerning the campaign is that Chirac was not so poor a second as to force him to quit. Given the ten points separating him from Balladur, the campaign itself would play a significant part in the outcome. A second point to note is that Chirac's disadvantage would be transformed into a devastating advantage if he could only catch up with Balladur in the polls (they crossed in late February). No candidate has ever recovered his position after being overtaken by a challenger from the same political family or associated families in the middle of the campaign. The classic cases are Chaban-Delmas in the 1974 presidential elections (overtaken by Giscard) and Raymond Barre in 1988 (overtaken by Chirac).

Jacques Chirac's Campaign

Chirac's campaign opened with a newspaper interview (*La voix du Nord*, 4 November 1995) which portrayed the candidate as an opposition leader calling for a clean sweep, and depicting the present government as the last of Mitterrand's fourteen-year presidency. This optical illusion (Chirac had himself been one of Mitterrand's Prime Ministers, one of Giscard's too...) was essential to the Chirac campaign. The image portrayed of Chirac was one of an outsider and a thinker who had withdrawn from the political mêlée to reflect on France's needs and had returned to his people not simply wiser, but a different man: more statesman-like (at 63 he seemed, in fact, physically more like a President than he had ever seemed before); more concerned about the people (he was flanked by the social Gaullist, Philippe Séguin); more centrist (his main lieutenant was Alain Juppé, a Chirac-Juppé team appearing less right-wing, in fact, than a possible Balladur-Pasqua one); more financially sound (he was also vigorously supported by Alain Madelin, a strong free-marketeer and leading member of the UDF); and more republican (he stressed again and again his belief in democracy and the republic). Armed with both a philosophy (published in his second small book of reflections which blended conservative ideas about economic performance with social-democratic ideas about social-mindedness),[15] and the army he had been drilling since the mid-1970s (his party, the RPR, with its national base and enormous experience at organising campaign rallies and at moblilising activists), Chirac portrayed himself as the true heir to the Fifth Republic. His supporters treated his major rally speech of 17 February as if it were the founding speech of a new Republic. In his TV and radio broadcasts, Chirac presented himself and was presented by his supporters as returning the Republic to Gaullism (he depicted the presidency as having become monarchical after Pompidou, a deviation the current Prime Minister would cultivate if elected). He also stressed the Gaullist style by stating his intention to use bold measures of state intervention to seal the current 'social fracture', and vigorously counter unemployment and 'exclusion', while patriotically striving to restore France's greatness. He depicted the current government as lacking these qualities, too willing to compromise, and lacking particularly the nerve necessary to take bold measures. Thus, the two-year interim government which Chirac had himself stage-managed became the object of his attacks in a way it could not have done had its principal representative not run against him. In fact, Balladur provided Chirac with a target and campaign themes he would have sorely lacked had Balladur remained his loyal servant. We shall come back to this point in our conclusion. Chirac, by giving his campaign a youthful emphasis, and a certain gaiety (cartoon-like apple trees being his main campaign symbol) Chirac distanced himself stylistically from his rival.

Edouard Balladur's Campaign

Apart from Lionel Jospin who did not declare his candidacy until 3 February, Balladur's candidacy (18 January) was one of the last declared. Jean-Marie Le Pen, Robert Hue, Dominique Voynet, Jacques Chirac, Philippe de Villiers had all declared before him. Nevertheless, it is arguable that Balladur declared too soon given that from 18 January the last three-and-a-half months of his premiership would constitute the bulk of a campaign which could only be a defensive one. Attacked from all sides and with no-one to attack himself, his 'campaign' appeared to be non-existent. His manifesto 'Croire en La France' did not appear for nearly another month, when Balladur presented his proposals at a news conference.[16] His first campaign meeting took place only in mid-February as he began to fall in the polls. He only reluctantly began citing Chirac openly from the end of March, weeks after he had been overtaken by him in the polls. Once Jospin had entered the race, he, Jospin, was able to conduct himself as if the conflict was between the left and right, Jospin and Chirac, as if Balladur were not important.

On many issues, the fundamentals between Chirac and Balladur's proposals were not very different. On public spending, the single currency, monetary policy, social security, pensions, employment, small industries and taxes, the two mainstream candidates had never really disagreed. Chirac, however, appeared throughout the campaign as offering more and the prospect of a more aggressive presidential style (while criticising the monarchical tendencies of others). On unemployment, for example, one of the major themes of the campaign, Balladur promised to reduce unemployment by one million by the year 2000 with a 4-5% growth rate. Even this claim was at the limits of real credibility. Chirac, however, always gave the impression that something even more dramatic could be done now (and was not being done), as if he could, if elected, solve problems immediately. It would, moreover, have been a contradiction of Balladur's pragmatic style were he to have promised more than a steady-as-she-goes set of policies. Presidential campaigns, however, by their intensity and focus upon individuals give the impression that voluntarist personal interventions can achieve much more. A great deal of Balladur's fortunes would depend upon his image as well as upon the organisation of his campaign.

Balladur's government had performed so well according to most of the normal scales of assessment – in investment, in containing inflation, in creating the conditions for economic growth, in maintaining overall the value of the franc – that a full-scale personal campaign based on style might have seemed superfluous. That would be, however, to misunderstand the nature of presidential elections. Besides, a substantive campaign on unemployment was unavoidable. As he was forced into the rough and tumble of campaigning, Balladur was deprived of his greatest – perhaps his only – weapon, namely, his image as a candidate whose legitimacy was drawn from his not needing to campaign at all. Unemployment, however, as in most of the Western democracies, had remained high and job security was perceived as more precarious, and redundancies were hitting social groups which hitherto had not experienced them. This climate of social malaise was given great prominence by the media and, as we have seen, was the central theme of Chirac's campaign. Balladur himself had referred to a 'pacte social' the previous year, referring to the need for effective social legislation. By the time of the campaign, 'le social' was a dominant theme, and the current government became the victim of accusations of inaction. Throughout the early months of 1995 there was a series of major strikes which added to the climate of social breakdown and the impression of governmental stasis, and therefore to the idea that the Prime Minister was losing his earlier control of the situation. In addition, because Balladur's popularity as Prime Minister was inextricably bound up with his probity and judgement, he was also extremely vulnerable to attacks on his integrity, far more vulnerable than any other candidate. A whole series of 'affairs' and 'scandals', some of which had been developing in the previous year, crashed over the government almost simultaneously in the run-up to the election campaign. By the time of the campaign, three government ministers had been forced to resign over corruption scandals. Perhaps most illustrative of the damage to the Prime Minister was a phone-tapping scandal that called directly into question the integrity not of Balladur but of the Minister of the Interior, Charles Pasqua, with whom, as we have seen, Balladur had become closely associated. Whether the Prime Minister was aware of the alleged improprieties (Pasqua was less under Balladur's control than any of his colleagues in government), it damaged the Prime Minister's reputation as it meant he had been either improper himself or else unaware and therefore less than completely competent. Overnight, all the potential advantage of the connection with Pasqua turned into a liability. In March, Balladur's own immense personal fortune was also revealed, marking him out as a highly privileged being in a society which contained many, and now media-saturated, pockets of real poverty. Given that his reputation was his most powerful electoral asset, the damage to it was inordinate. By mid-March (by late February according to some polls) Chirac's poll rating began to equal and then overtake the Prime Minister's. Balladur, having based his whole persona on not having even to stress his positive claims to the presidency, was now forced to defend himself against negative ones. After two months of relative campaign inertia he needed, in a word, to come out fighting. But campaigning now with his shirt-sleeves rolled up, and rallying support standing on tables (these occasions were given wide media coverage), Balladur – a man whose episcopal restraint had been the only image of him the public had known – seemed undignified. At a rally on 26 March Balladur's campaign team tried to change his image radically. Chanting 'Dou-Dou' (a diminutive of Edouard) and treating him as a lovable uncle figure, his supporters tried to will his popularity back. The approach was ill-judged: no-one was less of a 'Dou-Dou' than Edouard Balladur.

Meanwhile, the two other potential UDF candidates, Raymond Barre and Giscard d'Estaing, hesitated long enough (finally declining to run in declarations on 6 and 7 March respectively) to place a question mark over whether Balladur was the candidate of any of the major political parties. Nearly all the UDF did back him – the one major dissident element were the UDF's Clubs, Perspectives et Réalités, and several leading UDF figures like Alain Madelin, who had given his support to Chirac the previous November. Nevertheless, for UDF figures, campaigning for Balladur was like campaigning for another party's candidate. Moreover, the startling success of the left's candidate, Lionel Jospin (See Chapter 8), began in the closing weeks to reassert a left-right flavour to debate (which, of course, would dominate the second-round campaign), forcing the media and the public to pit a single party political representative of the right against the party political representative of the left. Relentlessly, Chirac appeared more and more the 'rightful' candidate, Balladur more and more the imposter. As Chirac climbed in the polls, he became more serene in his public appearances, while Balladur became more awkward and unsmiling. His main supporter, Pasqua, was now a liability, and the other leading Balladurians, Nicholas Sarkozy, François Léotard and François Bayrou seemed more bad tempered yet aimless in their public pronouncements; their claims that their champion was a real fighter contrasted sharply with the developing image of a potentially defeated man. When it came down to it, Balladur apparently had little to add to his 'Sleep now: I am watching over you'-style reassurance and self assurance of the previous two years. In fact, Chirac attacked this attitude with dignified outrage and sometimes humour in his campaign broadcasts, emphasising the gulf between their two styles to the detriment of the now *inappropriately* presidential Balladur style.

Whatever the role played by style, image and personal profile, by the time of the first round, Balladur had fallen in the polls to the old 'also ran' figure of around 16%, and Chirac was now accredited with figures in the high twenties. The closing moments of the campaign therefore made Balladur, now almost silent and looking ever more uncomfortable, look like the loser. The results, however, were as much an event as had been the Chirac come-back itself. Chirac beat Balladur 21% to 18.5%, but failed to achieve the runaway victory predicted. In fact, coming in a poor second to Lionel Jospin's 23.3%, Chirac did only marginally better than the scores he had achieved in 1981 and 1988. He was, however, through to the second round. And whichever of the two went through to the second round was almost certain to be the next President.

The Aftermath

Two views of Balladur prevailed in the days following his defeat. On the one hand, he appeared as the vain pretender to Chirac's rightful inheritance who, given the stewardship of the nation while his master contemplated the further horizon, had tried to outwit him. On the other, he appeared to many after his defeat as the best President France had just lost, a statesperson deprived of office because he did not know the street-fighting rules of party political clashes.

Balladur immediately called upon his voters to vote for Chirac in round two. He then solicited a one-to-one meeting with Chirac in order to maintain his hold over his votes and, as the champion of nearly half of the mainstream right's vote, to 'offer' them to Chirac. Chirac refused, agreeing only to meet all the representatives of the right, thus diminishing Balladur's claims by reasserting the parties' constituencies over momentary presidential ones. Ironically, but characteristically in terms of presidential rhetoric, Chirac claimed that he was doing the opposite, i.e. not recognising any intermediary between himself and the people. Balladur therefore withdrew from the scene, apart from one symbolic and silent appearance – as a member of the audience only – at the huge rally in favour of Chirac on 29 May. Chirac's refusal to negotiate with Balladur reflected a decision to try to eliminate Balladur from French politics after the decisive vote of 7 May; nevertheless, for two years vast swathes of the right's political establishment had been coaxed into varying degrees of submission to Balladur's maverick candidacy.

On the evening of Chirac's election, after beating Jospin 53 to 47%, the crowds in the place de la Concorde, whose gaiety was reminiscent of that of earlier Mitterrand victory celebrants, partially effaced the fact that Chirac had gained only 21% on the first round, far less than any previous successful presidential candidate; they also made Balladur, for two years taken for granted as the future President, seem like a distant memory. Chirac had won, but, to paraphrase Wellington, it was the damnedest near-run thing French presidential politics had ever seen, not between Jacques Chirac and Lionel Jospin, but between Chirac and his old friend, Edouard Balladur.

Conclusion

The respective fortunes of Jacques Chirac and Edouard Balladur in the 1993-5 period, a period which culminated in the victorious election of Jacques Chirac to the presidency of the Republic, highlighted the nature of presidentialism itself in the Fifth Republic. One of the secrets of Chirac's success was his ability to transmit to the electorate the idea that he was not an 'insider' but was symbolically from the 'outside'; that he had returned from across the desert and a period of reflection, armed with a philosophy which transcended the old ideologies and which was animated by a voluntarist 'gaullien' vigour. In inverse proportion to the depiction of Chirac's new 'vision' was that of Balladur as the old, the established, the overcautious, the uncourageous. Behind all this symbolic paraphernalia lay another no less significant element of the Fifth Republic's presidentialism, namely, the need for a very solid national and very unsymbolic party machinery upon which to depend, both in lean times and for the final stage – the campaign itself – of the twenty-year strategy to get Chirac into the Elysée.

In the case of Edouard Balladur, the strategic use of his opinion poll popularity and of his privileged access to television demonstrate a no less important feature of the Fifth Republic; namely, the mediatisation of a political personality and the profound political effects of this. For Edouard Balladur, using the media was an equivalent to Chirac's party machine. The problem for the former, however, was that the media was as capricious as it was powerful. Interestingly, the media's negative effect upon Balladur's popularity – severely disapproving of his insubstantial *Croire en la France* programme, for example – aptly demonstrated how the persona of a political leader, especially one without a sound party support base, is refracted through the media, and crucially dependent upon it.

Irrespective of what the media did to the Balladur campaign, his was also – like Raymond Barre's in 1988 – a demonstration of how not to run a campaign. However, its failings which we have discussed in this chapter and which serve as lessons in campaign management were arguably less significant than the shortcomings which had – paradoxically – given him such unprecedented popularity. That is to say that Balladur's status as a highly respected Prime Minister and assumed future President were strictly dependent upon his not needing to campaign for the presidency; the moment he did begin to campaign his image collapsed, the sudden loss of between ten and fifteen percentage points being the expression of this. The fall was all the more dramatic in that until the campaign or at least until 1995, Balladur's strategic choices, image and general political comportment had been exemplary. In terms of personal authority, moreover, he had been a far more effective Prime Minister than Chirac between 1986 and 1988.

It is perhaps true that the Balladur camp relied too much on the opinion polls, or rather upon the symbolism of Balladur's not needing to campaign, and that by the time he did need to, he and his team – like Barre before him – did not know how to. Chirac's not being Prime Minister also did allow him to do what he intended to do from the start, from 1993: he was able to comport himself as if he were truly playing out some epic role, returning to the Republic to restore it and invest it once again with its original Gaullist purpose. Balladur on the other hand spent the early part of his campaign attacking Jospin when he should have been countering Chirac, and the closing stages of the campaign trying to counter Chirac when he should have been attacking Jospin.

The Chirac-Balladur contest also tells us that the system, the regime, not only tolerates such crucial personal rivalry but institutionally *encourages* it. The need to survive over time and control the party machinery, the need to use the media, organise politically the five and seven-year cycles of the Assembly and the presidency, all show how the system encourages such rivalry. Equally, encouraging such rivalry means encouraging uncertainty and unpredictability: whereas Balladur's claim to the presidency was based upon an assumption that he would win, the success of Chirac's valiant campaign was based upon the assumption that he would lose. As the scales tipped, the uncertainty informing Balladur's chances of success turned into the irremediable collapse of his fortunes (down to the high teens bedrock support of the French centre-right); and, of course, the opposite was true for Chirac: as his forlorn efforts turned into hope, hope was dramatically amplified into runaway success. In the event, of course, Chirac did not see runaway success 'on the night', and we shall come back to this point in a moment. Another point to note regarding the uncertainty factor was that Chirac's fortunes were influenced by a completely extraneous event, namely the non-candidature of Jacques Delors: his 'withdrawal' in December 1994 (the irony of contingency being all the greater given that Delors never, in fact, was a candidate) reduced the imperative for an unequivocally supported right-wing candidate and allowed for the 'adventure' of the Jacques Chirac campaign, given that without Delors there no longer seemed to be any possibility that the right might conceivably lose. Without Delors, the right could enjoy the idea of two right-wing candidates (this too was undermined subsequently by the sudden popularity of Lionel Jospin which pushed the two right candidates into second and third place).

The dual between Chirac and Balladur was not only tolerated – even encouraged – by the system; by early 1995 it seemed to be willed by the electorate too, as if welcomed as an ultimate contest, given that the rivals had obviously not buried their differences. This is in part the reason for Giscard d'Estaing, Raymond Barre and Charles Millon's inability to get off the starting blocks: by February, they had become irrelevant, the two main rivals being the only ones of interest to the mainstream right's electorate, the media, and the nation more generally. Having said this, it is worth underlining the sad truth that in spite of the drama and the magnificent performance by Chirac, coming from way behind to overtake Balladur and eventually win the presidency itself, his 21% in the first round is testimony to how little he had really touched the hearts of his compatriots: his first round score in 1995 was barely more than that of 1988 or 1981. His years of campaigning had profited him little, and 1995 demonstrated how little faith the French really had in him. In hosts of towns and regions Chirac came third, overtaken, depending on the areas, by Jospin, Balladur or Le Pen. Unlike in 1988, however, the electoral arithmetic favourable to the right simply carried him from 21% in round one to 53% in round two and into the Elysée. From a cynical point of view, however, it can be argued that the style of Chirac's campaigns in both 1988 and 1995 were politically necessary i.e. he needed to eliminate the 'opposition' (i.e. right-wing rival) in round one, this being the only way forward into round two. In 1988 this led to certain defeat, in 1995 to certain victory, certain victory that is, in round *two*. By putting forward Edouard Balladur's name as Prime Minister in 1993, Jacques Chirac almost missed the opportunity to stand in round two of the 1995 presidential election campaign. Political observers will for years discuss whether Chirac's 1993-5 strategy was a political and psychological masterstroke or a blunder which almost brought his political career to an end. In the event, of course, he became the fifth President of the French Republic, inaugurating seven years of a Gaullist presidency and the political eclipse of Edouard Balladur, his friend for thirty years.

Notes

[1] For an analysis of the 1986-1988 period see John Gaffney (ed.), *The French Presidential Elections of 1988* (Aldershot, Dartmouth, 1989) pp. 4, 14-16, 48-53, 104-107. 1986 was the first time (1993, the second) that a President was faced with a hostile majority in the National Assembly. Observers had anticipated this happening in 1978 during the presidency of Valéry Giscard d'Estaing (1974-1981) when a left-wing majority might have been elected. In the event, the right won the elections.

[2] Presidential (pr) and parliamentary (pa) elections have taken the following erratic course, made more inconsistent by presidential dissolution of the Assembly (1962, 1981, 1988) or else the resignation or death of the President (1969, 1974): 1958 pr, 1958 pa, 1962 pa, 1965 pr, 1967 pa, 1968pa, 1969pr, 1973pa, 1974pr, 1978pa, 1981 pr, 1981 pa, 1986 pa, 1988 pr, 1988 pa, 1993 pa, 1995 pr.

[3] Chirac's only non-Gaullist rivals on the right throughout this period were Valéry Giscard d'Estaing and Raymond Barre. Within his own party, Michel Debré and Marie-France Garaud stood as Gaullist dissidents in the 1981 presidential elections but gained, respectively, only 1.1 and 1.3% of the national vote. After the 1988 elections, Philippe Séguin and Charles Pasqua entertained tentatively the idea of rivalling Chirac for the leadership of the RPR. Until the Balladur premiership, therefore, Chirac had had no serious rivals to his presidential claims.

[4] After Georges Pompidou's death, Balladur became President of the Friends of the Pompidou Centre. He also prepared Pompidou's memoirs for publication in 1975, was the executor of Pompidou's will, and remained a confidant of Pompidou's widow, Claude.

[5] His status was that of a deputy Prime Minister. 1986 was the first time Balladur was elected to Parliament. He was re-elected as an MP in 1988 and 1993.

[6] 'Etat-UDR' was used originally by the Radical politician Jean-Jacques Servan-Schreiber, UDR being the then initials of the Gaullist Party.

[7] The RPR and UDF had gone into the legislative elections of 1993 as the Union Pour La France alliance. Elected to the new assembly were 244 RPR and 213 UDF MPs.

[8] There are many accounts of this. See, for example, C. Nay, *Le Dauphin et le Régent* (Paris, Grasset, 1994), pp.346-361.

[9] Unemployment rose from 2.75 million in 1992 to 3.2 million in June 1993 and 3.3 million in June 1995.

[10] A very good example was his appearance on *L'Heure de Vérité*, 14 February 1994.

[11] In early 1995, the RPR had a membership of 140,000, 254 MPs, 85 Senators, and thousands of mayors and local councillors.

[12] During the campaign itself, television coverage of Edouard Balladur respective to the other contenders was reduced to compensate for what was regarded as earlier over-exposure. It is difficult to assess the effect of this, but it is likely that this damaged Balladur's campaign at a crucial moment (see Chapter 12).

[13] See J. Gaffney, 'France' in J. Lodge (ed.), *The 1994 Elections to the European Parliament* (London, Pinter, 1996), pp.84-106.

[14] *La France pour tous* was published three days after Chirac declared his candidacy.

[15] He had published articles in *Le Monde*, 17 November, 20 and 30 December 1995.

[16] *7 sur 7*, 11 September 1994.

Indicative Bibliography

Angeli, Claude and Stéphanie Mesnier, *Le nid'de serpents* (Paris, Grasset, 1995).

Bacqué, Raphaëlle and Denis Saverot, *Chirac Président* (Paris, Rocher, 1995).

Balladur, Edouard, *L'Arbre de Mai* (Paris, Jullian, 1979).

Balladur, Edouard, *Je crois en l'homme plus qu'en L'Etat* (Paris, Flammarion, 1987).

Balladur, Edouard, *Douze lettres aux Français trop tranquilles* (Paris, Fayard, 1990).

Balladur, Edouard, *Passion et longueur du temps* (Paris, Fayard, 1991).

Balladur, Edouard, *Des modes et des convictions* (Paris, Fayard, 1991).

Balladur, Edouard, *Dictionnaire de la réforme* (Paris, Fayard, 1992).

Brisard, Jean-Charles and Gérard Durand, *Charles Pasqua* (Grancher, 1994).

Charlot, Jean, *Pourquoi Chirac?* (Paris, Fallois, 1995).

Chazal, Claire, *Edouard Balladur* (Paris, Flammarion, 1993).

Chirac, Jacques, *Une nouvelle France* (Paris, Nil, 1994).

Chirac, Jacques, *La France pour tous* (Paris, Nil, 1995).

Clerc, Christine, *Jacques, Edouard, Charles, Philippe et les autres* (Paris, Albin Michel, 1994).

Cotta, Michèle, *Les secrets d'une victoire* (Paris, Flammarion, 1995).

Desjardins, Thierry, *L'Homme qui n'aime pas les dîners en ville* (Paris, Edition 1, 1995).

Domenach, Nicolas, and Maurice Szafran, *De si bons amis* (Paris, Plon, 1994).

Giesbert, Franz-Olivier, *Jacques Chirac* (Paris, Seuil, 1987).

Hecht, Emmanuel, and François Vey, *Chirac de A à Z* (Paris, Albin Michel, 1995).

Madjar, Robert, *L'Autre Chirac* (Paris, Lafon, 1995).

Nay, Catherine, *Le Dauphin et le Régent* (Paris, Grasset, 1994).

Scrutator, *Marathon pour l'Elysée* (Paris, Plon, 1995).

Seznec, Bruno, *Séguin* (Paris, Grasset, 1994).

de Vezins, Véziane, *Balladur de A à Z* (Paris, Albin Michel, 1995).

8. THE LEFT: JOSPIN, HUE AND LAGUILLER

DAVID BELL AND BYRON CRIDDLE

Introduction

The French Parti Socialiste (PS) won 38% of the vote in 1981, the year in which the presidency was won by François Mitterrand, the PS leader. This was the high point of Socialist electoral fortunes, but the party dominated the electoral landscape in the 1980s and appeared to be undergoing a cultural shift to become a 'party of government'. This was in contrast to the early years of the Gaullist Fifth Republic when it had been marginalised and found itself incapable of finding a candidate of presidential stature. Mitterrand occupied the presidency from 1981 until 1995. A series of Socialist governments held office, apart from the 1986-88 period, from 1981 until the legislative elections of 1993.

The party was transformed by the advent of François Mitterrand to its leadership in 1971, and the result was the victory in 1981. However, Mitterrand's strategy of alliance with the Communists which looked inevitable in the 1970s when the Communists polled over 20%, was impossible in the 1990s when the Communist Party had sunk to 6.5%. Moreover, the Mitterrand-dominated PS had only barely contained a succession of destructive factional quarrels amongst its Socialist 'barons' throughout the 1980s, and in 1990 these disputes burst out uncontained at the Rennes party congress: rivalries of personality and power were revealed to an astonished French public, and the party began to spiral down out of control. As it prepared for the parliamentary elections of 1993, a further series of difficulties was added. These were the Socialist government's inability to tackle the problem of unemployment and the steady stream of scandal about the party and the Mitterrand entourage.

Although the PS remained the dominant formation of the left in the 1990s, it was in a much diminished condition and in a changed ideological landscape. French politics had been transformed, and the old certainties of the left (anti-market, secular, Franco-centric) had been undermined, with new creeds yet to be established. Michel Rocard had, since the late 1970s, offered an alternative to Mitterrand's determined chase after the alliance with the Communists and preached a social democratic acceptance of the market and the possibility of an opening up of alliances with the political centre ground. This latter was never possible, even when he was Mitterrand's Prime Minister (1988-91), because of the President's opposition; only a few centrist personalities were enticed into the Socialist camp, most of whom subsequently returned to the centre. The limited experiment of centre alliance was ended when Edith Cresson was made Prime Minister in succession to

Rocard. This proved a catastrophe as Cresson struggled with a myriad of intractable problems and stinging electoral defeats. She was replaced in 1992 by Pierre Bérégovoy who did not have the time to make any impact on the party's declining fortunes. The Socialists were decisively ejected from office at the 1993 legislative elections by an electorate weary of high unemployment and endless scandals, polling their lowest vote (20%) since 1968 and reduced to a barely believable 67 seats in a 577-seat Assembly.[1] This drubbing was repeated at the June 1994 European elections when the list headed by Michel Rocard – now party leader – polled a meagre 14.5% of the vote (with a further 12% being polled by a Radical list headed by the louche business entrepreneur and one-time Mitterrandist minister, Bernard Tapie).[2]

Hence, from the middle of 1994 onwards the left suffered the same volatility which made the presidential election itself unpredictable. Moreover, with François Mitterrand still occupying the Elysée and the PS having been in government for ten of the fourteen years since 1981, the Socialist Party was in the peculiar position of running against the conservative majority whilst still being seen as the Establishment and as the incumbents; a comparable sort of ambiguity had existed at the time of the 1988 presidential election, but then to the advantage of the Socialists. In 1988, Mitterrand was still in his prime, a national father-figure exercising a role which seemed to blend the advantages – unimaginable in another West European country – of a presiding but non-governing monarch with leader of the opposition to the sitting conservative government. But in 1995, in place of a politically potent Socialist President was a man in terminal political and physical decline, whose own Prime Minister (Bérégovoy) had committed suicide, and whose private life and recently publicised Vichyite past gave a 'fin de siècle' look to the Fifth Republic's longest presidency. Other parties on the French left jockeyed to take advantage of a debilitated Socialist Party with a lacklustre leadership and no sense of strategy or direction. Because of the 1994 European election disaster, Rocard lost the leadership of the party as it drifted towards what some analysts at the time saw as an even worse disaster in 1995.

Thus the 1995 campaign appeared during the latter half of 1994 to promise a further surge of fragmentation on the left. After a brief period in which Bernard Tapie[3] gave the impression that, despite being disqualified as a potential office holder, he might actually run, he renounced the ambition to stand, leaving his Radical party in some confusion, whilst still trying to be kingmaker both in his party and within the wider left, as other names, including that of the charity organiser and popular ex-minister Bernard Kouchner,[4] were also floated. At the Radical Convention in February 1995, Jean-François Hory (Radical president) was nominated and launched his own abortive attempt to run as candidate in the absence of Tapie. The campaign was based on job creation (through reduction of the working week and public works), a defiant European federalism, and a libertarian revision of some of the conservative government's laws (notably the legalisation of soft drugs, ending of phone taps, and scrapping of the 'Pasqua' laws limiting French nationality) and social solidarity. Hory was supported by Radical groups which had a distinctly anti-Socialist position, whilst traditionalists within the party, schooled in the old Socialist-Radical alliance and with an eye on the town halls, mainly supported the PS. Coming at an inopportune time for the emerging PS candidate, Lionel Jospin (about whom Hory disobligingly commented that he had the image of a 'certain archaism'),[5] the Radical campaign may have been intended merely to influence the Socialist choice and to bid-up the price of Radical support for the Socialist candidate, but in the absence of Tapie the only Radical vote winner, it was an empty threat. Jospin's camp thought that the rebuilding of the left could not be done around a PS/Radical axis and certainly not with Hory.[6] The upshot was that Hory's brief campaign lacked impetus,

Table 1: Analysis of First Ballot Vote

	Laguiller	Hue	Jospin	Voynet	Balladur	Chirac	de Villiers	Le Pen
All Voters	5	9	24	3	19	20	5	15
Age:								
Men 18-24	6	7	19	4	10	32	3	19
25-34	6	9	21	3	16	23	4	17
35-49	5	10	24	4	16	19	5	17
50-64	4	8	21	1	24	20	5	17
over 65	2	10	19	1	35	16	2	15
Women 18-24	7	6	29	7	14	23	4	16
25-34	7	10	29	4	13	17	4	16
35-49	7	8	27	5	17	16	7	13
50-64	3	8	23	2	25	21	6	12
over 65	2	8	20	1	37	19	4	9
First time voters	6	7	23	5	13	21	3	21
Occupation:								
Farmer	5	5	13	1	24	29	9	14
Small business	3	5	8	1	27	28	7	21
Top prof./manag.	4	5	26	5	21	24	6	6
Middle prof.	7	7	31	5	17	19	4	10
White collar	8	10	23	3	15	17	5	19
Blue collar	7	15	21	1	10	15	4	27
Status:								
Salaried/waged	7	9	26	4	16	17	5	16
Self-employed	2	4	12	2	25	31	7	17
Unemployed	6	11	24	4	13	20	3	18
Housewife	3	6	20	3	24	20	8	16
Student	6	6	30	6	10	28	3	11
Retired	3	9	20	1	32	19	4	12
Religion:								
Practising Catholic	4	3	15	2	37	26	5	8
Non-pract. Catholic	4	7	21	3	21	23	5	16
No religion	9	16	32	5	8	12	2	15
Political origin:								
Extreme left	30	9	21	2	10	9	5	14
PCF	5	72	11	1	2	3	1	5
PS	6	5	78	2	3	2	1	3
Gén. Ecologie	10	3	23	35	4	6	7	11
Verts	8	2	12	52	4	13	3	5
UDF	1	1	2	0	73	15	5	3
RPR	1	0	0	0	25	61	6	7
FN	1	1	5	1	5	4	3	80
No party	10	6	13	4	23	19	9	15
Maastricht vote:								
Yes	4	6	34	4	22	21	3	6
No	5	13	8	2	18	20	8	26

Source: BVA *Le Monde*, 25 April 1995

had no influence on Jospin (despite his eventual use of Radical themes such as secular society, youth employment and citizenship), and Hory withdrew on 31 March just before nominations closed, opening the prospect for the PS of wooing Radical and 'Tapie' voters back to the mainstream left.

Another faction, Jean-Pierre Chevènement's Mouvement des citoyens (a 1992 split from the Socialist Party) which had taken most of the former left-wing CERES faction within the PS, proposed an 'alternative' policy in the 1994 European elections as a response both to the perceived rightward drift of the PS and to a prevalent French disillusion with politics. Mercifully for the PS, Chevènement's list polled a minute 2.54% in the European elections.[7] Chevènement's decision not to stand in 1995 left the Mouvement floating between Jospin, the Communist, Robert Hue, the ecologist Dominique Voynet, and even Jacques Chirac, though Chevènement himself supported Jospin.[8] In the event, four candidates fought the election from various positions on the left: Jospin, Hue, Voynet and the Trotskyist, Arlette Laguiller, thus mirroring a similar diversity on the right. The votes were distributed across the candidates in the way shown in Table 1 (above).

If we take Voynet to be part of the left, the left's aggregate was, at 41%, impossibly low for any expectation of an eventual victory. Excluding Voynet, it was only 38%, and taking only the Socialist-Communist aggregate – 33% – it was the left's second worst performance in the Fifth Republic, previous base levels having been 29% in the 1993 Assembly election and 36% in 1968. Even the widest possible definition of the 'left', therefore, gave it, with only two-fifths of the electors, no potential for a second ballot challenge. In order to avoid duplication of analysis, the Voynet candidacy will not be analysed in this chapter (see Chapter 9). We should however bear in mind that with several reservations, Voynet can be considered as part of the 'left' in electoral and in wider political terms.

Arlette Laguiller

In the event, the only force materially to benefit from the implosion of the non-Communist left was the small Trotskyist Lutte Ouvrière, an offspring of the Union Communiste Internationaliste created in 1939 and led by Arlette Laguiller,[9] the only known leader of a somewhat shadowy organisation which seems to have no international affiliation.[10] Unlike most other Trotskyist parties, Lutte Ouvrière has (since 1971) regularly contested elections. Although polling around 2%, and having some strongholds, the purpose has been to recruit and mobilise, rather than to win office.[11] In 1974, Arlette Laguiller was the first woman to run for the presidency, and with 2.33% out-polled the other Trotskyist, Alain Krivine, giving Lutte Ouvrière substantial momentum. In 1995, she was mounting her fourth presidential election campaign, having continuously run Lutte Ouvrière campaigns since 1973. The Laguiller campaign had the advantage of the disciplined Leninist-Trotskyite organisation and experience.

Laguiller was born in Paris in 1940 and left school at 16 to become a bank employee of Crédit Lyonnais. She was, at a young age, an anti-Algerian war activist in the left-wing Parti Socialiste Unifié. However, her main efforts were in union organisation, at first in the Communist CGT, and then in the non-Communist (Socialist-leaning) Force Ouvrière. Laguiller was instrumental in building up a strong Trotskyist presence in the FO unions[12] (more vulnerable to infiltration than the disciplined CGT), and the bulk of activist support came through the FO union movement where, by the mid-1990s, there was an established base for LO which has continued to recruit through radicalising strike work. Though claiming to be a bank worker, Laguiller appears to have spent most of her time on union activity since about 1970. Although one of the most secretive, Laguiller's

Trotskyist group was not one of the most sectarian, and had even made attempts to unite the Trotskyist movement, running a joint campaign with Alain Krivine's Ligue Communiste révolutionnaire in the European elections of 1979, and proposing an agreement with the PCF in 1988. Nothing came of the unifying ambitions which is hardly surprising given the historical tendency of the Trotskyite parties to quarrel and split, given also the iron discipline which imposes a line handed down from the top, and leads to a rapid turnover of activists (LO has perhaps, at most, 2,000 members), if not of leadership.

Although the campaign of Laguiller had undergone a rejuvenation, 'Arlette pour les travailleurs' revolved around the usual Trotskyist root-and-branch condemnation of the capitalist system, the bourgeois state, and of the elections themselves (which would 'change nothing').[13] To that extent, the message had remained the same since she first stood as a candidate against the Gaullist 'baron' Joël Le Tac in Paris (18th arrondissement) in 1973, the inflexibility of the LO's positions being quite remarkable, even on the extreme left. The denunciation of the 'scandals' which are inherent in 'the system' this time had a new resonance, especially for ex-Socialist voters. However, individual issues which were emphasised in 1995 included the re-nationalisation of all the banks, making sacking illegal, and the requisitioning of businesses which laid off workers. All salaries were to be increased by 1,500 francs, and a company tax of 50% was to be imposed. The campaign included a strong attack on the European Union, on the Maastricht Treaty and the Schengen agreements, countered by a (traditional) call for the creation of a 'United Socialist States of Europe'. Laguiller's anti-European Union stance, moreover, deprived the Communists of their usual monopoly of that position on the left. The Trotskyist movement also promoted and benefited from a wave of strikes in March 1995. Strikes during a presidential campaign are of course no novelty, but Laguiller's threat of a 'third round of social upheaval' (in effect a reprise of the old Trotskyist refrain of the general revolutionary strike which will surge up and overthrow capitalism), accurately translated the widespread discontent, a feeling that social issues were being neglected, and that no mainstream candidate had addressed the issue of social insecurity and persistent unemployment with sufficient determination.

The Laguiller vote on 23 April, at 5.4% (1.6 million), was the best ever Trotskyist presidential vote, rising above 6% in thirteen departments, and polling strongest in working class areas where protesting left voters rejected a compromised Socialist Party but were still not prepared to vote in protest for the Communist Party, even though it had held no portfolio in government since 1984. Not the least of paradoxes of presidential elections is that a first round vote can be cast with impunity: a protest can be registered with no direct transfer of power as a result. The persistent relatively good showing of minor parties at the first round of the presidentials is one manifestation of this possibility to register protest. The relatively small vote for Laguiller's candidacy should be seen in this context; nevertheless, the presidential election enables smaller formations to compete, if not in equality, at least with less disadvantage. For a short time, the Trotskyists had access to TV and to the national platform limited to them at other elections. They needed one good, experienced campaigner, and that they found in Arlette Laguiller.

Robert Hue

The Communist National Secretary,[14] Robert Hue, was running his first presidential campaign and the conditions could hardly have been more propitious. The Socialist Party was, initially at least, demoralised, discredited and preoccupied with its internal squabbles. The weakness of French social democracy has always been the Communists' good fortune; with the near collapse of the PS, the French Communist Party (PCF) had an unexpected opportunity to stop, or perhaps even reverse, its own vertiginous decline.[15] Hue came to the Communist leadership in January 1994 as a new face with the unexpected opportunity to renovate the Party. The election campaign enabled the introduction of a new style at the opposite pole from that of Georges Marchais' combative, aggressive 'workerism', with Robert ('Bob') Hue presenting himself as a decent, well-meaning, sincere, friendly man without affectation who (aided by his resemblance to a jolly garden gnome) came over well both on television and in large meetings.[16]

The Communist campaign effectively opened in the autumn of 1994, was well organised, and included over seventy public meetings. During these mass meetings, Robert Hue would read from a prepared text from a podium in the middle of an assembled group of carefully chosen 'representatives', and made a series of what were carefully tried jokes, remarks and sound bites. The meetings were standardised and organised to facilitate the bussing-in of Communist supporters from nearby districts to provide a good audience. This meant that meetings were full and enthusiastic and gave the impression of catching a rising tide. The evidence for a genuine 'Huemania' was, however, lacking, although polls, during the period of Socialist confusion (and their absence from the fight) gave Hue 12% at one time.[17] Hue, as is customary for PCF candidates, especially, collected endorsements from 'personalities', including, this time, the actor Roger Hanin (Mitterrand's brother-in-law), Gilles Perrault and the architect Roland Castro.

The man on whose shoulders the PCF campaign fell was, before the election, not well known to the public. He had entered technical college at 16 to start a career as a nurse, and briefly attended medical school before becoming absorbed in party politics, leaving the nursing service in the early 1960s to become a career bureaucrat in the Communist Party. He had the classic profile of the Bolshevik professional revolutionary and was the scion of a family which was Communist going back to his grandfather. He joined the Young Communists at 16 and made his way up as an apparatchik, through the initial Party school in 1954, the Federal school in 1967 and the national Party school in 1969. In 1973, he took the Party's intensive course for fast track promotions, and was put immediately in charge of the propaganda section of the Val-d'Oise federation in the Paris 'red belt'. He was elected mayor of the small town of Montigny-lès-Cormeilles in 1977, from where in February 1981 he first sprang to public attention by organising a demonstration against a Moroccan family accused of drug trafficking.[18] The incident was one of a series during Marchais' presidential campaign and caused widespread indignation at its racialist overtones (and implied Hue's closeness to Marchais' group).

The immediate outcome of the affair was that Hue was promoted to the leadership of the Communist Association Nationale des Elus Communistes et Républicains. Thereafter, his rise was even faster: in 1987 he was nominated on to the Central Committee, and in 1990 on to the Political Bureau. At the end of January 1994, Georges Marchais stood down after almost 25 years as the leader of the Party and Hue, a virtual unknown outside the Party apparatus, was nominated National Secretary (i.e. General Secretary). How much Hue was his own man and how much the renovation was of substance rather than presentation remained a moot point (somewhat uncomfortably underlined by Hue's bombastic assertion that he was under nobody's tutelage).[19] Hue had inherited the Marchais entourage; moreover, he was the choice of the outgoing General Secretary, a man not known for adventurous thinking, and, as we have seen, a pure product of the party machine. The apparatus, moreover, was concerned to retain its position and its power: a 'new' man in an old party. Marchais himself was never absent from the scene and in the election campaign itself made an unexpected twelfth hour TV appearance, commenting on the second ballot results. In the Party itself, Hue confirmed the democratic centralism inherited from the PCF's past and continued the fratricidal struggle against the 'refounders' and the party dissidents. In the meantime, at local level mayors of suspect opinion were quietly sidelined or evicted – better to lose a city than keep critical mayors.[20]

On the ground too, the evidence of Hue's reforming impetus and modernism was hard to find. The party continued its slow swing round from unconditional support for the former USSR which had started with the collapse of the Communist regime in Russia itself and the fall of Gorbachev. An admission during the pre-campaign of the PCF's 'backwardness' in drawing lessons from the Khrushchev speech of 1956 was hardly novel (a repetition of Marchais' view that it was the fault of Thorez nearly forty years before!) and the condemnation of Stalin hardly daring. Hue also asserted (inaccurately) that the PCF had ceased in the 1970s to admire Soviet society. If, at Hue's campaign rallies and meetings, there were strictures about how the Eastern Communist regimes had been a perversion of Socialism and not the real thing, and if the meetings were sprinkled with unorthodox quotations from de Gaulle, it was more style and presentation than substance. The same goes for Hue's intensive nationalism and emphasis on the need to protect the welfare state from the right and from Europe: the PCF's turn from philo-Sovietism to a left-wing defensive socialism (addressed by Hue to all those who 'want higher salaries, more jobs and the defence of social security') lay behind the covering fire of nationalist and anti-European rhetoric.[21]

Communist disarray was evident in the campaign documents, which resembled a series of negotiating positions, a shopping list designed to appeal to sectional interests in the Party's dwindling constituency. Hue's was never a governmental programme: he failed notably to ask the question about what would actually be done in government, let alone answer it. There were routine calls for a 35-hour working week (without loss of pay), a quadrupling of the wealth tax, the raising of lower wages (under 15,000 francs) by 1,500 francs per month, and cuts were to be made in defence spending. Part-time or temporary jobs were to be made into permanent ones and the industries privatised in 1986 were to be re-nationalised. A thread of Europhobia ran through the programme with condemnation of the Maastricht agreement (and the imputed consequences for unemployment and deflation), and there was a call for both radical reform and for a referendum on Europe in 1996. By the same token, the Party opposed the reintegration of France into NATO and the creation of a European army, and wanted the moratorium on nuclear testing to continue.[22] Campaign meetings usually included an assertion that Hue was the 'anti-Le Pen' candidate without going into detail on how or why (and this was in any case rich, not to say fruity, coming from the mayor of Montigny).

Where Hue's campaign again fell into a recognisable Communist pattern was in its attitude to the Socialist Party: it referred to the need to 'plumer la volaille', to pluck the socialist chicken by pulling away its support. The pre-election periods since 1974 have taken the form of an initial heavy barrage of criticism of the Socialists or their candidate, followed by a slight adjustment in order to condemn the conservatives and play up criticism of the right in the last few weeks and during the official campaign. Hue's campaign followed this overall pattern, but also employed the old tactic of the 'united front from below': that is, the effective refusal of negotiation or joint action with the PS leadership, accompanied by an appeal to Socialist workers and voters or, in current Communist jargon, a unified pact for progress a 'pacte unitaire pour le progrès'. The 'hesitation waltz' over the question of Communist ministers proposed by Jospin was an example.[23] Hue replied to this offer by remarking that the 'conditions for participation (in government) had not been fulfilled' – the PS had not kept its side of the bargain before. Meetings were salted with criticisms of the Socialist record and observations that Jospin had 'opted for continuity' when, Hue said, a radical 'alternative' approach and new union of the left were needed. As an open personality trying to rally all comers, Hue was, therefore, faced with the difficult task of trying to reject Jospin's overtures without appearing sectarian.

For the Communists, the Socialist nomination of Lionel Jospin was to revive the threat of marginalisation, and Hue was forced to campaign defensively against the 'wasted vote' argument (i.e. the tendency for Communist voters to vote for the better placed PS candidate even in the first round).[24] The last published polls before the first ballot dictated that the run-off might be between two right wingers (Balladur and Chirac). This inevitably pressured the Communist vote which comes from that part of the electorate most hostile to the right wing (and vulnerable to Jospin's squeeze). However, a further implication was that, having been asked by the Socialists to enter into a dialogue, the PCF and its candidate still counted. Beyond the presidential elections were the municipals in which the Socialists and Communists were going to be engaged in a defence of their town halls against an anticipated (but in the event, absent) right-wing surge in the 'honeymoon' period of a newly re-elected President of the right. The two principal parties of the left could not afford to be too hostile to each other during the presidential campaign for fear of endangering subsequently their last resource – their strong local government position. The logic of Hue's stance would have led to the refusal to endorse the Socialist candidate for the second ballot (leading activists to 'make up their own minds'), but the low vote for Hue and the fear of reprisals at the municipal election left him with no choice: Jospin was duly supported, if with some delay, three days after the first round results.

Hue's feverish campaign produced no more than a neutral result – a vote of 8.7%, which, though up on the 1988 result of 6.7%, was below the combined Juquin (dissident Communist) and Lajoinie vote of 1988 and the two digit figure indicated in early opinion polls in 1994 and 1995. The vote was only slightly ahead of the Trotskyist to whom many PCF voters had defected, and little more than half of the National Front. Hue polled above his national vote (see Table 1) amongst the least educated, those leaving school at 14, at 12%; the unemployed, at 11%; and manual workers, at 15%. But with barely half the number of workers voting for him as voted for Jean-Marie Le Pen, the first round confirmed how much recession and joblessness had favoured the populist right over the Marxist left. The party failed to break new ground or to provide a convincing new politics, but the campaign did enable it to recruit members and continue to play a role in national life. The organisation was proven and the PCF's role as an albeit semi-drained reservoir of votes from the PS was reconfirmed. Although this was no basis for a renewal, the final chapter of the PCF's long history had not yet been written. Hue himself must have been reinforced as leader both in the eyes of supporters, whom the campaign pulled into rallies, and in the eyes of the apparatus. This may not, however, have been enough to enable him to innovate, even assuming he wanted to. The PCF regained some credibility to the extent that an avuncular candidate and an appealing image had been laid over an apparatus which had proved extremely reluctant to change. At the policy level, however, a list of grievances, an old style rally of 'travailleurs en lutte', did not constitute a party programme.

At the beginning of the Mitterrand presidency the PCF was a powerful force: the right was united in opposition to it and the left was forced to come to terms with it. In 1995 it sought desperately to make an impact, and such influence as it did have came from its position in local government (where, in fact, Communists were strong). The Communist Party, however, through Hue's determined campaign gained a further extension of life and continued to perturb, and to pose a challenge to the unity of the left.

Lionel Jospin

The process by which Lionel Jospin came to be the Socialist Party's candidate in 1995 was a long and intricate one which started at the Party's defeat and discredit in the legislative elections in 1993, and the subsequent internal factional struggles. The principal line of cleavage pitted the heterogenous supporters of Mitterrand against those of Michel Rocard who proclaimed a 'modernism' along social democratic lines.[25]

The defeat of 1993, amidst accusations of broken promises, rising unemployment and social despair, as well as a series of embarrassing financial and political scandals, seemed to leave the party where Mitterrand had found it in 1971 – a marginal formation with a significant past but no future, holding on to national status only precariously thanks to its municipal bastions. In a startling coup in April 1993, Rocard ousted and replaced Laurent Fabius as party leader, inheriting, however, a moribund organisation, and facing unremitting hostility from the Elysée where Mitterrand had no intention of handing the inheritance to his long time enemy.[26] Rocard, the 'natural' presidential candidate (who had been Prime Minister in 1988-1991) became, in the course of a disastrous 1994 European election campaign, a spent force and a lost cause. The Socialist Party at those European elections took, as we have seen, a poor 14.5%, closely rivalled by Bernard Tapie's list which took 12%.

The defeat led to the eviction of Rocard as leader on 19 June 1994 by Henri Emmanuelli (who had supported his coup a year earlier). Emmanuelli's own coup was pushed by Fabius' mainly Mitterrandist coalition, and the experiment of social democratising the Socialist Party duly ended. The Party's front runner for the presidency for many years, in fact – along with Mitterrand – the party's only 'présidentiable' for the previous fifteen years and more, thus disappeared as a possible candidate, and one-by-one other figures were disqualified (Fabius, for example, was ruled out by an impending trial, for allegedly allowing Aids contaminated blood to be used for transfusions). At this point, the name of Jacques Delors began to be advanced with some insistence. Jacques Delors at the head of the European Commission had always maintained that he was not a candidate for the candidacy and that Rocard was the best placed Socialist. He was, in addition, although a member of the PS and a former Socialist government minister, not a natural politician, never having campaigned for other than local office, and was at odds with the factional and leftist Socialist Party. Had Rocard's modernisation succeeded, Delors would have been more at ease with the Party.

Yet Delors continued to lead the opinion polls throughout the summer of 1994 and was increasingly seen as the solution to the Socialist Party's problems. His status with the public revived the Socialists' governmental vocation and made credible again the possibility of national victory (something which had seemed beyond reach since the crushing defeat of 1993). Though Delors had given no indication that he would stand, the clamour in the party must have tempted him and it began to appear as a 'given' that within the party the next Socialist candidate had been identified. This was the mood in the autumn of 1994 as the presidential manœuvres started in earnest on the right, but Delors, still in Brussels, would make no firm decision.[27]

It was therefore a stunned Socialist Party which heard Delors' declaration on 11 December that he had decided not to be a candidate for the Presidency of the Republic, citing significantly his reluctance to be a President without a parliamentary majority – a realistic reading of the Socialist Party's inability to mirror presidential victories (1981, 1988) in parliamentary ones (defeats in 1986 and 1993 and a draw in 1988).[28] Chaos ensued as the leadership floundered around searching for a candidate who could lose with flair. First Secretary, Henri Emmanuelli, consulted former ministers Pierre Joxe and Robert Badinter, both of whom refused. Unnoticed, Lionel Jospin started to advance his name. Jospin had been First Secretary from 1981-1988 and Minister of Education in Rocard's government, but had almost quit active politics in 1993 (in fact, such near withdrawal was to become his great advantage). Although the President did not promote his interests, two other senior figures, Pierre Mauroy and Michel Rocard, were both favourable.[29] Henri Emmanuelli (his one time lieutenant) was not, nor was Jospin's rival, the former Prime Minister Fabius. Jospin appeared to be the continuation of Rocardism by other means, and the leadership went into furious spoiling action after Jospin's declaration of candidacy on 4 January, with a new left leaning collectivist, state planning and anti-capitalist party programme adopted to cause him maximum embarrassment.[30]

Thus was the Socialist Party's factionalism, never far below the surface, flailed into life again. The party leadership tried to wrong-foot Jospin by setting in train a formal procedure to choose the leader which could give them time to find and promote another candidate. Jospin had dismissed Tapie as 'amoral' in the past. Radical's J.-F. Hory also moved against Jospin (most notably at a 10 January meeting where a Radical candidate was promised).[31] Along with Emmanuelli, the Gauche Socialiste (a left-wing faction in the PS led by Senator Jean-Luc Mélenchon) also looked to the Radicals to provide the single candidate of the left within a PS and Radical institutional arrangement. Jack Lang, the Party's former Arts Minister who was still popular, declared his candidacy on 17 January and Emmanuelli (who had, he said, a 'certificate validated by psychiatrists and by the Vatican' that he would not stand) easily allowed himself to be pushed by the Gauche Socialiste into the fray as the peacemaker between Lang and Jospin. On 18 January, the same day as Balladur, Emmanuelli declared. Fabius asked Lang to withdraw. Lang, embittered, retired. There then remained two possible Socialist candidates: Jospin and Emmanuelli.

In a new and untried process set up *ad hoc* in December to impede any challenge to the leadership, the contest was fought out for the vote of party members (officially some 100,000 but in fact only about 60,000) and threatened to tear the party apart.[32] Dirty tricks were at a premium as Party personalities vied with each other to shape the Party's future. Emmanuelli had the support of 38 Federation secretaries and 50 deputies (including Fabius), as well as the Party apparatus.[33] This was the clash of the two cultures of French socialism. What was at stake was less the presidential nomination than the future of the PS after the elections and the identity of the people who would lead it into the next century. The Mitterrandists struggled to keep control.[34]

The fight did not follow exactly the lines of the Rocard/Mitterrand split but was recognisably similar. Emmanuelli was not a plausible presidential contender but was a Mitterrand loyalist (even defending the president's Vichy past) and was perceived as hard-line. Despite having presided over cutbacks as Secretary of State for the Budget in 1983, he presented himself as a reflationary leftist and opponent of austerity policies.[35] Brandishing the banner of the left, he was seen as sectarian and impatient. Positive about the Mitterrand years, he argued that if supporters were disillusioned it was from lack of socialist commitment. His language was aggressive in its denunciation of neo-capitalism and private property and in its obeisance to left-wing totems such as secularity. Jospin, chastened by the Mitterrand years, had already begun to distance himself from the President while still a minister in the late 1980s. The Rocardian restraint of the Jospin approach was palpable, and the refusal to provide 'miracle solutions' was derived from a realistic stance. His attention to detail was the counterpoint to Emmanuelli's suspicion of the culture of government. If Jospin was close to Rocard in his appreciation of the positive role of the market, he also emphasised the value of the public services.

The choice of Emmanuelli, not of presidential stature, would have been a refusal by the PS to engage in national politics and a return to municipal strongholds (as well as a reminder of the scandals in the Party's past, Emmanuelli being under investigation on corruption charges). The Party activists fully (and Mitterrand grudgingly) supported Jospin.[36] The man whom the Socialists chose had been a dull stalwart of the Mitterrand party – the President's stand-in as a leader from 1981 to 1988 – but had never been a 'courtier'. He had joined the Party in 1971 after its Epinay Congress and was elected on to the Secretariat in 1975. In 1979, he took over the party's International portfolio, and then from 1981 to 1988 was First Secretary. As First Secretary he was a loyal servant of the President but failed to build up a position for himself. In 1986, the first skirmish between Fabius and Jospin took place over who should lead the election campaign, and this quarrel had not only split the Party at that date but had survived into the subsequent presidential race.[37] Jospin was also a non-percussive minister for Education 1988-92, a crucial post in the Socialist governments. He was absent from the front rank of the political scene after 1992 partly through illness and because of doubts about the Socialist direction in government. His criticism of Mitterrand's excessive presidentialism was expressed in a book before leaving government (as were his presidential ambitions) and his highly individual stance was laid out in a lone contribution to the Party's Liévin Congress in 1994.

Jospin was austere, reserved and lacked the vitality and glad-handing abilities thought to be essential in a presidential candidate. This feature was regrettably confirmed in the first interview of his campaign (with Anne Sinclair on TF1 on 12 February) when he made no evident effort to convince. Jospin refused to rely on the Socialist Party to staff and run a campaign office, but took time to set up his headquarters. The first weeks were lost in unnoticed meetings with Party activists and major personalities. His background as a teacher and a former diplomat was reflected in the adagio first round campaign which the Elysée described as 'colourless'.[38] Such lack of pace enabled the PS leadership to make an unhelpful call for Mitterrand to intervene. But Jospin's personal wealth was artfully played down (he drove himself round in a small Renault), and his horribly serious, school-masterly, Protestant moral austerity worked to his advantage in a campaign mired on all sides in sleaze accusations.

Like Rocard, Jospin was suspicious of the Party, the institutional manifestation of this being the setting up of a campaign office separate from (and not supported by) the PS. This brought new people to the fore and gave the campaign a new face, but it also contributed to the hiatus in between the announcement of the candidature (followed by an upswing in the polls ahead of Chirac, then front runner) to the start of the campaign proper in April. Among the main figures in the office was Martine Aubry (former Employment Minister and daughter of Jacques Delors), who was the campaign spokesperson. A rising star in the PS, Aubry was not aligned with any of the factions, and the experience of the Jospin campaign would make her a national figure. Former industry minister Dominique Strauss-Kahn, co-ordinator of the experts advising the programme, was the other main team leader but, although also a rising star in the Party, he was less well known to the public. Jospin's long-time associate, the geologist, Claude Allègre, was his political chef-de-cabinet; Christian Sautter covered logistics and Daniel Vaillant was campaign organiser. The usually honorific presidency of the supporting committee was given to Jacques Delors who, however, took it on as a real campaigning job. Though the main roles went to new people, all the factions were represented in the campaign organisation. Jospin never, however, overcame the handicap of the slow start.

Jospin's platform – 'Propositions pour la France' – was slow to emerge from his committee of experts and was rewritten by him – to the infuriation of his staff – several times. It was modernist, moderate and detailed to a fault.[39] Although trapped by the legacy of the past, it was not a re-adoption of the right's agenda, and promoted neither Mitterrandist rhetorical leftism nor the old republican values of solidarity, justice and equal opportunities. The intention was to show that a viable non-Communist left still existed, to pull the left in behind the candidate and to mobilise enough support for him to reach the second round. On the key issue of unemployment – the left's most severe failure in power – Jospin was bullish, but the programme made no rash promises. The proposal on this front was for the reduction of the working week to 37 hours (with a further reduction to 35 in view), lower national insurance contributions, and public works initiatives to create jobs. The slight reflation proposed would not have run into the balance of payments problem which eventually ended the 1981 dash for growth, because France had a healthy surplus and inflation was low. A proposed increase in the minimum wage from 6,000 to 7,500 francs would, however, have had knock-on effects on other salaries. The problem here was that the policies of fiscal orthodoxy and price stability pursued in the past had caused job insecurity, and Jospin suffered from the same self-imposed incapacity to act on the labour market to create jobs as felled the Bérégovoy government in 1993 (when unemployment began to hit hard). Only Chirac, in his perfunctory bid for left voters with a 'Republican Pact', hinted at a departure from this philosophy of fiscal orthodoxy.[40] By the same token, Jospin's proposals on Europe were broadly in line with the other mainstream candidates, but the Socialists were hamstrung on this issue by the need for Communist support. Jospin's difficulty, saddled with this burden, partially explains why he never succeeded in intervening in the 'primary' on the right and imposing his own agenda on the election other than ensuring his presence at the second round.[41]

The platform departed from the Mitterrand orthodoxy in proposing a quinquennial presidential term and in recognising a French 'democratic deficit'.[42] The illicit disavowal of Mitterrand led to problems with the Elysée, which had supported Emmanuelli and then endorsed Jospin, but can hardly be said to have campaigned (and certainly not against Chirac). Under Jospin's proposals, ministers were to be excluded from executive positions in local government, referendums were to be held to ratify the main reforms, and the Prime Minister would submit the programme to the first sitting of the Assembly. The use of the controversial parliamentary guillotine under article 47 (3) was to be restricted, and proportional representation for legislative elections was an issue open for discussion. Jospin's programme had to enthuse (which it largely failed to do) and to unify (with sops to the Greens and the PCF). The purpose and effect of Jospin's campaign was to rebuild the Socialist coalition itself and beyond that the unity of the left. Hence the 'useful vote' argument was deployed with increasing insistence in the last week of the first ballot campaign. This was creditably achieved with the emphasis on the economic and social aspects of the programme and its proposed limiting of presidential power.

The first round results and the second round

Chirac had based his calculations on a first round vote of 23% and first place on the ballot. However, against all expectations, it was Jospin who took pole position with 24% to Chirac's 20%.[43] Socialist activists were galvanised and Jospin was visibly moved. The Chirac camp was demoralised and the campaign initiative passed to the left with Jospin on a new wave of confidence, certain, if not to be President, then to be the leader of the left. The campaign strategy then became one of trying to open up the gap between left and right. Jospin began to hammer the point that the RPR and Chirac had supported Balladur's government and that there was a web of policy between Balladur and the neo-gaullists. Chirac's 'Republican Pact' to improve social conditions was a mask for traditional conservatism, hence the slogan: 'Lionel Jospin le Président du vrai changement.' The other attack was on the 'RPR-state', the fear of an all-conquering Gaullist movement. However, the positive side of the platform was more difficult: Jospin struggled to convince the public that his proposals were much better than those of the right, and that a Socialist President – contrary to the experience of the last fourteen years – really would eliminate unemployment. Jospin's 24% was a success to the extent that he not only secured a place in the second ballot but also surprisingly led the field. It was, however, rather academic, bearing no comparison with Mitterrand's 26% at the first ballot in 1981, given the absence in 1995 of the full reservoir of Communist votes formerly available to Mitterrand. The social profile of the Jospin vote also revealed a problem for contemporary social democrats. He had support above his national vote amongst the middle classes (professional and managerial, 26%; middle ranking professionals, such as teachers, 31%; and students 30% – see Table 1); but support was below the Jospin national average amongst blue collar voters, only 21% of whom voted for him compared to Hue's 15% and Le Pen's remarkable 27%, the largest working class vote share of any candidate in the election. Moreover, although Jospin had achieved the unexpected, the left was split four ways. Although Laguiller would not call for the Lutte Ouvrière voters to support him, the imminent municipal elections (which depended on local coalition solidarity) would in fact serve to draw most in behind Jospin. He benefited from his constantly critical attitude to the Mitterrand legacy: voters were not being asked to affirm their support for the past. It was, however, a very recent past and its failures were stark.

In the second round, Jospin launched into a series of rallies (one each evening) and ended with the traditional mass meeting in Toulouse (50,000 attended). But the main 'event' of the second round was the 2 May television debate with Chirac, who had been the victim in a similar encounter with Mitterrand in 1988 but now had vast experience of TV 'face-à-face' debates.[44] This was not a debate which either could have won but it could have been lost by gaffes. The result was a remarkably passionless and courteous affair in which the two 'énarques' (both products of the prestigious Ecole Normale d'Administration) talked detail, and avoided the nightmare of a blunder. Jospin managed to present himself as being of presidential stature (in itself a victory) and had the only memorable sound-bite: 'Rather five years with Jospin than seven with Chirac'.[45]

On 7 May, from a first ballot left aggregate of 41%, Jospin narrowed the gap with Chirac by polling 47% (13.8 million) to the latter's 53% (15.8 million), taking 65% of Laguiller's vote; 86% of Hue's; 70% of Voynet's, and as much as 21% (one million) of Le Pen's.[46] He both out-polled his own national vote and beat Chirac among first time voters (52%), 35 to 49-year olds (52%), middle professionals – largely teachers – (55%), white collar workers (51%), manual workers (57%), wage and salary earners (53%), the jobless (58%), the non-religious (69%), and those who opposed the Maastricht Treaty in the 1992 referendum (54%) (see Table 2).

Hidden amongst these voters, however, lay the left's serious problem: its meagre 57% share of the blue collar vote compared with Mitterrand's 74% at the second ballot in 1988. Here lies the key to Jospin's failure. It is also worth noting that at the first ballot, candidates from the non-governing protest parties (PCF, Lutte Ouvrière, Front National, de Villiers' nationalists, and the ecologists) polled collectively 58% of the unemployed and 55% of the working class, evidence of working class estrangement from mainstream politics and, notably, from the Socialist left.

The task of overcoming the combined forces of the right proved, inevitably, impossible for Jospin who, in a farewell to campaigners after the election, declared that he had never really believed in victory.[47] But he had revived the Socialists' belief in their own force, recruited some 100,000 new members and placed himself at the head of the left, becoming, in effect, the leader of the Opposition. Within the PS, Jospin had been supported largely by minority groups and Rocardians, while the Fabius-dominated leadership ceased to be the key to the future (Fabius not having flung himself into the battle). Emmanuelli, realising this, offered his resignation in favour of Jospin. This was refused. During the subsequent municipal elections which reconfirmed his primary role, Jospin prepared a more audacious recomposition of the party which would make him President (a new office under a new constitution) and downgrade the position of First Secretary from leader-in-waiting to administrative secretary general. The challenge for Jospin was not just to renovate the PS but to end the destructive factional warfare and the debilitating internal squabbling. With the influx of new members, drawn in by Jospin's election campaign, calling on the Party activists to ratify his changes to the constitution and cutting out the Party's power brokers, this objective had for the first time since Epinay a strong possibility of success.[48]

Table 2: Analysis of Second Ballot Vote

	Jospin	Chirac
All voters	47	53
Age:		
18-24	49	51
25-34	48	52
35-49	52	48
50-64	43	57
over 65	36	64
First time voters	52	48
Occupation:		
Farmer	23	77
Small business	23	77
Upper prof./managerial	41	59
Middle professional	55	45
White collar	51	49
Blue collar	57	43
Status:		
Salaried/waged	53	47
Self-employed	22	78
Unemployed	58	42
Housewife	40	60
Student	46	54
Retired	40	60
Religion:		
Practising Catholic	26	74
Non-practising Catholic	41	59
No religion	69	31
Vote in Maastricht referendum:		
Yes	54	46
No	35	65

Source: BVA *Le Monde*, 10 May 1995

Conclusion

French social democracy, as represented by the Jospin vote at the second ballot in 1995, had recovered remarkably well from its dire electoral troughs of 1993 and 1994. Social democracy in general is not favoured during recession, nor by the process of globalisation which forecloses Keynesian and interventionist options. For some observers it is, in any case, little more than a creature of the Second World War and its attendant 'gemeinschaft' and the demands of post-war reconstruction, in short, of mid-century crisis. It faces, as well, the problem of an eroding social base and the need to assemble a disparate coalition of producers and consumers, collectivists and individualists, feminists in employment and men on the dole – all implying tensions liable to erupt in electorally-damaging factionalism. Evidence from other countries is less than encouraging. In Spain in 1995, presiding over mountainous unemployment figures and tarnished by corruption, a Socialist government tottered towards its nemesis. In Germany, the SPD failed in 1994 for the fourth consecutive time to regain power. In Britain, even though enjoying large opinion poll leads, the Labour Party had not, by 1995 won a general election for 21 years, and had only ever won twice. In America, Bill Clinton had won in 1992 on a lower share of the vote than Dukakis had lost with in 1988. Where social democratic parties had achieved office elsewhere, such as in Greece or Australia, it was often by exploiting populist nationalist sentiments which were not part of a traditional social democratic agenda. Compared to this record, Jospin's performance appeared to offer some hope, coming so soon after the 'failure' of a long Socialist presidency and government.

Nor was the Mitterrand inheritance perhaps as bad as it was conventionally painted by 1995, for it comprised a left converted from a culture of opposition to one of government, and its deradicalisation, through the decay of the Communists and through alternance and 'cohabitation' had made it a modern social democratic party with experience and potential. The left now faced a governing right with too much power – presidential, parliamentary, regional, departmental, municipal – and no alibis. The Chirac presidency, elected on an arguably bogus prospectus of 'social Gaullism' comprising promises of jobs, more welfare, higher pay, more education and housing, seemed unlikely to succeed where Mitterrand and the left had failed, and potentially large left gains in parliamentary seats beckoned in 1998. The collapse of full-time, stable employment and the divisiveness of European integration would take its toll on an incumbent right as it had on the left, with neither demonstrating that they had anything with which to counter the hard, populist right, which in 1995 was polling at a level almost equivalent to that of the large Communist Party of the 1960s and 1970s.

Any candidate of the left needs the support of the Socialist Party, given the difficulties Mitterrand encountered in the 1960s outside the main formation of the non-Communist left (the SFIO) when he struggled to unite the left from outside and was eventually sidelined by internal rivalries. It is likely that any future candidate will have to come from within the ranks of the PS and probably also have to be its titular leader. Jospin was able to enter the fray because the Party had been dispirited by a succession of failures and the prospect of another and possibly terminal defeat. The situation was adroitly used to rebuild the Party, to introduce new personalities and to set the agenda for the future, just as Jospin's 'brother enemies' within his own party had feared.

It was the presidentialisation of French politics which had caused the Socialist Party to turn to Mitterrand at the Epinay Congress of 1971 as the only plausible presidential candidate and as the one person who could revive the Party's flagging fortunes. In that limited sense, the Jospin candidacy is a replay of the Party's need for a presidential candidate in the van. However, Jospin also drew a number of lessons from the Mitterrand years. Presidential rivalries had fuelled the incipient factional competition in the Socialist

Party, a competition which had nearly torn it apart by 1990. This weakness Jospin was determined to overcome, and the momentum of the presidential elections gave him that possibility. His agenda included the need to replace the sterile personal wrangling (devoid of programmatic or policy implications) with the unity and harmony around a strategy needed in a party with a governmental vocation. That would not, of course, prevent internal debate, but would concentrate it on means, ends and prescription rather than on the procedural wrangling of the past. This was a tall order, nothing less than the final makeover of the French PS into a social democratic party, but it was nearer after the 1995 presidential election than at any time in the past.

It is not the least of the paradoxes of French politics that the rise of presidentialism, supposedly inimical to the left, had given the Socialists their longest ever tenure of power. However, through the Mitterrand imperatives imposed on the Party, presidentialism also led to the problems which by 1993 had made the PS virtually unelectable. Jospin, using the presidential platform and the campaign, was able to renovate the party and set the basis for the reconquest of power. But success in this venture would depend upon a continuing presidentialisation of the PS to an extent undreamed of in the 1970s when the Party first set out on the presidential campaign trail.

Notes

[1] P. Habert and P. Perrineau (eds.), *Le vote sanction* (Paris, *Figaro*/Fondation nationale des sciences politiques, 1993); O.Duhamel *et al.* (eds.), SOFRES *L'état de l'opinion 1994* (Paris, Seuil, 1994); D. B. Goldey, 'The French General Election of 21-28 March 1993', *Electoral Studies,* xii, 4, 1993, pp.291-314.

[2] For an analysis of the European Elections in France see J. Gaffney, 'France' in J. Lodge (ed.), *The 1994 Elections to the European Parliament* (London, Pinter, 1996), pp.84-106.

[3] *Le Monde,* 26 January 1995, and B. Kouchner, *Ce Que Je Crois* (Paris, Grasset, 1995).

[4] *Le Monde,* 24 February 1995, and J.-F. Hory 'Votez pour vous', 10 March 1995 (launch of the Radical campaign).

[5] *Le Monde,* 28 January 1995.

[6] *Le Monde,* 18 January 1995.

[7] *Le Monde,* 28 February 1995.

[8] *Ibid.*

[9] There is some doubt as to the unbroken continuity between LO and Union Communiste Internationaliste which was one of the earliest (if not the first) splits in the Trotskyist movement.

[10] See C. Bourseiller, *Les ennemis du système* (Paris, Laffont, 1989).

[11] *Le Figaro,* 22 February 1988 and *Le Monde,* 14 August 1987.

[12] *Paris Match,* 17 April 1981.

[13] A. Laguiller, *Moi, une militante* (Paris, Stock, 1974).

[14] At the PCF's 28th Congress in January 1994, the Party's leading authorities were renamed: the General Secretary became the National Secretary.

[15] J. Ranger, 'Le déclin du Parti communiste français' *Revue française de science politique,* Vol. 26, 1, 1986 (February) pp.46-62; P. Morris, 'French Communism and the End of Communism' in M. J. Bull and P. Heywood (eds.), *West European Communist Parties after the Revolutions of 1989* (London, Macmillan, 1994) pp.31-55.

[16] See report in *The Guardian,* 10 April 1995.

[17] *Libération,* 11 March 1995.

18 See *L'Humanité*, 10 February 1981.
19 *Le Monde*, 8 February 1995.
20 *Le Monde*, 28 March 1995.
21 P. Morris, *op. cit.*
22 *Le Monde*, 14 February 1995.
23 *Le Monde*, 12 March 1995.
24 Anicet Le Pors in *Le Monde*, 10 March 1995.
25 *Libération*, 12 October 1993.
26 R. Schneider, *La haine tranquille* (Paris, Seuil, 1992).
27 *Libération*, 26 January 1995 (report on the saga of Delors' non-candidature) and the subsequent rally of support for Jospin. For a detailed analysis of the PS during the period see J. Gaffney, *Socialism and Presidentialism: the French Socialist Party Conference, Liévin 1994* (Keele European Research Centre Papers, 1996).
28 *Le Monde*, 12 December 1995.
29 *Le Monde*, 6 January 1995.
30 Parti Socialiste, programme: *Le Monde*, 4 January 1995.
31 *Le Monde*, 1 and 3 February 1995.
32 *Le Monde*, 27 January 1995.
33 *Le Monde*, 20 January 1995.
34 *Libération*, 26 January 1995.
35 See *L'Express*, 11 October 1985.
36 See *Le Figaro*, 13 March 1995.
37 H. Portelli, *Le Parti Socialiste* (Paris, Montchrestien, 1992).
38 *Le Monde*, 14 March 1995.
39 *Le Monde*, 8 March 1995.
40 See R. Bacqué and D. Saverot, *Chirac Président* (Paris, Editions du Rocher, 1995).
41 *Le Figaro*, 24 April 1995.
42 *Le Nouvel Observateur*, 2 April 1995 and *Le Monde*, 2 February and 8 March 1995.
43 *Le Monde*, 25 April 1995.
44 *Le Monde*, 29 April 1995.
45 'Plutôt cinq ans avec Jospin que sept ans avec Chirac'. *Le Monde*, 3 May 1995.
46 SOFRES exit poll, 9 May 1995.
47 *Le Monde*, 8 May 1995.
48 Party restructuring started in July 1995. See *Le Monde*, 11 and 12 July 1995.

Indicative Bibliography

Bell, D.S. and B. Criddle, *The French Socialist Party* (Oxford, Clarendon, 1988).
Bergounioux, A. and G. Grunberg, *Le long remords du pouvoir* (Paris, Fayard, 1992).
Colombani, J.-M., *La gauche survivra-t-elle aux socialistes?* (Paris, Flammarion, 1994).
Estier, C., *De Mitterrand à Jospin* (Paris, Stock, 1995).
Gaffney, J., *Socialism and Presidentialism: The French Socialist Party Conference, Liévin 1994* (Keele European Research Centre Papers, 1996).
Giesbert, F.O., *Le président* (Paris, Le Seuil, 1990).
Jospin, L., *1995-2000 Propositions pour la France*, (Paris, Stock, 1995).
Portelli, H., *Le Parti Socialiste* (Paris, Montchrestien, 1992).
Rey, H., and F. Sublieau, *Les militants socialistes à l'épreuve du pouvoir* (Paris, FNSP, 1991).
Roucaute, Y., *Histoires socialistes* (Paris, Ledrappier, 1987).

9. THE OTHER CANDIDATES: VOYNET, LE PEN, DE VILLIERS AND CHEMINADE

CATHERINE FIESCHI

Re-alignment, de-alignment and electorate volatility: France in comparative perspective

The 1995 presidential election seemed to confirm a transformation in the preferences and orientation of the French electorate. Traditional voting patterns – according to race, gender and class (broadly defined) – which had been relatively stable since the advent of the Fifth Republic became from the early 1980s increasingly difficult to monitor; and the political allegiances, hitherto unchanged and therefore predictable, were thought to be undergoing rapid transformation. This de-alignment of the electorate, the electorate's desertion of its traditional poles of power, was evidenced by the shift to the left in 1981.[1] That year saw a Socialist victory in the presidential as well as the legislative elections, bringing the Socialist Party to power for the first time in the Fifth Republic. This, however, was followed by the Socialists' fall from grace, a fall which began as early as 1982 with by-elections and cantonal elections – traditionally favourable to the left – and the municipal elections of 1983. The decline was confirmed by the 1984 European and the 1985 cantonal elections. The French electorate, having supported the Socialists en masse (and ousted the Giscard government and the right in no uncertain terms), reversed their preferences in the space of a few months, castigating the left and supporting the right once again. This electoral volatility was the second indication of a transformation in the French electorate. Finally, the emergence of the FN and the record abstention rates (by the 1995 presidential elections they had reached 20.33%) suggested to political analysts and commentators that a de-alignment was occurring.

From a theoretical perspective France appeared an anomaly in Western European party systems. Whereas in other countries a fragmentation of the party system and a de-alignment of the electorate had begun to occur as early as the 1970s, France exhibited uncharacteristic stability on both these counts throughout the 1960s and 1970s. What occurred in many West European nations, namely a sudden growth in the number of parties and an increasingly volatile electorate, was often understood as the collapse of the post-war era's two main theses on party stability and electoral change. Both Otto Kirchheimer's thesis[2] which saw ideologically driven class-based parties being replaced by bland catch-all parties, and Anthony Downs' complementary theory[3] that a very small number of – barely distinguishable – catch-all parties were moving towards the political centre and dividing a stable, non-radical electorate among themselves, came under assault. These authors' findings, namely that smaller parties would have an increasingly difficult time emerging because of the systemic pressures exerted by huge catch-all parties on the party system, were being undermined both by what Crouch and Pizzorno – perhaps hastily – termed 'The resurgence of class conflict in Western Europe'[4] and by the plethora of new, small and sometimes radical parties in most West European democracies. The two models by Kirchheimer and Downs, drawn from their experience of the stability of an American-style two-party system and an affluent, secure and mature middle-class, were applied to Western Europe as the latter began siring stable democratic parties. However, the events of the late 1960s and their electoral consequences would disrupt this view of political competition. By the early 1970s, competition was back, old parties were challenged, new parties emerging, and new issues being articulated in the public and political spheres.[5] As has been pointed out by Peter Mair,[6] the literature on radical transformations and accelerated evolution of European party-systems has since become so plentiful that it has drowned out the dissenting voices seeking to discern elements of continuity and stability in a few countries.

Several explanations can account for the French system's belated transformation. The first (this also applied to Germany and Italy which exhibited some of the same tendencies) lay in the combination of the severity of the disruption caused by the Second World War and the institutional framework that was in place. The second and related explanation emphasised the weakness of party attachments in Fourth Republic France which bequeathed to the Gaullist Party a large, previously unattached pool of voters. This accounted for the French electorate's stability throughout the 1960s and 1970s and pinned it on the emergence of the hegemonic force of Gaullism in the 1960s.

For a long time, then, France, at least, seemed to confirm Kirchheimer's thesis: its party system revolved around a few major parties and the electorate gave no real sign of de-alignment. Commentators disagree on when changes began to occur in the French party system. David Cameron's influential thesis posits a first transformation of the Fourth Republic's notorious instability and weak government towards a catch-all party system; Cameron, paradoxically, termed the transformation a 'swing into partisanship' with the beginnings of the Fifth Republic.[7] Most commentators, however, were still unable to explain France's subsequent electoral quiescence. Some evidence lends credence to Michael Lewis-Beck's thesis that partisan attachments were stronger than had often been thought towards the end of the Fourth Republic, and that Gaullism, although ushering in major changes, capitalised on already existing ties of partisan attachment.[8] What is unquestionable is that, regardless of origins and causes, partisan attachment remained high and stable throughout the 1960s and 1970s and that it was the context of presidentialism that altered the roles and aims of parties. As John Gaffney writes:

> The developing presidentialism of the Fifth Republic saw the parties regaining their strength, but this according to the manner in which they adapted to the presidential contests. More fundamentally, the parties themselves were changing in their organisation, orientation, and eventually their ideologies, and were responding to the exigencies both of the presidential contests, as they perceived them, and of the wider political culture.[9]

The purpose of this chapter is to illustrate the manner in which a de-alignment in a system dominated by presidentialism will favour some parties and individuals over others and that, in France, this becomes manifest as of the mid-1980s, truly coming into focus with the 1995 presidential elections. In the first round of the presidential elections of 1995, 28% of voters (37% if we include the Communist Party) voted for what commentators termed 'peripheral formations'[10] (as compared to circa 25% in the 1988 election) of which 15% voted for candidates of the extreme right and 13% for the extreme left. If one adds to these figures the ·abstention rate of 21.62% (20.33% in the second round) and the 2.21% of spoilt or blank ballots, only 47.7% of registered voters voted in favour of a mainstream political party.[11] Chirac's 20.8% (15.8 % of registered voters) in round one illustrated the traditional parties' lack of appeal as well as a split in the mainstream right's vote.[12] The results of the 1995 presidential election indicate that voters used the election as an opportunity to protest. This warrants a few brief comments concerning both the electoral system in place and the manner in which it has been perceived and used by voters and candidates in the past.

A direct, two ballot, single constituency majority system has been in use for the designation of the President in France since the first election held by universal suffrage in 1965.[13] This is coupled with a similar two ballot, majority system in the legislative elections.[14] Traditionally, neither the presidential nor legislative elections have been used as vectors for protest. Even though the first round of the election has often been portrayed as allowing the population to express its preferences (whereas the second organises politically the formation of efficient government), the expression of dissent has generally been reserved for second order elections such as local, regional, and European elections in which smaller, more marginal or more recently formed parties generally fared better. With respect to the 1995 presidential election, Pascal Perrineau made the following assessment:

> For the first time in the history of the Fifth Republic we can talk of a real 'crisis election'(...) a whole series of voters used this presidential election as a means of protest. Up until now presidential elections had not fulfilled that role. The forces of protest occupied a much more marginal place. The French population generally aligned itself with the mainstream political forces and major candidates and voted 'usefully' right from the first round.[15]

In this way, 1995 represents a break with the past while being symptomatic of the increasing disaffection, volatility[16] and fragmentation of the French electorate which have plagued the French party system since the mid-1980s.

Let us now analyse the non-mainstream candidates in the 1995 presidential election in order to determine how they reflected, influenced and were influenced by the changes affecting the French party system.

The 'peripheral' candidates

We shall analyse four of the candidates labelled 'peripheral' by French commentators: Dominique Voynet, Jean-Marie Le Pen, Philippe de Villiers and Jacques Cheminade; the candidates Robert Hue of the French Communist Party and Arlette Laguiller, the seasoned candidate of Lutte Ouvrière are examined in Chapter 8. What each of the four had in common was that they sought, to differing extents and in different ways, to break with prevailing paradigms of French politics. The changes or reforms these candidates envisaged, regardless of their content, had much to do with modifying not only detailed or specific aspects of the policy spectrum, but the very 'form' of politics itself. Hence, despite their differences they could all be seen as seeking to implement changes reaching not just beyond traditional ideological lines (Chirac too claimed to be bridging the left-right gap), but often beyond the post-war conception of ideology itself. For example, the Greens tried to bring to the fore such concepts as gender-equality, while Le Pen attempted to bring back into the political mainstream ideas concerning race, which had been relegated to the scrap-heap of post-war politics. Some of these parties and candidates were calling for progressive change while others advocated regressive policies; each nevertheless shared a desire to move away from traditional politics and offered a radical re-thinking of politics in late twentieth century France. We shall present each of the candidates, his or her aims in running for the presidency, and highlight the distinctiveness of each one's campaign. We shall then examine how these candidates and their agendas benefited or suffered from the opportunities and constraints provided by the presidential framework.

Dominique Voynet and Les Verts

Turning a movement into a party: the cost of electoral competition

The changes in the French party system have not affected all peripheral parties in the same manner. The French Greens (Les Verts) led by Dominique Voynet were an example of a new force faced with a dual problem: first, that the Greens are essentially a New Social Movement (NSM) whose organisation and aims are antithetical to traditional political competition;[17] second, that electoral de-alignment and volatility have not spared the Greens. Just as traditional mainstream party support has been eroded by various economic, social and ideological forces, so these same forces have eroded the support-base of the Greens.

Along with this dual problem of the Greens' relationship to organised political competition, the French presidential system itself is a significant impediment to Green party power. Firstly, by structuring politics around strong parties and party-backing, it makes even more problematic an NSM's uneasy contact with traditional competition. Secondly, by drawing on a mythology (often rooted, paradoxically, in feminine representations) of a Republic dominated and safeguarded exclusively by male hero-leaders, it privileges male candidates to the presidency, while generally relegating women to the role of models for the latest sculptural and cultural update of Marianne. That the Green candidate in 1995, Dominique Voynet, was a woman was itself a significant statement about the nature of French politics; it nevertheless carried with it all the disadvantages it set out to highlight.

Over and above this, the French Greens are faced with the classic problem facing NSMs and left-libertarian parties: that of trying to revolutionise conceptions of the political (both the issues and the manner in which they are raised and brought into the public sphere) while being drawn into a political arena with whose rules and practices they are deeply disenchanted. For ecological parties throughout Europe, this has often meant that the basic rules of electoral participation have forced them to alter the internal organisation of their parties and movements. This had often been painstakingly conceived to mirror a concern for political equality, flexibility and grass-root participation. Failure to resolve this fundamental contradiction has been in part responsible for the French Greens' lacklustre performance in most electoral arenas and has prevented them from becoming a serious contender for political power.[18] During the 1970s and early 1980s, the ecologists' lashing critique of established political parties led them to reject the idea of becoming a party themselves, and their internal structure recurred as a theme in their debates. 1974, however, marked their electoral début, as René Dumont became ecology's first presidential candidate, receiving 1.1% of registered votes. This was a big step for the French ecological movement. But the campaign was fought on strictly environmental issues. Between 1974 and 1986, however, the ecologists became aware that their base was too narrow and that they were essentially a single-issue movement; they therefore attempted to broaden their sphere of concern. This entailed a re-examination of the meaning of 'ecology' and a questionning of the initial guidelines which defined the movement solely in environmental terms. Brice Lalonde was mandated by the party's rank-and-file to take this 'new and improved' ecological party to the voters in the 1981 presidential elections. The result was a less than significant 3.1%. 1984 saw the creation of a French Green party whose constitution and internal organisation reflected the movement's philosophy, its flexible structure and democratic power-sharing. The Greens then reverted to their initial ecological stance under the new leadership of Antoine Waechter. By 1986, Waechter, considering that the diversification strategy had failed, proposed a return to a strict environmental theme. In the 1986 legislative elections they secured only 1.21% but slightly improved their score in the 1988 presidential elections where they gained 3.8% of the vote. The Greens went on to a short-lived series of electoral successes, culminating in their 1992 score of 14.3% in the regional elections, but their score fell again to 3.32% in the 1995 presidential election. Alongside these varying fortunes the democratic and flexible party organisation led to a diversification of tendencies and differing ideological commitments within the party. These differences in turn led to the emergence of factions and later the creation of several separate parties; and to an ideological aimlessness and a failure to sustain a coherent discourse and clear positioning on the electoral spectrum.

Three lines of thought

Ecology has often portrayed itself as a 'global logic', an all-encompassing system which, in opposition to the Enlightenment's anthropocentric inheritance, does not place the human being at the heart of nature, taming it through work and ingenuity, but rather places human life within a natural system upon which it is dependent. Apart from a shared rudimentary critique of the state and of liberal-capitalist logic, however, there is little agreement between ecologist groups on the more intellectually refined developments within ecologist thought.

In an article published in *Notes et Etudes Documentaires*,[19] Michel Hastings distinguishes between three variants of ecological thinking in France: the first, which he calls 'neo-traditionalist', relies essentially on an idealisation of nature: the Earth, Gaïa, is transformed into a living, breathing being. Ties to nature – and hence to the soil to which one belongs – are seen as superseding all others. The second current, which Hastings calls 'libertarian', consists of a left-wing critique of capitalism and the state in which the desecration of the environment is thought of as the price-tag attached to liberal market economics. The philo-ecological treatise of the French philosopher, Michel Serres, *Le contrat naturel*,[20] is a good example of this view which, mirroring the social contract, asserts a natural contract between humans and the world they live in. The third current, labelled 'the reformists', condemns extremes in the name of political realism. For these, incremental change is the only effective real change, and real societal change can only be achieved through increased access to information. Their main aim is to democratise society through the democratisation of access to information. 'Ecology' is transformed into a vague metaphor in which political society is the living organism through which sap (information) flows freely, thus keeping it healthy and vibrant. These three currents correspond to a possible positioning on the ideological spectrum and more tangibly perhaps on the political stage. Since 1993, the French Greens have seen the fluctuations of these various lines of thought within the French ecological movement at large.

The different stances find their political embodiment in various splinter-parties and dissident groups present in France whose contributions to the political debate have been matched by the movement's overall ineffectiveness.

Of these three currents it is the reformists who are the best positioned to access political power. Such access, however, has been acquired not only at the cost of a dilution of ecological principles but also the encouragement of an often very unpragmatic tangle of personalities and rivalries. Brice Lalonde, president of Génération Ecologie (founded in 1990), fits the bill particularly well as the uninhibited pragmatist and reformer. A former Minister for the Environment in a Socialist cabinet, his political willingness to dilute the party message was not to everyone's liking, and in April 1994, Noël Mamère (vice-president of the party) censored Lalonde's internal decisions on the grounds that the latter and his supporters had become a minority within the party. Lalonde, as head of the party, challenged this decision and took it to the high court. Lalonde later had ministerial responsibilities in Edouard Balladur's right-wing government. Mamère went on to found his own movement Convergence Ecologie Solidarité (CES) with Andrée Buchmann (a former leading member of Les Verts). CES was then incorporated into Bernard Tapie's list Radical, which secured Mamère a seat as MEP in the European elections of 1994. Mamère's call to support Jacques Delors, however, caused increased friction between himself and Tapie and, in the wake of the European elections, while most Greens were still busy identifying the source of their electoral collapse, Mamère announced the creation of yet another group – a 'space for discussion' – bearing the label of Rassemblement pour une Ecologie Civique et Sociale, a group created according to Mamère in order to 'negotiate a contract with whatever candidate of the left [was] most apt to represent this type of ecology in the presidential election'.[21] The story of Lalonde and Mamère is a caricature of the 'participation' ethic taken to the extreme within a movement whose ideological boundaries are themselves so fluid, and it is arguable that the Green movement has suffered a great deal from the opportunism and rivalry of two of its leading members.

Antoine Waechter, ex-spokesperson for Les Verts, placed himself at the centre of a small circle of disciples, all Verts dissidents, with Le Mouvement des Ecologistes Indépendants (MEI) created in the autumn of 1994. In an interview granted to *Le Monde* in June of 1994, Waechter underscored his desire to create a party which would 'situate itself outside of the left-right cleavage, far from the ideological reflexes of the past'.[22] However stoic Waechter remained, his movement and his isolation failed to get him the necessary 500 signatures to take part in the 1995 presidential campaign. After announcing his intention to run for the presidency in January 1995, he was forced to withdraw in April.[23] This left Dominique Voynet as sole representative of the mainstream ecological movement amongst the presidential candidates of 1995. Her almost impossible task was to unite the various ecological currents under her electoral banner.

Dominique Voynet or how the Greens turned pink

Dominique Voynet[24] represents an attempt to reconcile the various strands of Green thought and ideology in France in a coherent and electorally sustainable position. Her election as leader of the Greens (replacing Waechter) in November 1993, signified a distinct shift to the left. The Greens' long-standing ambivalence as to whether to stay independent or to forge alliances with the left was thus resolved by a vote for Voynet. She, however, was always careful not to be seen as 'playing politics' in the manner adopted by Lalonde, hence her statement that 'we have to risk opening up, but that does not mean renouncing the independence we have always favoured'.[25] However independent, the Greens under Dominique Voynet anchored themselves squarely in the opposition left, thus benefiting from the support of the then Socialist leader, Michel Rocard. The Greens also benefited from the support of AREV – Alternative rouge et verte – itself a refuge for refoundation communists, and Convention de l'écologie politique made up of Greens and dissidents from Génération Ecologie. Voynet announced her candidacy following the meeting of the Green electoral college (23 October 1994) which designated her as Green presidential candidate. On 11 December Jacques Delors announced that he would not be in the running for the presidency. By pulling out (before actually having stepped in), Delors enabled Voynet to present her candidacy in a different light and take advantage of the political space available on the left. A few days after Delors's announcement, Dominique Voynet in an interview with *Politis* labelled herself 'the only real candidate of the left'.[26]

Voynet's strategy was to try to broaden the ecological issue not only through an increase in the number of themes the Greens were willing to address, but also by associating 'ecology' and the Greens in particular with a widening array of social movements. For example, they took to the streets in support of freedom of education (19 November 1994) and the Algerian democratic cause (3 December 1994); they were also associated with the fight against Aids and against homelessness (most especially during the crisis headed by the Emmaüs Association over Christmas 1994 during which they even approached the famous Abbé Pierre in the hope that he would agree to be their spokesperson). It is arguable, however, that Voynet's version of 'independence' involved a multiple allegiance, a serious dilution of the party's message and ideology, and a concomitant public confusion over what the Greens stood for.

This tendency towards becoming simply a 'candidate of the left' grew throughout the 1995 campaign. In an interview with *Politis* dated October 1994, Voynet described Green aims in the following manner:

> The Greens are not a lobby for the protection of the environment, they are not an opportunistic movement which sells itself to this or that majoritarian party in order to bring in the few missing percentage points, and to add a 'green touch' to a few policies without fundamentally altering the logic in place, they are not a social-democratic appendage given to selling off its votes in between the two rounds, or even earlier on, to the best-positioned candidate. [27]

Despite Voynet's clear and forceful manner, it is difficult to read these few lines as more than a defensive justification of what the Greens were not, with little information as to what they truly were.

However, although the combination of Jacques Delors' refusal to run and Lionel Jospin's late declaration of candidacy seemed to offer Voynet a period during which she could claim to be 'the only real candidate of the left', in reality the advantages were short-lived. Voynet's bid to be taken seriously as a presidential candidate of the left while keeping the idea of ecology in the public debate led her to espouse every cause and progressive position available: job equality between men, women and across racial divides; increased security measures on roads; social solidarity; social responsibility; a critique of liberalism; support for non-violence; research for Aids; help for the homeless; concern for education and health-care; a gesture against social and economic exclusion; a march for Bosnia... and, almost as an afterthought, protection of the environment and sustainable development. With the Socialist resurrection, however, the constituency targeted by Voynet's broad-based, left-leaning discourse reverted to its 'natural' leader, Lionel Jospin. By this point, it was too late for Voynet to retrench by shifting to the narrower 'ecological' discourse she might have adopted had Delors been a candidate or Jospin declared earlier.

Les Verts in numbers

In the event, Voynet's score in the 1995 presidential election demonstrated once again the dilemma with which such a party or movement is faced. Her score was a disappointing 3.32%. In the Nord-Pas de Calais, where Marie-Christine Blandin was a high-profile Green leader of the regional council, the result was a poor 2.30%. Even more disheartening was Voynet's mere 5% in her own home region of Franche-Comté where she was, respectively, regional councillor since 1989 and local councillor of the city of Dole since 1992.

This disappointment was in fact only the latest in a series from 1993 onwards. After exceeding 10% in the regional elections of 1989 and electing 9 MEPs to the European Parliament (10.59% of votes) in the 1989 European Elections, the Greens had moved towards what seemed enduring electoral success with a resounding 14.7% in the 1992 regional elections. The victory was short-lived, however, as the Greens met with defeat in the 1993 legislative elections where they failed to win a single seat. The 1994 European elections in which the combined lists of Brice Lalonde and Marie-Anne Isler-Béguin (Union des Ecologistes pour l'Europe) attracted 4.97 % of the vote (no MEPs elected) were the last in this series of electoral misfortunes preceding the election of 1995.[28]

Two conclusions can be drawn in the light of these results: firstly that the Greens tended to do better in regional and local elections (European results were mixed) than in presidential and legislative ones. This might be accounted for by either the French electorate's sustained reluctance to use the presidential election to protest, or as a logical consequence of the party's attention to its grass-roots membership. The Green movement has sought to escape the fate of mainstream parties, themselves notoriously removed from their rank-and-file; regional and municipal elections therefore allow Green candidates to reap the benefits of close contact with the public. The second conclusion is that the Green's relative failure, however, is due in part to the internal disputes which have plagued the movement since its inception. The discord stems in great part from the dilemma faced by any NSM which constitutes itself as a party and faces the competition of an electoral arena. In the context of a presidential contest such competition also involved several aspects for which the Green movement is ill-suited: the need for ideological coherence (or at least the image of such), the chance of being a winner, the ability to federate if not rally a sizeable constituency, the image of a united and coherent organisation, and of a leadership that is experienced, far-sighted, inspirational and preferably male. The Greens failed on each of these points, the National Front on none.

Le Pen and the Front National: growing electoral strength and the grooming of a 'présidentiable'

Jean-Marie Le Pen and Dominique Voynet are, at first sight, not the most comparable of candidates. Both were, however, clearly in the camp of the 'new' candidates. Moreover, they were candidates whose parties traditionally suffered from the tendency to the 'vote utile', the useful or strategic vote, thus making them both victims of France's majoritarian system. The Front National, however, initially dismissed as a short term protest-vote party, was, in 1995, the only progressing political formation, the only pole towards which there seemed to be any *re*-alignment. In other words, in the general context of an ongoing electoral de-alignment, Le Pen's party was the only one gathering what seemed like mainstream momentum. The evening of 23 April 1995 gave rise to yet another wave of disbelief as Le Pen's score rose to the 15% mark. Le Pen had steadily increased his support through the 1980s in electoral contests (with the slight exception of the 1988 legislative elections).With a resounding and – as he was quick to point out – historic vote of 15.25%, Le Pen, along with Jospin, was a 'winner' of the first round. To examine Le Pen's success, one has to consider the evolution of the candidate from extreme right-wing political agitator to popular, quasi-respectable and durable – although arguably no less politically menacing – figure of the extreme right. In the following section, we will outline and analyse his electoral performance to date, in particular the 1995 electoral success. Then, a brief comparative analysis of his 1988 and 1995 campaign literature will elucidate the subtlety and complexity of Le Pen's shifting political persona and message.

During the 1988 presidential campaign, a few days prior to the first round, a poll by the SOFRES revealed that only 28% of voters intending to vote for Le Pen believed that he would make a good President.[29] The first round of the election was already fulfilling a role of opinion outlet, and many of the votes garnered by Le Pen were but protest votes.[30] The period from the early 1980s up to 1988 was characterised by a strategy of consolidating an emerging power-base, and of asserting Jean-Marie Le Pen's presence on the French political stage through a 'credibility' offensive. The period from 1988 to the 1995 presidential elections saw the FN and its leader move further into the political mainstream in order to become 'présidentiable' and dispel doubts about Le Pen's suitability as a leader of the French Republic.

Le Pen's electoral ascent

1972-1984: achieving notoriety

While the Le Pen phenomenon is doubtless greater than the sum of its parts, Le Pen's career in the Fifth Republic – and thus the evolution of the FN – can be divided into three distinct stages: the first, from the FN's creation in 1972 to 1983/4 was marked by a barely disguised radicalism. Dressed in combat-gear and sporting a beret and eye-patch, Le Pen cultivated an aggressive public image. In spite of this, when the leaders of the extreme right movement Ordre Nouveau (founded in 1969) decided to create a movement more palatable to the electorate in the form of the FN, it was Le Pen whom they singled out as capable of transforming the image of the extreme right from a radical, anti-system, fascist current into that of a party which stood some chance of electoral gain, however marginal, in the March 1973 legislative elections. In 1972, when Le Pen created his Front National, it was with the distinct objective of re-integrating the extreme right into the parliamentary arena, a place it had briefly enjoyed in the 1950s[31] with the Poujadiste movement (of which Le Pen had been a part) but from which it had been virtually excluded since the Second World War.[32] Le Pen's task, therefore, was to assemble under the red, white and blue flame of his party's logo the diverse currents which made up the extreme right in France. As outlined by P. Milza,[33] this was an arduous task in the light of the failure of earlier extreme right movements. Le Pen's insight was to realise that in order to survive it was necessary to adapt. He almost immediately adopted the image of a man whose right-wing convictions were not extraneous to France's democratic tradition and Republican identity, while he at the same time presented a sufficiently radical image to gain notoriety on the political scene. Until 1984, the gains were insignificant: no score in the 1973 legislative elections; 0.7% in the 1974 presidential elections. In 1981, the FN did not run in the presidential elections as Le Pen failed to gather the 500 necessary signatures, and in the legislative elections which took place a month later the FN scored 0.3%. Yet in the 1983 municipal elections the FN candidate Jean-Pierre Stirbois gained 16.7% of the votes for the FN list in Dreux (Eure-et-Loire). The reasons behind this surge in support remain to be explained. The reason most often invoked is a backlash effect against the left (in power since 1981). Discontent which might have stemmed from radical socialists disappointed in Mitterand's performance as well as from right-wing supporters hardening their stance in view of the left's power, account in part for the electorate's sudden interest in Le Pen's party. The 'Dreux effect', as it came to be known, signalled the beginning of the FN's electoral emergence and paved the way for the 1984 11.1% breakthrough in the European elections. For the FN, these scores were a confirmation of the efficiency of their tactics: the strategic combination of extremist discourse and democratic allegiance had enabled the extreme right to re-enter the realm of parliamentary politics.

Most commentators agree that Le Pen was paying only lip-service to Republican and democratic ideals, values which, however scorned by supporters of the extreme right, are nevertheless necessary to achieving a credible and respectable image.[34] Le Pen's public allegiance to broad democratic ideals played a significant role in the rehabilitation of the extreme right and in his political rise to power. [35] As Taguieff and Milza[36] make clear, the FN espoused a strategy consisting of a suave blend of legalistic tactics, centrist propositions and radical ideas in its conquest of the electorate.[37]

By 1984 a first step had been made; the FN was still perceived as a protest movement rather than as the expression of a coherent political opinion but had succeeded in de-ghettoising the extreme right.

1984-1988: from notoriety to credibility

The period from 1984 to 1988 saw the FN establishing itself as a fixture in French political life. Whereas the ten preceding years had been spent using a strategy capable of yielding an electoral breakthrough, the period between 1984 and 1988 harnessed this emerging electoral strength to an even more 'democratic' image in order to achieve durability and political credibility. 1984 marks the beginning of Le Pen's great professions of faith as well as the beginning of his more insistent and public re-definition of himself through books and declarations. He increasingly used the term 'democrat' to label and define himself.[38]

His score of 14.39% in the 1988 presidential election confirmed his political success but also the continuing reluctance, even of many of his supporters, to perceive him as more than a first-round presidential candidate.[39] He was a credible enough candidate to attract a vote which could not easily be dismissed by other politicians. Another tactic was needed, however, if he was to achieve a political image which could be harnessed to win the respectability necessary for 'presidentiability'.

1988-1995: from credibility to respectability

The attempt to achieve the necessary respectability to become 'présidentiable' evolved along two lines, both of which were crucial. One concerned Le Pen's electoral attitude, the other a more general transformation of his discourse. Le Pen's discourse varied according to his audience. There was a marked difference between Le Pen's rhetoric and discourse while on the campaign trail and the more radical and unashamedly racist and offensive discourse he was more well known for off the trail, in between major electoral contests. This was, for example, readily apparent in 1988, when after having endlessly justified himself so as to regain a measure of credibility with respect to a statement in which he referred to the holocaust as a 'point of detail',[40] he slipped back into this mode shortly after the election with a pun on Nazi crematoriums. The contrast between the 'campaigning' Le Pen and the 'real' Le Pen still existed at the time of the 1995 elections:

while he was uncharacteristically subdued – as we shall illustrate below – during the campaign, he was unable to contain his anger and frustration against all of his 'enemies' upon hearing of the definitive results of the first round, and thus could not resist the appeal of a rhetorical rampage. His anti-semitic comments on the Jewish pop singer Patrick Bruel when the latter cancelled his shows in the cities where an FN mayor had been elected in the municipal elections of June 1995, were also revealing after his carefully controlled discourse during the presidential campaign. Even on that occasion, however, although anti-semitic, Le Pen's attacks were again much less strident than those levelled against Jews earlier on in his political career. To this dual attitude dictated by electoral contests, one must, therefore, add a broader transformation of Le Pen's discourse between 1988 and 1995 rooted in his quest for respectability. The import of his discourse remained offensive, nationalistic, implicitly racist and continued to smack of national-populism.[41] But his rhetoric shifted from the crudely explicit to the more sophisticated. Perhaps the underlying assumptions and ideas remained the same, but their verbalisation became tamer and perhaps their acceptability greater.

While he still oscillated between his more radical non-campaigning persona and a softer personality, groomed to seduce the electorate, Le Pen also altered his general discourse qualitatively in order to appear more statesmanlike.[42] The debate surrounding the Maastricht treaty and the shape of the new Europe, as well as Le Pen's leadership of the Groupes des Droites Européennes afforded him a double opportunity to work on his more politically mainstream image. It first and foremost saw him speak to such distinguished assemblies as the European Parliament. More importantly, however, his notorious opposition to a federal Europe allowed him to target pro-European politicians and their 'cosmopolitan' views of Europe as the cause of unemployment (since it was their philosophies which allowed for growing numbers of immigrants into nations such as France). This in turn enabled him to attack all politicians more freely by accusing them of all being part of the same plot to annihilate the French nation. Well known examples from the 1988-95 period were Le Pen's puns on the 'Maastricheurs' (the 'Maastricheats') and the 'Fédérastes' ('federal' being equated in Le Pen's repertoire with 'pederast' as another abnormal compulsion). This period marked the beginning of the real shift in his discourse toward an attack on the politicians rather than on the immigrants themselves. The debate on Europe, and more specifically, from 1992, on Maastricht, can be seen as having afforded Le Pen an opportunity to appear as a political actor preoccupied with affairs of state in a prestigious and validating environment. It also allowed him to alter his rhetoric without appearing to be selling out in the eyes of his supporters.

The 1995 presidential campaign came after yet another series of electoral successes. The 1988 elections were followed by an 11.8% score in the 1989 European elections, 12.5% in the 1993 legislatives, and 10.5% in the 1994 European elections. The 15.25% 1995 presidential score appalled many, but surprised no one.

Le Pen's 1995 campaign: continuity and change

Le Pen's 1995 presidential campaign was marked by continuity and change. The continuity was readily apparent, not just in the electoral success, which was predictable and in line with what Le Pen had come to expect since 1988, but also in Le Pen's campaigning style. However, this campaign also saw a marked willingness by Le Pen to tone down the racist rhetoric and adopt a more subdued mainstream manner. This suggests that Le Pen, recognising that his 'natural' electoral constituency was limited, decided to broaden his appeal to new segments of the electorate. This last point should also be understood in the light of the possible de-alignment and re-alignment occuring within the French party-system in the 1990s through which a paradox emerged:

widespread disaffection with the mainstream parties and an increasing number of economically and socially deprived voters led to a situation whereby the mainstream voter and the disaffected – and hitherto marginal – voter became one and the same. Let us highlight the differences and similarities between Le Pen's 1988 and 1995 campaigns in order to see how altering his discourse enabled him to broaden his electoral constituency beyond defined lines and appeal for support from the more mainstream, disaffected voter.

Continuity

The first element of continuity is that the 1995 campaign, in terms of organisation and timing, did not differ significantly from the previous one. As in 1988, Le Pen began campaigning early: he officially announced his candidacy on 17 September 1994, but the campaign had already begun in fact as early as January 1994 as Le Pen set out on his campaign for the cantonal elections, and then in the Spring for the European elections. Both of these campaigns were for all intents and purposes pre-mobilisation exercises for the 1995 presidentials. By the time Le Pen officially declared his intention to run for the presidency in his closing speech of the Bleu-Blanc-Rouge meeting in September 1994 in Reuilly, he had already attained campaign momentum. And from September, Le Pen set out to canvass the country once more. Like Chirac's, his was a dynamic grass-roots campaign using whatever local support was available to create the feeling of an unstoppable popular wave spreading across France.[43] This popular rubbing of elbows fitted neatly with the image of the 'little man' who has done well for himself yet not forgotten past setbacks, the ordinary person in touch with the plights and problems of average French citizens.

The manner in which he presented himself to the voters in his 1995 presidential manifesto is a good illustration of the relationship between himself and the ordinary – potential – voter.

> As candidate to the post of President of the Republic, I am nothing more than a French citizen like any of you. War orphan, state-funded pupil, student activist, combat officer, businessman, family man, national and European MP, I know your fears, your problems, your worries, your distress and your hopes because I have felt, and continue to feel them.[44]

This 'popular touch' has been a trade-mark of Le Pen since his earliest days. The now well-known blend of populist-nationalism of his discourse, his repeated attacks on immigration, his rejection of bureaucracy (French or European) and mounting critique of government élites as well as his strident nationalism confounded analysts and commentators alike.[45] Le Pen's trump-cards were his easy manner and forthcoming style, his oratorical skills and the strength and discipline of his party-machine; but more useful still was his ability to come across as both a French visionary and a man involved in the necessary struggles of politics and of war (he made much of his involvement in Indochina and other military services rendered). All of these combined to create the paradoxical image of a visionary pragmatist: in touch with both the prestige and honour of the French nation and the daily well-being of citizens.

Change

The 1988 campaign was marred by Le Pen's dismissal in late September of 1987 of the holocaust as a 'point of detail'; no such monstrous remarks were made during the 1995 presidential campaign, and few offensive declarations were reported by the press.

However, although this campaign did not suffer from verbal media gaffes, it was placed under the sign of violence and the FN saw itself twice accused of having blood on its hands. On the night of 21 February 1995, FN supporters putting up posters murdered a young Comorian, Ibrahim Ali, and on 1 May (during the FN traditional May Day parade) a young Morrocan, Brahim Bouarram, drowned in the Seine after having been thrown off a bridge, allegedly by FN supporters. The loathsome and explicitly racist nature of both these crimes angered much of the French population and Le Pen was asked to justify himself and his party on several occasions. But on these two matters again, Le Pen succeeded in appearing circumspect (in the case of the second murder he refused to accept responsibility, blaming instead a 'Chiraquian manipulation'[46] destined to mobilise anti-racist opinion against the FN). The tone adopted by Le Pen on both occasions was almost appropriately regretful, in particular during his appearance on the French political show *La France en direct*, during which he reacted violently against an interviewer who insinuated that Le Pen could not have cared less about Ibrahim Ali's death in February.[47] On neither occasion did Le Pen seem altogether 'repentant': of course, he did not accept responsibility for either 'accident' (as he called them), but his reaction was far removed from that which one might have expected in 1987 or 1988. It seems that the high cost of the 1987 'detail' of the gas chambers, and of his virulent discourse more generally, might have led the FN leader to reappraise the efficiency of this sort of attitude, especially while on the campaign trail.[48] Furthermore, Le Pen seemed to have mastered the art of distancing himself from the FN at crucial times so as not to appear as one of its more radical elements, while at others, such as in times of electoral contests, he showed himself consistently capable of mobilising party support and activists. Thanks to this strategy, Le Pen often came across as the one whose strength and inspiration inspired the party, but who, nevertheless, could not be held accountable for members' individual actions and statements. This in turn enabled him to appeal to groups both on the extreme and on the mainstream right. The FN maintained its extreme right credentials by forging links with Catholic, fundamentalist, pro-life groups (Comités Chrétiens Solidarité, Centres Charliers, Laissez-les Vivre, SOS Tout Petits) through the likes of the FN's Bernard Antony. At the same time, the FN's ties to the moderate right were strengthened through links with associations such as the more mainstream Club Renaissance.[49]

Perhaps the most important point regarding Le Pen's respectability offensive during this campaign concerns his discourse surrounding immigration. Whereas Le Pen remained as anti-immigration in 1995 as he had been in 1988, analysts such as Pascal Perrineau[50] noted a shift in Le Pen's discourse. First, Le Pen evoked the themes of immigration and insecurity far less in 1995 than in 1988, concentrating rather on unemployment. Secondly, the immigration issue was increasingly dealt with by attacking 'inept politicians' rather than the immigrants themselves. During several television interviews, Le Pen explicitly questioned government figures regarding the immigrant population in France; and he accused the French government of lying to the public, of doctoring official statistics and questioned its ability to maintain the distinction between legal and illegal immigrants.[51] Le Pen's attacks on politicians were not new, but whereas he had previously attacked the immigrant population itself, the politicians of both left and right were the exclusive targets of Le Pen's criticisms during the 1995 electoral campaign.

Le Pen's campaign flyers are a good illustration of the manner in which the treatment of the immigration issue evolved between 1988 and 1995. They also illustrate the broader evolution of Le Pen's discourse between the two elections, and the increased mainstream appeal of his discourse to a new group of voters, mainly the unemployed and those living in increasingly precarious conditions – in essence, those who would not vote for an outwardly racist discourse. The comparison also illustrates Le Pen's bid for presidential credibility by portraying himself, as most other candidates traditionally do, as someone who is of the people but has an added experience of political life.

Le Pen's 1988 campaign claim that he was unlike any other running politician put him in a difficult situation for 1995: on the one hand, it was crucial that he maintain the requisite distance between himself and all the others in order to condemn political corruption without any risk of being assimilated to those he criticised. On the other hand, it was essential for the election that he shed his 'outsider' image which he had explicitly cultivated in 1988 (one of his three electoral posters pitched him against the background of a horse race with the caption 'L'outsider défend vos couleurs' ('the outsider champions your interests')). The figure of the outsider was precisely what Le Pen needed to transform his image into that of someone who was as 'présidentiable' as the other candidates. As such, where the 1988 flyer demarcated him from the rest of the political class, the 1995 flyer, while it could not afford to place him squarely on the 'inside' lest he be tainted, placed him *amongst us*. His insistence in 1988 that he was the only candidate able to offer such a programme, that he was a solitary visionary, was replaced in 1995 with a discourse of his belonging to France. 'I am like no one else' had been replaced by 'I am like you'. Where the 1988 flyer centred on what Le Pen would do were he to be elected, the message in 1995 centred on who Le Pen was and where he came from. In the 1995 *Appel aux Français* (on the reverse side of the flyers), presenting a programme became secondary to presenting Le Pen as a credible candidate for the presidency. Replacing 1988's risky 'Osez voter pour vos idées, Osez voter Français' ('Dare to vote for your ideas, Dare to vote French') with the bland 1995 caption 'Avec vous une France pour tous les Français' ('With you a France for all French people') confirmed the desire to turn a protest-vote into a mainstream vote. Even though a superficial knowledge of Le Pen's ideas casts exclusionary light on the words, their explicit message was tame. The 'tous les Français' implied a broad notion of citizenship on the basis of a *jus solis* as well as the intended *jus sanguinis*.

In the corpus of the letter he refers to those who have lost their jobs, who fear for them, and those whose children have been unable to find a job. He then refers to those who fear for their pensions (an attempt at targeting the elderly population which had until then consistently been reluctant to vote for him: only 12% of the over 65 vote in 1988).[52] Immigration is mentioned only once in the 1995 flyer, and then only amongst a variety of other elements. The 1988 flyer on the other hand, gave a far greater impression of a nation under siege, with Le Pen referring to 'immigrants, assassins, terrorists and drug-dealers'. The urgency and violence of 1988 gave way to a more fashionable worried concern.

Lastly, the bullet-point section of the flyers of 1988 and 1995 was altered subtly. Two elements are readily apparent: the first is that Le Pen kept 1988's 'why would they [the political mainstream] do tomorrow what they couldn't do yesterday?' slogan. However, unlike the 1988 flyer which went on to swamp the reader with statistical information concerning numerous issues, the 1995 flyer simply reminds the reader of the other candidates' affiliation with the current (scandal-tainted) political class implicated in the nation's decline. The section closes with the caption 'A vote for Le Pen is a useful vote right from the first round', an ambivalent appeal to perceive Le Pen as both a 'useful' first-round candidate and an imaginable second-round one. This is not Le Pen the real outsider but a candidate asserting his rights to be considered a true insider.

The second change in the bullet points was that while both flyers organised the ten points by theme, the themes adopted in 1988 were all at once hard-hitting and static ('Immigration'; 'Security'; 'Housing' etc.), followed by very short, direct, aggressive descriptive paragraphs. The 1995 flyer also offers ten bullet points, but the thematic headings and the present infinitive infuse the sentence with a directness and sense of purpose: 'Offrir un travail à chaque Français; Garantir la santé publique; Reconquérir la souveraineté française' ('giving work to all French persons; guaranteeing public health; reclaiming French sovereignty'). Furthermore, unlike the agressivity of 1988, the 1995 headings were more cryptic, giving the illusion of someone delineating both a programme and a vision rooted in classical values. For example, 1988's fifth point entitled 'L'Europe: pour l'Europe des patries' ('Europe: For a Europe of fatherlands') is transformed into 1995's tenth and last point 'Reconquering French sovereignty' followed by several illustrative points of which renegotiating Maastricht is but one. Without going into further detail here, we can see that there is a shift between 1988 and 1995, from an emphasis on Le Pen's knowledge to an emphasis on Le Pen's vision. The 1995 document targeted a much broader audience by means of a more mainstream right-wing discourse. It targeted the large section of the electorate which was concerned with unemployment, pensions and security. Its language was therefore necessarily closer to the political mainstream than in 1988, as its aim was to present Le Pen as someone whose vision, broad understanding of issues and capacity for action made him an ideal candidate for the presidency.

Room for manœuvre

Le Pen's 1995 campaign cannot be examined without taking account of the manner in which the Chirac campaign and campaign style impacted on Le Pen's. It is not within the scope of this chapter to analyse Chirac's campaign (See chapter 7); nevertheless it is important to emphasise the manner in which a 'kinder, gentler' Chirac would affect Le Pen. The 'conversion' of Le Pen's arch-enemy to a form of consensus politics which, as Chirac often put it, tried to 'bridge the left-right cleavage' (this after his long flirtation with more markedly right-wing politics) can be interpreted as having had a double effect on Le Pen. On the one hand, a more centrist Chirac allowed a wide open space on the extreme right for Le Pen. Unlike in the 1983 municipal elections whose aftermath pushed everyone to the right, and the 1988 presidential elections in which Chirac rivalled the leader of the FN in terms of iron-fisted politics and nationalist fervour, in the 1995 presidential contest Le Pen was able to depend on the extreme right vote with little or no competition (contrary to what he claimed, Le Pen did not significantly lose votes to de Villiers). This partly accounts for his ability to avoid using his more extremist vocabulary. On the other hand, given Le Pen's desire to cloak his campaign in respectability and his hesitation to use his usual tone, Chirac's move to a centrist but populist rhetoric created a superficial similarity between the two candidates' style and discourse which may indeed have cost Le Pen some votes, and blurred his 'new' identity. However, some commentators have underscored the degree to which Chirac's conversion to a variant of populism may have helped legitimise Le Pen's discourse and thought. Pascal Perrineau makes the following points:

> When one grants the extreme right what might be termed 'an official outlet', one contributes to its legitimation. (...) Jacques Chirac's anti-élite discourse can be labelled populist. His denunciation of the establishment, of technocrats, of a form of monologic thought (la pensée unique) and all that..., we have been reading about this for years in the extreme right press. Chirac's 'social fracture' discourse is also a favoured theme for someone who, like Le Pen, has been calling for a radical change in the rules of the political, economic and social realms. (...) Of course these themes pander to a certain public [not necessarily Le Pen's]. But even though Le Pen has exploited these themes in a different way, their use – by others – has granted him a political space.[53]

What is undeniable is that, while Le Pen and Chirac might have shared themes, Le Pen went as far as witholding his support for Chirac in the second round (making the scornful statement that 'Chirac, c'est Jospin en pire' [Chirac is Jospin, only worse]). Le Pen was also able to stress his importance and political weight in the French electoral arena by keeping the country guessing for over a week while he decided whom he would support in round two.

An evolving discourse for an evolving electorate

The most striking aspect of the Le Pen's 1995 vote was not the score. His 15.2% was indeed historic but it was not surprising, and, in fact, only represented a 0.8% gain over the 1988 score. What evolved more dramatically between 1988 and 1995 (in fact, from 1986) was the social composition of his electorate. Le Pen's initial vote was in a sense a protest vote of the provincial 'petite bourgeoisie';[54] but by 1994, Le Pen had become the clear winner in the popular sectors and amongst workers.[55] 1995 also confirmed the geographical as well as the social penetration of Le Pen's constituency: the Le Pen vote was maintained in its original areas of predilection while adding more to its list of sympathetic regions; it confirmed its hold on the eastern parts of France and the regions bordering the Mediterranean coast, and gained strength in the industrial North and centre of the country. Hervé le Bras (director of the Laboratoire de Démographie Historique) noted this shift and characterised it as one from a protest electorate to a disaffected electorate.[56] Le Bras also underscored the increasing differentiation between the electorate of the South of France and the electorate of the North. He refers to the southern 'ideological' vote and the Northern 'sociological' vote[57] and points to Le Pen's capacity to tap into various forms of resentment, disaffection and fear. In essence, Le Pen developed a discourse and programme which exploited the resentment of the industrially burnt-out zones of northern France, the fears stemming from the insecurities bred by the living conditions and social isolations of the Parisian suburbs and, finally, the disaffection of a southern electorate which resented the strain of an ill administered, poorly managed and economically deprived immigrant population. The southern electorate had for a long time constituted Le Pen's main electoral pool, but the former two represented a relatively new and growing phenomenon which could provide him with an expanding (and young) pool of voters.

In Jean-Marie Le Pen's presidential campaign, the factor of real importance was the deepening of the 'respectability' strategy and the tactics associated with it (toning down of the immigration issue, a relative absence of explicitly offensive remarks, and a generally more mainstream rhetoric); this accompanied a new drive for the diversification of the FN's electoral base. The results of this strategy are apparent, not so much in Le Pen's score, but in the sociological composition of his vote. The FN has been able to position itself as much more than a single-issue/single-electorate party and has the potential to act as a rallying point for the disaffected as a social category. In 1995, there was, apart from Jean-Marie Le Pen, another attempt to garner the votes of those to the right of the mainstream right, and it is to this that we now turn.

Philippe de Villiers and Le Mouvement pour la France

Philippe de Villiers, a relative newcomer to high-profile politics who had gained over 12% of the vote in the 1994 European elections, is interesting to compare with Le Pen in terms of both strategy and style. Despite protestations on both their parts, the media and the general public linked the two inextricably during the 1995 presidential campaign. De

Villiers was plagued by questions on the nature of his electorate and his ideas in comparison to those of Le Pen. After the 1994 European elections in which Philippe de Villiers' surprising 12.33% of the vote had outscored Le Pen's list, analysts hypothesised as to whether the extreme right's power had to be interpreted as having doubled overnight and whether de Villiers was not only complementing but replacing Le Pen's populism. The presidential campaign was therefore a test of de Villiers' support made possible by his resounding success in June 1994 . His resounding defeat in 1995 made the hypothesis irrelevant, and reasserted Le Pen's privileged yet questioned place in the leadership of the extreme right.

Let us look at de Villiers' background and campaign for the 1995 presidential elections, establish what differentiated the two candidates, and assess the degree to which de Villiers' campaign suffered from being associated with Le Pen.

Tradition and inherited respectability

Alumnus of the Ecole Nationale d'Administration (ENA), President of the Conseil Général de Vendée, former member of the Parti Républicain (PR), the Viscount Philippe le Jolis de Villiers de Saintignon did not have to struggle for his respectability. In fact, his political appeal was based upon the respectability of his family and heritage, harnessed to his conception of how this – France's – heritage might best be preserved.

De Villier's credentials to represent a political current lay in his brief period serving in the 1986 Chirac government (he was billed as one of the new generation of ultra-liberals which had come to prominence in the Reaganite/Thatcherite climate of the mid-1980s). In 1987, de Villiers gave up his position in the Chirac cabinet to take up once again the post of MP for the Vendée region, and in 1989, after a clear victory in the 1988 legislative elections, he became President of the Conseil Général de Vendée. It is from 1988-89 onwards, therefore, from his nationally known local base, that de Villiers started to cultivate his political specificity, denouncing corruption and the decline of morals, and developing an increasingly hostile stance to Delors' Europe.

Founding his movement Combat pour les Valeurs in 1992, de Villiers appeared as the incarnation, for some the spectre, of an old extreme right: far from Le Pen's populist appeal and self-made convictions, de Villiers displayed an old regime blend of arrogance and charm, traditional, reactionary morals, and a vocabulary and speaking style which evoked France's aristocratic and royalist tradition. In each of his subsequent election campaigns he called for a return to a moral order, to Catholic and family values and to economic and financial protectionism. De Villiers had participated in the anti-Maastricht crusade led by Charles Pasqua and Philippe Séguin in 1992. It was the still largely unresolved Maastricht issue – despite the treaty's ratification – which enabled him to present his successful list L'Autre Europe for the 1994 European elections. With the help and seemingly limitless funds of financier Jimmy Goldsmith, his anti-Maastricht programme expressed a growing disillusionment with the European Union and scepticism about Maastricht.[58] On 16 September 1994, still basking in the glow of his June success, de Villiers resigned from the PR and two months later on 20 November 1994 unveiled the Mouvement pour la France: (MPF) 'The Mouvement pour la France is not an electoral machine', said de Villiers at the time, (...) 'I want it to be a compass for France and an anchor for the governing majority'.[59] The MPF was to be the party machine which carried him through to the presidential election. When he announced his candidacy on 8 January 1995, the polls did not credit him with more than a few percentage points' worth of support, and when he held his first electoral meeting near Mulhouse in February the figure remained the same: 2-3%. To this de Villiers replied that three weeks before the European elections the polls had credited him with only 3% of the vote.

However, the presidential campaign of 1995 deprived de Villiers of all that had made him a force to contend with in the previous June: most notably, the absence of Delors deprived him of an adversary against whom his anti-European discourse might have been directed. In fact, Delors' absence kept the European issue out of the presidential campaign almost entirely, thus removing the main plank of de Villiers' platform, leaving him with only his anti-corruption crusade. He had left the PR in the thick of the corruption storm which was to force its president, Gérard Longuet, to abandon his post as Minister for Industry. His own opportune departure allowed de Villiers to champion the fight against corruption. The consequence, of course, was increasing political isolation.[60] Standing out against the political establishment in a country with strong political loyalties was a long haul. De Villiers' electoral base was as fragile as it had been successful. He attempted early to counter this by pledging to support the right-wing candidate in the second round, a pledge which, in fact, diminished his claim to distinctiveness while not really increasing his attractiveness. Such a position also revealed the weakness of his overall political identity: that he was acting for disaffected though ultimately loyal supporters of the governing majority.

De Villiers' presidential campaign

Philippe de Villiers announced his candidacy on the weekly political television programme *7 sur 7* on 8 January 1995 during which he declared that he had listened carefully to Chirac's ideas but had not found them to be 'fit for the gravity of the challenge that lay ahead'.[61] Ironically, it had been on this same programme a month before that Delors had announced his decision not to run for the presidency, thus obliterating de Villiers' main platform even before the presidential campaign had begun. This irony set the tone for what was to be an almost exclusively 'televisual', though lacklustre, campaign.

De Villiers' campaign on the ground remained uneventful; he repeatedly seized the opportunity to underscore the resemblance between Chirac and Balladur; and from the date of his first electoral rally in Blotzheim near Mulhouse (1 February 1995) to his last in Nice (21 April 1995), de Villiers exhorted the public not to sell France to a European future 'which would leave no role for the President but unveil a few German monuments while bringing a bunch of flowers to the Bundesbank'.[62] Apart from this, de Villiers' campaign was spent not defining his difference from Chirac and Balladur but countering accusations likening his programme and his ideological stance to Le Pen's. Though it was thought that de Villiers could hijack votes from both the Balladur and Le Pen electorates, it became clear during the campaign that even as Balladur's campaign lost steam there was to be no transfer of votes in de Villiers' favour. As for Le Pen's electorate, it became apparent that none of it was to be swayed by de Villiers' style and manners. It is interesting to note that Bruno Gollnisch (vice-president of the FN) thought that any parasitic aspect of de Villiers candidacy would be compensated for by the fact that de Villiers would act 'as a broadcaster of the FN message'.[63] Gollnisch was right inasmuch as the policies advocated by de Villiers now made the FN seem an integral part of the political culture where policy differences may distinguish candidates, but underlying values were shared. Strategically, de Villiers would have needed to couple his campaign with a kind of personality contest in which he defeated Le Pen and assumed the mantle of the extreme right's leadership. This he could not do. Electorally, moreover, in the political scenario of 1995, de Villiers' constituency did not exist. As we have seen, without Delors' candidacy, there was no further reason why parts of Chirac's, Balladur's or Le Pen's electorate should steal away from them to give their first round support to de Villiers, indeed, no reason to even include him as one of the imagined options for a right-wing voter given these other candidates of the right.This last point leads us to our main concern which is de Villiers' brand of extreme right politics and how it compared to Le Pen's.

The Le Pen element in the de Villiers campaign: revolution vs. reaction

The links between Le Pen and de Villiers can be understood as operating on three levels. On a first level, that of broad political families, Le Pen and de Villiers are clearly first cousins. They were united in their dislike for liberal democratic regimes (loosely defined), their abhorrence of cosmopolitanism especially in the form of universal values, and in their tendency to look to their nation's past glory for political inspiration. As such, they were both right-wing, reactionary, authoritarian and prone to discrimination based on narrowly nationalist objectives and criteria. Second is the question of style. For a long time it appeared as though the main difference between Le Pen and de Villiers was stylistic. The message was thought to be the same (anti-Europe, anti-immigration, pro-family, pro-church, pro-capital punishment); indeed the only difference seemed to be that de Villiers was protectionist while Le Pen's economics were ultra- or neo-liberal; yet each was seen as capturing the votes of a specific electorate, with de Villiers catering to the reactionary provinces, in particular his own region of Vendée, while Le Pen expanded his hold on the more urban areas. De Villiers and Le Pen therefore appeared to be sharing the spoils of an extreme right based on the same aims but differing in its methods and style so as to pander to different segments of the population. Further, de Villiers' preference for a 'zero level immigration'[64] and his attitude towards religion and the family created a further superficial likeness between the two politicians that tended to reduce differences to a question of style. The two were using the same catch-phrases ('values', 'family', 'nation', etc.), but closer analysis shows that these words and symbols were used to different ends. Style mediated both differences and similarities between the two men. When the two figures are seen in the broader French social, political and cultural context, fundamental, defining differences appear.

This third level invites the question of which themes in right-wing thought they expressed. Some of the differences between the two men were, for example, rooted in radically different conceptions of the family and of religion.[65] For Le Pen, religion was a form of folklore which functioned as a shared experience between people. As for the family, it was seen as a kernel of identity upon which nationhood could be established. For de Villiers, religion was a set of morals on which one should depend for order, while the family was the basic cell of social control. These two concepts are useful in distinguishing the two politicians and their form of radical right politics, since from these two concepts stemmed their vision of what needed to be done. For Le Pen, these concepts served nationalistic purposes, in that folklore and identity were the basis upon which one would be able to distinguish the truly French from the non-French. De Villiers' system on the other hand, made less of nationhood in that his aim was not so much to separate the French from the non-French but, rather, to control the forces of change. As such, de Villiers' politics were a clearer expression of the fear of loss of status or privilege such as is delineated in theories of relative deprivation,[66] and thus can be traced to French counter-revolutionary forces. Le Pen's brand of extremism, in contrast, while it shared with de Villiers its sense of loss of past glory, owed more to Vichy's national populism.[67] So, while the two could share Pétain's famous slogan 'travail, famille, patrie', the words would be destined to produce different resonances and emanated from different aspects of French history.

Other factors

The results of the first round, which revealed a 4.74% score for de Villiers, also highlighted other factors. The first was that de Villiers had been a single-issue candidate in the European elections and that, deprived of the possibility of debating this issue, he was unable to mobilise support (the extreme right was content in voting for Le Pen's programme, and the provincial bourgeoisie for Balladur). The first round result also underscored the fact that, as noted by Hervé le Bras, the de Villiers score, unlike Le Pen's, did not have a national resonance. Le Bras pointed out, however, that the de Villiers phenomenon should not be understood as an epiphenomenon: de Villiers supporters were the extreme right of Northern France, they were substantially the same electorate that supported Poujade in 1956 and, more tellingly even, Jean Royer who, in 1974, had started an anti-pornography and anti-supermarket crusade: 'it is just like a benign infantile disease, an eruptive manifestation which reappears once in a while in the same spots,' wrote Le Bras somewhat disparagingly.[68]

De Villiers was the 1990s manifestation of a deep-rooted reactionary vein in French politics: and although this particular manifestation might perhaps be ephemeral enough, its relationship to French republican politics raises major questions as to the strength of the liberal democratic heritage of the Revolution.

The difference between Le Pen and de Villiers can be summed up if we see de Villiers as a reactionary of the traditional type. His aims were largely a return to the moral and social order characteristic of the pre-revolutionary period. As argued earlier on, his main aim was to resist change and to preserve order. The issue of Europe which for so many continued to represent an unknown future perhaps marked by drastic change and growing insecurity and a loss of French nationhood, was a perfect issue on which to graft de Villiers' forces of reaction. Le Pen on the other hand embraced the forces of change more wilfully in an attempt to alter fundamentally the political topography, seeking what in effect would be a revolutionary change under the benign heading of the Sixth Republic. Although both on the extreme right, each therefore expressed different aspects of France's wider culture of reaction.

Let us now look briefly at the true outsider in the presidential race, Jacques Cheminade.

Jacques Cheminade and the Fédération pour une Nouvelle Solidarité

Although a graduate from the Ecole Nationale d'Administration, like so many of the French political class, Jacques Cheminade is difficult to situate in French politics. He had already attempted to run for the presidency in 1981 and 1988. Leader of the Parti Ouvrier Européen (POE) (which became the Fédération pour une Nouvelle Solidarité in 1991) and an ex-high civil servant in the French department of Finance, he labelled himself a 'dissident Enarque' (student of the ENA), and called for a new 'republican front' while remaining closely associated with the American right-wing extremist and leader of the US Labour Party (of which the POE was the European counterpart), Lyndon Larouche.

In 1984 and 1989, while secretary general of the POE, Cheminade presented lists at the European elections. In 1984, he scored 0.08% of the vote. He reached 0.17% in 1989. In March of 1993, Cheminade tried his luck in the legislative elections and ran for a Paris district: his efforts won him 0.33% of the vote. In September of 1994, as a candidate in a by-election in the Puy-de-Dome region he obtained 0.58% of the vote against former President of the Republic, Valéry Giscard d'Estaing. In 1995, Cheminade succeeded in getting the necessary 500 support signatures to run for the presidency – he obtained 556 – and was thus able to participate in the contest.

Two things are of interest with respect to his candidacy. The first was his political orientation, which in spite of his strange right-wing associations was difficult to define. The second was the manner in which he was able to garner the 556 signatures, given his abysmal scores in all political contests to date.

Cheminade: right or left?

Cheminade's close association and friendship with Lyndon Larouche had led to his being promptly slotted in the extreme right. Cheminade consistently fought against this label and repeatedly denied it during the 1995 presidential campaign. At a press conference, on 13 April 1995, for example, he declared that he had no links whatsoever with the extreme right and asked to be judged on his actions rather than on rumours 'I am the victim of a lynching operation, of a cabal (...) because I have some things to say, I have a project, a commitment to certain things'.[69]

It is difficult to judge Cheminade on his actions, so marginal was he to political life, but his presidential flyers give an idea of the complexity of the character. In his campaign literature as well as in his speeches, Cheminade came across as the champion of the little man. Most of his declarations attributed the failings of modern society to the preponderance of the market. More precisely, it was the inability of politicians to rein in capital and harness it to the forces of progress for the many as opposed to profit for the few which Cheminade primarily targeted:

> A speculative cancer has infested the world in the past twenty years: money is increasingly absorbed into buying and selling operations which produce no tangible riches. This financial cancer is destroying the body of the productive economy by siphoning the flow of credit and money away from it. (...) this cancer is the cause of unemployment.[70]

After this diagnosis of the causes of France's current difficulties, Cheminade went on to spell out the remedies, the main tenets of his project, which addressed principally the plight of rural France and the social and economic situation in deprived suburbs. Aside from an idyllic and paternalistic view of the French rural dweller, nothing in Cheminade's campaign literature could really be connected to the extreme right. In fact, confusingly enough, most of his proposals could well have been associated to a socialist manifesto. One of his commitments was a bizarre insistence on the necessity to expand and/or revitalise France's space programme. In a section entitled 'Remettre l'Espace à l'Horizon' ('Putting Space Back on our Horizon') Cheminade explained – in great detail and with singular enthusiasm – the need to participate with others in the great adventure of the 'conquest and industrialisation of the solar system' in order to create at least 15,000 jobs in space engineering and re-ignite our 'spirit of discovery'.[71]

Cheminade's campaign literature was a collection of essays on disparate themes, and the views expressed ranged from the benign to the outrageous. Not all that Cheminade said seemed far-fetched, but the 'package' was, in its multifaceted whole, bizarre for a presidential, indeed for any, political campaign. At best it could be seen as the reflection of an eclectic mind, at worst as a smoke-screen for something more cynical or else quite scatty.

The confusion and oddness of Cheminade's candidacy, indeed its inappropriateness, meant that his campaign was virtually (although not completely – see below) ignored by the media. The manner in which Cheminade gathered his support signatures therefore raises questions about access to political competition at the national level.

Cheminade set out to gather the necessary 500 support signatures in a most methodical manner. Three of the mayors whose signatures he had enlisted subsequently declared that they had been duped and regretted having supported Cheminade. Cheminade's campaign had been meticulously planned: first, a package containing Cheminade's CV and campaign flyer was sent to each of France's 36,500 mayors. Then, a telephone campaign targeted thousands of possible signatories. Finally, the decisive offensive was launched in January and February of 1995 when the front troops of the FNS were sent – in pairs – on a cross-country, door-to-door mission destined to wrest definite support from the convinced few. In each of the seventy canvassed regions, the emissaries of FNS distributed a smattering of Cheminade's writings (such as his impassioned introduction to the early twentieth century Socialist leader, Jean Jaurès's *De la réalité du monde sensible*). The canvassers omitted a few troubling details such as Cheminade's having been found guilty of fraud in 1992.[72]

When the story of the Cheminade fraud was revealed by the press, each of the three angered mayors, in an attempt to untangle themselves from the mess, wrote to Cheminade claiming that they had spotted contradictions in his political views which placed him sometimes on the right and other times on the left. Jacques Velghe, the Socialist mayor of the small village of Saint Christophe, wrote the following in his letter 'I am profoundly disappointed in the misrepresentation of your political career and I will not be an accomplice to such actions.'[73] Indeed, the charge of misrepresentation characterised Cheminade's campaign; the ambiguity of his candidacy did much to explain the public's suspicious attitude toward such a character, and thus his poor electoral result, 0.27%.

Conclusion

The impact of peripheral forces on the 1995 presidential election provides evidence as to the strength and condition of presidentialism in late twentieth century France. The fate of the Greens and of the FN are vivid illustrations of the workings of presidentialism in a period of electoral volatility and simultaneous de-alignments and re-alignments. The context of presidentialism demonstrates the problems faced by peripheral parties in majoritarian systems: despite obvious ideological differences, the Greens and the FN shared the same electoral dilemma. Initially delineated by Adam Przeworski with respect to working class parties hesitating between isolation and electoral competition,[74] this consists in trying to develop a viable electoral stance in the face of the 'combination of minority status with majority rule'.[75] The dilemma could apply to any party suffering from numerical inferiority resulting from its radical platform's appeal to a finite electorate; as such, the FN and the Greens both suffered, to different extents, from their initially defined, radical platforms and non-catch-all nature. They were both placed in a position where the prospect was either resounding defeat (the Greens) or stagnation (Le Pen). Both had to decide whether or not to broaden their electoral appeal. As we have seen in the case of the Greens, the dilemma was more pronounced given their NSM status. They were faced with the dilemma of constituting themselves as a competitive electoral force and participating in a system whose rules and aims they were severely critical of and which they hoped to change.[76] They were faced also, like the FN, with the electoral dilemma proper which forced them either to broaden their platform in order to increase their appeal outside their natural constituency or maintain a distinct platform and identity but forfeit any hope of widening their constituency. This is a dilemma because there is a very real element of risk involved: broadening one's appeal and attempting to sway new segments of the electorate necessarily involves a transformation, usually a 'dilution' of the original, radical party platform. This dilution may well bring in new voters but may simultaneously alienate the 'natural constituency' of the party or movement.

In 1995, Le Pen's dilemma was this: he had to increase his score of 1988 by making a broader appeal which entailed toning down his more strident stance and opinions while still differentiating himself from the other candidates. Here, Le Pen needed to assess how far he could move to the centre and into the mainstream without alienating those who voted for him precisely because he was radical. The 1995 electoral campaign saw Le Pen taking careful steps toward the centre and testing the waters of mainstream right-wing discourse. The steps were tentative but the results were clear: as the sociological composition of Le Pen's vote shows, a portion of the unemployed and the so-called disaffected voters moved towards him from the centre as he simultaneously inched towards them.

The possibility of this move from the extremes of the right to a more mainstream right by the FN illustrates presidentialism's power to shape political parties. Although the electoral dilemma stems from the nature of electoral competition itself in any majoritarian system, the presidential system renders the dilemma more acute by placing great emphasis on the presidential candidate's party-backing, the strength of his/her party machine and the candidate's capacity to appear as though he/she is both deriving power from the party as well as imparting discipline to it.[77] In a chapter entitled 'Sources of Party Transformation: The Case of France', Frank Wilson explains how the introduction of a presidential system (and direct presidential elections) in France affected the terms of competition and thus led to a deep, if belated, transformation of the party system and the parties themselves. According to Wilson, the fact that the presidency became the chief prize of political competition affected the system profoundly: parties needed new structures and strategies and these were to prove particularly difficult to construct for small parties.[78] The broadening of their mandate to national proportions meant that small parties would need to reform under the weight of a new type of competition and adopt organisational structures either beyond their means or, more importantly perhaps, beyond their ideological and organisational scope. Further, the importance of the presidential race and the resources and attention devoted to the grooming of a 'présidentiable' within each party meant that internal discord and competing view-points took on new forms.[79]

Understanding the pressures of the electoral dilemma helps our understanding of the actions and transformations undergone by radical parties. These, however, shed only partial light on our case studies. The electoral dilemma needs to be seen also in the context of presidentialism itself. The Greens and the FN faced the same electoral dilemma, yet the FN fared much better in its attempt to adapt than did the Greens (who, in fact, also moved squarely into the mainstream). It is the context of presidentialism which accounts for this difference: where the FN boasts a well-organised, disciplined party and an undisputed leader, the Greens made headlines because of their internal splits and persistent discord; this last point weakened Dominique Voynet as a political leader in the eyes of the public. Thus the move to the centre is only successful if coupled with electoral attributes made all the more necessary by a presidential context: a unified party and strong leader.

The impact of presidentialism goes further: by transforming the presidency into the only real political prize, and the race for the presidency into the most important national, political competition, presidentialism draws into the presidential electoral arena parties, such as the Greens, whose defining features and political identity make them necessarily hostile to and unfit for a presidential race. Yet the presidential context leaves little choice to smaller, less unified parties other than to respond to presidentialism at enormous costs to their identity and political organisation. On the other hand, parties like the FN, whose ideological definitions do not include a true commitment to grass-root voices or to institutionalised dissent, and which is itself fashioned by the myth of the strong hero-leader, are poised for a measure of success.

A related point is that presidentialism clearly allows for, even encourages, peripheral parties of the authoritarian type more than left libertarian ones, for the Fifth Republic is based upon a mistrust of parties and the perceived need to counter factionalisation and even 'party government' by privileging strong leaders. This is, however, framed by the electoral dilemma of a two-ballot system and by presidentialism itself. A radical leader will stand no chance of presidential success no matter how disciplined and strong his/her party is, unless the latter has already diluted its platform. Because the presidential context has turned the presidency into the most sought after electoral prize, extreme right-wing parties will continue to measure themselves against this contest, and will either successfully be kept at bay by the acuteness of the trade-off required of them or else achieve success only at the cost of their extremism.

In conclusion, we might ask whether electoral volatility, voter indecision and the emergence of the FN should be taken as symptoms of the de-alignment of the French electorate. What the 1995 presidential election highlights is that accompanying the de-alignment from the mainstream parties has been a re-alignment in favour of the FN (the FN's position was confirmed in the municipal elections of June 1995 following the presidential elections of May). That this de-alignment occurred later in France than in other Western European nations has been discussed in our introduction. We can raise the further question here of the extent to which this movement of the electorate is also indicative of the development of strategic voting in France. A. and M.T. Lancelot have noted that it has become increasingly difficult to predict and/or monitor French voters according to socio-economic status:

> The explanation of social and political behaviour seems to be increasingly rooted in an allegiance to certain social and cultural values and in a strategy. It stems less and less from the feeling that one belongs to an objectively defined category.[80]

Perrineau sees the Le Pen vote as a strategic vote ('un vote sur enjeux'), 'These voters use their vote for Le Pen to signal their rejection of immigration and their preoccupation with the issue of security'.[81] It is what A. and M.T. Lancelot refer to as a vote motivated by resentment rather than allegiance,[82] a classic protest vote. Yet we should also note that those who voted for Le Pen did so as a category: those who had the most to lose from the economic and social situation in France. The category may no longer be defined along traditional class-lines, but it nevertheless reflects a group of persons whose situation is, or is potentially, precarious. If the FN has become the party of the disaffected then an element of social class obviously enters the analysis. This in part contributes to a paradoxical situation in which a party whose target group is the socially, economically and electorally disaffected electorate is also moving toward the mainstream in terms of its images, style and discourse.

This raises the further question of why a similar development has not been seen in the fortunes of other political parties, in particular the Greens. We may conclude by saying that the FN's greater success is in part due to its responding not only to the dilemmas created by the shifts in the nature and behaviour of political constituencies but also to the exigencies of presidentialism within the Republic.

Notes

[1] Many commentators underscore the fact that this Socialist victory could subsequently be interpreted as the right's defeat. The left's first round score of 47.25% constituted a tiny increase compared to its 1974 score of 46.08% and the defeat was by no means crushing for Giscard. For a discussion see A. and M.T. Lancelot 'L'évolution de l'électorat français' in G. Ross and S. Hoffman (eds.), *L'expérience Mitterrand: continuité et changement dans la France contemporaine* (Paris, PUF, 1987), pp.105-31.

[2] Otto Kirchheimer, 'The Transformation of Western European Party Systems' in J. la Palombara and M. Weiner (eds.), *Political Parties and Political Development* (Princeton, N.J., Princeton University Press, 1966), pp.177-200.

[3] Anthony Downs, *An Economic Theory of Democracy* (New York, Harper and Row, 1957).

[4] C. Crouch and A. Pizzorno, *The Resurgence of Class Conflict in Western Europe since 1968* (London, Macmillan, 1978).

[5] Picked up in the late 1970s as an increasingly strong trend which showed little or no signs of subsiding, the weakening of traditional parties and their ties to the traditional party base as well as increasing electoral volatility spawned a vast amount of literature. Ronald Inglehart diagnosed a cultural shift toward post-materialist values (R. Inglehart, *The Silent Revolution: Changing Values and Political Styles amongst Western Publics* (Princeton, N.J., Princeton University Press, 1977)); Gurr identified mounting 'relative deprivation' conducive to collective mobilisation in the face of idle institutions (T. Gurr, *Why Men Rebel* (Princeton, N.J., Princeton University Press, 1970)). Some looked for causes which might explain the radical transformation undergone by Western party systems and their voters. Early explanations included the *embourgeoisement* thesis which pointed to unprecedented levels of comfort and security as the underlying source of the emergence of a new more confident voter who, having slowly divested him/herself of the strait-jacket of class-based voting, took an additional step consisting of shedding his/her attachment to bland, non-ideological, catch-all parties (See S. M. Lipset, 'The Changing Class Structure and Contemporary European Politics', *Dædalus*, 93, 1964, pp.271-303). The related theories of social mobility and increased educational access point towards a more discerning, educated and therefore refined kind of voter. All of these theories inform the more recent understanding of electoral change in industrial democracies and only a combination of all of them can shed light on a process which began with the unrest of the 1960s and continues to this day to bewilder political scientists.

[6] P. Mair, 'La trasformazione del partito di massa in Europa', in M. Calise (ed.), *Come cambiano i partiti* (Bologna, Il Mulino, 1992), pp.99-120.

[7] D. Cameron and R. Hofferbert, 'Continuity and Change in Gaullism: the General's Legacy', *American Journal of Political Science*, 17, 1, 1973, pp.78-83; see also D. Cameron, 'Stability and Change in Patterns of French Partisanship', *Public Opinion Quarterly*, 36, Spring 1972, pp.19-30.

[8] M. Lewis-Beck,'France: the Stalled Electorate' in R. Dalton, S. Flanagan and P.A. Beck (eds.), *Electoral Change in Advanced Industrial Democracies: Realignment or Dealignment?* (Princeton, N.J., Princeton University Press, 1984), pp.428-433.

[9] J. Gaffney, 'Introduction: Presidentialism and the Fifth Republic' in J. Gaffney (ed.), *The French Presidential Elections of 1988* (Aldershot, Dartmouth, 1989), p.10.

[10] SSU-CSA poll in *Le Monde*, 26 April 1995.

[11] Pascal Perrineau, *Le Monde*, 26 April 1995.

[12] In 1981, Mitterrand had a 26% initial support base (*Le Monde*, 26 April 1995).

[13] For details on de Gaulle's decision to adopt universal suffrage see Edmond Jouve, 'Modes de scrutin et systèmes électoraux', *Documents d'études: droit constitutionnel et institutions politiques* (Paris, La documentation Française, 1986).

[14] All legislative elections take place under a majority system, except for the legislative elections of 1986 which took place under a law passed in 1985 instituting proportionnal representation. The law was abolished in July of 1986 and the previous system was re-instated.

[15] Pascal Perrineau, *Le Monde*, 26 April 1995.

[16] Voter indecision, which often goes hand-in-hand with volatility, seems to have been one of the hallmarks of this election. According to a CSA first-round exit-poll, 12% of voters made up their minds at the very last minute inside the voting booth, while 16% made up their minds in the last few days leading up to the election; *Le Monde*, 26 April 1995.

[17] See in particular R. J. Dalton, 'Strategies of Partisan Influence: West European Environmental Groups' in J. C. Jenkins and B. Klandermans (eds.), *The Politics of Social Protest: Comparative Perspectives on States and Social Movements* (UCL Press Limited, University of Minesotta, 1995), pp.296-323.

[18] Thereby illustrating once again the apparently inevitable trade-off faced by any organisation between being democratic and being efficient.

[19] Michel Hastings, 'Le discours écologiste: un exemple d'hermaphrodisme idéologique', special issue of *Notes et Etudes Documentaires,* Pierre Bréchon (ed.), 'Le discours politique en France', 1993, pp.115-136.

[20] Michel Serres, *Le contrat naturel* (Paris, F. Bourin, 1990).

[21] Interview with Antoine Waechter, *Le Monde*, 28 June 1994.

[22] *Ibid.*

[23] Waechter announced the creation of his *Mouvement des écologistes indépendants* in June 1994, but it formally came into existence at the beginning of September 1994. He announced his candidacy on 8 January 1995 and withdrew from the presidential race on 5 April 1995.

[24] Born in 1958, Dominique Voynet is an anaesthetist. She has been *Conseillère régionale* of Franche-Comté since 1992 and *Conseillère municipale* of the city of Dole since 1989. She was a founding member of the Greens and has been their spokesperson since 1992.

[25] Dominique Voynet, cited in 'Divided French ecologists meet to ponder the future' *Reuter News Service/Western Europe online*, 26 June 1993.

[26] Dominique Voynet, interviewed by Jean-Louis Peyroux in *Politis*, 15 December 1994.

[27] Dominique Voynet, interviewed by Bernard Langlois in *Politis*, 20 October 1994.

[28] John Gaffney, 'France', in J. Lodge (ed.), *The 1994 Elections to the European Parliament* (London, Pinter, 1996), pp.84-106.

[29] SOFRES poll conducted 1 and 2 April 1988, cited by J. Jaffré in 'Le Pen ou le vote exutoire', *Le Monde*, 12 April 1988.

[30] Pierre Bréchon for example, describes the vote for the FN as a 'social protest vote' ('un vote de protestation sociale') in his article 'Qui choisit le Front National?', *Etudes*, 1 January 1992, p.47.

[31] The extreme right's previous public achievement had been the 4.3% polled by Jean-Louis Tixier-Vignancour in the1965 presidential election.

[32] For a discussion of the Poujadiste movement in France see Dominique Borne, *Petits bourgeois en révolte? Le mouvement Poujade* (Paris, Flammarion, 1977).

[33] P. Milza 'Le Front National: droite extrême ou national-populisme?' in J.-F. Sirinelli (ed.), *Histoire des droites en France* (Paris, Gallimard, 1992), pp.691-697.

[34] The view that democratic values and the discourse associated with them were understood by Le Pen as nothing more than instruments in gaining electoral strength was even supported by Le Pen's ex-wife Pierrette who candidly admitted to the French weekly *LíEvénement du jeudi* that 'He thinks that authoritarian regimes are more efficient. Democratic regimes, he thinks that's just something you have to put up with for a while.' *LíEvénement du jeudi,* 28 March 1985.

[35] The latter also points to the fact that Le Pen's feigned conversion to democracy and his endorsement of the Republican framework should also be seen as part of a wider movement begun as early as 1962 by Europe-Action and followed by the rest of what was to be known as the French New Right, and which consisted in 'combat through wits and ideas rather than through force'. Thus spoke Dominique Venner, leader of Europe-Action, in *Défense de l'Occident,* 26 November 1962, pp.46-52.

[36] Some accused Le Pen of being a wolf in sheep's clothing and of harbouring authoritarian tendencies behind a veil of democratic discourse. Others, such as French historian and political scientist René Rémond, go as far as to wonder whether one could apply the 'extreme right' label to an organisation 'whose relatively moderate and legalistic character would prevent one from associating it with the counter-revolutionary tradition and the agitation of the Leagues', cited in P. Milza, *op. cit.* pp.699-700.

[37] This strategy, which forced commentators and adversaries of Le Pen to seek new lines of inquiry into the FN phenomenon and new ways of countering its brand of racism and radicalism, in no way diminishes the threat a figure such as Le Pen posed for the democratic process, quite the opposite. As Milza writes 'Strident anti-parliamentarianism and direct action can constitute some of the hallmarks of related organisations, but they do not exclude the presence of legalistic currents that are temporarily ready to play the parliamentary game for tactical reasons.(...) With regard to the FN as it stands today, and while we struggle to pinpoint the subtle difference between the extreme right and the extremes of the right, let us keep in mind that the leagues of the 1930s pale in comparison to the activism of the FN's origins, the clearly expressed tactical choices of its founders who established that the FN was to camouflage its true colours and its consistently and resolutely anti-system discourse. Finally let us keep in mind its verbal violence which, in terms of the critique of the party system, of its xenophobia, of the denunciation of cosmopolitanism and its designation of minorities in more or less coded manner is again no tamer than that which we find in other explicitly extremist movements and parties of the inter-war years'. P. Milza, *op. cit.*, pp.699-700.

[38] On Le Pen's strategy of credibility and respectability between 1974 and 1988 see specifically section II, part A/1 'Le vent en poupe: une stratégie prometteuse de crédibilisation and de respectabilisation' in Christophe Hameau, *La campagne de Jean-Marie Le Pen pour l'élection présidentielle de 1988* (Université de Paris II, Travaux et recherches Panthéon-Assas, 1992), pp.55-66.

[39] See footnote 15.

[40] For a discussion of this and other gaffes and their implications and consequences for the 1988 campaign see Christophe Hameau, *La campagne de Jean-Marie Le Pen pour l'élection présidentielle de 1988*; in particular annex 13.

[41] P. Milza, *op. cit.* pp.699-700; and P. A. Taguieff, 'Un programme révolutionnaire' in N. Mayer and P. Perrineau (eds.), *Le Front National à découvert* (Paris, Presse de la FNSP, 1989), pp.27-61.

[42] See Catherine Fieschi, 'The Discourse of Jean-Marie Le Pen: a Case Study in Ambiguity' in H. Drake and J. Gaffney (eds.), *The Language of Leadership in Contemporary France* (Aldershot, Dartmouth, 1996), pp.107-132.

[43] This was reminiscent of what in 1988 was dubbed the 'tournée des plages' (the beach tour) which saw Le Pen on a summer campaign tour of major French beaches making the most of the opportunity to chat with locals and tourists.

[44] J.-M. Le Pen, *Appel aux Français*, 1995 presidential campaign brochure *Le Pen président* (Saint-Cloud, Publications du Front National, 1995).

[45] P. Milza's thesis, expounded in the article cited, that Le Pen's brand of rhetoric and political thought owes much, not only to the ideas of the counter revolution, but also to those of Vichy's national-populism is arguably the most convincing.

[46] On this occasion, Le Pen made specific reference to the desecration of a Jewish cemetery in Carpentras in 1990 of which Le Pen supporters had been hastily accused and which turned out to have been carried out by a gang of bored teenagers not even remotely associated with the FN. The accusation had been made in haste and far too pointedly for Le Pen not to seize the opportunity to masquerade as scape-goat and martyr. On Le Pen's declaration about the two murders, see Renaud Dely 'Le Pen se place dans l'opposition', *LíEvénement du jeudi*, 8 May 1995, p.11.

[47] See Le Pen's inflamed reply on *La France en direct*, France 2 Television, 13 March 1995.

[48] It is interesting to compare Le Pen's self-control with Chirac's who was incessantly portrayed in satirical television programmes as having the choice between keeping quiet or risking another gaffe; Chirac's *Guignols* puppet was thus constantly seen clasping his hands over his mouth and repeating mantra-like statements in an attempt to keep his cool and avoid costly slips of the tongue. On this, see the section on media satire in chapter 12 of the present volume.

[49] For further information concerning the FN's web of alliances and associations see Nonna Mayer, 'The Dynamics of the Anti-National Front Countermovement', paper delivered at the *Annual Meeting of the American Political Science Association*, Chicago, 31 August -3 September 1995, pp.3-5.

[50] Robert Schneider, 'Qu'est-ce qui fait monter Le Pen...' interview with Pascal Perrineau, *Le Nouvel Observateur*, 6 April 1995, pp.30-31.

[51] *La France en direct*, France 2 Television, 13 March 1995; *Face a la une*, TF1 Television, 23 March 1995. See also Le Pen's *Appel au Français* 1995 presidential campaign brochure.

[52] C. Hameau, *op. cit.* p.101.

[53] Robert Schneider, 'Qu'est-ce qui fait monter Le Pen...' interview with Pascal Perrineau, p.30.

[54] Robert Schneider, *Ibid.*, p.31.

[55] *Ibid.* p.31.

[56] Hervé Le Bras, interview in *Le Monde*, 14-15 May 1995.

[57] Hervé Le Bras, *Ibid.*

[58] Estimates of campaign costs for some of the 1994 European election lists indicate that de Villiers' *L'Autre Europe* list was the most expensive at 27 million francs as compared to the 1.3 million spent by *Génération Ecologie*, the 15 million spent by

L'Europe Solidaire (Socialist) and the UDF-RPR's 20 million francs campaign. See J. Gaffney, 'France' in J. Lodge (ed.), p.105, fn. 5.

[59] Ph. de Villiers, *Le Monde*, 22 November 1994.

[60] This isolation was compounded by de Villiers' propensity to make career moves which in retrospect suggest a penchant for defection rather than political savvy.

[61] Ph. de Villiers, *Le Monde*, 10 January 1995.

[62] Ph. de Villiers, *AFP online*, 21 April 1995.

[63] C. Chombeau, 'Le Pen lance sa campagne', *Le Monde*, 16 January 1995.

[64] When he launched the MPF in November 1994, de Villiers said that he would call for 'zero level immigration', *AFP online*, 20 November 1994.

[65] The support which de Villiers draws from Catholic church authorities is no secret, and many of the individuals who support de Villiers are themselves leaders of Catholic groups: for example Françoise Seillier, vice-president of the National Confederation of Catholic Family Associations or Christine Boutin, MP for the Yvelines region, both active members of de Villiers' group *L'Europe des nations* in the European Parliament. Most of the group's declarations so far have centred on the promotion of 'ecological birth control' and anti-contraception exposés. For more on this topic see an excellent report entitled *Le retour de l'ordre moral* compiled by *Le Réseau Voltaire* (a non-partisan organisation dedicated to the promotion of freedom of speech) and published in *Le Journal Radical*, 17 October 1994, pp.29-37.

[66] Ted Gurr, *Why Men Rebel* , *op. cit.*

[67] For more on this topic see the section on Le Pen in the present chapter.

[68] Hervé Le Bras, interview in *Le Monde*, 14-15 May 1995.

[69] *AFP online*, 13 April 1995.

[70] *Les Engagements de Jacques Cheminade, Le projet de J. Cheminade* (Paris, 12 rue Dupetit Thouars, Spring 1995), p.1.

[71] *Les Engagements de Jacques Cheminade*, pp.4-5.

[72] In 1992 Cheminade was sentenced to a suspended prison sentence of 15 months for fraud. This was brought about when the children of an elderly woman who had died of Alzheimer's disease in 1986 accused Cheminade of having taken advantage of their mother's illness to obtain over 1 million FF for his party. The children of Mrs. Pazery had taken legal action claiming that their mother could not have voluntarily handed over such a sum of money. *AFP online*, 7 April 1995.

[73] Letter of Jacques Velghe to Jacques Cheminade, cited in *AFP online*, 10 April 1995.

[74] A. Przeworski, *Capitalism and Social Democracy* (Cambridge, Cambridge University Press, 1985).

[75] A. Przeworski, *op. cit.*, p.24.

[76] To some extent Ordre Nouveau might have been faced with a similar dilemma when they decided to create the FN in order to broaden their appeal.

[77] J. Gaffney, 'Introduction: Presidentialism and the Fifth Republic', *op. cit.*, pp.1-36.

[78] Frank L. Wilson, 'Sources of Party Transformation: The Case of France', in Peter Merkl (ed.), *Western European Party Systems: Trends and Prospects* (New York, The Free Press, 1980), p.41.

[79] See John Gaffney, *The French Left and the Fifth Republic* (London, Macmillan, 1989).

[80] A. and M.T. Lancelot, *op. cit.*, p.122.

[81] Pascal Perrineau, *op. cit.*, p.31.

[82] A. and M. T. Lancelot, *op. cit.*, p.109.

Indicative Bibilography

Calise, M., *Come cambiano i partiti* (Bologna, Il Mulino, 1992).

Chebel d'Appollonia, A., *L'extrême-droite en France de Maurras à Le Pen* (Paris, Editions Complexes, 1987).

Dalton, R., S. Flanagan and P.A. Beck (eds.), *Electoral Change in Advanced Industrial Democracies: Realignment or Dealignment?* (Princeton, N.J., Princeton University Press, 1984).

Drake, H. and J. Gaffney (eds.), *The Language of Leadership in Contemporary France* (Aldershot, Dartmouth, 1996).

Gaffney, J. (ed.), *The French Presidential Elections of 1988* (Aldershot, Dartmouth, 1989).

Hameau, C., *La campagne de Jean-Marie Le Pen pour l'élection présidentielle de 1988* (Université de Paris II, Travaux et recherches Panthéon-Assas, 1992).

Hastings, M. 'Le discours écologiste: un exemple d'hermaphrodisme idéologique', Pierre Bréchon (ed.), special issue of *Notes et Etudes Documentaires,* 'Le discours politique en France', 1993, pp.115-136.

Inglehart, R., *The Silent Revolution: Changing Values and Political Styles amongst Western Publics* (Princeton, N.J., Princeton University Press, 1977).

La Palombara, J. and M. Weiner (eds.), *Political Parties and Political Development* (Princeton, N.J., Princeton University Press, 1966).

Le Bras, H., *Les trois France* (Paris, Editions Odile Jacob, 1995).

Merkl, P. (ed.), *Western European Party Systems: Trends and Prospects* (New York, The Free Press, 1980).

Perrineau, P. and N. Mayer, *Le Front National à découvert* (Paris, Presses de la FNSP, 1989).

Przeworski, A., *Capitalism and Social Democracy* (Cambridge, Cambridge University Press, 1985).

Ross, G. and S. Hoffman (eds.), *L'expérience Mitterrand: continuité et changement dans la France contemporaine* (Paris, PUF, 1987).

Serres, M., *Le contrat naturel* (Paris, F. Bourin, 1990).

Sirinelli, J.-F., (ed.), *Histoire des droites en France* (Paris, Gallimard, 1992).

10. THE BUSINESS COMMUNITY AND THE ELECTION

MAIRI MACLEAN

The 1995 Presidential elections: business as usual?

The battle to secure France's greatest political prize – the presidency of the Fifth Republic – began for some candidates, overtly or otherwise, as early as the return of the right to government in the Spring of 1993. For others, lacking the support of a party machine, circumstances dictated a much shorter-lived campaign; or even, in the case of some would-be contenders, spectacularly absent from the fray, none at all.[1] But whatever the duration or orientation of the various campaigns which made up this bitter presidential election, candidates from all points on the political spectrum would have derived from their dealings with the business community an overriding impression of 'business as usual',[2] bordering on indifference.

Officially, the main employers' organisation, the Conseil National du Patronat Français (CNPF), professed neutrality towards the elections. Unofficially, however, this veneer of aloofness seemed to mask a reality which was potentially more disturbing: 'We are disconnected', claimed one CNPF official,[3] almost as if 'splendid neutrality' were in fact a convenient disguise for lack, or loss, of interest. The business magazine *Capital* described the election as a 'bizarre campaign', characterised, paradoxically, by consensus, bickering and silence,[4] an indication perhaps of a business community somewhat at odds with the world of politics.

There was apparently little logical reason for the business community to become impassioned by the campaign. After all, the financial markets had clearly anticipated the victory of a right-wing candidate – as predicted by countless opinion polls since March 1993, when the left had been so unceremoniously ousted from government with 17.6% of the suffrage, and as confirmed by the left's performance in the European elections of June 1994, when they sank to a new low with only 14.5% of votes cast. The identity of that presumed conservative victor, on the other hand, seemed to matter relatively little. Neutrality was, of course, a safer option than favouritism: currying favour with one conservative candidate to the annoyance of the other would have been an unnecessarily risky strategy when a right-wing victory seemed guaranteed. The currency markets assumed that, whether Jacques Chirac or, more probably, Edouard Balladur were at the helm (the latter's success being taken as a foregone conclusion when he announced his candidacy on 18 January 1995), 'la politique unique' would continue, that is to say, the franc would continue to be pegged to the mark within the Exchange Rate Mechanism of the European Monetary System. Introduced by the Socialists in the late 1980s, this policy of keeping a strong franc, 'le franc fort', had come to epitomise financial orthodoxy. It had been maintained by the right-wing majority since 1993 – even if, with the franc buffeted by the turmoil in international currency markets triggered by the sudden collapse of the dollar vis-à-vis the yen and the mark in the Spring of 1995, the policy of the 'franc fort' had of late given way almost imperceptibly to the new and more achievable policy of a 'franc stable'. The victory of outgoing Prime Minister Edouard Balladur would thus guarantee continuity. At no point before the first round of the election did the markets seriously consider the possibility that a left-wing candidate might conceivably be returned to the Elysée. In the event, the unexpected victory of Lionel Jospin in the first round on 23 April caught the markets off-guard. The franc lost value overnight, falling from 3.57 francs to the mark on Sunday evening to 3.585 by Monday morning, close to its record low of 3.59, achieved on 8 March 1995.[5] The uncertainty caused by Jospin's surprise first-round win was, however, less significant than that prompted by the previous week's spat between Jacques Chirac and the governor of the Bank of France, Jean-Claude Trichet, when Chirac had hinted that there might be higher priorities than the defence of the currency. Then the loss in the value of the franc had been greater (from 3.4814 francs to the mark to 3.5250),[6] a sign perhaps that financial orthodoxy and currency stability – the guarantee of continuity – mattered more to the markets than any political 'upset'. These were incidental events. On the whole, the markets took the 1995 presidential elections in their stride, less concerned by the actual outcome than by future presidential and government action, for which (potentially at least) they reserved their sanction.

The second reason for the business community's apparent indifference to the election had to do with the very limited margin of manœuvre for action which any President would have at his disposal. The concept of a limited margin of manœuvre is a familiar one to French businessmen: 'Marge' and 'Manœuvre' even appear as comic characters in a regular column in the business monthly *Alternatives économiques*! It was precisely because of such restricted room for manœuvre, both economic and political, as well as for personal reasons that Jacques Delors, an early opinion poll favourite to win the race to the Elysée, took the decision in December 1994 not to stand for election.[7] Having enjoyed for a decade the far-reaching powers which accrue to the President of the European Commission, Delors had no desire to play the much diminished role of an 'idle king', which would have been compounded in his case by a massive right-wing majority in the National Assembly.[8]

So, despite the incessant chorus of change on the part of those who, in the Spring of 1995, emerged as the three leading contenders (the only three of nine pretenders to the Elysée who could seriously presume to succeed),[9] the business community did not apparently expect change to occur. On the contrary, it assumed that the liberal economic programme combined with tight monetarist and budgetary policies pursued before the election (summarised by one former director of a leading French petrochemical company as 'Jacobin liberalism watched over by the State'[10]) would continue thereafter. The increased internationalisation of world economies in the 1970s and 1980s had curtailed the powers of the state to effect change at a national level. This had been the hard lesson learned by the first Mitterrand government experiment of 1981-1982. In the teeth of acute competition in global markets, which government action is almost powerless to allay, it is understandable that big business in particular should see the cut-and-thrust of electoral debate as largely irrelevant to its concerns. As Jean-Louis Servan-Schreiber writes:

The disappearance of planning, the lowering of protective barriers, the global trivialisation of technical competence, the melting-pot of international finance, the undermining of the collective representation of business (professional associations and the CNPF) are all symptoms of the same phenomenon: the intensification of competition, of the combat engaged in by each enterprise against all others.[11]

Government room for manœuvre, already severely curtailed by the realities of economic interdependence, had been further and most dramatically reduced by the Treaty on European Union signed at Maastricht in February 1992. Critically, in preparation for economic and monetary union (EMU), the Treaty had established a number of 'convergence criteria', designed to ensure the close coordination of economic policies and the sustained convergence of economic performances among European Union member states. Two of these convergence criteria were of particular import: the size of government deficits and levels of national debt. An excessive deficit was defined as one which exceeded 3% of gross domestic product (GDP), whether forecast or actual. At the same time, the stock of national debt was to be monitored in member states, and where the ratio of debt to GDP was greater than 60%, punitive measures against the recalcitrant member state would be triggered.[12] Sanctions included inviting the European Investment Bank to reconsider its lending policy towards the state concerned, obliging the member state to make a sizeable, non-interest-bearing deposit with the Community until the deficit had been corrected, and imposing fines of an appropriate size.[13] A meeting of heads of government was arranged for 31 December 1996, at which point it would be decided whether a sufficient number of member states fulfilled the necessary criteria for the adoption of a single currency. Those that did not would be dubbed 'member states with a derogation',[14] and their voting rights on the Council of Ministers suspended accordingly. But it is clear that, for France, far worse than the threat of any sanctions would be the threat of not qualifying to proceed to the next stage of EMU. If it were indeed the case that an inner core of high performance member states were to move on to EMU in advance of the others, the blow to Gallic pride were France to be excluded from the 'high table' through failure to qualify was not one which could easily be countenanced.

In December 1993, with the French budget deficit running at 6.1% of GDP, the Balladur government had set a government deficit target of 2.5% of GDP by 1997. Nevertheless, after considerable efforts at economising on the budget,[15] several privatisations later[16] and despite a healthy growth rate of 2.6% for 1994,[17] on the eve of the presidential election campaign France was still running a budget deficit of some FF442 billion,[18] equal to 6% of a gross domestic product worth FF7,376 billion. Meanwhile, the size of the national debt had swollen to FF2,900 billion. It was predicted to rise to FF3,200 billion by the end of 1995 – this being the best case scenario, good management permitting. But by the end of June 1995, the Budget (the *loi de finance initiale*) had already been revised to allow for increased expenditure. And while this level of debt did not infringe the Maastricht Treaty's convergence criterion regarding debt, merely to service it would eat up one fifth of annual tax receipts.[19] It would appear then that, in France in the 1990s, prudent fiscal management (which Balladur strove to embody, and almost succeeded, give or take the odd scandal!) is not in itself sufficient to reduce the budget deficit, nor is healthy economic growth adequate to cut unemployment,[20] which remained obstinately stuck at 12.6% throughout 1994 – a reflection, perhaps, of just how narrow are the straits which define the limits of government action.

Finally meaning business? The thorny issue of employers' charges

French business is not, of course, a homogeneous bloc, but a patchwork of some 4 million businesses, large and small, represented in their dealings with government by a wide variety of trade associations, lobbies and pressure groups, each waving the banner of its own interests. In these circumstances, is it really possible to speak of a cohesive business community unified by common concerns?

There was one issue which came to the fore during the election which did matter to employers, indeed which mattered very much despite their ostensible neutrality, and where, in contrast to inimical global waters which businesses must navigate unaided, the new President might well be in a position to make a sizeable difference to their lot. This was the thorny issue of tax and social security payments by employers, heavier and more punitive in France than in any of her major competitors or European partners. In 1994, the monthly cost to an employer for each employee earning the minimum wage was in excess of FF8,000, more than FF2,000 above the minimum wage itself (FF6,000), once national insurance payments ('cotisations maladie') and family allowance benefits ('allocations familiales') were added. (In other European countries, the latter are paid for centrally rather than by employers). In the run-up to the 1995 presidential elections, French employers demanded a reduction in these social charges, as indeed they had many times in the past. Championing their cause was the new President of the CNPF, Jean Gandois, elected as the successor to François Périgot in December 1994. A product of the prestigious 'grandes écoles' (the Ecole Polytechnique and the Ecole des Ponts et Chaussées), and formerly chairman of the aluminium and metal container giant Pechiney, Gandois sought to counter his image as a 'big company man' by seeking also vigorously to represent the small and medium-sized business sector, whose interests are normally the preserve of the CGPME (Confédération Générale des Petites et Moyennes Entreprises).[21] What is noteworthy about the 1995 presidential elections is that for the first time it seemed as if employers' demands did *not* fall upon deaf ears; on the contrary, all three leading candidates took note; and one of these, Jacques Chirac, seemed to take particular note.

The burden of social welfare on employment had long been a cause of friction between employers and government. Under the centre-right administrations of Valéry Giscard d'Estaing (1974-1981), compulsory deductions ('les prélèvements obligatoires') had increased by one percentage point per year from 35% of GDP in 1974 to 42.5% by the end of his presidency, as the French economy went ever deeper into recession.[22] The CNPF had already burnt its boats with Giscard, having withdrawn its support from him during his 1974 presidential campaign, preferring neutrality. Its bargaining power thus diminished, an uneasy stalemate between 'patronat' and President ensued throughout his mandate.[23]

With the election of François Mitterrand in 1981, relations between 'patronat' and government turned overtly hostile. This was hardly surprising. The brunt of the costs of the radical social programme implemented by the new left-wing administration immediately following its accession to office was borne by business. These included the 39-hour week; the fifth week of paid holiday; the Auroux laws; the raising of the minimum wage; the increase in social security payments by employers; and the increase in the business rate ('taxe professionnelle').[24] The CNPF calculated the cost on business of the first two items alone to amount to FF60 billion, with the additional charges bringing the total costs to FF95-100 billion. The result was a tax and social security burden on French business which, the CNPF claimed, was twice that of its principal competitors.[25] On 10 March 1982, in an interview published in *Le Monde*, the then president of the CNPF, Yvon Gattaz, himself an entrepreneur, denounced the 'bleeding dry' of business by government: 'I know that our discourse on employers' payments is always greeted with a certain scepticism. [...] But it is as an economic expert that I raise the alarm [..]: our firms are being bled dry; we must put a stop to this haemorrhage imposed in the name of social progress'.[26] What is interesting about this remark is that the refrain which Yvon Gattaz reiterated many times to the Prime Minister of the day, Pierre Mauroy, would not have been out of place in 1995 delivered by Jean Gandois to the principal presidential hopefuls:

> If you want to cut unemployment, Yvon Gattaz repeated unremittingly to Pierre Mauroy, you must stimulate growth. If you want to stimulate growth, you must respect economic balance. If you want to respect economic balance, you must encourage exports. If you want to encourage exports, you must improve the competitiveness of firms and stimulate investment. If you want companies to invest, you must allow them to improve their margins, reduced to an all-time low in 1981, and to achieve that you must stabilise and then reduce employers' tax and social security payments. If you want firms to take on more workers – in particular the small- and medium-sized sector, with its greater scope for recruitment – you must cut the cost of employment, by lessening the dual burden of employers' payments and legal constraints. If we remain in an 'open economy' [...], it becomes all the more imperative to draw this series of conclusions.[27]

Relations between 'patronat' and government became less conflictual with the left's U-turn on economic policy in 1983 and subsequent 'discovery of the firm' in 1984. There emerged a successful and enduring consensus; but the effect of the rehabilitation of the firm in French public opinion paradoxically was to undermine the CNPF as a representative body. In the early 1990s, the organisation was further damaged by the sheer number of prominent companies or business figures tainted by allegations of financial scandal or improper meddling in politics. In 1994, Budget Minister Nicolas Sarkozy was able to dismiss the CNPF as merely another 'lobby' – a remark Gandois, then campaigning for its presidency, found 'insulting', but which nevertheless reflected the relative decline of its power base. Employer tax and social security charges had continued their relentless rise throughout the Mitterrand presidency, despite the clamour for their reduction which was heard once again in the run-up to the 1988 presidential elections.[28] They subsequently enjoyed a brief decline, only to rise again in 1989. On the eve of the 1995 presidential elections, compulsory deductions accounted for more than 50% of GDP. This compared with much lesser burdens on France's main competitors: approximately 44% in Germany, 42% in the UK, 33% in the United States, and 29% in Japan.[29]

Why, then, should presidential candidates be more receptive to employers' arguments about tax and social security payments in 1995, when these had not been heard in 1974 or 1981, and only partially in 1988? The explanation for this lies in the domain of perceptions as much as in that of statistics. Two themes had come to particular prominence in the run-up to the election: unemployment and exclusion, the first perceived as the antichamber to the second. If, in the summer of 1994, 3.338 million were registered as active job-seekers with the Agence Nationale pour l'Emploi (ANPE),[30] in reality as many as 5 million individuals were believed to be outside the system. Getting more people into work seemed the obvious way of combatting the developing phenomenon of social exclusion. The 'fight for jobs' became the hobby horse for all candidates, and 'the absolute priority, to which everything else must be subordinate' for the eventual victor Jacques Chirac.[31] By its scale and persistence even in times of economic growth (forecast at 2.9% for 1995),[32] France's unemployment had revealed itself as structural, not cyclical. And while the root causes of the problem were debatable,[33] the onerous cost of employment was pinpointed not only as a major culprit (being at once a disincentive to hiring and an incentive to firing), but also as something which a new President could actually do something about. While in 1994 the cost to the firm of an employee earning the minimum wage was estimated at FF96,000 per annum, the cost to society of the average unemployed person was calculated at the significantly higher annual rate of FF122,700.[34] Any cheaper alternative to existing policies was *de facto* worthy of consideration. The additional burden on business of an overly generous pay-as-you-go pension scheme, whereby employers and employees pay directly for those who are retired (the height of absurdities being that in France the average pension exceeds average earnings!), without the pension funds urgently needed to make the system sustainable, was a separate but related issue. Therefore, Chirac argued, borrowing from the ideas of the arch-liberal Alain Madelin and, to a lesser extent, the social Gaullist Philippe Séguin, it was time to alleviate the burden on business. In particular, the social security contributions for certain categories of workers should be reduced in the hope that this might stimulate job creation on a scale sufficient to bring down unemployment:

> We need a global policy more favourable to employment and the entrepreneur: more accessible financial resources, a tax and social security system more favorable to employment and investment, an administrative burden considerably lightened. [...] We need a great taxation reform to encourage business initiative.[35]

The French business class is used to being blamed for France's misfortunes, the classic example of this being de Gaulle's celebrated rebuke, 'Où étiez-vous, messieurs?', following allegations of collaboration during the Occupation. In 1995, the finger was again being pointed at employers, this time for their perceived 'headlong rush to productivity',[36] for having become exclusively preoccupied with competitiveness and profitability to the detriment of wider social considerations, with the result that in the industrial sector, employment had consistently declined as efficiency gains were achieved. The remedy, in Chirac's eyes, was the creation of 'l'entreprise-citoyenne': a corporate sector exercising civic responsibility, playing an active role in the battle against unemployment and thereby helping to remedy the effective exclusion of many of the labour force from the prospect of real work.

The original linkage of business enterprise with citizenship was certainly not Chirac's. He did, however, discuss the idea at length in both *Une Nouvelle France* and *La France pour tous*. Chirac conceived of citizenship as the successor to de Gaulle's dream of 'the association of capital and labour' which he later came to call 'participation'. Interestingly, Jean Gandois had played a major role in the recent promotion of 'l'entreprise-citoyenne'. Despite the traditional CNPF emphasis on the virtues of free enterprise and the employers' right to represent their own interests, it was precisely on this platform that Jean Gandois campaigned for the presidency of the organisation. More consensual than previous CNPF presidents, Gandois proposed that national negotiations should be held between employers and trade unions after the elections, in order to debate what could best be done by both sides to stimulate employment and create a healthier social and industrial milieu. Given this shared ideal, a meeting point was thus possible between 'patronat' and government – or at least between Gandois and Chirac – based on the following deal:

> the purpose of a firm cannot be reduced to its ability, which is clearly necessary, to make a profit; it must become a place of citizenship and, to that end, welcome young people in search of their first job as well as adults engaged in retraining. Let us give entrepreneurs the means to achieve this, by including part of their social security

payments in the general budget. One simple principle must prevail: it is far better to pay for an unemployed person to return to work than to pay him to do nothing.[37]

Reduced to its essentials, the promise held out by Chirac to the business community was effectively one of a 'partnership' between government and business, whereby government would assume a share of the burden of employers' social security payments by incorporating these into the general budget, in return for which business would behave in a more socially responsible manner, particularly with respect to the recruitment of the young and long-term unemployed, to the benefit of society as a whole.

If the focus of much of this chapter has been on Jacques Chirac, to the exclusion of his rival candidates, this is not because the 1995 presidential elections represented a one-horse race; they did not. They were, as suggested in our introduction, a *three*-horse race; but one in which one of the non-runners (Delors) featured more prominently than some of the also-rans (Voynet, de Villiers and Cheminade). However, there is a very real sense in which Chirac sought to reach out to the business community and its concerns in a way in which the others did not.

Business community perceptions of the key contenders

All three main candidates claimed that the election was not intended as a war of personalities: Chirac urged 'a real debate of ideas, eliminating, for once, the perpetual rivalries of personalities'[38]; Balladur aimed to run a campaign which would be 'positive, serene and optimistic'[39]; while Jospin sought to focus the debate on the traditional left-right divide. But with vagueness on the part of all three main candidates clouding much of the debate, coupled with differentiation between Balladur and Chirac necessitating fratricide at the heart of the RPR (Rassemblement pour la République), it was in fact the individual personalities of the contenders which in many ways came to the fore. These – or rather perceptions of these – became the centre of their appeal (or lack of appeal) to the business community.

Edouard Balladur: forgotten promises, abortive projects?[40]

For the CNPF, a major achievement of Balladur's premiership was undoubtedly his role in the successful conclusion of a GATT deal (General Agreement on Tariffs and Trade) in December 1993, rendered all the sweeter by the last-minute concessions for French agri-business and the audio-visual sector wrest by Balladur from the negotiations. On the other hand, his effective surrender to striking Air France employees only one month before, in November 1993, was perceived as a major defeat, both real and symbolic. To the CNPF, Balladur was perceived above all as a man who promised much but who ultimately failed to deliver, held in the immobilising grip of 'an excessive degree of caution',[41] whose new legislation was extensive, but the application of which was continually found to be wanting, whose projects began with a reassuring bang only to end in a disappointing whimper.

There are many illustrations of this. In 1993, for example, the Balladur government had engaged in 'une relance sans le dire', a reflation which did not speak its name. Lacking the necessary impetus, however, it ultimately proved to be abortive. Likewise, on 25 August 1993, Balladur announced that long-term business gains on shares in SICAV ('sociétés d'investissement à capital variable'), taxed at 25%, would henceforth be tax exempt, provided that the proceeds were invested in property. Two days later, Budget Minister Sarkozy elaborated on the proposal, this time specifying an upper limit of FF 1,200,000, and explaining that the measure applied to couples only, with a personal limit of FF600,000 each. In other words, during the intervening forty-eight hours the goal-posts had moved: the measure did not now concern corporate investors, who nevertheless would have been in a position to stimulate the stagnant property market.[42] Promises to reform the business rate ('taxe professionnelle'), as part of a great 'revolution' carried out by Interior Minister Charles Pasqua, were side-stepped. And while Balladur promised to double the number of young people engaged in training programmes and apprenticeships, the reality fell considerably short of the desire. The number of those participating in such schemes increased only slightly: from 406,000 in March 1993 to 432,000 by September 1994.[43] The CNPF's overall verdict on Balladur can be summarised as follows: 'He didn't want to take any risks, he didn't want to change the course of history'.[44] Reviewing Balladur's achievements over two years, *Le Monde* drew the same conclusion: 'His initiatives appear more like a panoply of texts signalling good intentions [...]. This is clearly the case as far as unemployment and employment are concerned'.[45] Chirac was in evident agreement with this analysis: 'When prudence is everywhere, courage is nowhere'.[46] In Balladur's defence, however, one might say that one was treating the regent as if he were the king. Whoever ultimately became President in 1995, the cohabitation of 1993-95 was essentially an interim, when no major economic projects could be realised on a grand scale, given the nature of the political conjuncture.

Lionel Jospin: an honest broker, promising little

The business community never seriously entertained the possibility of a left-wing successor to Mitterrand. That said, and despite Jospin's relatively late entry to the race (not until February 1995 did he secure the Socialist Party's nomination), the CNPF did prepare in-house briefing notes on Jospin in January 1995. These notes, intended to brief the CNPF executive on presidential candidates, sought to outline Jospin's politics and preferences. Inevitably sparse, Jospin being something of an unknown quantity at the time, they highlighted in particular his reserve regarding the *franc fort* and the Maastricht Treaty. His reticence regarding the Socialist Party's programme as agreed in 1994 was approved, notably his silence over the stated objective of a 35-hour working week. Jospin's attitude to employers' social security payments was, however, seen as less encouraging. In Jospin's view, the state should not to have to 'pick up the tab' for what he perceived as employers' attempts to cut costs:

> What is the point of systematically cutting the cost of labour [..] at the microeconomic level, at the level of the firm – in the name of adjusting to international competition – if the burden is merely shifted to the macroeconomic level, to the level of society as a whole, which finds the cost ever harder to bear?[47]

Jospin's economic programme later crystallised around several key concepts: a 37-hour week by 1997; higher salaries in the interests of a fairer distribution of profit; and the exemption from social security contributions of the first FF5,000 of monthly salary. The business community's general perception of Jospin was of an honest broker who, in his favour, had refrained from making too many promises which he might one day have to betray. In the run-up to the second round, the view was even expressed by the business community that a victory for Jospin, who had promised relatively little, might even be better than one for Chirac, who had raised so many expectations that, with the margins of manœuvre such as they were, he could not fail to disappoint.

Jacques Chirac: a kick-start to the economy?

Throughout his campaign, in contrast to his rivals, Chirac had seemed at least to try to put himself in the shoes of France's businessmen, forever frustrated in their attempts to bring down employer tax and social security payments. He stressed his appreciation of their efforts, striving in particular to reach out to the small businessman:

> I know and appreciate the formidable potential of our large industrial and service companies [...]. But I would like to emphasize one of the particularities of our country: the strength of the small- and medium-sized business sector. This accounts for almost 6 jobs out of every 10, more than 50% of our national wealth, and an irreplaceable share of our exports.[48]

Chirac had certainly listened attentively, much of his campaign material giving the concerted impression of a pensive Chirac hearing and heeding France's calls for help. For employers, what he promised amounted almost to the perfect package: reduced employer social security contributions for lower salaries, and lower taxes (a reformed succession law in particular). His *pièce de résistance* was a job-creation scheme designed to encourage employers to recruit the long-term unemployed, the 'contrat initiative-emploi' (CIE). According to this, employers would receive the sum of FF2,000 per month for a period of two years for hiring an unemployed person who had been registered with the ANPE for over a year (less than a year for jobless over fifty years of age, as it emerged when the proposal became law on 1 July 1995).[49] During this time, employers would be exempt from paying social security charges for that part of the employee's salary equal to the minimum wage. The CNPF's view was that such measures, together with lower taxes, would help to produce the necessary 'kick-start to get the French economy moving'.[50] But the problem was that Chirac had promised 'all things to all men': wage rises for the salaried; salaries for mothers; the maintenance of the minimum wage; more spending on health, education and culture. At the same time, he was also proposing to get the budget deficit down and reduce the national debt! And all of this was to be financed purely by a slight increase either in the CSG ('contribution sociale généralisée') or in the rate of value-added tax (VAT), the 'kick-started' economy (according to the ideas of Alain Madelin) being relied upon to provide the wherewithal to fund all the rest.

The 'patronat' at the polls

Overall, the preferred candidate of an initially indifferent 'patronat' in the 1995 presidential elections became Jacques Chirac. In fact, Chirac emerged as the business community's favoured candidate prior to becoming front runner in the national polls. Previously, Balladur had been the favourite to succeed. An opinion poll carried out by *L'Expansion* in January 1994 revealed that 53% of business heads considered Balladur the best man for the job, as against only 21% for Chirac. By the summer of 1994, however, the tide had turned in Chirac's favour.[51] A panel of businessmen consulted by *L'Expansion* in June forecast a clear win for Chirac (47%, as against 42% for Balladur). When probed as to their personal preferences, the result was somewhat closer, with 38% supporting Chirac and 34% Balladur. No Socialist candidate was considered to be in the running. With a score of only 2% (prediction to win) and 6% (personal preference), Delors achieved the highest of any figure of the left – although we must remember that this was in the immediate aftermath of the European elections, so disastrous for the Socialists.[52]

Meanwhile, a regular opinion poll measuring the satisfaction of business chiefs with the Balladur government (carried out by Louis Harris for *Enjeux-Les Echos* and *France Info*) found the business community relatively satisfied with the government's performance for most of Balladur's premiership. The turning-point occurred with the revelations over the Halphen-Schuller-Maréchal phone-tapping scandal in February 1995, tarring Balladur himself with the brush of sleaze which had been gradually tainting so many of his cabinet.[53] Interestingly, this particular poll remarked on a difference of opinion between the heads of large and small businesses. Those in charge of large enterprises (more than 200 employees) were more likely to be relatively satisfied with the government's performance, whereas those running smaller businesses were more likely to express discontent, reflective of a desire for far-reaching change. On the date of the first round of the election, when the panoply of choice was still theirs, 33% of those describing themselves as 'heads of industry and commerce' voted for Chirac as against 25% for Balladur, 13% for Jospin and 12% for Le Pen.[54]

After the election: continuity or change?

Great expectations, if unfulfilled, can lead to great disappointment. President Chirac promised sweeping change in his election manifesto, and a clean break with the previous two years of 'cohabitation'. No longer should priority be given to reducing the budget deficit at the expense of employment. No longer should the running of the country be in the hands of technocrats and 'énarques',[55] dominated by fiscal and budgetary concerns which stifle investment and initiative. No longer should entrepreneurs have to compete in a business world rendered more hostile by the severity of the tax and social security contributions imposed on them by their own government. But, as we remarked at the beginning of this chapter, with the margins of manœuvre so tight, how was such an ambitious electoral programme to be put into practice? More importantly, how was it to be funded?

Chirac had carefully stuck to the broad outline of his programme during his presidential campaign, steering clear of the distasteful details of costs. But with election to high office comes the need to address such matters. In June 1995, far from lowering taxes as promised, the VAT rate was raised from 18.6% to 20%. Admittedly, Chirac had signalled a likely increase either in the CSG or in the VAT rate in the event of his being elected; but VAT is an indiscriminate tax which hits hardest at the lowest paid, unemployed and excluded. The rise, though inevitable, ill suited Chirac's new and much cultivated image of a caring President with a social conscience. VAT was not, however, the only tax to be raised immediately. In a symbolic gesture, signalling that times were hard and that the rich should therefore also feel the pinch, the higher rate of wealth tax ('l'impôt de solidarité sur la fortune') was increased by 10%. Chirac had deliberately comforted the French electorate with the illusion that tax reform meant tax reduction, despite the obvious question mark over the funding of his job creation scheme. No country in Europe had been blessed by tax cuts since 1992, and it was inconceivable that France, which already had one of the lowest rates of income tax in the EU,[56] should hope to buck the trend in the prevailing climate. Surveying the minefield of 'droits acquis' (tax exemptions which, once acquired, assume the status of rights too sacred to withdraw)[57] which is France's tax system, and musing on the difficulty of implementing tax reform in a country where the electoral sun never sets, the business magazine *L'Expansion* concluded: 'The fiscal "big bang" will not take place'.[58] For the time being, it seemed that Chirac would have to wait to fulfil his election promise of tax cuts. However politically desirable the latter might be, economic realities, the constraints of Maastricht and even his own job creation scheme demanded that a much tighter ship be steered across troubled economic waters.

The tax increases which occurred in the wake of the presidential elections were, nevertheless, relatively minor. They were certainly unequal to Chirac's ambitious job-creation scheme (particularly since tax receipts were found to be down for the year 1995), swiftly implemented on 1 July with, as promised, a monthly subsidy of FF2,000 to employers coupled with the anticipated reduction in social security contributions for workers recruited under the scheme. What this initiative would cost was anybody's guess. The new government under Alain Juppé floated the figure of FF28 billion.[59] Less optimistically, and doubtless with malicious intent, the Balladur camp had already costed Chirac's electoral programme at the enormous figure of FF500-600 billion.[60] To fund it, in their view, would necessitate a 4-5% increase in the VAT rate, far in excess of the actual 1.4% rise introduced.

At the G7 summit of industrial nations held in Halifax, Canada, in mid-June 1995, President Chirac sang a different song to the one he had intoned throughout his electoral campaign. Barely five weeks after his election to the Elysée on a platform of prioritising employment, Chirac now promised to make it his priority after all to keep public spending down in order to meet the Maastricht criteria for monetary union. With the hole in the social security fund growing (FF65billion at the time of Chirac's election, and expected to reach FF120 billion by 1996), with privatisation receipts for 1995 now expected to yield only FF40-45 billion as opposed to the FF55 billion originally estimated – proceeds which, in any case, could no longer be used to fund current expenditure, given the Maastricht rules – the margins of presidential manœuvre were as tight as ever before. Only two weeks into Chirac's mandate, a report on the future of France to the year 2000 announced that job creation on a scale sufficient to bring down unemployment was quite simply incompatible with parallel attempts to reduce public deficits. Predicting a negligeable improvement in the unemployment rate by the turn of the century (200,000 fewer jobless), the author noted: 'This result derives from the context of a policy to reduce public deficits which is particularly *ambitious*. It follows that a budgetary policy which aimed at a more *progressive* reduction of public deficits would result in a more rapid increase in jobs created'.[61]

In view of the sweeping promises made by Chirac to the business community, there is good reason to assume that the *patronat* will once again be frustrated in its demands, and that the next presidential election will find it with new grounds for remaining at one remove from the electoral process. Perhaps by then it will have learned, as Chirac himself learned through Balladur's betrayal, that promises in politics commit nobody but those who listen to them.

Conclusion

'Politics', Chirac said somewhat unoriginally during his election campaign, 'is the art of making possible that which is necessary'. French entrepreneurs, who, together with tax-payers, had shouldered for too long the burden of balancing the books of government spending, were in no doubt as to what precisely was necessary in 1995: large tax cuts in order to stimulate investment, thereby creating the vital conditions for healthy economic growth which alone could shrink the dole queues. Their relative indifference to the electoral process can be explained by the continual failure of former Presidents and their respective governments to get to grips with this crucial matter. This time, such a course was urged by free-marketeer Alain Madelin as the only one capable of achieving the reduction in unemployment which had been President Chirac's stated priority throughout his election campaign. Madelin's dismissal from the post of Finance Minister only three months after his appointment, however, suggested that it would not be followed. The 1996 budget, unveiled in September 1995, revealed itself as an austerity package which, while designed to reduce the public deficit to 3.55% of GDP in 1996, nevertheless did no more than tinker with its root cause: government spending, which had long been out of control. Without much needed tax reform, without the unpalatable policies needed to curb public spending, the prognosis for private enterprise remained gloomy indeed. Business investment continued to suffer from the government's greed for funds, while monetary union, now firmly at the top of the priority pecking order, may well be achieved by the end of the century – but perhaps only at the expense of further inflated dole queues. Ultimately, one is forced to conclude that while presidential candidate Chirac justly perceived what was necessary, President Chirac perhaps lacked the political courage to – in his own words – make the necessary possible.

Notes

(The author wishes to thank Jacques Lauze and Michel Drain of the Commission des Finances, Assemblée Nationale, Jean-Pierre Helbert of the CNPF and Alain Raoux of the Présidence, Assemblée Nationale, for their kind assistance in the research for this chapter).

[1] The familiar faces of Raymond Barre and Valéry Giscard d'Estaing were conspicuously absent from the final line-up of candidates. Similarly absent was the notorious entrepreneur, Bernard Tapie, long tipped by opinion polls as a potential contender for the Elysée, but in the event prevented from realising that ambition had he so desired by a prison sentence for match-rigging in connection with his football interests. Jacques Calvet, head of Peugeot-Citroën SA, had announced his candidature for the presidency as early as 1991, but subsequently withdrew from the contest: this was a publicity stunt designed to focus attention on the July 1991 car agreement between the European Commission and Japan's Ministry of International Trade and Industry (MITI), which Calvet regarded as being against the interests of French and European manufacturers. But the most noticeable absentee of all was of course Jacques Delors, expected to secure the presidency in the autumn of 1994, only to renounce the challenge in December.

[2] The title of George Jones's chapter on the business community and the 1988 presidential elections: 'Business as usual: the employers', in J. Gaffney (ed.), *The French Presidential Elections of 1988: Ideology and Leadership in Contemporary France* (Aldershot, Dartmouth, 1989), pp.185-210.

[3] Personal interview with the author, January 1995, Paris.

[4] 'Election présidentielle', *Capital*, April 1995, p.18.

[5] See 'Les marchés financiers pris à contre-pied ont réagi par un repli immédiat', *Le Monde*, 25 April 1995.

[6] See 'Risques monétaires pour l'après-présidentielle', *Le Journal de Finances*, 22 April 1995.

[7] See for example 'Delors bows out of contest for French presidency', *The Financial Times*, 12 December 1994.

[8] *Ibid.*

[9] 'The choice is between continuity and change', ran Chirac's campaign refrain; 'change without rupture' was adopted as Balladur's slogan; while '*real* change' became Jospin's catch-phrase, particularly following his first-round win.

[10] Personal interview with the author, January 1995, Paris.

[11] 'La disparition de la planification, l'abaissement des barrières protectrices, la banalisation mondiale des compétences techniques, les brassages financiers internationaux, l'affaiblissement de la représentation collective des entreprises (fédérations professionnelles et CNPF) sont les symptômes d'un même mouvement: l'intensification de la concurrence, du combat mené par chaque entreprise face à toutes les autres'. Jean-Louis Servan-Schreiber, *Le Métier de patron* (Paris, Fayard, 1990), p.192. Unless otherwise indicated, all translations are the author's.

[12] See 'Protocol on the excessive deficit procedure' annexed to the Maastricht Treaty, articles 1-3.

[13] See article 104c of the Maastricht Treaty.

[14] *Ibid.*, article 109k.

[15] FF18 billion of public expenditure had been frozen by the Balladur government.

[16] During the Balladur premiership, the following state-owned companies were privatised: BNP (Banque Nationale de Paris) in 1993; Elf-Aquitaine, UAP (Union des Assurances de Paris) and Renault in 1994; and SEITA (Société Nationale d'Exploitation des Tabacs et Alumettes) in 1995. Altogether as much as FF93.4 billion was raised from their sale. Balladur intended to use the bulk of the proceeds to fund 'les dépenses courantes' of the State, that is to say routine expenditure which would normally be funded by the budget. However, according to the Maastricht Treaty's convergence criteria, member states are not permitted to use the proceeds from the sale of state-owned assets to reduce their budget deficits. This is to facilitate comparison between federal states, such as Germany, and non-federal states. The proceeds may, on the other hand, be used to reduce the national debt.

[17] Figures given in 'Les comptes de la nation', *Politique économique française ('Les notes bleues de Bercy')*, no. 64, 1-15 June 1995, p.4.

[18] The 1994 deficit was compounded by the writing-off of FF 22 billion of debt owed by developing African nations and former French colonies. Four (Cameroon, Congo, the Ivory Coast and Gabon) had their debt halved, while ten others (Benin, Burkina Faso, Comoro, Guinea, Mali, Niger, the Central African Republic, Senegal, Chad and Togo) had their debt written off completely.

[19] CNPF, 'Il n'y a pas de marge de manœuvre budgétaire', *Cartes sur table 1994*, p.27.

[20] France enjoyed sustained, if modest, economic growth from 1990 to 1995, with the sole exception of 1993, when growth declined by 1.4%. *Ibid.*, p.3.

[21] See 'CNPF: budgétiser les cotisations maladie', *L'Expansion*, 6-19 February 1995, p.88. By representing the interests of the small business sector, Gandois hoped also to arrest the relative decline of the CNPF as a representative organisation.

[22] See Henri Weber, *Le Parti des patrons: le CNPF (1946-1986)* (Paris, Seuil, 1986), p.330.

[23] Joseph Szarka, *Business in France: an Introduction to the Economic and Social Context* (London, Pitman, 1992), p.173.

[24] Broadly comparable to the British business rate, the *taxe professionnelle* is paid to the local authorities (*communes*), which have the right to tax economic activities taking place on their territory. For a detailed discussion of this tax, see George Jones, *op. cit.*, pp.193-194.

[25] The Mauroy government disputed these calculations, estimating the combined cost to business of the 39-hour week and the fifth week of paid holiday at FF15-18 billion, with the additional financial charges bringing the total to FF20-23 billion.

26 'Je sais que notre discours sur les charges est toujours accueilli avec un certain scepticisme [...] C'est en expert économique que je lance ce cri d'alarme [...]: les entreprises sont exsangues, il faut stopper les saignées qu'on leur impose pour financer le progrès social'. Cited in Weber, *op. cit.*, p.330.

27 'Si vous souhaitez faire reculer le chômage, répète inlassablement Yvon Gattaz à Pierre Mauroy, il faut relancer la croissance. Si vous voulez relancer la croissance, il faut respecter les grands équilibres. Si vous voulez respecter les grands équilibres, il faut relancer les exportations. Si vous voulez relancer les exportations, il faut améliorer la compétitivité des entreprises, stimuler leurs investissements. Si vous voulez que les entreprises investissent, il faut leur permettre de reconstituer leurs marges, tombées à un minimum historique en 1981, et pour cela stabiliser puis réduire leurs charges. Si vous voulez qu'elles embauchent – en particulier celles qui pourraient le faire, les PME –, il faut réduire le coût du travail, sous la double forme d'un allégement des charges et des contraintes légales. Si l'on reste en 'économie ouverte' [...], cette chaîne de déductions s'impose avec une force contraignante'. *Ibid.*, pp.323-324.

28 See Jones, *op. cit.*

29 CNPF, 'La dérive des dépenses collectives', *Cartes sur table 1994*, p.19.

30 The seasonally adjusted number of unemployed, according to the norms of the International Labour Office, totalled 3,175,000 in August 1994.

31 Jacques Chirac, *Une Nouvelle France: rélexions I* (Paris, Nil Editions, 1994), p.19.

32 Economist Intelligence Unit forecast. *EU Country Report: France*, 1st Quarter 1995, p. 7.

33 'Est-ce le coût trop élevé du travail, la crise internationale, l'ouverture des marchés ou le dumping des pays en développement? Doit-on s'en prendre à notre système d'éducation et de formation, à une politique monétaire trop rigoureuse, à une erreur d'appréciation qui nous a conduits à privilégier le traitement social du chômage par rapport à l'effort d'insertion?' Jacques Chirac, *Une Nouvelle France*, *op. cit.*, pp.15-16.

34 Jacques Chirac, interview published in *Les Echos*, 16 January 1995.

35 'Il faut donc une politique globale plus favorable à l'emploi et à l'entrepreneur: des ressources financières plus accessibles, une fiscalité et des charges sociales plus favorables au travail et à l'investissement, des contraintes administratives considérablement allégées. [...] Il faut entreprendre une grande réforme fiscale qui favorise l'initiative'. *Ibid.*

36 Jacques Chirac, *Une Nouvelle France*, *op. cit.*, p.24.

37 'L'utilité de l'entreprise ne se résume pas à sa capacité, évidemment nécessaire, à dégager des profits; elle doit devenir un espace de citoyenneté et, à ce titre, accueillir aussi bien des jeunes en quête d'insertion que des adultes en cours de reconversion. Donnons-en les moyens aux entrepreneurs, en budgétisant une partie des charges sociales. Un principe simple doit prévaloir: mieux vaut payer pour qu'un chômeur retrouve un emploi plutôt que de le payer à ne rien faire'. Jacques Chirac, *La France pour tous* (Paris, Nil Editions, 1994), p.92.

38 Jacques Chirac, *Une Nouvelle France*, *op. cit.*, p.141.

39 Balladur's televised speech in which he announced his candidacy, 18 January 1995.

40 The views put forward in this section are based on interviews carried out by the author at the CNPF, as well as on in-house briefing reports on the main candidates produced by the CNPF between November 1994 and January 1995.

41 Personal interview with the author, CNPF, January 1995, Paris.

[42] The Paris basin, home to the vast majority of large French companies, had been particularly badly affected by tumbling property prices since 1989.

[43] 'Les promesses oubliées de la "réforme"', *Le Monde*, 19 January 1995. This article provides a full account of legislation introduced by the Balladur government, documenting its lack of tangible effect.

[44] Personal interview with the author, CNPF, January 1995, Paris.

[45] 'Les promesses oubliées de la "réforme"', *op. cit.*

[46] Jacques Chirac, *Une Nouvelle France, op. cit.*, p.140.

[47] 'A quoi sert d'alléger systématiquement le coût du travail [...] au niveau macro-économique, au niveau des entreprises – au nom de l'ajustement à la compétition – si le fardeau se retrouve au niveau macro-économique, au niveau de la société toute entière, qui a de plus en plus de mal à en supporter le coût?' From CNPF, 'Les orientations économiques et sociales de Lionel Jospin', 12 January 1995, cited in *Le Monde*, 11 January 1995.

[48] 'Je connais et j'apprécie le formidable potentiel de nos grands groupes industriels et de service [...]. Mais je voudrais insister ici sur une singularité de notre pays: la place occupée par les petites et moyennes entreprises. Près de 6 emplois sur 10, plus de 50% de la richesse nationale, une part irremplaçable de nos exportations'. CNPF, 'Jacques Chirac – éléments de programme présidentiel', 21 December 1994, taken from *Une Nouvelle France, op. cit.*, p.122.

[49] See 'Le contrat initiative-emploi bénéficiera surtout aux chômeurs âgés', *Le Monde*, 21 June 1995.

[50] Personal interview with the author, CNPF, January 1995, Paris.

[51] See 'Les patrons plus confiants', *L'Expansion*, 6-19 January 1994, p.43.

[52] 'Les patrons préfèrent Chirac à Balladur', *L'Expansion*, 30 June-12 July 1994, p.41.

[53] See 'Les chefs d'entreprises préfèrent désormais Chirac à Balladur', *Les Echos*, 6 March 1995, pp.2-3. The level of satisfaction with government performance dropped to 38% in February 1995, as against 55% the previous October.

[54] Percentages according to an exit poll carried out by CSA for *Le Parisien*. See 'Qui a voté pour qui au 1er tour', *Le Parisien*, 24 April 1995.

[55] *Grandes écoles* graduates from the Ecole Nationale d'Administration in particular (of which Chirac himself was one). Chirac denounced their stranglehold on France in his debate with Jospin (also a product of the same system), 2 May 1995.

[56] Only one in two of France's 28 million households pays income tax, which in 1993 yielded only 21.67% of tax receipts totalling FF1,429.63 billion, as against the 43.53% provided by VAT.

[57] These include tax breaks for civil servants and more than a hundred cushioned professions: subsidies are enjoyed by novelists and fashion models, for example. Others, less fortunate, pay income taxes of up to 58%.

[58] See 'Le *big-bang* fiscal n'aura pas lieu', *L'Expansion*, 20 March-2 April 1995, pp.78-81.

[59] Personal interview with the author, June 1995, Commission des Finances, National Assembly, Paris.

[60] Figure cited in 'Les chefs d'entreprise préfèrent désormais Chirac à Balladur', *op. cit.*, p.2.

[61] 'Ce résultat est obtenu dans le cadre d'une politique particulièrement *ambitieuse* de réduction des déficits publics. Aussi faut-il en déduire qu'une politique budgétaire qui viserait une réduction plus *progressive* des déficits se traduirait par une augmentation plus rapide de l'emploi'. Bernard Barbier, 'Une Projection à moyen terme (1944-

2000): tendances macroéconomiques et perspectives pour les finances publiques', *Les Rapports du Sénat*, no. 293, p.14.

Indicative Bibliography

Balladur, E., *Je crois en l'homme plus qu'en l'Etat* (Paris, Flammarion, 1987).

Barbier, B., 'Une Projection à moyen terme (1994-2000): tendances macroéconomiques et perspectives pour les finances publiques', *Les Rapports du Sénat*, 293, 1995.

Chirac, J., *La France pour tous* (Paris, Nil éditions, 1994).

Chirac, J., *Une Nouvelle France: réflexions 1* (Paris, Nil éditions, 1994).

CNPF, *Cartes sur table 1994: vérités sur l'économie française* (Paris, CNPF, 1994).

Delors, J., *L'Unité d'un homme* (Paris, Odile Jacob, 1994).

Demotes-Mainard, M., 'Les comptes de la Nation en 1994', *Politique Economique Française* (*Les notes bleues de Bercy*), 64, 1995.

Peyrelevade, J., *Pour un capitalisme intelligent* (Paris, Grasset & Fasquelle, 1993).

Servan-Schreiber, J.-L., *Le Métier de patron* (Paris, Fayard, 1990).

Szarka, J., *Business in France: an Introduction to the Economic and Social Context* (London, Pitman, 1992).

Weber, H., *Le Parti des patrons: le CNPF (1946-1986)* (Paris, Seuil, 1986).

11. THE TRADE UNIONS AND THE ELECTION

SUSAN MILNER

Introduction

The importance of trade unions in the major defining event of French political life, at a time when France is recognised as having the lowest unionisation rate (around 9%) in the industrial world, may seem rather dubious. But in a country with a traditionally low propensity to join parties and associations and participate in political activism, trade unions remain the single largest form of organised collective action. A membership of around two million may be dramatically low in comparison with France's neighbours (the single largest confederation in Germany, IG Metall, covering only the metal-working industry, boasts more members) but it still dwarfs membership of political parties; the largest confederation alone (the Confédération Française Démocratique du Travail, CFDT) has more members than all France's parties put together. Opinion polls continue to show that a large majority of French people view the trade union movement as indispensable to the practice of democracy. This is not to deny that French trade unions face a crisis of legitimacy. Indeed, the question of their relationship with the political world, which was raised during the 1995 elections with renewed acuity, placed further pressure on the trade unions to define and justify their role. This questioning of the trade unions' position within the polity and within wider society formed the backdrop to events as they related to the trade unions in 1995.

To some extent, the trade unions themselves were marginal actors in the events surrounding the campaign. Two interconnected features of the campaign set the agenda for them. The first was the wave of strike movements which broke out early in 1995. The major trade unions were as ever quick to organise and channel the movements around key demands, but in many cases (as is the norm in France) the conflicts had broken out spontaneously, with specific local or company-based demands. The second was Jacques Chirac's campaign which, in order to mark an ideological separation from the Edouard Balladur government and to increase his own populist appeal, criticised the prevailing orthodoxy of wage restraint. As a result of these twin phenomena, the 1995 presidential campaign was unusual in the prominence given to 'le social'. Elyane Bressol (editor of the weekly magazine published by the second-largest union the Confédération Générale du Travail, CGT) called it an 'atypical' campaign, and forecast an equally atypical post-electoral period.[1] She was right on both counts.

The background

In 1988, the issues defined by the leading candidates (particularly François Mitterrand) cast the presidential campaign in traditional left-right terms which allowed the trade unions to make a choice in favour of the left in the name of republican values, whilst directly trade union issues (such as pay or labour law) were effectively side-stepped. The trade unions were thus able to justify their explicit (CGT) or implicit (CFDT and Force Ouvrière) voting instructions as 'guardians of the republican tradition'.[2] In 1995, however, their position had changed to become, in Michel Noblecourt's words, that of 'spectateurs engagés' ('spectators who felt involved').[3] The trade unions participated much less in the political debates than previously, wanting to retain their autonomy as 'social partners'. Since the outcome of the election was generally expected to be a right-wing victory, this meant neutrality. It was also, commented Noblecourt, as if they had lost their illusions about the nature of power and the ability of politicians to deliver the reforms and guarantees they wanted. More specifically, this disillusionment affected the trade unions' relationship with the left.

This political shift was also logical for the trade unions in terms of their own membership and, perhaps more importantly, the possibility of recruiting new members. A poll carried out in December 1994 showed that 73% of French people found the existence of trade unions 'useful'. The breakdown of the result according to voting intentions in the first round of the presidential elections was particularly interesting. Among left-wing sympathisers, this figure was predictably higher: 97% of communist voters and 86% of socialist voters. But it was also high among intended de Villiers (76%), Barre (72%), Chirac (66%) and Balladur (66%) voters. The Le Pen electorate placed rather less worth (59%) on trade unions. According to Jean-Paul Jacquier, the results of the poll showed that the old left-right division on trade union activity (right = bosses, left = unions) was now redundant.[4] Whilst this is something of an oversimplification (and it should be noted, too, that the poll may be taken as an expression of electoral fluidity rather than entirely at face value), the results reflect a new uncertainty in the political landscape in which the trade unions find themselves.

Moreover, it was already clear in the 1980s that trade union members themselves were far from constituting a solid left-wing electorate. Force Ouvrière, the third-largest confederation, always contained within it a remarkably heterogeneous mixture, with a strong leaning to the right and the far-right as well as a vociferous Trotskyite fraction. The smaller Confédération Française des Travailleurs Chrétiens (CFTC, a Catholic confederation) and Confédération Générale des Cadres (CGC, the supervisory and lower-management union), both traditionally right-wing, were known to contain a disproportionately large group of voters receptive to de Villiers.[5] The exit poll conducted after the first round of the election among members and sympathisers of the main trade unions did not, therefore, contain many surprises, although the fact that twice as many FO as CFDT sympathisers voted for Robert Hue is striking, as is the level of teachers' support (FEN: Fédération de l'Education Nationale, traditionally known as socialist- or communist-leaning) for Le Pen. One suspects, given the CGT's failure to endorse Hue at confederal level and its generally low-key campaign on his behalf at local level, that the bigger proportion of the CGT sympathisers' vote given to Jospin than to Hue was not entirely unexpected. What Table 1 shows (below) is that the trade union vote was diverse and overall rather fragmented, with the persistence of left-wing (particularly socialist) voting among CFDT and CGT sympathisers.

Table 1: Exit poll (CSA-SSU) after first round of presidential elections (figures show % of votes cast)

	Laguiller	Hue	Jospin	Voynet	Balladur	Chirac	de Villiers	Le Pen
CGT	4	35	39	3	4	6	2	7
CFDT	7	4	45	5	14	16	3	6
FO	10	8	15	3	20	25	3	16
CFTC	1	2	17	1	42	21	11	5
FEN	4	4	54	3	9	6	3	17
CGC	1	-	9	1	25	35	5	24
Other	4	9	18	3	21	24	13	8
None	4	4	15	5	21	24	6	21

Source: *La Tribune-Desfossés*, 25 April 1995

Opinion polls from the 1970s onwards showed consistently that the negative image of French trade unions was closely associated with their perceived 'politicisation': thus, in a SOFRES survey published in February 1995, 40% of those questioned attributed the steep fall in union membership to 'politicisation' (the largest single response).[6] In order to reverse the ebbing membership tide, unions desperately needed to convince workers that their priorities were based on workplace demands, not politics. The trade unions were therefore happy to portray themselves as outsiders, remaining outside the policy process and influencing politics as autonomous actors. Furthermore, the strike movements allowed them to emphasise their role as social and economic actors ('the struggle on the streets' and in the workplace) rather than political advocates.

This explains the vehemence with which the trade union leaders, particularly Marc Blondel (FO), rejected government initiatives to bring unions and employers together. In Summer 1993, Balladur's Labour Minister, Michel Giraud (reportedly acting under direct orders from the Prime Minister), broke with practice by using the June meeting of the National Committee on Collective Bargaining to appeal to the 'social partners' to mobilise together 'for employment'. He called for 'a modern system of collective bargaining which allows the skills which enterprises need to be defined and career paths to be mapped out, and which ensures employees a just compensation for the efforts in terms of acquiring skills, or of mobility, which are expected of them'.[7] President Mitterrand in his 1994 New Year's message called for a 'new social pact', and Balladur similarly invited the social partners to get together 'to see how we can arrive at 200,000 fewer unemployed in 1995'. Union leaders responded by accusing the Prime Minister of attempting to shift attention away from his own employment record and confuse the roles of politicians and social actors. After the presidential elections, new Prime Minister Alain Juppé attempted a similar overture to unions and employers, only to receive a reprimand from union leaders. Employers, too, were keen to remind politicians to keep out of the social partners' legitimate sphere of action. Presenting a joint declaration to mark the opening of talks between employers and unions on 28 February 1995, Jean Gandois (president of the employers' confederation, the Conseil National du Patronat Français, CNPF) explicitly dissociated the talks from state action and called for more freedom from political interference: 'For the last twenty years we have headed towards an ever greater economic liberalism, but we have also headed towards an ever greater 'dirigisme' in social affairs. This situation must be corrected: the social partners must resolve their social problems themselves.'[8] The 28 February meeting opened up a new era for industrial relations in France, offering the chance for an autonomous sphere of action.

Talks between trade unions and employers: towards a new role for the social partners?

The year 1995 saw several 'firsts' for the French trade union movement. In January, the new CNPF president, Jean Gandois, astonished observers by establishing bilateral contacts with the CGT leader, Louis Viannet. Gandois' election at the head of the employers' confederation had been heralded as the start of a new direction for social relations in France. Known for his promotion of 'l'entreprise citoyenne' ('the civic firm', a French term approximating to the British notion of industrial democracy), Gandois had campaigned for the post on the theme of a 'renewal of bargaining policy'. On election, he immediately announced plans to hold national-level talks, first bilaterally with each confederation, then with all the confederations together. Interestingly, the CGT's reaction to Gandois's new policy was cautiously welcoming. True to the CGT's line, Viannet remarked in January 1995 that he counted on the strength of grassroots discontent rather than the goodwill of employers to ensure change, but he acknowledged the CNPF's change of tone and, perhaps most importantly, did not dismiss it outright.[9]

Gandois was not acting alone. Some observers saw in the CNPF's initiative the hand of the powerful mining and metal industries lobby (the Union des Industries Métallurgiques et Minières, UIMM). Arnaud Leenhardt, chair of the CNPF's social affairs committee and president of the UIMM, became one of the key actors in the historic joint employer-union talks launched in February 1995. The UIMM's concerns (beyond its traditional Catholic-inspired social paternalism) were largely fuelled by the fears of unrest in companies: a survey of several thousand human resources and personnel managers published early in 1995 showed that 19% of them anticipated a 'tense social climate' in their companies in the next nine months, whereas six months earlier only 10% of them had expressed similar fears.[10] Viannet was right: the strike movements, which affected both public and private companies all over France, played a large part in coaxing employers to the table. But the UIMM had another set of reasons for wishing to promote 'social dialogue': the reform of the tripartite management of the social protection system and particularly a clarification of the state's role. The state appeared to be reneging on its responsibilities to co-finance the costly system, particularly unemployment benefit, and it was therefore in the employers' and trade unions' interests to work together to force the state's hand. It was no coincidence that on 2 May, Leenhardt presented a CNPF discussion document calling for a rethinking of the tripartite arrangements and a more flexible management system, with more autonomy for the social partners in matters relating to employer and wage-funded contributions and state involvement where state finance was needed. Union responses to Leenhardt's discussion document were predictably negative (since they suspected employers of trying to back out of financial responsibilities), but the CNPF's strategy may have been to agree to talks on issues of interest to the unions (notably working time) in exchange for an airing of the social protection issues.

The employer-union talks which opened on 28 February 1995 can therefore justifiably be termed 'historic', even though little was achieved in the way of concrete agreement. The employers agreed to open discussion on ways to reduce unemployment, including reduction and reorganisation of working time, whereas previously they had always refused even to consider summit-level talks with unions on these themes. Given the traditional hostilities between French employers and unions, as well as the power games involved in any negotiation process, it is not surprising that progress remained slow.

When the working group on employment met on 27 April, Gandois appeared to scupper the talks by refusing to entertain any discussion of working hours. The trade unions, particularly the CFDT, had made this a central demand in the talks. However, later on 16 May, the CNPF withdrew its veto and reopened the question of working time. On 7 September, the social partners reached an agreement on early retirement 'solidarity' schemes whereby those over fifty-five would receive pre-pension benefits and be replaced by a young worker. Not only did the trade unions confound all predictions by presenting a united front, they also proved able to reach a compromise with employers and force the new government into honouring its commitment on financing unemployment benefits (albeit in instalments), which it had earlier refused to do. Thus, the talks appeared to bear fruit. Moreover, they augured well for a more constructive role for trade unions in the French economy and a way out of the impasse caused by reliance on political change from above.

Not all the changes took place at confederal level. The French trade unions have been keen to shake off their 'insider' image in another sense. A 1991 European Commission report suggested that unemployment in France was likely to keep rising because the insider group (workers on relatively stable contracts) retained the bargaining power to maintain its own position at the expense of the unemployed, and employment policies tended to perpetuate this division.[11] There is no doubt that unemployment and 'precarious' forms of employment have driven a wedge between different categories of worker and considerably eroded worker solidarity. Around half of the jobs created in 1994 were on fixed-term contracts. Conscious of the negative effects of their image as 'protectors of the privileged' (that is, workers in stable jobs), trade unions and workplace committees have developed a series of initiatives at local level to promote employment and reintegrate redundant workers.[12] The CFDT has been particularly active in promoting this type of action, but in some cases, concern to mobilise all those concerned by the threat of unemployment has led local unions to create new, united structures across the traditional confederal divisions: for example, the idea of a joint employer-union departmental employment observatory monitoring labour market trends in the Ardèche department was proposed by a cross-union 'intersyndicale' in 1991.[13] If unemployment and new forms of employment help to explain the current crisis of trade unionism, they also suggest the need for new responses, and in particular the need to overcome traditional divisions. This calls into question the capacity of the trade union movement to act not only as interest groups defending the interests of their core members, but also as pressure groups promoting a wider vision of society, without falling into the trap of 'politicising' their demands.

The presidential campaign and the 'social question'

The theme of unemployment and its relationship to trade union demands underlay much of the presidential campaign. Unemployment was cited by 71% of the electorate as the determining factor influencing voters.[14] Speaking on the radio shortly after the elections, FO leader, Marc Blondel, cited a SOFRES survey indicating that 92% of the population expected the new President to solve the unemployment crisis.[15] In their campaigns, all the presidential candidates claimed that employment was their number one priority, with Chirac putting forward his 'Contrat d'initiative pour l'emploi' to replace existing active labour market measures, and Jospin proposing a four-point investment plan to create low-skilled public utility jobs. Moreover, the campaign in its later stages was remarkable for the emphasis placed by all the candidates on measures in favour of low-income groups. As the theme of social inequalities took centre stage, the dominant discourse shifted significantly away from the previous orthodoxy of economic rigour and wage restraint.

In 1994, Prime Minister Balladur had set up a widely publicised planning group with the task of presenting scenarios for 'France in the year 2000'. The group was headed by Alain Minc, the centrist businessman and economic expert known to be close to Balladur. The group's report warned above all against the temptation of loosening economic rigour, and presented the issue as a choice between higher wages and lower unemployment.[16] Balladur took up this theme of wage moderation in his public pronouncements: 'wage demands destroy jobs'. However, an influential INSEE report published early in 1995 suggested that whilst oversupply had initially plunged France into recession, insufficient demand was preventing an economic upturn and depressing employment levels. Moreover, wage moderation had not borne the promised fruits in terms of job creation.[17]

Meanwhile, the increasing number of strikes across the country suggested the unpopularity of Balladur's message. Wage demands were prominent in most of these strike movements, although many strikes were also triggered by redundancies (for example, at Bull or Elf), by demarcation and status disputes in the public sector, or by a whole range of grievances linked with bonuses and working conditions.[18] Workers felt all the more justified in their actions because in most cases the companies refusing to give wage increases had announced huge rises in profits. The profits of the twenty-five largest French companies doubled in 1993-94.[19] Moreover, several magazines lifted a taboo by revealing details of top directors' salaries, showing that their salaries and perks had rocketed over the period when workers had been asked to tighten their belts. Thus, for example, the long-running dispute at GEC-Alsthom in late 1994 was sparked off by a 2% wage rise, offered at the same time as the company announced record profits from its international operations and the managing director's salary was revealed by a magazine to be in the region of a billion francs a month. This allowed the trade unions to shift the debate from the 'higher wages = unemployment' equation to a vociferous condemnation of inequalities.

Survey after survey indicated that the sacrifice of recent years had not been evenly spread. In 1992, household gross disposable income had increased by 2.3%, but only by 0.8% in 1993 and 0.6% in 1994. The proportion of labour costs in value added had dropped from nearly 70% in 1980 to 60.8% in 1992, 60.7% in 1993 and 60.1% in 1994.[20] In 1993, 38% of companies had given no wage rise at all. Wage restraint was hitting workers at the bottom end of the wage scale particularly hard as pay differentials widened. The gap between management and supervisory staff on the one hand and blue-collar workers and clerical staff on the other had been increased by performance-related pay for the former categories, allowing employers to negotiate limited or zero overall rises whilst rewarding their highly trained staff. In 1995, middle management earned 2.7 times more than blue-collar workers on average, but in some companies it could be as much as nine or ten times more.[21] The wave of discontent even prompted Gandois, head of the employers' confederation, to concede that wage restraint at a time of increased profitability could be seen as a 'provocation', and he advised companies to loosen their grip on wages.

Finally, workers and the trade unions were able to claim the moral high ground not only because of the perceived inequalities in wage structures, but also because in many cases businesses and employers had become tainted by financial corruption. Pierre Suard, the head of Alcatel-Alsthom, continued to hang on to his post during the election campaign despite having been imprisoned for financial impropriety. His was not the only case to hit the headlines. The business scandals which emerged in 1994-5 combined with high-level political scandals (from which the Balladur government was not exempt) to create a climate in which politicians could no longer preach financial rigour to hard-pressed working-class and lower-middle-class households.

The candidate in the best position to capitalise on both public concerns about the rising unemployment rate and individual economic grievances was, of course, Jacques Chirac. At the same time as he was exhorting young workers to take jobs at lower rates than the minimum wage, Prime Minister Balladur was found to be drawing wages from a computer company on top of his ministerial salary. His aristocratic manner and lifestyle made him an easy target. Revelations about corruption within his government dealt a fatal blow to his campaign. Chirac was quick to take advantage, repeating early in his campaign that 'wage demands and jobs are not in opposition with each other'. Balladur tried to backtrack after the publication of the INSEE report, but it was too late. As for Jospin, he was reportedly prevented from making incautious promises of income redistribution by his advisor Martine Aubry (the former Labour Minister), and he spoke cautiously of 'a controlled increase in wages'. His apparently hesitant approach to social affairs was shown in his declarations on working time: Jospin called rather timidly for a reduction from thirty-nine to thirty-seven hours a week rather than the thirty-two hours put forward by the work-sharing lobby. This caution contrasted with Chirac's populist appeal for a break with orthodoxy ('la pensée unique') and willingness to make incompatible promises to various social groups. Indeed, Chirac's discourse brought him closest to the trade unions' demands, to the extent that Marc Blondel (FO) was accused of campaigning for Chirac in his support of the strike movements. Blondel, undoubtedly a supporter of Chirac although scrupulously neutral in his public pronouncements, replied indignantly that the trade unions had been putting forward their case long before the presidential campaign.[22]

Chirac's ability to tune into the mood of the country and turn public discontent to his advantage meant that, once in office, he was able to look to both the trade unions and employers for support for his policies. The trade union confederations, even the CGT which might have been expected to denounce the return of a right-wing President, gave Chirac a cautious welcome. If anything, it was the employers who started to feel worried about his spending promises. However, it was also clear in the summer of 1995 that the new President had left himself a hostage to many demands for economic redistribution, which were all the more powerful for having simmered under the surface since the onset of economic austerity under the Socialists in 1982-3.

Conclusion

The trade unions' strategy of distancing themselves from the political world and pursuing high-level talks with employers was aimed at strengthening their position and helping them to overcome their chronic organisational weakness. For this strategy to succeed, it was important for the trade unions to remain aloof from party politics and the state institutions during the presidential campaign; in other words, to remain 'outsiders', albeit outsiders with a stake in the electoral outcome and a specific message to the new incumbent. To a large extent, they managed to achieve their ends. The summit-level talks between unions and employers remained largely undisturbed by electoral turmoil. A first agreement on working time was signed on 31 October 1995, although it disappointed the trade unions by concentrating on the employers' demands for flexible working hours rather than aiming at a universal reduction of working time. Perhaps more important than the content of the agreement was the trade unions' united front during these negotiations, which augured well for continued rapprochement and joint cross-federation action, even if full organisational unity seemed unachievable in the medium term (and could well be an unhelpful distraction).

One problematic area which remained was the relationship between private and public sector workers within the trade union movement. In France as elsewhere in Europe in the

1990s, public sector workers formed the largest section of union membership. As demands for public spending squeezes intensified, public sector workers found themselves increasingly under pressure, and their fight to save their jobs and their status seemed set to dictate trade union demands. As we noted earlier, this left the trade unions open to accusations that they act as 'insiders' within the system, fighting to retain their 'privileges' at the expense of the unemployed and those suffering low wages and precarious conditions in the marketplace. Since, in the age of economic scarcity, the art of politics had increasingly become a matter of playing off one social group against another, the tension inherent in trade union activity between the defence of members' interests and wider social demands made the position of trade unions fragile, especially in relation to public opinion. French trade unions' dependence on public sector membership made them particularly vulnerable to 'insider' accusations. The struggle to defend their members' interests whilst reaching out to other social groups (notably those in the unprotected, temporary and part-time work sectors and the unemployed) seemed therefore inevitably to constitute the major challenge for French trade unions of the post-Mitterrand era.

Notes

[1] E. Bressol, 'Rendez-vous présidentiel', *Hebdo de l'actualité sociale Vie Ouvrière*, no. 2645, 3 May 1995, p.84.

[2] See S. Milner, 'Guardians of the republican tradition? The trade unions', in J. Gaffney (ed.), *The French Presidential Elections of 1988* (Aldershot, Dartmouth, 1989), pp.211-239.

[3] *Le Monde*, 23 May 1995.

[4] *Le Figaro*, 15 February 1995.

[5] *Le Monde*, 23 May 1995.

[6] *Les Echos*, 16 August 1995.

[7] 'France: collective bargaining in 1992', *European Industrial Relations Review*, no. 236, September 1993, pp.29-31, p.29.

[8] *Le Monde*, 2 March 1995.

[9] E. Bressol (interview with Louis Viannet), 'Si les salariés se placent à l'offensive', *Hebdo de l'actualité sociale Vie Ouvrière*, no. 2630, 20 January 1995, pp.68-70: p.70.

[10] L. Bernard, 'Le ras-le-bol des salariés non cadres', *L'Evénement du Jeudi*, 16 February 1995, pp.58-67: p.60.

[11] Commission of the European Communities, *Country studies: France*, Economic Papers no.5, p.10.

[12] See D. Labbé, *Syndicalistes et comités d'entreprise face à l'exclusion* (Paris, Conseil National pour l'Insertion par l'Activité Economique, 1994).

[13] See *Libération*, 28 November 1991.

[14] See *L'Evénement du Jeudi*, 20 April 1995.

[15] *Objections*, France Inter, 9 May 1995.

[16] A. Minc, *La France de l'An 2000* (Rapport au Premier ministre de la commission présidée par Alain Minc, Commissariat Général du Plan), (Paris, Odile Jacob/La Documentation Française, 1994).

[17] See *Le Monde*, 18 March 1995.

[18] See *Libération*, 13 April 1995.

[19] *Le Monde*, 30 March 1995.

[20] *Le Monde*, 18 March 1995.

[21] Bernard, 'Le ras-le-bol des salariés non cadres'.
[22] Editorial, *Force Ouvrière*, no. 2244, 29 March 1995, p.3.

Indicative Bibliography

Bernard, L., 'Le ras-le-bol des salariés non cadres', *L'Evénement du Jeudi*, 16 February 1995, pp.58-67.
Blondel, M., Editorial, *Force Ouvrière*, no. 2244, 29 March 1995, p.3.
Bressol, E., 'Rendez-vous présidentiel', *Hebdo de l'actualité sociale Vie Ouvrière*, no. 2645, 3 May 1995, p.84.
Bressol, E., 'Si les salariés se placent à l'offensive', *Hebdo de l'actualité sociale Vie Ouvrière*, no. 2630, 20 January 1995, pp.68-70 (interview with Louis Viannet).
Commission of the European Communities, *Country studies: France*, Economic Papers no.5, 1991.
European Industrial Relations Review, 'France: collective bargaining in 1992', no. 236, September 1993, pp.29-31.
Labbé, D., *Syndicalistes et comités d'entreprise face à l'exclusion* (Paris, Conseil National de l'Insertion par l'Activité Economique, 1994).
Milner, S., 'Guardians of the republican tradition? The trade unions', in J. Gaffney (ed.), *The French Presidential Elections of 1988* (Aldershot, Dartmouth, 1989), pp.211-239.
Minc, A., *La France de l'an 2000* (Rapport au Premier ministre de la commission présidée par Alain Minc, Commissariat Général du Plan) (Paris, Odile Jacob/La Documentation Française, 1994).

12. THE CAMPAIGN AND THE MEDIA

PAMELA M. MOORES AND CHRISTOPHE TEXIER

Introduction

In the French presidential elections of 1981 and 1988, the future of the French media, especially broadcasting, was a major issue of concern. François Mitterrand's undertaking to liberalise radio in 1981 was rapidly translated into a phenomenal proliferation of community and commercial radio stations. The advent of independent radio marked the beginning of a new libertarian culture, and the end of a post-war era during which broadcasting had been regarded as an instrument of the State. By 1988, this liberalisation had extended to television, with the launch of the subscription channel Canal Plus in 1984, followed by commercial channels La Cinq and M6 in 1986, and the controversial privatisation of TF1, the country's main television channel, in 1987. However, whereas free radio had been perceived as a left-wing expansion of freedom of information, the opening up of television to commercial forces led to right-wing liberalism and domination of the market by competing financial interest groups. Heated debates raged over the respective merits of public service broadcasting and commercial television; and the issue of control of broadcasting continued to be a source of conflict. The supposedly independent broadcasting authority, the Haute Autorité de la Communication Audiovisuelle, created in 1982, was quickly replaced by the Commission Nationale de la Communication et des Libertés (CNCL) as soon as the right came to power in 1986, and this was succeeded in turn by the Conseil Supérieur de l'Audiovisuel (CSA) in early 1989, following Mitterrand's re-election. In principle, broadcasters had been granted autonomy, but politicians nonetheless exerted significant influence over their activities insofar as political officeholders (principally the Presidents of the Republic, the National Assembly and the Senate) were responsible for appointments to the supervisory authorities. As a result, nominations were often politically motivated, especially in the case of the CNCL in 1986. The rapid succession of regulatory authorities, and the concomitant changes of personnel inspired by political priorities, convincingly demonstrated that, in the eyes of government, media control remained an important political issue.

By 1995, however, as the relative longevity of the CSA suggested, the situation had stabilised, and media reform was not an issue in the election. Professional journals interviewed candidates about their policies on the press,[1] and specialists such as Dominique Wolton challenged them to initiate a debate on the media,[2] but to little effect. Candidates' election material devoted space to cultural and audio-visual policy,[3] but nothing new or controversial emerged to generate wider interest amongst the electorate. Arlette Laguiller was the only presidential candidate to take up a current media controversy explicitly in an official campaign broadcast.[4] The satirical weekly, *Le Canard enchaîné*, had recently been condemned for receiving stolen goods in the form of the tax returns of the managing director of Peugeot, Jacques Calvet, which the newspaper had used to substantiate its accusations that Calvet had taken a handsome pay increase for himself while refusing workers' pay demands.[5] Laguiller defended *Le Canard*'s actions, and made a plea for greater freedom of the press. However, her aim was to prevent exploitation of the workforce by ensuring financial transparency and accountability in industry; freedom of the press was merely an instrument to this end, not a campaign issue in its own right. Jacques Toubon, the Minister for Culture, talking to a group of media professionals, asserted that although Jacques Chirac recognised the potential of developments in new technology, he did not regard the media as a crucial campaign issue, given the country's more pressing problems.[6] On this, the candidates appear to have agreed. Accordingly, this chapter will concentrate on what proved a more significant issue in 1995, namely the role of the media in facilitating the electoral process, that is, informing the public, effecting communication between candidates and the electorate, and providing a forum for political debate.

The changing role of the press

Historically, the French press has been politically diverse and influential, with titles reflecting every strand of political opinion. However, in the 1990s, French newspapers are less politically outspoken than their predecessors (or their contemporary British counterparts). The communist press (*L'Humanité, L'Humanité Dimanche*) and extreme right-wing titles (*Minute, National Hebdo*), whose circulation is limited, are notable exceptions to this rule. Broadly speaking, newspapers are becoming ever less politicised under the Fifth Republic. The presidential regime and the rise of television have led to increasing personalisation of political debate. Also, the fall in circulation of daily papers since the Liberation, and the declining number of surviving titles, deter the press from adopting a partisan stance, for fear of alienating potential readers. Analysis of the 1995 presidential election confirms the decreasing political influence of the press, however full the newspaper coverage of the campaign.

Late 1994 and early 1995 were particularly difficult times for many titles, beset with financial difficulties and preoccupied by internal restructuring. Prominent left-of-centre national newspapers *Le Monde* and *Libération* were both undergoing editorial and financial reform in an attempt to balance the books and regenerate a declining readership. A new formula *Libération*, commonly referred to as *Libé 3*,[7] was launched in a burst of publicity on 26 September 1994, while the new management team of *Le Monde*, with Jean-Marie Colombani at the helm, negotiated a substantial injection of fresh capital prior to launching a new version of the paper in January 1995. July 1994 had seen the final collapse of Philippe Tesson's twenty year old *Le Quotidien de Paris* as a result of dwindling sales, despite the launch of a new formula only three months earlier, and this served to underline the precarious state of national dailies.[8]

The regional press was faring little better. *Sud-Ouest*, one of the leading regional dailies, had suffered repeated strikes and industrial conflict since the beginning of 1994, causing publication to be suspended on several occasions. Despite some improvement in its situation by the time the election took place, the fundamental problems remained unresolved. *La Voix du Nord*, another major provincial title, was preoccupied with diversification and restructuring, and launched a new formula on 11 April 1995, a matter of days before the election.[9] Such difficulties did not prevent the press from devoting extensive coverage to the election, and *La Voix du Nord* benefited from the special privilege of publishing the announcement of Jacques Chirac's candidacy in its columns on 4 November 1994. However, newspapers generally adopted a cautious approach, hesitating to display bias. *Le Figaro*, which had come out strongly in favour of Jacques Chirac in 1988 at the expense of his right-wing opponent, Raymond Barre, and had suffered a fall in circulation as a result, was careful not to repeat the mistake in 1995, appearing unwilling to choose overtly between the two RPR candidates, Chirac and Balladur (even if subtle bias in favour of the former may nonetheless be detected). The Socialist Party's dithering over its choice of candidate, and public discontent with fourteen years of Socialist presidency, no doubt played a part in *Libération*'s relative lack of enthusiasm for Lionel Jospin's candidacy in comparison to its wholehearted support of Mitterrand in 1981 and 1988. It is hard to dispel the suspicion that general self-restraint and reluctance to single out one candidate for unqualified support might also be linked to dependency of the French press on State subsidy (a reliance alien to the British newspaper industry). It may not have been sheer coincidence that Nicolas Sarkozy, the Minister responsible for Communication, and staunch supporter of Edouard Balladur, announced a new programme of government aid to the press only three days before the first round ballot.[10]

Where election coverage in the press did provoke controversy, it was on the grounds of abdication rather than abuse of political influence, as a result of excessive reliance on opinion polls. Long before potential candidates had even made up their minds as to whether or not to stand, their popularity ratings appeared throughout the press, helping them to make this decision.[11] From November 1994 onwards, *Le Figaro*, with the help of SOFRES, regularly devoted a special column to polls examining the electorate's main preoccupations. From February 1995, readers of *Libération* were treated to a weekly 'Présidoscope' concocted by IFOP, relaying apparent movements of public opinion in relation to prospective candidates. Even the traditionally circumspect *Le Monde*, which prides itself on a reputation for sound judgement, succumbed to this obsession. On 12 January 1995, before the Socialist candidacy was even finalised, an extensive article in *Le Monde* by Jérôme Jaffré, director of political research for SOFRES, announced Edouard Balladur's unrivalled lead in the polls under a bold headline extending the full width of the page: 'According to public opinion, the result of the presidential election is a foregone conclusion'.[12] Reservations about the reliability of such predictions were conveniently minimised. Not surprisingly, the decision to devote so many column inches to a pollster, and to announce his findings in so sensational a fashion, provoked furious accusations of manipulation, disinformation and, at the very least, unprofessional reporting.[13] However, *Le Monde* had clearly been infected by the widespread intoxication with the polls. On the last weekend before the first ballot, it led with a front page article boasting its publication of the last poll of voting intentions permissible before the inception of the official one week pre-election ban.[14] This tendency, even from the most traditional quarters of the media, to conceive of their role as dramatising, self-perpetuating mirrors of public opinion seems more likely to serve the interests of candidates' campaign strategists than those of the electorate. In the case of the 1995 presidential election, although newspaper sales increased for the coverage of results following the first ballot,[15] over the campaign period as a whole, circulation figures did not experience the boost normally associated with a major election.

The electorate was evidently looking elsewhere, and primarily to television, for its main source of information on candidates and their policies. In Régis Debray's terms, we have moved from the 'graphosphère' to the 'vidéosphère', from the age of print to domination by the film or television image.[16] More than 95.5% of French households have at least one television set[17]; the average adult watches three hours of television per day; and one in every two French adults watches the evening news on television. Above all, surveys demonstrate that the majority of the electorate turn to television as their principal source of political information. When questioned about the media most useful to them in deciding how to vote at an election, and given a choice between television, radio, print media, conversations, meetings, tracts, posters and polls, the overwhelming response of voters is television.[18]

Regulation and the pursuit of balance

The central importance of television in 1995 was also reinforced by the effects of new legislation governing candidates' electoral expenses. Following a number of scandals concerning the financing of political parties, a consensus had emerged on the need to limit campaign expenditure, level the playing field for candidates of different financial means, and curb the trend to American style commercialisation. A law was passed on 15 January 1990, forbidding the use of commercial hoardings for political posters during the pre-election period,[19] and the 1995 election was the first presidential contest to be fought since the introduction of this legislation. Only the standard, smaller posters which had been formally approved for display on official election noticeboards were legally permitted (although activists continued to liven up the streets and corridors of the metro with illicit publicity). Looking back to the famous advertising campaigns of 1981 and 1988, enthusiasts regretted the absence of the huge billboard images which had become almost an art form in their own right. Predictably, political marketing consultants such as Daniel Robert and Jacques Séguéla condemned the restrictions, claiming that the 1995 campaign was dull and colourless, because candidates had not been forced to reflect sufficiently on creating a distinctive image.[20] Commentators on the 1993 legislative elections had already observed that the new restrictions resulted in a more sober and discrete campaign,[21] and in marketing terms the 1995 campaign was low-key. Activist graffiti artists who had previously enjoyed adding carpet slippers to the 'Génération Mitterrand' poster, or a letter 'p' transforming 'La France unie' into 'La France punie', found more limited sources of amusement, the humorists' attention focusing primarily on the series of jokes sparked off by the apple tree used as a logo in Jacques Chirac's campaign.[22] Candidates produced a plethora of publicity: pamphlets, eye-catching stickers, tee-shirts, even free cassette recordings of speeches from Jean-Marie Le Pen, which were distributed to voters' letter boxes. However, since all such material had to be accounted for in the record of a candidate's expenditure, and as financial limits were now stricter, advertising was inevitably rationed.

In contrast, radio and television appearances cost nothing, and therefore assumed even greater importance than previously. Political advertising in the press in an election period has been banned in France since 29 December 1966, and on 13 December 1985 this principle was extended to broadcasting. However, from the early years of the Fifth Republic, namely 14 March 1964, all candidates at a presidential election have been guaranteed equal access to radio and television.[23] In 1995, it was the responsibility of the Conseil Supérieur de l'Audiovisuel to ensure balanced radio and television coverage. Outside election periods, government, majority and opposition are entitled to equal air time. In a pre-election period the rules are more complex. For a three month period prior to the ballot, on this occasion from 1 January until the opening of the official campaign on 7 April 1995, the governing principle was that of equity or balance. This meant that all prospective candidates were entitled to coverage proportional to their perceived political importance. Subsequently, once the official list of candidates had been published, all candidates were to receive equal air time.

The presence of a system of regulation designed to ensure pluralism and equality of access to broadcasting is undeniably a plus for democracy, but the increasing sophistication of political communication, and also the rapidly changing and intensely competitive context in which broadcasters now operate, mean that the regulatory framework requires constant review. One long-standing problem in the French system which affected coverage of the 1995 campaign stemmed from the fact that, whereas a candidate's appearance on different programmes at different times of day corresponded to entirely different audience figures, the CSA simply added up and reported total minutes of coverage for candidates and their supporters, as if this were directly proportional to impact and influence. Some of the fundamental principles of regulation also required clearer definition: the concept of equity had never been officially translated into specific measurable criteria, and remained a matter of interpretation. The Council took account of notoriety, the number of votes cast in previous elections, and standing in the polls. However, the fact that the weighting of these factors was not revealed meant that the CSA and broadcasting organisations could not be satisfactorily called to account. Moreover, presidential elections centre on individual candidates, not parties; did the CSA simply look back at Chirac's vote in 1988, or was it faced with the difficulty of how to divide up between Chirac and Balladur all votes previously cast for RPR candidates in recent elections? Clarification of such points was not forthcoming. Further problems stemmed from the inherent difficulty of categorising some contributors to political debate. The CSA recorded not only the time allocated to a candidate's own words, but also the contributions of prominent supporters to be credited to his or her account. How then was Bernard Tapie to be classified in 1995? One has to assume that he was counted initially as a supporter of the Radical leader, Jean-François Hory, and subsequently as a defector to Lionel Jospin's camp. The difficulties were exacerbated as Balladur's standing in the polls declined, and centre-right politicians hesitated between him and Chirac, often switching allegiance to the latter's camp. The situation was so fluid that establishing the precise moment of transfer proved problematic, thus highlighting the somewhat artificial character of the process in many instances.

CSA figures demonstrate that whereas, during the official campaign, lesser known candidates were relatively well served by the principle of equal coverage,[24] the criteria underlying the notion of equity, applicable from 1 January to 7 April, inevitably discriminated against newcomers lacking an established political base. The CNCL had noted the limited attention the latter received in 1988,[25] and it was in response to their report that the CSA, in its recommendations of 20 and 27 September 1994, explicitly asked broadcasters to ensure fair coverage of all prospective candidates in the three-month pre-campaign period. However, three months before the election, it was still by no means obvious who all the candidates were to be. In January, the CSA diligently monitored air time devoted to Antoine Waechter, Brice Lalonde, Bernard Kouchner, Charles Millon, Raymond Barre and leaders of the Radical Party, all potential candidates who ultimately did not stand. On the other hand, Jacques Cheminade did not figure in the CSA calculations, and took the media by surprise in early April when it transpired he had secured the five hundred signatures necessary to enter the presidential race.[26] From the broadcasters' point of view, there is increasing pressure to secure high audience ratings, and it is clear that they quickly decided who were the three main contenders with genuine prospects of success, and focused on them at the expense of 'minor' candidates. The latter found repeated cause to complain to the CSA. The Council's own monitoring services confirmed this imbalance in January, and again to a lesser extent in February, but despite their summons to redress the balance, it was not until March that the situation improved.[27] In its final report in May 1995, the CSA was forced to admit that 'minor' candidates had indeed been disadvantaged, and had not received their fair share of air time.[28]

The most publicised example was the 'injustice' suffered by Jean-Marie Le Pen. His proportion of the vote at the first round was approximately three quarters of the score achieved by Chirac and by Balladur, and yet, in the pre-campaign period, they had generally received roughly six to eight times as much attention as him in news bulletins (with some variation in the degree of disadvantage from one channel to another). Le Pen has always posed problems for the media. In the past, the most common criticism levelled against broadcasters was that they had encouraged the growth of the Front National by paying Le Pen too much attention and providing him with a platform.[29] Conscious of this danger, in 1995 as in previous elections, news broadcasters erred in the opposite direction, grossly underestimating his following. They did their professional reputations little good, and Le Pen's cause a great service, by giving him the opportunity to trumpet so loudly, and with such apparent justification, that he was the victim of an establishment conspiracy.[30] Le Pen was invited on to magazine programmes and political shows more routinely in 1995 than in the lead up to previous elections, and CSA monitoring demonstrates that the disadvantage he suffered in this respect, although considerable, was less marked than in the case of general news coverage.[31] Nonetheless, the image of Le Pen the victim was given further credibility by the refusal of Anne Sinclair, host of the important magazine programme *7 sur 7* on TF1, to interview him in person (because he had been abusive to her previously on account of her Jewish origins). To completely exclude Le Pen from appearing on *7 sur 7* would have been interpreted as clear evidence of political prejudice but, equally, the decision that, exceptionally, TF1's news director Gérard Carreyrou should replace Anne Sinclair on 26 February 1995 for the interview with Le Pen, only reinforced the view that the leader of the Front National was singled out for special treatment.

Balladur's 'privileges'

Even more controversial was the prominence given to Edouard Balladur in the media in the early months of the year. Opinion polls of voting intentions in 1995 proved unreliable, most notably the predictions of a Balladur landslide. However, if media coverage is determined in part by pollsters' findings, this sets up self-perpetuating movements in a candidate's popularity ratings and consequent share of air time, which have no basis in terms of confirmed electoral support.[32] Balladur had long been accused of spending his time in office ensuring that his own allies occupied positions of power in broadcasting: Jean-Pierre Elkabbach at France-Télévision, Patrice Duhamel at Radio France, Catherine Nay at Europe 1. He had also appeared on television on a record number of occasions since he became Prime Minister, twenty-eight appearances in all, and thirteen of these on TF1,[33] where he and his lieutenant, Nicolas Sarkozy, were said to enjoy a special relationship with the channel's president, Martin Bouygues. Balladur's announcement, on 18 January 1995, that he would be a candidate for the presidency was broadcast direct from the Prime Minister's official residence at the Matignon Palace, underlining his privileged position. However, recent French history demonstrates that even direct influence over broadcasting cannot guarantee success at the ballot box. In 'La croyance en la croyance'[34] the media sociologist, Jérôme Bourdon, suggests that what is significant is not so much that television actually exerts a decisive influence on elections, but rather that there is a widespread belief that it does. This point would seem to be borne out by the contrast between widespread accusations that Balladur was benefiting from abuse of privilege, and his ultimate fate in the ballot box. Indeed, his apparent privileges with regard to the media may in fact have worked to his disadvantage: Chirac and other opponents seized every opportunity to denounce 'l'Etat-Balladur', and the Prime Minister did himself no service by having his campaign spokesman, Nicolas Sarkozy, appear repeatedly in the media on his behalf, while continuing to assume ministerial responsibility for broadcasting. This was at the very least a naive error of judgement, laying him open to charges of abuse of influence.[35] Such damage to Balladur's reputation was all the more harmful as his popularity in the polls had been due to his standing as a cautious man of integrity, untouched by the scandals which had beset so many politicians. Added to the Maréchal-Schuller revelations which dented his pristine image in early 1995,[36] the presence of powerful friends in the media became more of a liability than an asset as Balladur was increasingly portrayed as a complacent establishment figure, fending off Chirac the underdog and people's champion.

Resentment of Balladur's 'advantages' was also fuelled by the official CSA report on media coverage of presidential candidates during January (released on 15 February), which demonstrated that he and his supporters had benefited from far more air time than any other candidate, namely 6 hours 41 minutes in total, as compared to 4 hours 19 minutes for Chirac, for example. Moreover, if one examines coverage on the TF1 news at 8 pm, an important moment in the daily schedule in terms of audience figures, Balladur had received 52 minutes, as compared to a mere 21 minutes for Chirac.[37] This confirmed the validity of the complaints which representatives of other candidates had been making to the CSA for some time. Anticipating problems, Balladur's allies argued that any extra attention he received was an inevitable consequence of his carrying out his official functions as Prime Minister. The new CSA regulations adopted on 20 September 1994 made no reference to the distinction (previously operated by the CNCL in 1988) between appearances in an existing official capacity and statements or appearances which could be specifically related to electoral prospects. To the annoyance of some opponents, the CSA, under the new direction of Hervé Bourges, was persuaded to reintroduce this distinction on 8 February, on the grounds that it would otherwise make it very difficult in future for a Prime Minister in office to stand for the presidency. In practice, the hasty introduction of this distinction made very little difference on this occasion,[38] and may have simply served to exacerbate resentment of Balladur's position.

Increased air time clearly does not automatically favour a candidate, and the very basis of CSA monitoring appears flawed insofar as it was purely quantitative as opposed to qualitative. Reports associating Balladur and the Maréchal-Schuller affair were scarcely likely to serve the Prime Minister's cause, but if they were situated in the electoral context, they would have been added to his tally. CSA measurement took no account of whether coverage was positive or negative. Moreover, the focus was exclusively on candidates and their supporters, paying no attention at all to the potential influence of intermediaries, analysts and commentators. These shortcomings were recognised by media specialist Jean-Marie Cotteret, who was newly appointed to the CSA on 23 January 1995 to take special responsibility for the supervision of election campaigns. He soon confirmed that evaluation of journalists' contributions and some form of content analysis would be under consideration for the future.[39] However, the practical implications of such a complex enterprise scarcely bear contemplation. Not surprisingly, concrete proposals in this respect did not figure in the reforms recommended by the CSA in the autumn of 1995.[40]

The battle between broadcasters

Wide review was clearly called for nonetheless, because the system of regulation was conditioned by the priorities of a bygone era when the main concern was to guard against political bias under a State monopoly. Since the introduction of independent television in the mid-1980s, this is no longer the most evident danger. Interviews with journalists prior to the 1995 election confirm that, not only on grounds of professional ethics, but, more compellingly, out of pure self-interest, there was little temptation for them to be partisan.[41] Their job security depended on advertising revenue which is determined by audience ratings. So whereas they had been under pressure to please their political masters when media organisations were under the direct control of government, they now sought to safeguard their future by surpassing commercial rivals. This encouraged a consensual approach to politics: success depended on attracting the maximum audience, that is, in political terms, appealing to all sections of the general public by avoiding offending anyone. This is a further explanation for reluctance to devote attention to a controversial figure like Le Pen. Ironically, although his appearances were known to boost viewing figures on account of his sheer entertainment value,[42] they also attracted adverse publicity. As far as mainstream presidential contenders were concerned, it would not have been in broadcasters' interests to risk revealing a preference for any one candidate.

The question of fair competition between television channels, especially between independent TF1 and public service channel France 2, was a matter of considerable concern for CSA representatives responsible for scheduling the official campaign broadcasts. After 30 September 1986, only public channels were obliged, or even permitted,[43] to carry official election broadcasts. In so doing, they sacrifice viewers. Audience figures for presidential campaign broadcasts in 1988 were poor. It was the first presidential contest since the introduction of independent television and the consequent increase in choice of programming available to viewers, and the public demonstrated their lack of enthusiasm for the official campaign by switching to alternative forms of entertainment.[44] This is why, in 1995, the longer (15-minute) broadcasts were scheduled in the middle of the night, showing only to an audience of insomniacs. This was the result of an unhappy compromise between the candidates, who felt they were entitled to the opportunity for serious in-depth discussion, and the CSA, which was unwilling to impose this burden on public service broadcasters at peak viewing time.[45] Thus, the paradoxical outcome of commercial pressures was a programme schedule in which the length of an official election broadcast was, as a general rule, inversely proportional to its potential audience at the particular time of day. Nonetheless, after the election, the CSA reported with some satisfaction that the cumulative audience for the televised campaign broadcasts was 132.8 million viewers, 93.9 million for the first round, and 38.9 million for the second.[46] The figures were unprecedented for official election broadcasts, a success which was probably due in part to the new production conditions introduced in 1993, and applicable for the first time in 1995 to a presidential election.[47] The new regulations permitted candidates to incorporate their own video and sound sequences (prepared at their own cost) for up to 40% of the long or medium-length programmes, and up to 50% of the shorter programmes. This enabled them to produce less static, more colourful, varied, and technically sophisticated television, enhancing interest in the 1995 campaign.

Outside the official campaign broadcasts, television coverage of the election was dominated by the desire of competing channels to outdo their rivals at all costs, but purely in terms of maximising audience ratings. In the early months of the year, despite CSA warnings to pay more attention to 'minor' candidates, the media were obsessed with the bitter in-fighting between the RPR rivals, because of the emotional suspense and human drama inherent in the conflict between supposed 'friends for thirty years' who were now intent on one another's downfall. Televised politics tends to focus on events not policies, on soundbites not substance, and cut-throat commercial competition only aggravated this. Following the evening of the first round ballot, representatives of France-Télévision and TF1 were formally reprimanded by the CSA because they had infringed legislation by announcing their estimated results several seconds before 8pm, that is before all polling stations in mainland France were even closed! The intention was evidently to attract viewers to their channel by stealing the advantage in the hope of maintaining the audience thereafter. On the weekend of the second ballot, France-Télévision took out a full page advertisement in *Le Parisien*, 6-7 May, boasting its audience figures for coverage of the first round results and the televised debate between the two second round candidates on 2 May, proudly declaring itself the winner, and advertising its forthcoming coverage of the second ballot. The result of the first round contest between TF1 and the combined forces of France 2 and France 3 is open to interpretation, according to the precise selection of audience figures (both organisations invariably citing those figures which showed their own performance in the best light).[48] However, what is clear is that television channels were at least as preoccupied with their own contest as with the battle between presidential candidates. In the France-Télévision advertisement, and also on air, viewers were repeatedly thanked for their loyalty in choosing to watch France-Télévision. Late on 7 May, they were treated to the celebratory finale of France 2 coverage, a futile race around Paris in the company of the journalist Benoît Duquesne and a fleet of SFP motorbikes,[49] in hot pursuit of the car carrying a victorious Chirac and his wife. The couple were relentlessly pestered for a statement, but in vain, except for Bernadette Chirac's expressions of concern for the safety of the reckless motorcyclists. The audience was repeatedly reminded of the three hundred technicians required to bring them these shots live, and the unprecedented nature of the technical feat they were witnessing. In short, television coverage on such occasions was dominated by the drive for excitement and spectacle, and became self-conscious, self-centred and, paradoxically, extraordinarily banal in its dogged pursuit of sensation.

Candidates' media strategies

In 1988, Mitterrand had kept his distance, refusing to be drawn into the media 'hype' surrounding the presidential election. He had risen above the banality of television, maintaining interest and suspense by rationing his appearances, and alternating them with radio broadcasts and press releases. His *Lettre à tous les Français*, published in leading dailies, had all the more impact as it represented a traditional, and yet, in the contemporary electoral context, unexpected form of communication.[50] Perhaps Chirac was taking a leaf out of Mitterrand's book when he chose to announce his candidacy in *La Voix du Nord*, a provincial newspaper based in Lille, the birthplace of General de Gaulle. It was a way both of appealing to tradition, and also of adopting a distinctive, unexpected approach, a sign of independence, and refusal to be drawn into the mêlée. The effect was to distinguish Chirac's declaration from subsequent announcements on television by potential contenders, whether it be Jacques Delors' 'no' or Philippe de Villiers' 'yes', both delivered on *7 sur 7*, or Valéry Giscard d'Estaing's 'no' on *Face à la une* (all exercises in stage-managed suspense which, in their own way, were equally inspired by Mitterrand's example in 1988). Further indications of a trend to revalorisation of the written word were to be found in the repeated use of written slogans on the television screen in Chirac's campaign broadcasts, and also in the series of books published by candidates, actual and potential, in the period leading up to the 1995 election: *Ma vérité* (Jacques Delors), *La France pour tous* (Jacques Chirac), *Textes et discours* (Edouard Balladur), *Dans cinq ans, l'an 2000* (Valéry Giscard d'Estaing), *Discours encore et toujours républicains* (Philippe Séguin), *La Tentation du conservatisme* (Charles Millon, UDF) and *Ouragan sur la République* (Hervé de Charette, UDF), etc. Such publications represented a means of self-promotion, a pretext to generate media attention, yet without appearing to seek it deliberately. They also carried particular weight in the presidential context insofar as authorship of a book – an elitist, cultivated, literary form of expression – gave some measure of the qualities of the individual intellect and personality, and was likely to be regarded as more prestigious than yet another appearance on a television chat show. Developing one's thoughts in a book, making public statements in a carefully chosen place and in one's own time... these were tactics designed to confer the presidential qualities of being reflective, aloof, and in control.

Nonetheless, for the majority of contenders, free access to television for the campaign constituted an unrivalled opportunity to promote the candidate and his or her policies, especially for a little known figure like Jacques Cheminade. Even for more established politicians, including Lionel Jospin (because of his late selection as the Socialist candidate), maximum television exposure was crucial in order to establish legitimacy. In the cases of Chirac and Balladur, however, since both had already enjoyed a prominent profile as Prime Minister, and it seemed clear from the summer of 1994 onwards that they were determined to remain in the race, there was time and good reason to reflect on a more subtle strategy. The comparison of their approaches is interesting because it suggests the dangers of relying too exclusively on broadcasting. Balladur was generally considered to perform well on television, and appears to have concentrated his efforts here, rather than campaigning on the ground, since he had little experience of the latter, and felt ill-equipped for the task. By early March 1995, however, journalists noted a change in his tactics,[51] as politicians close to him openly acknowledged his miscalculation. With his popularity in the polls waning, Balladur was forced out on to the streets of depressed Parisian suburbs and into the country to press the palms of the population, but he was visibly uncomfortable on walk-abouts, and his ineptitude merely reinforced the image of a detached, aristocratic figure who had little in common with the people. The sight of Balladur climbing on to a table to address a crowd, or surrounded by pigs in a farmyard, was far from natural or convincing.

In contrast, Chirac, the party man, with years of experience of mixing with ordinary people, had a reputation for being excitable, unduly aggressive and ill at ease on television, and preferred to address mass rallies and meetings, tirelesssly touring the country. It was a central plank of his campaign that he had taken time out of government to keep in touch with the people. It is true that only the party faithful and keen supporters turn out to rallies, whereas the crucial section of the electorate, whom the candidates needed to reach, were those who had not made up their minds, and they were more numerous than usual in 1995 according to the polls. On the other hand, floating voters with no strong political allegiance are those least likely to be attracted by television programmes which are explicitly identified as political. Today's viewers, accustomed to regular doses of advertising, are only too aware that official broadcasts, political interviews and studio debates constitute a carefully constructed, synthetic and contrived form of communication with transparent objectives. In contrast, images on the evening news showing a candidate being thronged by enthusiastic crowds of 'ordinary people' excite curiosity and enhance a candidate's credibility. Such images are more compelling because they maintain the illusion that a candidate has not specifically sought the coverage. Television cameras and journalists are on the spot as impartial reporters carrying out their duty to cover the news, and viewers assume that the event is authentic because there is a pretence that the candidate does not know he is being watched, even if, in reality, political meetings are highly stage-managed, especially in terms of their media presentation.

Comparison of Chirac's and Balladur's strategies suggests the merits of a flexible, multi-faceted campaign, continually staging events which will be reported in the media so as to keep the candidate in the public eye. Although television is undoubtedly important, it is unwise to spend too long in the studios; the candidate needs to be seen out and about in the country, in order to create a dynamic of movement and action. Occupying the screen incessantly is counterproductive, since the public loses interest. It was in mid-February, just when the CSA was reporting that Balladur had received disproportionate media attention, particularly on TF1, that his popularity in the polls began to fall. By now, Balladur had used up so much air time that, precisely when it was important for him to have the opportunity to redeem his reputation following the Maréchal-Schuller affair, the only channel keen to receive him was the news channel, LCI,[52] which attracted low audience figures. The main television channels had been warned by the CSA to restore the balance, and were now allocating time to his opponents. Planning a presidential media campaign could be compared to planning a middle distance race: you need to keep something back for the final sprint, and this was all the more important as the 1995 election campaign had started so early, and the electorate's interest was flagging.[53]

When one compares the official broadcasts on television prior to the first round of the election, it is evident that Chirac adopted a different strategy from his rivals. The CSA regulations require that a candidate be present both in image and voice in each of his or her broadcasts, but do not stipulate for what proportion of the time. With the exception of Arlette Laguiller (who resolutely stuck to the traditional close-up shot, focused on the upper part of the body, as she talked direct to camera), all the candidates in 1995 exploited the dialogue format, engaging in question and answer sessions with members of the public. Several called upon well known figures to testify on their behalf.[54] Nonetheless, in these cases, the candidates themselves remained central to the broadcast and dominated proceedings in terms of their physical presence. Chirac, however, rationed his direct personal exposure. In a series of broadcasts prior to the first round, it was his close allies Alain Juppé, Philippe Séguin, Hervé de Charette, Charles Millon and Alain Madelin, who played the central role, answering questions on his behalf. His only contribution to these broadcasts was to appear in pre-recorded clips, with his image inset against the pages of his campaign brochure 'La France pour tous', speaking between printed inverted commas. The latter technique emphasised the logic of continuity with other elements of his campaign, while the delegation of responsibility took some weight off his shoulders during a hectic period of campaigning, enabling him to exploit the undoubted asset of a strong supporting team. This strategy also meant that when he personally came to dominate the broadcasts in the 'final sprint', there was the sense of reaching a climax following a build-up of suspense, and his personal appearances still retained some degree of novelty.

For Lionel Jospin, the novelty of his candidacy, initially viewed as a handicap, was ultimately used to good effect. A latecomer to the race, following Jacques Delors' decision not to stand and the consequent ballot to select the Socialist candidate, Jospin had received little media attention since leaving the government in 1992, and therefore benefited from the natural curiosity of the voting public. His campaign got off to a slow start, because he needed time to establish himself in relation to the party and an electorate which had appeared keen to support the more prominent Delors. The introductory sequence to each of Jospin's official broadcasts prior to the first ballot showed him being greeted by rapturous crowds at rallies, thus suggesting the progress his campaign had already made. The main body of these early broadcasts then went on to present him on safe, familiar territory in the role of sympathetic but authoritative pedagogue, leading round-table studio discussions with a judicious selection of 'ordinary French people', including some particularly articulate representatives of the young. Despite the static, contrived context and occasional awkwardness on Jospin's part, changes of speaker and unconventional camera angles introduced a sense of movement which was reinforced by the ongoing dialogue from one broadcast to the next, as viewers returned to the same table, but to a new topic of discussion, gradually building up familiarity with the candidate and his policies.

Buoyed up by his impressive first round victory, Jospin grew visibly in self-confidence and learned to relax in subsequent broadcasts, allowing occasional glimpses of a smile to light up his austere demeanour.[55] His rise in status was reinforced by the extensive and strictly egalitarian media coverage enjoyed by Chirac and himself between the two rounds. A remote hypothesis had been transformed into a feasible proposition, and in interviews Jospin appeared more comfortable than previously, using the future tense (as opposed to the conditional) when talking about his presidency. Capitalising on his ascendancy, he spoke of the movement, dynamism and birth of new hope he represented,[56] and this became the theme of his second series of campaign broadcasts. Instead of focusing on Jospin the individual relating to fellow citizens, the lively opening sequence of these broadcasts rapidly juxtaposed symbolic travelling shots of a blue river flowing through verdant countryside, swaying crops, a handful of earth, a flight of birds in a blue sky... thus metaphorically elevating Jospin's candidacy to a transcendent plane, while embodying the interests of the nation. Whereas Chirac at this point was talking nostalgically of restoring France to its former glory, Jospin the newcomer projected the image of a man determined to look resolutely ahead. Having established his personal credentials, he no longer needed to worry about rivals in his own camp, and in his official broadcasts it was now his turn to call upon well-known figures who had rallied behind his campaign to testify on his behalf.[57] Thus it was that the novice established his personal reputation first, and then displayed his new-found supporting team, whereas the more experienced Chirac adopted the reverse sequence in his broadcasts. Chirac first undermined his RPR rival by demonstrating that he, rather than Balladur, had attracted the support of leading right-wing figures, and subsequently dominated personally. In both cases, however, there was a clear progression maintaining momentum.

The media play-off between finalists Jospin and Chirac was the televised debate on 2 May. This had been billed as the great media event of the election, with numerous articles situating it in a historical tradition first established by the memorable encounter between Giscard and Mitterrand in 1974. On this occasion, however, the unanimous verdict was that the contest ended in an honourable but disappointing no score draw for the candidates and television channels alike. Following difficult negotiations, during which the CSA had acted as intermediary, the debate was finally carried live by both TF1 and France 2, thus attracting an impressive total of 16.8 million viewers.[58] It was refereed by journalists associated with the two channels, Guillaume Durand and Alain Duhamel respectively, their selection being approved by the candidates themselves. The order of play, the topics to be covered, the questions permitted, every detail was so restrictively defined in advance that public service journalists protested that there was no room for a worthwhile exchange of views.[59] In the event, the two journalists in the studio were reduced to the docile role of timekeepers, as the candidates engaged, uninterrupted, in long-winded monologues. They themselves were ultra-cautious, intimidated by historical precedents and fear of putting a foot wrong. Although it might be argued that their refusal to succumb to personal antagonism, and their insistence on exploring detailed matters of policy, produced a technically rich and informative exchange, the result was dull television. The best that media commentators could find to say about the candidates' performance was that it had been civil, courteous and modest. It was almost as if the weight of the occasion, the desire for dignity, and also the burden of regulation, ensuring balance but imposing restraint, had spoiled the one genuine opportunity for a frank, gloves-off confrontation. This was certainly not a dramatic clash of personalities and philosophies, or the exciting climax viewers had been led to expect. Jean-Pierre Joulin, news editor for the radio station Europe1, was heard to remark that this would be the end of televised presidential debates of this sort.[60] Perhaps it was in reaction to this atmosphere of restraint, and the dull, consensual nature of much television coverage, that political satire, an inherently creative and fundamentally critical genre, outside the scope of existing regulation, enjoyed such a revival in 1995.

The success of satire

Both in print and in broadcasting, political satire had grown in popularity from the early 1980s onwards, attracting its largest audiences since May 1968. In 1995, the famous satirical weekly *Le Canard enchaîné* claimed average circulation figures of 500,000 copies, while the new *Charlie Hebdo*, the 'silly, nasty weekly', as its founders liked to call it,[61] was selling approximately 52,000 copies per week. *Charlie Hebdo* had been relaunched in 1992 after over a decade's absence due to falling readership and lawsuits, but was now boasting around 200,000 readers. Election periods, with their intrigue and conflict, have always proved a fertile terrain for satirists, and 1995 was no exception. *Le Canard*, for example, unearthed a rich vein of scandal in Chirac's questionable administration of the city of Paris, accusing him of misuse of his influence as Mayor in order to make personal gains in the property market.[62]

In addition, there was a flurry of new publications: *L'Enveloppe électorale*, a spoof version of candidates' campaign statements from the authors of the television show *Les Guignols de l'info*; *Elysée Massacre*, a sensational supplement from the right-wing weekly *National Hebdo*; and *Les Dossiers secrets des renseignements généraux*, secret files from the Intelligence Services supposedly stolen from the desk of the Interior Minister, Charles Pasqua. The latter was the work of the press group Jalons, which already had a reputation for its spoof publications: *Le Monstre (Le Monde)*, *L'Aberration (Libération)*, and *Le Cafard Acharné (Le Canard enchaîné)*.[63] On the Monday following the second ballot, Jalons also brought out *Le Journal du Lundi* (parodying the Sunday newspaper *Le Journal du Dimanche*). The front page headlines read: 'Surprise: Chirac beaten! Lionel Jospin elected President',[64] and the paper went on to announce that the entire political situation had changed overnight owing to an error in calculation. A new satirical paper *Le Cactus* had also been launched as the campaign got underway in early April.[65] Admittedly, the print runs of such newspapers were relatively small, but their very proliferation and their financial viability were clear evidence of the strong appeal of satire at a time when traditional newspapers were experiencing difficulties maintaining circulation figures.

It was in broadcasting above all, however, that satire had its greatest impact on the general public, through the daily radio programme *Rien à cirer* presented by Laurent Ruquier on France Inter, and more particularly, through the French counterparts of the British television programme *Spitting Image*, namely the *Bébête Show* and *Les Guignols de l'info*. In May 1995 (according to TF1 press services), the *Bébête Show* was attracting an average audience of 6.5 million viewers per day, while *Les Guignols de l'info* (to which fewer people have access since it is broadcast on the subscription channel Canal Plus) boasted 2.9 million viewers daily.[66] Surveys suggest that the audience of the *Bébête Show* was generally older, more conservative and working class, while viewers of *Les Guignols de l'info* tended to be younger, more urban, better educated and more left-wing.[67] Whatever the precise audience profile, a clear majority of the French population, 63% in 1993, admitted to enjoying these programmes.[68] In 1988, the *Bébête Show* had already dramatically outstripped the audience figures of the official campaign.[69] In 1995, the additional impact of *Les Guignols de l'info* (which had been launched in 1988 after the presidential election) generated a cumulative audience for political satire on television of nearly ten million viewers, thus representing a significant potential influence.

Moreover, on 7 May *Les Guignols de l'info* boldly broadcast its own election special, scheduled to compete directly with the announcement of the results on France 2 and TF1. This was a direct challenge to conventional media treatment of politics, tempting the electorate to revel in parody of the predictable reactions of politicians and journalists, in preference to a 'serious' treatment of the outcome of the presidential election.

This is why some critics, including the former Minister of Culture, Jacques Toubon, claimed that such satire damages the image of politicians and fosters anti-democratic sentiments. Charles Pasqua went so far as to declare that the programmes undermined the office of the presidency itself.[70] Resentment had been especially acute after the suicide of Pierre Bérégovoy in 1993, when close friends confided that he had been deeply hurt by the corrupt image he had been given in the *Bébête Show* and *Les Guignols de l'info*. Nonetheless, politicians were coming to recognise that they could not afford to ignore or stigmatise a genre which enjoyed such popular support. Jacques Chirac, who was caricatured mercilessly by *Les Guignols de l'info* in the two years preceding the 1995 election, professed that he enjoyed the programme all the same. According to his daughter and public relations counsellor, Claude Chirac, he even asked for a selection of excerpts from the show as a sixtieth birthday present.[71] The President of the Centre for Civic Information, Jean-Christian Barbet, maintains that the programmes contributed to political apathy in France and abstentions at elections.[72] However, a 1995 survey designed to shed light on the influence of the *Bébête Show* and *Les Guignols de l'info* on the electoral process was largely inconclusive.[73] Political scientist Stéphane Rozès argued that the enthusiasm for political satire was a consequence rather than a cause of depoliticisation,[74] but even this view oversimplifies the situation insofar as a detailed knowledge of current politics is a prerequisite for appreciating the genre. It would appear that the public increasingly distanced themselves not necessarily from politics per se, but from a complacent and compliant presentation of politics by the mainstream media.

Paradoxically, and perhaps because 'there is no such thing as bad publicity', there are potential benefits in satire for the politicians themselves: they can learn to correct their own tics and weaknesses, and improve their public performances. Claude Guillaumin, formerly an editor on France Inter radio, recalled how Michel Rocard learned to speak more slowly and intelligibly by studying how the impressionist Laurent Gerra mimicked him on *Rien à cirer.*[75] The ethnologist and media specialist Walter Detomasi also talked of the positive, demystifying effects of caricature which humanises politicians, brings them down to earth and makes them more accessible to the general public. Chirac's success in 1995 was frequently said to owe something to the vulnerable image he had acquired thanks to *Les Guignols de l'info*. The show's comic portrayal of him on the verge of a nervous breakdown induced by Balladur's betrayal may have helped to endear him to the public. If this were the case, it would simply underline the fundamental limitations of a narrow system of regulation, which ignores qualitative analysis, disregarding the role of satirists or the bias of interviewers, for, as argued previously, it is precisely the less obvious and more indirect influences of television which are likely to be the most persuasive.

Detailed examination of *Les Guignols de l'info* (over the period 10 April to 10 May 1995) does not suggest that any individual candidate was deliberately favoured, either in terms of exposure or political bias. Arlette Laguiller alone may have derived some satisfaction from the treatment she received, insofar as she appeared frequently and in a relatively favourable (albeit ironic) light, as the last true representative of the working class. This is not to say that she was not mocked for her 'obsolete' ideas, but she at least appeared refreshingly sincere and genuine. Balladur was systematically ridiculed for his clumsy attempts to become as common and vulgar as his compatriots; Jospin, the newcomer, who did not even figure in either the *Bébête Show* or *Les Guignols de l'info* at the beginning of 1995, was presented as a simpleton who had been unemployed and was thrilled to find work[76]; Chirac, for his part, emerged as an opportunist, torn between innate conservatism and a recent conversion to social democracy. Despite concern about the effects of satire on voting behaviour, it seems unlikely that such portrayals would have influenced voters significantly in one direction rather than another, as opposed to simply reinforcing existing prejudices.

What is more significant for our discussion is the implicit attack on the media which lies at the heart of these satirical broadcasts and publications, and most explicitly so in the case of *Les Guignols de l'info*, whose title might be loosely translated as 'Clowns in the news'. In decor, format and cast, the show was based on the 8pm news, and amongst the two hundred puppets portraying sports, pop and showbiz personalities, were leading media figures like Christine Ockrent, Serge July and Gérard Carreyrou, who were as much the butt of humour as were politicians. The choice of PPD as the programme's central character underlined its intentions. PPD was clearly a caricature of Patrick Poivre d'Arvor (known as 'PPDA'), the famous TF1 news presenter who, despite his popularity, had come to embody the worst in journalism for many professionals. Guilty of misrepresentation and clever use of archive material to fake an interview with Fidel Castro in 1991, and more recently implicated in the Botton affair which brought down Michel Noir (Mayor of Lyon), he was accused by the profession of an unscrupulous disregard for ethics, and complicity with politicians. He was even quoted in *Le Monde diplomatique* as saying that the journalist's job was 'to give a smooth, untroubled view of the world',[77] thus reducing news to a reassuringly conformist, vacuous source of entertainment far removed from the idealist conception of the media's function as a challenging fourth estate. PPD's greeting at the opening of the show on 7 May, a slight variation on his usual quip, was: 'You are watching too much election coverage on television.'[78] This paradoxical greeting gives an indication of the central thrust of the show, whose aim was to undermine conventional media treatment of political life while parodying political debate. In an interview with *Libération*, Jean-François Halin, one of the show's three scriptwriters, illustrated this point:

> Frankly, the French press does not home in on the issues it should be tackling, it has lost its sense of priorities. As we are outside the system, we are still in a position to express our view. (...) French journalists are in cahoots with those in power, in government and business. They give a soft, consensual view of things. (...) They have lost all critical acumen.[79]

In 1995, the absence of a critical, challenging voice was evident in many of the television interviews with presidential candidates, who were rarely forced to reconcile the inherent contradictions in their arguments. With journalists increasingly interpreting their role as bearers of the latest poll results, rather than as active intermediaries between public and politicians, the latter were often able to turn electoral debates to their own favour by dictating the agenda. The lack of informed, penetrating and determined questioning from journalists gave politicians unprecedented room for manœuvre.[80] Although, in their official broadcasts, the majority of candidates chose to stage a dialogue rather than directly addressing the electorate, not surprisingly they generally dispensed with a professional intermediary, preferring to respond to questions put by 'ordinary individuals' – students, the unemployed, immigrants – carefully selected 'representatives of the general public'.[81] All in all, the traditional journalist found himself dispossessed, and the satirists came into their own in response to public frustration and boredom.

Conclusion

We mentioned above that two parallel contests were underway in this election, the political battle between challengers for the presidency, and the media battle between competing TV channels. The high score of more extreme candidates at the first round was widely interpreted by commentators as an expression of dissatisfaction with mainstream politics. Similarly, as regards the media, the rise of satire, especially the success of *Les Guignols*, represented a protest, and a search for an alternative to the sanitised, consensual treatment of politics which saturated the television screens of France-Télévision and TF1. The presidential contest, in which personality is particularly important, lends itself to caricature, but this was even more true of an election where mainstream candidates were so transparently at pains to suppress or disguise their natural temperament. Not only was Balladur intent on developing the common touch; the televised debate between Chirac and Jospin was also an endurance test in self-control. The success of satire was to highlight the inadequacies of journalists and politicians. The challenge for the future which thus emerged for broadcasters and government from the 1995 election was how to reconcile the complex task of achieving political balance with new market pressures to succeed in terms of audience ratings, and yet, despite these constraints, give journalists the freedom and self-confidence necessary to generate the open and dynamic debate which was so evidently lacking on this occasion.

Notes

[1] For example, 'Quatre candidats à la présidentielle. Au nom de l'indépendance de la presse', *L'Echo de la Presse*, no. 59, April 1995, pp.53-55.

[2] 'Télévision et présidentielle', *Libération,* 9 March 1995.

[3] See, for example, Jospin's three hundred words on the topic under the title 'Relever le défi culturel et audiovisuel' (Meeting the challenge in cultural and broadcasting policy) in his policy document *Résumé des orientations et propositions de Lionel Jospin,* p.7.

[4] On France 2, at 1.30 pm on 10 April 1995.

[5] On 27 September 1989, *Le Canard enchaîné* had published details of Jacques Calvet's tax returns in order to demonstrate that while he was limiting employees' pay increases to 1.5%, his own salary had apparently increased by 45%. The courts found that *Le Canard* had not committed an offence in publishing the material which was valid information. However, on 3 April 1995, the Court of Appeal's verdict that the newspaper was guilty of being in receipt of stolen goods (in the form of the tax returns) was upheld. This provoked indignation from media professionals since it limited the scope for exposure of wrongdoing: if a newspaper could present no proof, it was guilty of libel; if it obtained the necessary proof, it could be condemned for being in receipt of stolen goods.

[6] Reported by Philippe Gavi, 'Médias', *Le Nouvel Observateur*, 16-22 March 1995.

[7] *Libération* was first published as a leftist paper in 1973; its second, more moderate version was launched by new director Serge July on 13 May 1981 following Mitterrand's presidential election victory; the 1994 relaunch therefore constituted *Libé 3*.

[8] An entirely new daily paper entitled *Le Quotidien de Paris* was launched by Nicolas Miguet on 15 February 1995, but this is a flimsy, extreme right-wing rag, and should not be confused with its respected predecessor.

[9] See Alain Salles, '*La Voix du Nord* accentue sa diversification', *Le Monde*, 11 May 1995.

[10] See A. Salles, 'M. Sarkozy présente dix mesures d'aide à la presse', *Le Monde*, 22 April 1995.

[11] Valéry Giscard d'Estaing's decision not to stand was widely attributed to his poor ratings in the polls. Similarly, it is doubtful whether Edouard Balladur would have entered the race if the pollsters had not rated his chances so highly.

[12] 'Pour l'opinion, l'élection présidentielle est déjà jouée'.

[13] See the detailed discussion of this incident in Roger Delpey, *Nicolas Bazire, Edouard Balladur, Nicolas Sarkozy en examen pour manipulation des sondages* (Paris, Jacques Grancher, 1995), pp.73-77.

[14] 'Jacques Chirac confirme nettement son avance sur Edouard Balladur et Lionel Jospin. Le dernier sondage publiable...', *Le Monde*, 16-17 April 1995.

[15] *L'Echo de la Presse (La Lettre Hebdo)*, 28 April 1995, reported the following short-term increases in circulation: *Le Figaro*, 770,000 (normally around 550,000); *Libération*, 550,000 (normally around 240,000); *Le Monde*, 825,000 (normally around 520,000); *Ouest France*, 1,100,000 (normally around 850,000).

[16] R. Debray, *Cours de médiologie générale* (Paris, NRF Gallimard, 1991).

[17] See figures given by D. and M. Frémy, *Quid 1995* (Paris, Robert Laffont, 1994), p.1311.

[18] See Roland Cayrol, 'Le rôle des campagnes électorales' in Daniel Gaxie (ed.), *Explication du vote. Un bilan des études électorales en France* (Paris, Presses de la Fondation nationale des sciences politiques, 1985), pp. 386-387; also R. Cayrol, *Les Médias: presse écrite, radio, télévision* (Paris, Presses Universitaires de France, 1991), pp.453-454.

[19] For these purposes, the official pre-election period began on 1 January 1995.

[20] See Martine Esquirou's interview with Séguéla, 'L'élu sera le plus télévisuel', *Libération*, 29 March 1995, and Laurent Neumann's interview with Robert, 'Daniel Robert: "Rendez-nous les publicitaires" ', *L'Evénement du jeudi*, 20-26 April 1995. Séguéla undermined his own argument about the positive role of advertisers in reinforcing distinctiveness, however, when he also asserted that Chirac's slogan 'La France pour tous' had been devised by him, a few months earlier, for Michel Rocard, when the latter was still a potential presidential candidate. This claim only served to reinforce the view that the slogans and images of such poster campaigns were largely interchangeable and meaningless. (Giscard d'Estaing had apparently turned down the slogan 'La force tranquille' before it went on to be associated with Mitterrand's success in 1981.)

[21] See 'Campagne intime. Moins d'affiches publicitaires, plus de contacts directs: la loi limitant les dépenses électorales a produit ses effets', *Le Monde*, 15 March 1993.

[22] Jospin's campaign team responded to Chirac's apples with a poster depicting a young girl asking, 'Monsieur Chirac, votre programme électoral ne nous prend-t-il [*sic*] pas un peu pour des poires?', that is, 'Doesn't your electoral programme rather take us for mugs?'

[23] See article 12 of decree no. 64-321, 14 March 1964.

[24] A detailed breakdown of coverage during the official campaign period is provided in *La Lettre du CSA*, no. 68, May 1995, p.7.

[25] *Election du Président de la République. Rapport sur la campagne à la radio et à la télévision (22 février - 8 mai 1988)* (Paris, CNCL, 1988), p.55. Detailed discussion of the imbalance between established candidates and less well known rivals can also be

found in Marlène Coulomb-Gully, *Radioscopie d'une campagne. La représentation politique au journal télévisé* (Paris, Editions Kimé, 1994), and in G. Sainteny, 'Le Cens médiatique. L'accès des petites forces politiques à l'audiovisuel', *Médiaspouvoirs*, no. 38, April-June 1995, pp.91-102.

[26] After the election, reviewing its own effectiveness, the CSA proposed that the law be changed in order to establish the final list of candidates earlier, so as to ensure more equal access to the media (*La Lettre du CSA*, no. 73, October 1995, pp. 9-10).

[27] In principle, CSA sanctions were extensive, and included suspension of the operating licence; in practice it relied on formal warnings, fines and the effects of public disapproval.

[28] See *La Lettre du CSA*, no. 68, p.4, and the evidence provided by a detailed breakdown of coverage on p.6.

[29] See, for example, Philippe Maarek, 'Le message télévisé a-t-il besoin du discours politique?', *Mots*, no. 20, September 1989, p.26.

[30] Le Pen opened his official campaign broadcast on 20 April 1995 with a table of CSA figures for the period 1 January to 6 April 1995, demonstrating the considerable disadvantage he had suffered.

[31] See contrast between figures for 'les journaux télévisés et les bulletins d'information' and for 'les magazines d'information' in *La Lettre du CSA*, no. 68, pp.6 and 8, respectively.

[32] In her study of the 1988 elections, Coulomb-Gully (*Radioscopie d'une campagne*, pp.68-69) observed a close correlation between a candidate's fate in the polls and the level of interest shown by broadcasters, the latter amplifying any supposed movements of opinion registered by the polls.

[33] According to Renaud Revel, 'Présidentielle: TF1 bétonne', *L'Express*, 2 March 1995, p.21.

[34] 'Belief in belief', in *Médiaspouvoirs*, no. 38, April-June 1995, pp.48-52.

[35] See, for example, the accusations made by Roger Delpey in *Nicolas Bazire, Edouard Balladur, Nicolas Sarkozy*. The notion of a ruthless conspiracy to neutralise Chirac and promote Balladur had also been developed by Ghislaine Ottenheimer, *Les deux Nicolas. La machine Balladur* (Paris, Plon, 1994).

[36] In December 1994, Judge Eric Halphen was asked to investigate the financing of the RPR party in the Hauts de Seine department, a bastion of Edouard Balladur's supporters (including Charles Pasqua, Nicolas Sarkozy and Patrick Balkany). Rumours suggested that Halphen's father in law, Dr Jean-Pierre Maréchal, had been paid one million francs by Didier Schuller, a leading local RPR politician, to influence the outcome of the investigation. It was then discovered that Balladur had authorised the bugging of Dr Maréchal's telephone, and this news provoked a scandal since it was considered a misuse of the Prime Minister's powers for party political purposes.

[37] A full breakdown of coverage for all candidates and their supporters on all channels during January is reproduced in *La Lettre du CSA*, no. 66, March 1995, pp.10-12.

[38] A full breakdown of media coverage for February, incorporating this distinction, is given in *La Lettre du CSA*, no. 67, April 1995, pp.4-10.

[39] Jean-Baptiste de Montvalon, 'Jean-Marie Cotteret, membre du CSA. "Il faudrait parvenir à un pluralisme qualitatif"' *Le Monde*, 1 March 1995.

[40] See 'Election présidentielle et télévision: un cadre juridique à revoir', *La Lettre du CSA*, no. 73, October 1995, pp.7-10.

[41] See Cécile Maveyraud, 'France 2 et TF1. La course à l'élection' and Frédéric Péguillan, 'TF1. Gagnons, gagnons sans déranger', *Télérama*, 5 April 1995.

42 See Sheila Perry, '*L'Heure de Vérité*: televised democracy?', *French Cultural Studies*, vol. 4, February 1993, p.2.

43 The ban on independent channels showing official campaign broadcasts was intended to avoid disruption of the strict observance of equality enforced on public service channels, but in October 1995, in view of the new, more specialised television offerings being anticipated, such as a channel devoted to parliamentary proceedings, the CSA recommended that all channels be permitted to screen the broadcasts in future, subject to strict CSA supervision and conformity with the principle of equality (*La Lettre du CSA*, no. 73, October 1995, p.10).

44 Coulomb-Gully (*Radioscopie d'une campagne*, p.72, note 10) reports that, in 1988, the obligation to broadcast the official campaign probably meant a 30% reduction in audience for public service channels at that point in their schedules .

45 Minutes of meeting with candidates' representatives, 9 February 1995 (CSA internal document).

46 *La Lettre du CSA*, no. 68, May 1995, pp.4-5.

47 'Conseil Supérieur de l'Audiovisuel. Décision no 95-95 du 20 mars 1995 relative aux conditions de production, de programmation et de diffusion des émissions relatives à la campagne officielle en vue de l'élection du Président de la République (23 avril et 7 mai 1995)', *Journal Officiel de la République française*.

48 See Philippe Boubeillon, 'Au premier tour, France 2 parvient à talonner TF1', *Libération*, 25 April 1995.

49 Société Française de Production.

50 For more detailed discussion, see John Gaffney, 'Language and style in politics', in C. Sanders (ed.), *French today. Language in its social context* (Cambridge, Cambridge University Press, 1993), pp.187-198.

51 See, for example, Claude Askolovitch, 'Une plante d'appartement au grand air. Quand Edouard se convertit en candidat', *L'Evénement du jeudi,* 9-15 March 1995.

52 La Chaîne de l'Information, a cable and satellite news channel run by TF1.

53 Mitterrand had already demonstrated this in 1988. The President had rationed and timed his television appearances carefully, while Chirac had received so much more coverage that the CNCL was finally obliged to warn TF1 that it must redress the balance. Mitterrand delayed matters until, on the eve of the first round, he finally granted a television interview to Patrick Poivre d'Arvor. Coulomb-Gully (1995, pp.243-246) concludes that Chirac used television more intensively, Mitterrand more intelligently. Chirac was not to forget the lesson in 1995.

54 For example, René Dumont and Charles Fiterman lent their support to Dominique Voynet, while Georges Marchais appeared on behalf of Robert Hue.

55 During his thirty minute appearance on *Face à la une*, TF1, 28 April 1995, Jospin admitted, 'J'ai fissuré l'armure' ('I have split open my protective armour').

56 These points were well illustrated in *Face à la une,* 28 April 1995.

57 Contributions were made by Martine Aubry, Bernard Kouchner, Pierre Mauroy, Jean Lacouture, Jacques Le Goff, Patrice Chéreau, Cécile Novak, and even Marie-Claire Mendès France.

58 Reported by Renaud Dely, 'Débat télévisé: les deux camps se satisfont du match nul', *Libération*, 4 May 1995, p.4.

59 See J.-B. de Montvalon, 'Les journalistes de France 2 critiquent l'organisation du face-à-face télévisé', *Le Monde*, 28 April 1995.

60 Reported by Ariane Chemin, 'Le PAF s'ennuie studio 109', *Le Monde,* 4 May 1995.

61 *Charlie Hebdo* – 'l'hebdomadaire bête et méchant'.

[62] 'Une société d'HLM a vidé sa tirelire pour empêcher Chirac d'être expulsé', *Le Canard enchaîné*, 29 March 1995, and 'Chirac ment comme il réside', 5 April 1995.

[63] In English 'cafard' translates as 'depression' or 'cockroach'; 'acharné' means 'relentless'.

[64] 'La Surprise: Chirac battu! Lionel Jospin élu Président'.

[65] See 'Les journaux satiriques s'emparent de la campagne', *Le Monde*, 14 April 1995, and further information in *L'Echo de la Presse*, 12 May 1995.

[66] Sources : TF1 and Canal Plus press services.

[67] See the results of the surveys conducted by *Le Point*, 20 November 1993, and the Louis Harris Institute (February 1995) analysed by Emmanuel Fraisse, 'Les politiques et leurs marionnettes à la télévision', *Médiaspouvoirs*, no. 38, April-June 1995, pp.103-9.

[68] See Michel Pascal, *Le Point*, 20 November 1993.

[69] 'Avec les Bébêtes, chaud l'air de la campagne', *Libération*, 19 April 1988.

[70] Both quoted by Christine Deymard, 'L'année du latex', *Le Nouvel Observateur*, 23 December 1993.

[71] Reported by Jean-Claude Raspiengeas, 'Les Français votent Guignols', *Télérama*, 16 March 1994.

[72] Quoted by Isabelle Berdoll, 'Les marionnettes sont-elles vraiment inciviques?', *Le Quotidien de Paris*, 1 January 1994.

[73] See Louis Harris survey, February 1995, analysed by E. Fraisse in 'Les politiques et leurs marionnettes à la télévision'.

[74] Quoted by Joël Duru and Alix Mazeran in 'La dérision politique est-ce bien raisonnable?', *Médiaspouvoirs*, no. 35, July-September 1994, p.9.

[75] Cited by Raspiengeas in 'Les Français votent Guignols'.

[76] Jospin was referred to as 'la bonne poire' (literally the 'good pear') of the Socialist party. Translated more generally as 'mug' or 'sucker', this nickname was intended as a satirical allusion to the apple used in Chirac's campaign, and to a series of jokes about apples and pears which stemmed from this.

[77] 'Nous sommes là pour donner une image lisse du monde'. Quoted by Serge Halimi, 'Un journalisme de révérence', *Le Monde diplomatique*, no. 491, February 1995.

[78] 'Vous regardez trop les élections à la télévision'. His usual greeting was simply, 'Vous regardez trop la télévision', that is, 'You are watching too much television'.

[79] 'Franchement, la presse française ne met pas le doigt où il faudrait le mettre, elle ne hiérarchise plus. Comme nous sommes à l'extérieur de ce système, nous avons encore le loisir de parler. (...) Les journalistes français sont acoquinés avec le pouvoir et les grosses entreprises. Ils donnent une vision molle et consensuelle des choses. (...) Ils perdent tout esprit critique'. Quoted by Jean-Pierre Pisanias, 'Les Guignols ouvrent leur campagne électorale', *Libération*, 24 February 1995.

[80] See Sylvie Briet, 'Les émissions politiques, du débat idéologique au règne des sondages', *Libération*, 18-19 March 1995.

[81] See A. Chemin, and J-B. de Montvalon, 'Les anonymes ont envahi la campagne officielle', *Le Monde*, 23-24 April 1995. The rare exceptions were the journalists Cathy Capvert of *L'Humanité*, who interviewed Robert Hue for his official campaign broadcasts, and Bernard Langlois of *Politis*, who interviewed Dominique Voynet.

Indicative Bibliography

Bourdon, Jérôme, *Haute Fidélité. Pouvoir et télévision, 1935-1994* (Paris, Seuil, 1994).

Collovald, Annie, 'Le Bébête Show, idéologie journalistique et illusion critique', in *Politix*, no. 19, 1992, pp.67-86.

Coulomb-Gully, Marlène, *Radioscopie d'une campagne. La représentation politique au journal télévisé* (Paris, Editions Kimé, 1994).

Coulomb-Gully, Marlène, 'Les "Guignols" de l'information, une dérision politique', in *Mots*, no. 40, September 1994, pp.53-64.

Delpey, Roger, *Nicolas Bazire, Edouard Balladur, Nicolas Sarkozy en examen pour manipulation des sondages* (Paris, Jacques Grancher, 1995).

Drouot, Guy (ed.), *Les Campagnes Electorales radiotélévisées* (Presses Universitaires d'Aix-Marseille, Economica, 1995).

Election du Président de la République. Rapport sur la campagne à la radio et à la télévision (22 février - 8 mai 1988) (Paris, CNCL, 1988).

Elections et télévision, Actes du Colloque, Valence, 1-4 April 1993 (Valence, Centre de Recherche et d'Action Culturelle, 1993).

Guénaire, Michel and Grégoire Triet, *La nouvelle communication en période électorale. Analyse de la loi du 15 janvier 1990* (Paris, Gide Loyrette Nouel, 1992).

Halimi, Serge, 'Un journalisme de révérence', *Le Monde diplomatique*, no. 491, February 1995.

La Lettre du CSA, nos. 66-73, March-October 1995.

'Les Médias font-ils l'élection?', *Médiaspouvoirs*, no. 38, April-June 1995.

13. THE POLLS AND THE 1995 ELECTION

JEAN AND MONICA CHARLOT

Introduction

The 1995 election was marked by what the political commentator Georges Suffert termed 'Poll-mania'[1] and *Le Monde* 'Polling disease'.[2] It is true that the French political élites consider that opinion polls have so great an influence on voters that on 19 July 1977 a law was passed to prevent 'the publication, circulation and commentary' of any opinion poll 'having a direct or indirect link with the election during the week preceding each ballot and on election day itself'. Public opinion polls are indeed seen as a mixed blessing. On the one hand they are a desirable addition to the democratic decision-making process, on the other they are deemed a threat to responsible élite politics.

The 1995 presidential election was no exception to the rule. In the 105 days of the pre-election period, 114 opinion polls gave the voting intentions of the public, an average of 1.08 polls a day.[3] What is it that has caused the French to be so keen on polls? Various explanations have been advanced ranging from a fascination with numbers or a love of horse-racing, to the more psychological explanation that the individual fears solitude and is therefore happy to find her or himself part of a group. Whatever the reason, there is no doubt that opinion polls affect not only public perceptions, but also the perceptions of the politicians, the candidates' campaign strategies, and the morale of the parties. The polls, however, do not make the election; if they really did, Edouard Balladur, and not Jacques Chirac, would have been elected President in 1995.

There are six major polling organisations: SOFRES (founded from the SEMA group in 1963) comes top of the market. Its principal outlet in the press is the Hersant group (*Le Figaro*). It publishes (with Seuil) an annual book of its polls under the title *Opinion publique*. BVA, founded in 1970 and linked to *Paris-Match* for its political barometers, comes second. IFOP-Etmar, founded in 1938, is the oldest polling institute in France; it publishes its polls in *Le Journal du dimanche*. IPSOS, founded in 1975, is associated to *Le Point*; Louis Harris France, founded in 1976, is financially linked to SOFRES; and CSA is a more recent breakaway from Harris.

The result of a presidential election had never been as unpredictable as it was in 1995: the voters could not make up their minds, nor could potential candidates decide whether to stand or not. And yet two years earlier things had seemed relatively simple. François Mitterrand's age, 78 at the time of the election, and his state of health made it obvious that he would not stand again. There were some pollsters who persisted in testing the hypothesis of a third mandate for the incumbent but no one really believed it possible and this was confirmed by the results of these 'fictional' polls.[4]

The Socialist dauphin, despite the President's dislike of him, was Michel Rocard. Pierre Mauroy had spoken of him in 1992 as the Socialist's 'virtual' candidate, the 'natural' candidate, and in April 1993 Rocard had taken over the leadership of a defeated Socialist Party which was looking for a saviour. On the right, the major artisan of the legislative victory of the RPR-UDF was Jacques Chirac and his only rival at the time was thought to be the former President, Valéry Giscard d'Estaing, whose presidential future was considered doubtful even by his supporters within the UDF. The persistent, unpredicted popularity of the new RPR Prime Minister from 1993, Edouard Balladur, transformed the situation.[5] 1993 became 'Balladur's year'.[6] The pollsters were intrigued by the phenomenon. According to Pierre Giacometti (BVA) it was the pivotal position of Edouard Balladur on the right-left scale which explained the popularity of the Prime Minister-President.[7] He was neither on the left nor on the right in the eyes of the centrists, while being on the right for both the right and the extreme right.

Jean-Luc Parodi (IFOP) explained: 'It is the disillusionment with the Socialists that has created the belief in Balladur, by responding to a need for confidence among voters. Nonetheless', he added, 'the so-called qualities of calmness and moderation may tomorrow be seen as lethargy and apathy; today's need for confidence may become tomorrow's disillusionment'.[8] Stéphane Rozès (CSA) went further, calling Edouard Balladur 'a colossus with feet of clay', a man who ran the risk of being deserted by the hard core of right-wing voters[9]; and Jérôme Jaffré (SOFRES) noted the paradox between the popularity of the Prime Minister – which remained at its zenith – and the pessimism among the French, which reached an absolute record, making 1993 a dark year of despair.[10] Contrary to the more critical views of these pollsters, however, the media and public opinion were inclined to see only the rise and rise of Edouard Balladur,[11] his 'presidentialisation' and increasing claim to credibility as a future President – and the consequent eclipsing of Jacques Chirac.

In June 1994, the European elections caused the Socialist left in its turn to have doubts as to the identity of its presidential candidate. When the list led by Michel Rocard obtained only 14.5% of the votes, he lost both the leadership of his party and his role as Socialist presidential candidate. Six months later, on 11 December 1994, Jacques Delors, President of the European Commission and a member of the Socialist Party, withdrew from the presidential race. He had been the polls' favourite together with Edouard Balladur, and the last hope for the left. The Socialist Party was left without a candidate only four months before the first round.

The uncertainty on both sides – with no candidate on the left and too many on the right – led the pollsters to increase the number of possible combinations when testing voting intentions. This meant that the pollsters were led to explore an uncertain political landscape and to anticipate what the political actors would do. In such uncharted territory, they had to rely for the most part on contradictory clues and, above all, on their own intuition.

The first question they had to answer was that of Edouard Balladur's candidacy. Would he finally stand despite the theory that a Prime Minister 'cohabiting' with a President of the opposite tendency should not stand as a candidate, a theory that Edouard Balladur himself had publicly put forward in 1990 before he became a 'cohabiting Prime Minister' and after witnessing the resounding defeat of Jacques Chirac in 1988? All the polling institutes, with the exception of BVA (said to be close to Jacques Chirac), believed Edouard Balladur would stand and tested his candidacy from their very first poll on presidential voting intentions. (BVA only included Edouard Balladur in their questionnaires from mid-October 1993 when the rift between Edouard Balladur and

Jacques Chirac had become public).[12] The second question was: since Balladur was a potential presidential candidate, did the rivalry between Chirac and Balladur, both 'companions-in-arms of the RPR', and 'friends for the past thirty years', mean they would fight one another on election day, or that the least well placed would stand down before the first round in order to avoid a damaging contest?

Neither Edouard Balladur's silence nor Jacques Chirac's ambiguous statements in September 1993, declaring that he would never 'be a rival' of the Prime Minister, helped pollsters see what the future had in store. IPSOS was the first institute to simulate a first round opposing Jacques Chirac and Edouard Balladur. It did so in its very first presidential voting intentions survey on 27-31 August 1993; the other institutes followed suit in 1994: SOFRES in March, BVA in April, CSA in June, IFOP in September, Harris only in October. All the institutes, except for IFOP and CSA, took the precaution of also testing the hypotheses of only one of the two – Chirac or Balladur – standing in the first round.[13] The final problem for the first round, for both the RPR and UDF, was: would there be a UDF candidate – Giscard or Raymond Barre for instance? Disquieted by the rallying of the UDF to Edouard Balladur (himself a member of the RPR), the President of the UDF – Valéry Giscard d'Estaing, still a potential presidential candidate – was determined that the UDF should be present in the first round, and said so publicly in February 1994. It was not until both Raymond Barre (6 March 1995) and Giscard d'Estaing (7 March 1995) had, only weeks before the first round, declared they were not standing that it became clear there would be no UDF candidate. All the polling institutes had from the start included a UDF candidate – usually Giscard – in their voting intention surveys. This hypothesis was to be maintained right into 1995 when the various institutes abandoned it one after the other.[14] It was no doubt their scores in the various polls that led both Barre and Giscard not to enter the presidential reckoning.

With regard to the Socialist candidate, pollsters and public alike were led astray until mid-December 1994, first by the dilemma of whether the candidate would be Rocard or Delors, then by the rise in popularity of a Delors candidacy. During the first phase, the pollsters included a Delors hypothesis even when Michel Rocard was seen as the 'natural' candidate of the Socialist Party. This was no doubt due in part to a certain 'Mitterrand effect': the well-known hostility of the President to Michel Rocard made Jacques Delors, from the start, a credible alternative candidate for the Socialists.[15] After Michel Rocard had been eliminated in June 1994, given the Socialists' disastrous European election results, all the institutes concentrated on the candidacy of Jacques Delors until he withdrew his name from consideration on 11 December 1994. The collapse of the Delors hypothesis disrupted the presidential race for the second time since the beginning of the pre-campaign. As in the case of Edouard Balladur in 1993, the results of the polls, and to an even greater extent the commentaries of the pollsters, had in part created a Delors phenomenon. As early as 1993, the press had underlined the gap in popularity and potential presidential credibility between Jacques Delors and Michel Rocard and had begun comparing Delors and Balladur. 'Within party logic nothing has changed', wrote the *Nouvel Observateur*, 'Jacques Chirac and Michel Rocard are the natural candidates. But in public opinion they have already been replaced: the only credible candidates are Edouard Balladur on the right and Jacques Delors on the left'.[16] After the eviction of Rocard, and during the summer and autumn of 1994, the Delors phenomenon was considerably strengthened. On 30 August, *Le Monde* published a cartoon entitled 'Opinion Polls'. Balladur followed by Delors – both with their hands clasped behind their backs – were depicted climbing the upward slope of the opinion polls. 'Je ne sais pas où on va, mais on y va' ('I don't know where we're going but we're off'), Delors was saying, while Balladur looked down over his shoulder, replying 'Plaît-il?' ('I do beg your pardon?'). Jérôme Jaffré also in *Le Monde*, claimed in September that 'for the choice of candidates, the preferences of the voters measured by the opinion polls weigh more than the choices of the political parties', and concluded that: 'If there is no change only Edouard Balladur, Jacques Chirac and Jacques Delors have any hope of becoming the next President of the Republic'.[17]

Within a few weeks, the polls of voting intentions had taken Jacques Delors from the position of challenger to that of favourite, overtaking Edouard Balladur. IPSOS in mid-September put him first in the first round and the winner against Jacques Chirac in the run-off. From mid-October onward all the surveys confirmed his rise, giving him 30% of votes on average, as against 25% to Edouard Balladur and only 16.5% to Jacques Chirac. Second round voting intentions from the beginning of October showed him winning consistently and easily against Jacques Chirac. BVA saw Delors as the winner against Edouard Balladur for the first time on 17-21 November 1994. From then on Jacques Delors was catapulted into a commanding lead and, in the simulations, won in the second round whoever stood against him: until 11 December 1994, when the favourite of the polls, the only hope of a victory for the left, dropped his bombshell – he had finally decided not to stand. Jacques Chirac, on the contrary, held steady in his determination not to withdraw, despite the polls and the pressure put on him by the Balladurians who characterised him as a loser and urged him to stand down. Jacques Chirac was to say in Colmar on 23 September 1994: 'Let's forget about opinion polls, those so-called certainties we cling to in uncertain times, this electoral arithmetic',[18] and on 12 November, quoting the Christian democrat philosopher, Jean Guitton, he said: 'to be popular, to rise on the breeze is actually to be blown around like a dead leaf'.[19]

With Delors gone, the pollsters, right up to Lionel Jospin's investiture by the Socialist Party on 5 February 1995, tested various solutions for the left. IFOP and IPSOS were the first to put Jospin forward, in mid-December. All the institutes in their simulations of 'Socialist primaries' found him behind Jack Lang, but in front of Henri Emmanuelli. The candidacy that the Socialist Party activists preferred was thus not in the first instance the person the voters would have preferred. CSA had, in fact, measured Jack Lang's potential score from the end of April 1994, and Lionel Jospin's only from mid-January 1995.

In January, only three months before the election, the uncertainty concerning the candidates on offer was still so great that the surveys of voting intentions continued to present a surprising number of hypothetical combinations of candidates for the first round: 6 for BVA, 5 for SOFRES and IFOP (3 at the end of May), 4 for Harris, CSA and IPSOS (2 at the end of May for the last two). This uncertainty was linked to three factors: the presence or absence of Giscard or Barre; the identity of the Socialist candidate; and the emergence or not of a maverick candidate such as Bernard Kouchner on the centre-left. In other words, the accurate first round combination – Jospin, Balladur, Chirac – without Giscard or Barre – was known only very late in the day.

Harris and IPSOS were the first to offer it, in the first half of January; then BVA and SOFRES in the second half of the month; IFOP did not do so until the end of February, followed closely by CSA. The hesitation as to the second round candidates was equally strong. IPSOS and CSA only systematically tested the Jospin-Chirac hypothesis from mid-February. We need to stress here, however, a point of fundamental importance: voting intentions which date back to several months before all the major candidates are known have, in fact, no predictive value for the second round. Before the campaign starts, voting intentions measure not votes but the 'attraction' candidates have for voters. This is fragile, and tends to overestimate two kinds of potential presidential candidates: those already in positions of power, who have greater legitimacy and inspire deference; and popular personalities who are regarded positively by people of all sorts of political persuasion who do not necessarily vote for them when the election comes. This had been the case for both Jacques Chaban-Delmas and Raymond Barre in former presidential elections, and for Simone Veil, as leader of a list in the European elections of 1989; Delors' popularity – had he decided to stand – would probably have suffered too. Edouard Balladur, in January 1995, had the advantage both of being in power, and of being popular – Jacques Chirac on the other hand had never been among the stars in the popularity ratings and was, in addition, playing the role of a more and more critical supporter of a popular government whose leader was from his own party. The number of votes which Edouard Balladur was said to command was thus inevitably overestimated, as was Jacques Chirac's underestimated. Lionel Jospin was late in emerging as the Socialist candidate and suffered both from the fact that his credibility as a potential President was uncertain, and that in any case there was a strong reaction against the Socialists after President Mitterrand's fourteen years in office. It was thus obvious that, over time, support for Lionel Jospin, as measured by the polls, would increase. He was presented as a decent, honest man and as the only hope of rebuilding a credible opposition force on the left. In other words it was, all in all, singularly imprudent to think that the election had already been won by Edouard Balladur. That is, however, what Jérôme Jaffré, director of political studies at the SOFRES and one of the subtlest connoisseurs of French politics seemed to believe when he published in *Le Monde* on 12 January 1995 an article entitled 'For public opinion, the presidential election has already been won'.[20] Jaffré underlined the favourable image Edouard Balladur had in public opinion and showed that this was confirmed by his score of voting intentions. He had the double advantage of being able to count both on the political links between the UDF and RPR supporters and on the sociological links between the right and the centre. Jaffré did not take into account the fact that Raymond Barre had been in a similar position in 1988 and had run into trouble. Lionel Jospin, moreover, Jaffré explained, was not Mitterrand, and was far less likely to draw votes away from Balladur than Mitterrand had from Chirac in 1988. For Jaffré, the government's record was in Balladur's favour this time and not in Chirac's. Moreover, the fact that Edouard Balladur was a member of the RPR gave him an influence that Barre could never have hoped for within the RPR electorate. As for Jacques Chirac's attempt to by-pass Edouard Balladur by means of a grass-roots campaign appealing to the people against the élites, this was hindered by his former image and by the durability of the division between left and right. Jaffré's only reservation was the volatility of the electorate, in particular within the governing majority. But this was seen essentially as the result of the delay in the declaration or designation of the principal candidates. He concluded: 'It is still too soon to say, but if M. Balladur is elected [...] it can be said that the presidential election was won even before it was fought'.[21] He illustrated his argument by opinion polls, thus seeming more scientific than politicians' statements or journalists' commentaries. But there was a double flaw in such reasoning: it overestimated the solidity of public opinion three months before the first round, and underestimated the impact Chirac's energetic, iconoclastic social campaign was to have.

The purpose of pre-campaign polls

Because they cannot see into the future, does this mean that the opinion polls served no purpose and were even harmful? They were in a sense harmful for those who drew too much from them. They had, for instance, a boomerang effect on the Balladurians, in that too much confidence was placed in them, leading to a concomitant lack of vigour invested in campaigning itself. One thing is certain: the polls did not prevent the voters from making up their own minds. The voters reversed the ratings of Balladur and Chirac around 21 February 1995 and the order in which Chirac and Jospin came on the first round on 23 April. If the polls put Edouard Balladur at the top, they did not at any time indicate – as they had done for Valéry Giscard d'Estaing – that Jacques Chirac had become marginalised. Chirac remained the outsider before becoming, late in the day, the favourite. Opinion polls, when used with the necessary precaution, enabled commentators to interpret a situation which was rendered complex by the record number of *potential* candidates (Balladur, Chirac, Rocard, Delors, Giscard, Barre, Fabius....). The polls were of course only one of several indicators used in political decision-making. They did not prevent Jacques Chirac from soldiering on, nor Jacques Delors from giving up. They did not decide who would stand – that remained firmly in the hands of the individuals concerned. It is the political actor who weighs up his or her chances and the political cost of standing, basing decisions on a more or less rational interpretation of the polls – but also on the belief in his or her ability to change people's opinions and the conviction that the candidacy serves a purpose.

The polls are an excellent scapegoat when things go wrong and when a candidate who was expecting to win loses, as the attacks of the Balladurians – who had used the polls against Jacques Chirac – showed on the evening of the first round. Was defeat due to 'manipulation'? 'We must have it out',[22] declared François Léotard, Balladur's strongest supporter. The publishing of the opinion polls had 'led public opinion astray', Simone Veil, another Balladur supporter, added. And Edouard Balladur's spokesman, Nicolas Sarkozy, underlined 'the formidable defeat'[23] of the opinion polling institutes, guilty, in his opinion, of having told the French near polling day that the election had already been won by Jacques Chirac.

Were the opinion polls biased?

The evolution of the ratings of Balladur and Chirac (see graph 1) is the most spectacular illustration of how the polls progressed from the time when the polling institutes first successfully predicted the actual line-up of major candidates.[24] The intersection of their respective graphs on 21-22 February 1995 came as a surprise, and upset many calculations. The dispersal of the results of the surveys around the average of the various polls at each moment of the campaign rarely exceeded the normal margin of error (2 to 3 percentage points for a sample of around 1000 people). It must also be stressed that there was a consensus among the polling institutes up until 20 February with all the surveys putting Chirac behind Balladur. On that date came the first poll (BVA) to put Jacques Chirac on an equal footing at 21% with Edouard Balladur. This was confirmed on the following day by an IPSOS survey placing them both at 22%. From then on all the institutes put Balladur behind Chirac, with only one exception, a survey by SOFRES (21-23 Feb.) who subsequently fell into line with the other institutes.[25] Chirac's poll rating rocketed, while Edouard Balladur's crashed after a faltering start to his campaign. It must be said that if there was an error it must have been the error of all the polls, all the time, a most unlikely scenario, especially given that the institutes are commercial rivals and therefore not actively seeking a consensus; and that they use different sampling and weighting methods. It should be stressed, moreover, that they have very rarely been wrong in their predictions since pre-election polls first flourished in 1965, on the occasion of the first presidential election.

Accusations have been levelled at pollsters to the effect that some candidates have a poll rooting for them – SOFRES for Edouard Balladur, for instance, or BVA for Jacques Chirac, and perhaps even IPSOS against Lionel Jospin. We can assess this by comparing the results of individual institutes with the average results of all six institutes. Does a particular poll overestimate one candidate or underestimate another in a repeated, regular fashion? Out of 11 surveys, SOFRES put Edouard Balladur above the average six times, below four times, and once exactly on the average; as for Jacques Chirac, SOFRES put him higher than the average of the polls three times and below eight times. The bias against Chirac, although it is not systematic, is perceptible. BVA ran ten surveys in all and put Jacques Chirac above four times, below four times and on the average twice. So there was no obvious advantage for Jacques Chirac. But BVA put Edouard Balladur eight times below the average, and only twice above. Here again if there was a bias it was negative rather than positive, since Chirac was not systematically overevaluated whereas Balladur was underrated. IPSOS – nine surveys – overestimated Edouard Balladur (six times above, three times below); with regard to Jacques Chirac the results seem neutral (four times above, four times below the average), while during the dominant Chiraquian phase IPSOS was more pessimistic than the opinion polls as a whole and more optimistic for Balladur. With regard to Lionel Jospin, IPSOS put him twice above the poll average before the beginning of the campaign in January but after that underestimated him continually. IPSOS was the only institute to predict (wrongly, on the 21 April in its last, unpublished, poll before the first round), the elimination of Jospin and a second round involving Chirac and Balladur.[26] All the other institutes pitted Chirac against Jospin.

Bias when it exists is thus extremely limited, being probably due to methodological options (methods of weighting for instance) rather than to political choices. There is no evidence of a deliberate attempt at manipulation.

The error of the first ballot

The error of the polls in the first round must, however, be explained. In the second round there was no error since the evolution had been clearly revealed in the final confidential surveys (see Tables 1 and 2, below).

None of the polling institutes gave the results of the first round in the right order. It is customary not to pay too much attention to the over- and under-evaluation of candidates in the polls, provided they give the candidates in the right order. All the polls had given Chirac a clear-cut lead in this first round of voting. He was seen as coasting serenely towards the Elysée. In the event, Jospin headed the only poll that counted – the election result itself. IPSOS was also mistaken as to the runner-up, putting Edouard Balladur and not Jospin in second place behind Chirac.

All the institutes underestimated Jospin (2.5 points minimum SOFRES to 5 points maximum IPSOS); all overestimated Chirac (2.5 points minimum IPSOS to 4 points maximum BVA); four institutes out of six predicted Balladur's score accurately (Harris gave the result exactly; IFOP, CSA, IPSOS to 0.5 point) but two overestimated it (SOFRES by 2 points, BVA by 3). The deviations remained within the normal margin of error, as far as the results of Le Pen, Hue, Laguiller, Voynet and Cheminade were concerned. Only de Villiers among all the lesser candidates was overestimated by 1 to 1.5 points by all the institutes.

An examination of voting intentions during the last phase of the first round gives us some clues as to the reasons for the polling error.

If we look first at the underestimation of Jospin (Graph 2), one hypothesis was that on the day, voters on the left had not wanted to waste their votes on minor candidates and thus cause the major candidate on the left to be eliminated.[27] Voting intentions on the eve of the first round would not have enabled one to predict this: polls showed a rise in the ratings of the minor candidates on the non-Socialist left from the end of the first week in April,[28] whereas Jospin's score, from the end of the first week in March, stagnated. Nonetheless, an in-depth analysis of voters' responses to the IFOP exit poll of 23 April 1995 shows that Lionel Jospin reached his score of 23% of votes cast by taking four points from voters who had initially intended to vote for Robert Hue, and two points respectively from those who were in favour of Arlette Laguiller and Dominique Voynet.

Table 1

The results of the final (unpublished*) polls and the election results in the first round, on 23 April 1995 (% cast in metropolitan France)

Candidates	rounded results	HARRIS 19-20/4	IFOP 20-21/4	CSA 20-21/4	SOFRES 20-21/4	IPSOS 21/4	BVA 22/4
1 Jospin	23	20 (-3)	20 (-3)	19.5(-3.5)	20.5(-2.5)	18(-5)	20 (-3)
2 Chirac	20.5	24 (+3.5)	24 (+3.5)	24 (+3.5)	24 (+3.5)	23(+2.5)	24.5(+4)
3 Balladur	18.5	18.5(=)	18 (-0.5)	19 (+0.5)	16.5(-2)	19(+0.5)	15.5(-3)
4 Le Pen	15	14.5(-0.5)	14 (-1)	14 (-1)	14 (-1)	14(-1)	14.5(-0.5)
5 Hue	8.5	9 (+0.5)	9 (+0.5)	8 (-0.5)	9.5 (+1)	9 (+0.5)	9 (+0.5)
6 Laguiller	5.5	4.5 (-1)	5 (-0.5)	6 (+0.5)	5 (-0.5)	6 (+0.5)	5 (-0.5)
7 de Villiers	5	6.5 (+1.5)	6.5 (+1.5)	6 (+1)	6 (+1)	6 (+1)	6.5 (+1.5)
8 Voynet	3.5	3 (-0.5)	3.5 (=)	3.5 (=)	4 (+0.5)	5 (+1.5)	4.5 (+1)
9 Cheminade	0.5	0 (-0.5)	0 (-0.5)	0 (-0.5)	0.5 (=)	0 (-0.5)	0.5 (=)

Major candidates
(1 + 2 +3)	62	62.5(+0.5)	62 (=)	62.5(+0.5)	61 (-1)	60(-2)	60 (-2)

Minor left-wing candidates
(5 + 6 + 8)	17.5	16.5(-1)	17.5(=)	17.5(=)	18.5(+1)	20(+2.5)	18.5(+1)

Minor right-wing candidates
(4 + 7)	20	21 (+1)	20.5(+0.5)	20 (=)	20 (=)	20(=)	21 (+1)

Total Left + Ecologists
	40.5	36.5(-4)	37.5(-3)	37 (-3.5)	39 (-1.5)	38(-2.5)	38.5(-2)

(Variance)		(+/-1.22)	(+/-1.22)	(+/-1.27)	(+/-1.33)	(+/-1.44)	(+/-1.55)

* unpublished given the ban imposed by the law to publish or comment on opinion polls in the week preceding a ballot (Law of 19 July 1977).

Table 2

The results of the final (unpublished) polls and the election results in the second round, on 7 May 1995 (% votes cast in metropolitan France)

Candidates	rounded results	HARRIS 4 May	CSA 3 May	SOFRES 4-5 May	IPSOS 5 May	BVA 6 May	IFOP 6 May
1 Chirac	52.5	52 (-0.5)	53 (+0.5)	53 (+0.5)	53 (+0.5)	52 (-0.5)	53.5 (+1)
2 Jospin	47.5	48 (+0.5)	47 (-0.5)	47 (-0.5)	47 (-0.5)	48 (+0.5)	46.5 (-1)

On the other hand, those who had hesitated between Jospin and another candidate of the left were in the event more faithful to Jospin. He only conceded four points to the three minor left-wing candidates. So overall he gained four points, sufficient to make the difference between the last polls and the actual result. This rallying to Jospin in the polling booth itself is in keeping with what the exit polls tell us about the political motivations of the Jospin vote. Here we might note in particular the IFOP poll according

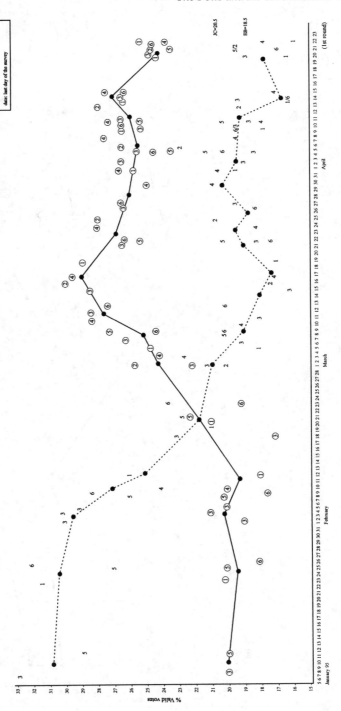

Graph 1. Evolution of voting intentions (1st round): J. Chirac against E. Balladur

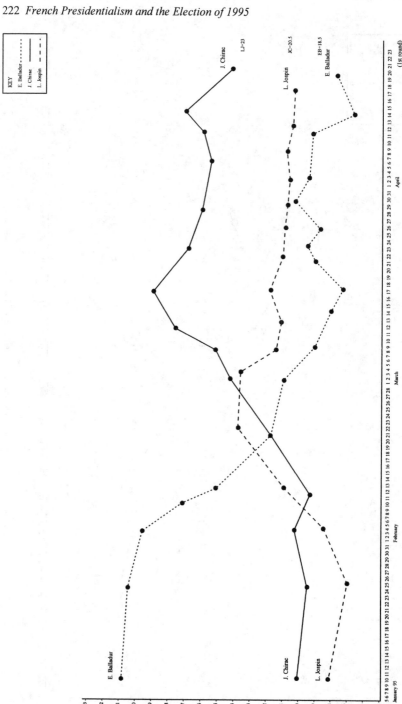

Graph 2. Evolution of voting intentions (1st round): J. Chirac, E. Balladur, L. Jospin

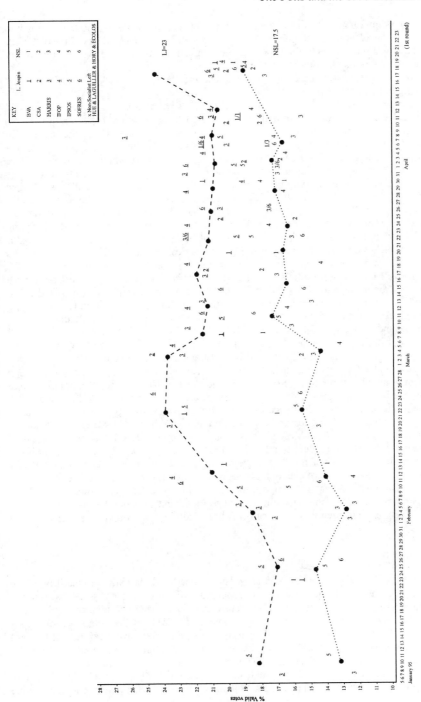

Graph 3. Evolution of voting intentions (1st round): Lionel Jospin and the Non-Socialist Left

to which only 50% of Jospin voters chose him on the first ballot in the hope he would 'become President of the Republic', whereas 65% of Balladur voters and 73% of Chirac voters chose their candidate in the hope he would enter the Elysée. The second major motivation for Jospin voters was 'for him to be a candidate in the run-off'.[29] In other words these voters wanted a left-right contest and that meant backing Jospin and not wasting their votes.

The overestimation of Jacques Chirac on the first ballot was a different matter. Did potential voters who would normally have selected Jacques Chirac believe him to be so far ahead in the polls that they did not bother to vote? The analyses of the increase in abstentions noted on the first round (21.6% of those on the electoral register, as against 18.6% in 1988 and 18.9% in 1981) do not enable us to identify whether there were more abstentions among Chirac's voters than among those voting for other candidates. There was a higher level of non-voting in Paris, one of Chirac's strongholds: 27% as against 23% in 1988 and 22.5% in 1981. But in Corrèze – the other main Chirac heartland – there were only 14% of non-voters and the department had the highest turnout in France.

Another explanation was the possibility of tactical voting: Chirac supporters casting their votes in favour of Lionel Jospin to keep out Balladur and prevent a Chirac-Balladur fight on the second round. There certainly was tactical voting but the number of voters concerned was too low for it to be apparent in the surveys.

In fact all the opinion polling institutes had registered a clear fall in the Chirac vote from 26% on average to 24% between the last published polls (eight days before the first round) and their unpublished surveys on the eve of polling day. The dip in Chirac's score was expressed by the pollsters. It was partly due to a last-minute rise in Balladur's score – from around 17% on the 14-15 April to 18% on the 20-21 April. According to the IFOP exit poll, Chirac finally gained 4.5 points from voters who had hesitated between him and Balladur, 2 points from those who had been attracted to Jean-Marie Le Pen in the first instance, and 1.5 points from those who were inclined to vote for Philippe de Villiers: this amounts altogether to an 8 point progression. But Chirac lost 10.5 points among voters hesitating between him and another candidate – 6 to Balladur, 3 to Le Pen and 1.5 to de Villiers. Jacques Chirac was, therefore, on a downward slope – which advantaged Edouard Balladur and to a lesser extent Le Pen and de Villiers. Could Edouard Balladur have caught up with him? Most pundits thought it impossible for this new reversal of opinion to benefit Balladur greatly. The lead taken by Jacques Chirac after 20-21 February had come sufficiently late in the campaign to be interpreted as the *outcome* (for most voters) of a process of electoral choice and not as a transitory preference for floating voters. The other indicators of public opinion – in particular what voters wanted the outcome of the presidential election to be, and the extent to which the main candidates were seen as 'présidentiable' – confirmed the solidity of voting intentions at that moment.[30]

Conclusion

When they were wrong-footed, all the pollsters underlined the extreme volatility of the voters and talked of the new and exceptional difficulty of their work as election predictors. The argument is not without substance. But it must be tempered. First, this volatility was not totally new. According to SOFRES, 23% of the voters, in mid-April 1988, said they might still change their minds; a similar poll gave a result of 29% (+6) seven years later.[31] Second, the volatility was not equal in all the electorates and usually concerned neighbouring electorates. The major candidates – Chirac, Jospin and, to a lesser extent, Balladur – and the small extreme candidates (Le Pen, Hue) had a more stable electorate than the others. Most floating voters hesitated between candidates who were politically close, like Chirac and Balladur or Jospin and Hue, or even Chirac and Le Pen. The difficulty in measuring the volatility of voters for the pollsters and other election pundits raises a scientific challenge: but it is not because a situation becomes more complex that the expert should give up.

Notes

1. 'Sondomanie'. *Le Figaro*, 8 February 1995. Unless otherwise indicated, all translations are the authors'.
2. 'Sondagite'. *Le Monde*, 9 February 1995.
3. CB News, 2 May 1995.
4. According to BVA (28-29 January 1994 for *Figaro Magazine*), François Mitterrand would be beaten in the second round by Edouard Balladur (65 to 35) and by Jacques Chirac (54-46). He would scrape through against Valéry Giscard d'Estaing (51-49). According to Harris (24-25 June 1994 for *VSD*), all three leaders of the majority would beat him: E. Balladur (59-41), J. Chirac (57-43) and V. Giscard d'Estaing (56-44).
5. From late March to early April 1993, the popularity scores of Edouard Balladur were at a record level of 'confidence' (73% – SOFRES), of 'good opinions' (58% – BVA) and of 'satisfaction' (56% – IFOP). In September this honeymoon period, contrary to normal circumstances, continued and had indeed become even more positive.
6. *Le Sondoscope* (the French review of opinion polls), 94, January 1994 used the expression 'l'année Balladur' after the *Financial Times* had declared that 1993 was Balladur's year on 31 December 1993.
7. 'La popularité présidentielle d'Edouard Balladur', *Le Figaro*, 8 October 1993.
8. 'Le désir de confiance', *Le Figaro*, 25 November 1993. ('C'est d'abord la désillusion Socialiste qui fait l'espérance balladurienne, en créant un "désir de confiance" dans l'électorat. Cependant les qualités dites de calme et de modération du Premier ministre peuvent demain se décliner sur le mode de l'inaction et de l'apathie, et "le désir de confiance" d'aujourd'hui devenir le désabusement de demain'.) See also, by the same author, 'De la popularité comparative', *Le Figaro*, 11 March 1994.
9. See Gilles Paris, 'La popularité relative du premier ministre', *Le Monde*, 27 November 1993.
10. 'L'humeur paradoxale des Français', *Le Monde*, 24 December 1993.
11. See Jean Charlot's article: 'Le point de vue d'un politologue. Savoir lire les sondages. Tout est-il donc joué pour 1995?', *Le Figaro*, 22-23 January 1994. Charlot stressed that the election was still 15 months away (an 'eternity'), that nothing was settled and that too much must not be read into the opinion polls.
12. An attempt was made at public reconciliation during the RPR's parliamentary study days at La Rochelle at the end of September 1993.
13. Over a more or less lengthy period in 1994: IPSOS until July, SOFRES until September, BVA until October, and Harris until December. Most of the time a UDF rival (Giscard or Barre) was envisaged against Balladur and against Chirac. But BVA – from November 1993 to October 1994 – and SOFRES – from January to September 1994 – would also test the hypothesis of Balladur or Chirac as the single candidate for the RPR and the UDF in the first round.
14. Harris and IPSOS in January, BVA and SOFRES in the second half of February, CSA and IFOP at the beginning of March 1995.

[15] Only Harris from early January to early April 1994 tested Rocard without testing Delors in a whole series of surveys.

[16] Robert Schneider, 'Balladur s'envole, Rocard plonge', *Le Nouvel Observateur*, 20 May 1993 (commentary of a SOFRES barometer). See also the commentary of a Harris poll in 'Le sacre de l'automne. Edouard Balladur et Jacques Delors sont pour l'instant sans rivaux. Avantages et limites de la non-candidature', *Valeurs Actuelles*, 13 September 1993. Schneider wrote in the *Nouvel Observateur*: 'In terms of the parties, nothing has changed: Jacques Chirac and Michel Rocard remain the natural candidates. But according to public opinion, they have already been superseded: the only credible candidates are Edouard Balladur on the right and Jacques Delors on the left' ('Dans la logique de parti, rien de changé: Jacques Chirac et Michel Rocard restent les candidats naturels. Mais, dans l'opinion, la relève a déjà eu lieu: il n'y a plus de crédibles qu'Edouard Balladur à droite et Jacques Delors à gauche').

[17] 'La présidentielle hors partis', *Le Monde*, 29 September 1994. ('...dans le choix des candidats les préférences des électeurs, mesurées par les sondages, pèsent davantage que les voeux des formations politiques [...] sauf bouleversement, seuls Edouard Balladur, Jacques Chirac et Jacques Delors peuvent espérer devenir le prochain Président de la République').

[18] 'Oublions les sondages, ces tables de la loi des temps incertains. Oublions les arithmétiques électorales'.

[19] 'Etre dans le vent c'est souvent avoir le destin d'une feuille morte'.

[20] 'Pour l'opinion, l'élection présidentielle est déjà jouée'. *Le Monde*, not Jaffré, gave the article its title.

[21] 'Il est encore trop tôt pour le dire, mais si M. Balladur est élu [...] on pourra dire que l'élection présidentielle était jouée avant même que d'être écrite'.

[22] 'Il faudra s'expliquer'.

[23] 'la formidable défaite'.

[24] Apart from some minor details – like the presence of Antoine Waechter and Brice Lalonde (ecologists) who finally did not stand, or that of François Hory (Radical) or again that of Charles Millon (UDF); not to mention the surprise candidate who did stand, Jacques Cheminade.

[25] Survey conducted between 21 and 23 February 1995, by the *Nouvel Observateur* which credited Edouard Balladur with 23.5% and Jacques Chirac with 19% of votes cast.

[26] IFOP and SOFRES overestimated Jospin during the campaign in comparison with the other institutes but were probably nearer the truth if one considers the result on the first round. CSA and BVA underestimated him, as did IPSOS. Harris was constantly around the average of the polls concerning Jospin.

[27] See in particular Jérôme Jaffré's 'Les sondages ne sont pas de la magie', *Le Figaro Magazine*, 28 April 1995; Claude Weill's 'Voici pourquoi les sondeurs se sont trompés', *Le Nouvel Observateur*, 27 April-3 May 1995; Gérard Le Gall's 'Présidentielle 95: une opinion indécise', *Revue politique et parlementaire*, 976, March-April 1995, pp.10-17.

[28] This coincided with the opening of the official television campaign and gave the 'minor' candidates the same amount of free television as the 'major' candidates.

[29] 17% of Balladur's voters and only 8% of Chirac's said they voted to ensure that their candidate would be present in the second round. The exit poll carried out by BVA confirmed this: 53% of Jospin voters 'really hope Jospin will win' (as against 65% of Balladur voters who 'really hope Balladur will win' and 70% of Chirac voters who

'really hope Chirac will win'). 42% of Jospin's voters had decided to vote for him because 'rather Jospin than either of the others'.

[30] 2.25 points more for Jacques Chirac on 23 April than for Edouard Balladur may seem so low as to be reversible. Except if one considers that 2.25 points represent 689,500 voters.

[31] IFOP found a greater difference of electoral volatility, from 13% to 34% (+19) between 1988 and 1995. The fact that the institutes gave very different figures is a problem. During the last (confidential) surveys on the first round, the proportion of floating voters varied from 27% (BVA) to 37% (CSA) and probably even more for IPSOS (figure not published).

Indicative Bibliography

Bacqué, Raphaëlle and Denis Saverot, *Chirac Président – les coulisses d'une victoire* (Paris, du Rocher/DWB, 1995).

Charlot, Jean, *Pourquoi Jacques Chirac? Comprendre la présidentielle 95* (Paris, de Fallois, 1995).

Cotta, Michèle, *Les Secrets d'une victoire* (Paris, Flammarion, 1995).

Ottenheimer, Ghislaine, *L'Impossible victoire* (Paris, Robert Laffont, 1995).

'Haro sur les sondages?', Round table, *Revue politique et parlementaire*, 977, May-June 1995, pp. 4-26.

SOFRES, *L'Etat de l'opinion 1996* (Paris, Seuil, 1996).

14. POLITICS AS NARRATIVE: THE MEDIA, THE POLLS AND PUBLIC OPINION

CATHERINE PRADEILLES

Introduction

A first observation to make about the 1995 presidential campaign is that none of the things which were expected actually happened. Accounts of the events which took place in the months leading up to the campaign, of the campaign itself, and of the outcomes can be summarised as a long list of surprises: from the list of candidates, to the voters' interests, from the thrust of the campaign to the electoral results themselves.

Firstly, the definitive list of candidates was in itself a surprise. Leading in the opinion polls throughout 1994, Jacques Delors, President of the European Commission from 1985 to January 1995, had been expected to stand for the left, and only put an end to the suspense regarding his candidacy by revealing his decision not to compete in December 1994.[1] Lionel Jospin officially became the candidate of the Socialists only at the beginning of February 1995.[2] During this long run-up to the election, the uncertainty about the identity of the Socialist candidate misled commentators, who believed that the PS, the party of government for over a decade, was going to be unable not only to gather enough support to prevent the right from winning the presidency, but even to mount a creditable challenge.

As for the other candidates and their position in the race, the first round was generally expected to be a re-run of the European election of 1994. This election had questioned the dominance of the so-called ruling parties, of both the right and the left, and had launched new movements and leaders. On the left, the election had benefited Bernard Tapie, business tycoon and TV personality, using the small left-wing Mouvement des Radicaux de Gauche (MRG) as his base. Political commentators predicted that he would feature heavily in the presidential race: instead, Bernard Tapie disappeared, discredited in a series of trials for financial fraud. His successor as the candidate of the MRG (renamed 'Radical'), Jean-François Hory (dubbed 'Monsieur demi-point' for his 0.5% score in opinion polls), had to withdraw for lack of support. On the right, a similar process of marginalisation occurred, at the expense of Philippe de Villiers. A Catholic conservative from the Vendée, a staunchly conservative region, de Villiers obtained an astonishing result in the European election,[3] on the strength of his nationalist and traditionalist ideals. He seemed to appear as the respectable alternative to Jean-Marie Le Pen, the successful leader of the racist Front National. Although Philippe de Villiers indeed became a candidate in the presidential election, the score he obtained was dismal, two thirds of his electorate in the European election deserting him. Confusion was heightened when two out of the three potential ecologist candidates, Brice Lalonde and Antoine Waechter, dropped out, incapable of gathering the minimum number of signatures required to stand, making way for Dominique Voynet. In the last days of the pre-campaign period, an unknown figure defying categorisation, Jacques Cheminade, appeared out of the blue. The strangeness of his largely-ignored candidacy only underlined the bizarre nature of the overall line-up.

Another surprise was that the general picture depicted by the media prior to the election did not, as it turned out, correspond to the voters' interests. The swings and turnarounds in the last weeks of the campaign and the quite unexpected outcome of the first round showed that neither the protagonists nor the themes highlighted throughout 1994 and 1995 were those that the voters ultimately regarded as the most important.

Further surprises were in store as far as the personal conflicts and the balance of power were concerned. Both the public and many commentators, assured that the famous left-right distinction was now *passé* and that French people had become 'depoliticised',[4] expected a duel between Edouard Balladur, Prime Minister (RPR) in office since the victory of the right in the 1993 legislative elections, and his political mentor, Jacques Chirac, founding president of the RPR and Mayor of Paris since 1977. The outcome was expected to be a Balladur win.[5] And yet the campaign of the second round proved to be a traditional left-right confrontation. Charles Pasqua, the powerful Interior Minister of the Balladur government in office since April 1993, was deemed to be the kingmaker on this occasion, and tipped to be the next Prime Minister. Instead, he disappeared from the political scene in February 1995, discredited by a politico-judicial scandal; and it was Alain Juppé, main advisor to Chirac during the campaign while at the same time Foreign Minister in the Balladur Government, who became Prime Minister after Jacques Chirac's victory.[6] Ironically, it was the cold technocrat Juppé who triumphed over the colourful and politically legendary Pasqua; and this alongside his master, Chirac, who spent much of the campaign fulminating against the technocrats.

As for the themes of the campaign, expectations were, once again, unrealised. Everyone expected European integration to be one of the core themes of the campaign, in anticipation of the 1996 European summit and in view of the war in Bosnia and the difficulties encountered in the implementation of the Maastricht Treaty.[7] Similarly, the fight against unemployment, running at a very high level in France, seemed a burning issue (although voters apparently had very little confidence in their politicians to solve the problem).[8] But for reasons we shall examine below, Europe ceased, mainly because of the internal debates of the right, to be a feature of the campaign. As for unemployment, Jacques Chirac succeeded in conflating this theme with the concept of 'exclusion', creating a new sphere for his discourse to develop. In so doing, Jacques Chirac's campaign sidestepped the difficult issue of unemployment, minimising its dramatic character by contrasting it with the even greater misery of exclusion from the basic rights to food, accommodation and healthcare: homeless people, sleeping rough and begging on the streets embodied the notion of exclusion for the media.

Regarding the general thrust of the campaign, the surprise was even greater. Voters, weary of politics and wary of vain electoral promises, were expected to be either timid or blasé. Campaigns such as Edouard Balladur's were expected, constructed upon the achievements of his government and upon a refusal to make wild promises. Instead, however, Jacques Chirac's campaign signalled the victory of the rhetoric of change and of voluntarism.[9] Jacques Chirac would not (to paraphrase him) be restricted to making new proposals, but set out to exemplify a new way of thinking and acting in the political realm; in this way Chirac reintegrated the voluntarism of old Gaullist rhetoric back into the discourse of presidentialism.

The electoral results came also as a surprise and proved everyone wrong, especially after the first round.[10] The right was expected to triumph on the evening of the first round, but the Socialist candidate came first.[11] Balladur was for a long time (until February 1995) deemed a sure winner, and Chirac was elected instead.[12] The Greens were expected to make a reasonable showing, if they presented a single candidate; they did, but instead it was Arlette Laguiller, legendary figure of the revolutionary left, who did better than expected.[13] In short, the whole campaign unfolded and was fought under the sign of misinterpretations: not a single institution was able at the time to keep up with what was really going on.

In view of this catalogue of surprises and disappointments, it is clear that an analysis is required of some of the circumstances that brought them about, and of the sources of information which contributed to and reported them, in order to throw light upon voters' expectations and their relationship to the political process on the occasion of this sixth election of the President of the Republic by universal suffrage.

Public opinion and élite interpretations

It is clear from what we have said above that we cannot rely upon what the media, politicians and political experts, expressing themselves during the campaign, put forward as the opinion of the French people. A great number of errors of analysis occurred, and even after the election few gave a clear view as to why a majority voted Jacques Chirac into the presidency. Nor can we rely on the results of opinion polls alone, inspired as they are by certain expectations and preconceptions for they tend to lead to sets of closed questions which, in turn, condition the answers of interviewees and the interpretation of those answers by the pollsters. At their best, opinion polls give only a partial picture. A consensual picture of public opinion is nowhere to be found, election results themselves testifying to the fragmentary nature of 'public opinion'. An election is a decision-making process: its purpose is to choose, in a constitutional framework, an individual and a programme, supposedly meeting the expectations of the nation. At the same time, the effectiveness of this decision does not rely on a consensus, but on the agreement of a simple majority. In fact, of course, there are probably as many different expectations as there are voters; and people are, or feel, involved in their political institutions to varying degrees. It is instructive to explore why the task of surveying their views is so complex.

How do we account for the many surprises and misperceptions outlined above? Two institutions can be said to be responsible for spreading most of the errors in forecasting and in interpreting voters' expectations: the media and the political analysts. As the discourse of the media and of French political scientists is one of the most important primary sources for understanding the period, it is vital to be clear as to the difficulties associated with this material.

Starting with the media, we need to ask what the nature of the relationship between public opinion and the media is. Aside from any theoretical debate, let us focus on a practical observation: in the absence of strong political activism and of a strong social framework, it is principally through mediation by the media that most citizens perceive themselves as members of a national political community. Through such mediation, individuals also have an opportunity to evaluate the position of their personal opinion against the full scale of public opinion, particularly when presented with numerous opinion poll results; and the broadcasting of a political image of the community contributes to the shaping of these same individual opinions. In addition to this mission of the media, i.e. to represent the national community and inform the nation as a whole, the media and their discourse(s) are informed in their turn by their own constructed view of the expectations of their audience. As part of the economic imperative of the media, they must attract the largest audience possible. They must, therefore, anticipate daily what people are expecting to watch, read and listen to. As a result of these two constraints – a mission to give the nation a picture of the entire community, and the need to appeal to a large audience – the media do not voice public opinion directly; they are nevertheless a leading force in the shaping and dissemination of public opinion.

Sociologists and political analysts are, in France, courted by the media and by politicians seeking rational, scientific legitimation of their activities. Whether journalists, political writers, or renowned academics, these experts model and interpret the evolution of public opinion, which is then disseminated by the media. We can name here just a few of these sought-after specialists: Alain Duhamel, François-Henri de Virieu (France 2 Television); Ivan Levaï (France Inter); Anne Sinclair, Gérard Carreyrou (TF1); Philippe Alexandre, Michèle Cotta (RTL); Franz-Olivier Giesbert (Europe 1) are all commentators and highly-informed interviewers; Jérôme Jaffré (Sofres), Roland Cayrol (CSA), and Jean-Luc Parodi (Ifop) are eminent pollsters, Jean-Marie Colombani (Le Monde) is an eminent editorialist; Professors Georges Vedel and Jean-Louis Quermonne are authoritative analysts of institutional matters; Olivier Todd is an equally eminent academic whose ideas were a possible inspiration for Chirac's campaign. The many mistaken expectations we have mentioned, however, suggest a marked discrepancy between the real voters' expectations, and the images of public opinion disseminated by the media and given discursive shape by the experts. In order to look at this discrepancy between the discourse of the media and voters' behaviour, let us consider two examples, one during the first round of the campaign, the other during the second.

When the media and commentators highlighted the Chirac-Balladur duel, because the two candidates were old friends and belonged to the same party, and when, between the two rounds, they emphasised the televised Chirac-Jospin debate, hoping to focus on its conflictual potential, it is not that they misread the expectations of their audience, since the 'epic' nature of these confrontations had indeed claimed the attention of the public. But neither 'duel' lived up to its potential entertainment value: there was, in fact, no confrontation to speak of in the end. Instead of being fought between two rivals on the right, the second round fell in the traditional mould of a left-right contest. As for the televised debate between Chirac and Jospin, the two winners of the first round settled for dialogue rather than bellicose exchange, each refusing to submit to the scenario predicted by the media. These two examples show how different was the version of the campaign anticipated and disseminated by the media from what actually happened as far as the voters were concerned.

The media, then, recreate an image of current affairs. In view of their prevalence in the public space and their mission to inform immediately, they are responsible for broadcasting an intelligible account of the present. In so doing, they are subject to a first constraint of clarification which, of course, leaves room for misrepresentation, however minor. The media are also subject, as we have seen, to economic constraint, that of audience ratings, which reinforces the story-telling tendency to dramatise, as much in the choice of events as in their commentaries. For example, the expression 'more and more' is used over and over again by the French media whatever the nature of the event commented, to imply a narrative dynamic suggesting a progression or series of events that are, literally, 'news': there is 'more and more' violence in our cities, the young are 'more and more' disillusioned with politics, etc. In the case of political analysts, constantly called upon by the media to prepare and comment upon numerous opinion polls – there were more than two new political opinion polls published every day on average during the campaign[14] – they were expected to enlighten audiences; on the whole, they made fools of themselves instead.[15] The results of opinion polls, including those prepared with the greatest scientific integrity, were subverted by the interpretative imperatives of the media and by the popular desire for narratives, which transformed into forecasts simple snapshots of public opinion. Even political scientists themselves, despite being conscious of possible pitfalls and margins of error, fell prey to the pressure for clarity and story-telling, repeatedly emphasising the so-called 'increased volatility' of the electorate.[16] Less involved, less motivated, more undecided, more than a third of the electorate was said to be behaving in a fickle and unpredictable, even rebellious, manner, choosing either not to participate at all (the decline of electoral participation rates in the Fifth Republic is often interpreted as a sign of protest) or else to react to social, economic and political circumstances by voting for candidates and parties with aggressive electoral manifestos, particularly in the areas of immigration and taxes. Whatever the wider explanations for such unpredictable and rebellious voting, one of the variables rarely taken into consideration is the voter's own reaction not only to his or her own circumstances but also to the (potentially contradictory) scientific discourse of experts, and to the commercial mission of the media, as well as the general public's taste for dramatic narratives, and this, of course, in the context of the epistemological impossibility of fully understanding or of anticipating the immediate future.

A further factor to consider, and perhaps the most paradoxical phenomenon of all, is that the whole group of protagonists, voters, politicians, journalists and analysts, exalted the presidential function during this campaign, at the same time as they were confronted with the institutional reality of a weakened, impotent, almost absent President.[17] The real paradox, however, is the unspoken reverence the French have for the office. This is not always apparent, especially from polls and surveys. To illustrate public perception of the presidency, however, we should look at the symbolic aspect of the transfer of power between François Mitterrand and Jacques Chirac. In January 1996, seven months after the election of Chirac, at the time of the death of François Mitterrand, there was an extraordinary outpouring of public devotion for the man who for fourteen years had embodied the French Republic. In view of the intensity of this emotion, some commentators were able to say, that not until this moment was Jacques Chirac able to claim for himself the quasi-sacred dimension of the President, transcending the ideological opposition between himself and his predecessor; and that it was only upon the death of Mitterrand that the true transfer of power took place. To the extent that these insights are true, we can see from such mythifying of the men and the office involved that the very notion of presidential power exceeds by far that inscribed in the constitutional text of 1958.

This raises fundamental questions about the very nature of people's relationship with their political institutions. Just as the aura of power of the President exceeds his constitutional competences, the expectations of French public opinion in this campaign far exceeded the technical issues listed in the official manifestos and the media. The fight against unemployment, wages, social security, pensions, taxes, European policy, the place of the young and of women in society, the fight against Aids, this ready-made list of topics about which people have to express their concerns when interviewed by pollsters, does not even begin to address the full extent and the true nature of voters' expectations. Just as voters probably expect the President to embody a certain idea of power, and of the relationship between the citizens and their institutions, their expectations in social, economic, institutional, and international fields are vaguer, more various, and wider ranging than the media, the politicians, the pollsters and researchers can ever suggest.

In these circumstances, then, what do voters' expectations consist of, and where should we look for their manifestation? The most likely hypothesis, and this is the implication from the thrust of our discussion so far, is that these expectations are the product of a mix of rationality and affectivity, of preoccupations not merely restricted to institutional matters, but involving everyday issues and worries, and more or less accurate memories of the institutional past and of political and philosophical views of the world, however sophisticated or unsophisticated. In order to address the significance of these influences, we need first to ask whether there is actually a theoretical difference between the notion of *public opinion* and that of *voters*.

Are voters' expectations before an election just expressions of public opinion on political issues? This is the broad assumption made by the polling institutes. Do the French become voters only on election days when they vote? Before and after such days, is the opinion which a pollster can collect of a different nature? On a factual level, it is true that only on election days does the expression of a personal preference coincide with a performative act of decision, rich in consequences for the future of the community. In the French Republic, one can observe on election days a phenomenon which is at the heart of the notion of national unity: the normal fragmentation of society into groups, classes, professions and interests disappears to make room for the expression of a public will. Contrary to the situation in monarchical regimes, the election of the President of the French Republic is the constitutional step which most specifically embodies this symbolic transmutation of French society into one indivisible people. This phenomenon has been referred to as 'presidentialism'.[18] The notion of presidentialism tends, among other things, to symbolise a balanced and complex institutional system where the executive power is dominant, but shared between the President and (in France) the Prime Minister, who needs to be supported by the Parliament. The President embodies the political unity of the national community, through his single and powerful persona, a role which has reinforced the tendency to personalise in French politics.[19] The singular mystique of the relationship between voters and President, specific to the Fifth French Republic, goes back formally to de Gaulle's 1962 reform of the electoral law regarding the election of the President by universal suffrage. Since then, the presidential election has become the high point of French political life. This phenomenon reinforces the unique value of election day, and the unique status of voters on that particular day.

Before and after an election, then, the analyst will meet only with 'public opinion'.[20] The links between public opinion on the one hand, and voters on the other, have not been established scientifically, and they are not stable – one of the factors preventing the use of political opinion polls in anticipating the outcome of a vote. 'Public opinion' is a vaguer notion than 'voters', and manifests itself in a considerably wider range of ways. In order to establish an accurate expression of public expectations, we need to reassess the sources available, and to pay more attention to the events most likely to influence these expectations. Comparing these sources with the outcome of the vote is one of the more efficient means of understanding the nature of, and shifts within, people's aspirations.

Where then, if not in the discourse of the media, are these aspirations to be recorded and deciphered? Many institutions exist which are meant to represent people's opinion or interests, and could therefore be expected to voice their expectations: legislative and consultative bodies, political parties, unions, associations, lobbies. For many of them, however, the French people are often more of a target than an authentic inspiration,[21] and the image they portray of their constituents may be just as prone to error as is the media. We can take political parties as an example. It is the work of politicians and political parties to anticipate the major preoccupations of public opinion and to shape the proposals which will meet with public support. It is the work of the candidate to embody these themes and proposals, synthesised in the shape of a certain vision of France. But this anticipation is also prone to error: error about the state of public opinion (diagnostic error); error about the expectations and the level of support in public opinion (error about proposals and means); error about the person and vision of the candidate (error of image, of reputation, of symbolism).

This brings us to a final important factor which also needs to be taken into account during election periods: the events themselves. There can be no doubt that the anticipations, the proposals and the personal chemistry of each candidate in 1995 were continuously confronted and compared during the campaign, not only with those of other candidates, but also with a continuum of events apparently external to the electoral sphere. This being the case, the interactions and chain reactions which take place, not only between the various actors of public life but also between them and current affairs, pull the strategies of each camp into a particular dynamic, and give the election campaign its shape and rhythm, as we shall demonstrate in the following section. This dynamic is not neutral, because it displaces perspectives and modifies the electoral priorities of both candidates and the public, and creates a context, a background against which the candidates' rhetorical effects are projected and distorted. The impact of current affairs on public opinion is another way in which the media manifests itself, not only projecting a given image of public opinion and of the national community as a whole, but also offering a way to perceive the meaning and impact of current affairs.

It is clear, then, that *something* happened to French public opinion in the months preceding the election, and that the unravelling of this sequence of events is a key element in understanding electoral priorities and, more broadly, the realities of French politics. It is this *something*, which is not just a sequence of events but belongs to the realm of perception, that we shall attempt to identify in the next section of this chapter. It is also clear, however, that the task of documenting and analysing voters' expectations in 1995 is a complex one, requiring a careful assessment of potential sources and an approach which addresses the dynamics and volatility of the electoral period. In order to frame our enquiry, therefore, let us summarise the sources and approach adopted in our analysis.

Interpreting the campaign

Sources and method

The media, first, and notwithstanding our reservations about their 'objectivity', are central to an understanding of the period under study. This is so because, as we have seen, they a) broadcast a global political image of the community; b) amplify the interpretations of political experts and the stances of the politicians; and c) present current affairs to the public. The media produce a continuous and continuously shifting dramatised picture of French society, as well as a metaphorical story of current politics. Our analysis is based on detailed study of the influential dailies *Le Monde* and *Le Figaro*, and of the following magazines, from October 1994 to May 1995 (and before or after these dates *ad hoc*): *Enjeux-Les Echos, L'Entreprise, L'Evénement du Jeudi, L'Expansion, L'Express, Le Nouvel Economiste, Le Nouvel Observateur, Le Point*, and *Problèmes politiques et sociaux*, published by La Documentation française. Our corpus also includes the important 1.00pm and 8.00pm news programmes on TF1 and France 2 both before and during the official campaign.

Our second source was opinion polls: not only the many polls assessing the relative popularity of presidential candidates, but also those which address the whole range of social and political issues. Opinion polls are significant in two respects: because they give a picture, through the scope of their questions as much as through the answers given, of the view of public opinion dominant at the time; and because they are very often commissioned by the media, and their results widely debated. In addition to the study of the polls by the media, we have made extensive use of the specialised journal *Le Sondoscope*, and referred to the publications of polling institutes and specialised organisations such as SOFRES, *L'Etat de l'opinion 1994* and *1995*; *Enquêtes Louis-Harris 1995*; *L'Etat de la France 1994-95* and *1995-96* studies of the CERC (Centre d'Etude des Revenus et des Coûts); and studies of the INSEE (Institut National de la Statistique et des Etudes Economiques).

The third source consists of candidates' manifestos. All of the candidates' manifestos contained, in different orders, similar themes. Looking at the manifestos of the three main candidates, for example, these items are: the fight against unemployment, education, housing, taxes, social protection, the reform of the Republic's institutions, politics at local level, justice, the environment, European and international politics. One finds the same topics listed in special issues and studies undertaken by the media and the polling institutes.[22]

Our method has been to look at the shifts of public opinion as expressed through all of the above sources, and to scrutinise these against current events as reported in the French media in 1994 and up to May 1995. Two wide-ranging exercises contributed to this appraisal. First, a comprehensive comparison of the polls given by the specialised journal *Le Sondoscope*; we shall discuss below the place and importance given to various polls in the headlines of the main press, radio and television during the pre-election and campaign period. Second, scrutiny of the way in which candidates themselves represented voters' interests in their communications, and of the gap which existed so often between the themes highlighted and categorised in political manifestos (employment, taxes, social protection, republican institutions, justice, housing, Europe, etc.), and those which effectively captured the headlines during the campaign. These comparisons are the basis for our account, below, of the interaction between political expectation and political reality. (As the reader will have observed, a selection of the many sources exploited, together with explanatory details of events, are referred to in footnotes, as a potential source of information for other researchers and also to avoid excessive digressions within the main body of this chapter).

For clarity of presentation we have divided the election into two periods. The first, from mid-1993 and spanning almost the whole of 1994, was characterised by consensus amongst the media, commentators and, to some extent, the political classes themselves: the presidential election was to be a matter for the right, and Balladur would emerge victorious over Chirac. The left was divided, suffering from uncertainty over the choice of PS candidate and weakened by the shadows cast by the end of Mitterrand's term in office. The second period included an intermediate phase from November/December 1994 to the beginning of February 1995, and encompasses the growing number of scandals tainting Balladur's image, the campaign itself, and Chirac's eventual victories, disappointing on 27 April, undeniable on 7 May. What is of interest here is the disequilibrium between the duration and calm of the first period, almost eighteen months, and the upheaval and drama of the second, barely three months. This tells us a great deal about some of the influences upon French presidentialism and the relationship between presidentialism and the presidential contest itself. Let us now analyse these two periods in more detail, looking at the way voters' expectations emerged in them.

The first period: the art of the status quo

Until the Autumn of 1994, public debate and the media were marked by the same characteristics: restraint, moderation, even silence on certain subjects. The Balladur team's response to his persistent popularity was to cultivate a public image of concern, conviction and reassurance. Firstly, it worked to present the image of a country damaged by more than ten years of socialism; secondly, it informed the French of the hard work, well publicised deeds and remarkable achievements of the Balladur government; finally, it offered congratulations for the results achieved so far, and hinted at greater things to come. This excellent communication strategy was aimed at controlling public discourse and expectations, and at promoting the political stability needed to highlight the value of governmental achievement. To reinforce the message, most of the main pieces of legislation passed by the government from 1993 onwards were long term in nature, their effect spanning the next five years, such as the budgetary laws for 1995 and 1996, and the 'Five-yearly employment law'.[23]

From the time of Edouard Balladur's investiture as Prime Minister and of his general policy declaration on 8 April 1993 his team portrayed the premiership as the start of a new era: the social and economic situation of France was disastrous and the French would have to accept sacrifices. The country was on the verge of bankruptcy and of serious social divisions. A policy of common sense, austerity and realism would have to prevail. A team of professionals was in place, whose hard work would be rewarded in the end. A discourse emphasising governmental concern yet the need for austerity characterised this period. Edouard Balladur sought to prolong this phase of stability, forbidding his ministers to discuss the forthcoming presidential election, and refusing to confirm his possible candidacy. Speaking about the presidential election was synonymous with *bad* politics; *good* politics was about managing France efficiently and telling the French people the truth as to the state of their country.[24]

When commentators called into question the ability of the government to get things done, it referred to the hard work it had already done and to signs of hope for the future. In large measure, the Balladur government appealed to the popular vote through themes of cultural identity: the fight against immigration, under the authority of the formidable Charles Pasqua, or the protection of French agriculture, and of the French culture and language. The Pasqua laws on immigration restricted the granting of French nationality and the right of asylum. In agriculture and culture, the Balladur government succeeded in preserving French interests in the very high profile GATT negotiations.

At the end of 1994, the third aspect of the government's image, reassurance, became more prominent as the first successes began to appear. The most spectacular concerned unemployment: after a marked deterioration in 1993, unemployment stabilised in 1994. December 1994 even brought a slight improvement in the official statistics. Relying on the new employment law, the government was able to issue forecasts of future decreases (200,000 annually).

What does this first period tell us about representations of power to public opinion? The images of power were made essentially through Balladur's communications, and the response of public opinion was consistent and stable for a long period of time. There were a number of elements to the stability of Balladur's image. The first was the appearance of tranquil and sober competence, expressed through examples and symbols of restraint and skilfulness. It was accompanied by tough stances on populist issues, but also by a tendency to retreat in the face of rebellion: Edouard Balladur bypassed, in August 1994, presidential opposition to the Pasqua laws;[25] on the other hand, he withdrew the education bill, aimed at allowing local authorities to finance private schools, and the bill on training for the young unemployed,[26] designed to authorise firms to pay young workers less than the minimum wage. These withdrawals took place in response to demonstrations by the supporters of state run schools in the first case, and strikes and sometimes riots by pupils and students in the second case. Critics talked about weakness and immobilism concerning the government's U-turn over the Air France strikes in October 1993, but opinion preferred to see the Prime Minister as flexible rather than weak. Much of the government's image was controlled through the monopolisation of discourse and the suppression of debate. Edouard Balladur and 'his' ministers (Charles Pasqua, Simone Veil, François Bayrou, François Léotard, all regular guests on politics programmes and the news) gave expansive exposés of governmental action which were in stark contrast to the secrecy and silence imposed upon the parliamentary majority. Debate was suppressed through a refusal by the Prime Minister's team to acknowledge dissension in the Majority, and the invention of the 'presidential taboo'; for months, Matignon asserted the view that the French did not want to hear about the presidential election too soon, and that they were sick of party politics. This later transformed itself into the theme of the 'rejection of polemics'.[27] In the meantime, the long monologue of 1994 took place against the backdrop of 'the necessity of a great debate of ideas'.[28]

The strategic aim was the preservation of calm and social stability, and a semblance of unity in the parliamentary majority. This allowed public attention to focus solely on the paternalistic figure of Edouard Balladur. Recalling the circumstances of ex-Prime Minister Pierre Bérégovoy's suicide, following a harsh campaign for the 1993 legislative election, public attention was drawn to the risk of corruption inherent in political responsibility. The Balladur government set about correcting this negative image of the political class. More importantly perhaps, the constant explanations – clear without being simplistic, convincing but not demagogic, grave but not affected – given by Edouard Balladur to the French people, and in regular appearances on television and in articles published in *Le Monde*, conferred a flattering sense of importance upon the audience. Because Edouard Balladur was able to find a tone far removed from political cant, and seemed to express, through his constant care to explain everything, the value he attached to the support of the French people, he assigned to the voter a prominent place in the topography of government and politics as recipient and judge of the political action carried out in his/her name.

This first period ended with the capture by the French authorities, between Christmas and New Year 1994, of Algerian terrorists who had hijacked an Air France plane. This dramatic affair projected the image of a determined, clever and protective government extending, even into the realms of international relations and terrorist violence, the image of cool-headedness, and of the control and efficiency detailed above.

The second period: transition and instability

The second period started slowly as other potential candidates, Jacques Chirac among them, tried to claim back the initiative. In spite of the efforts of the team in office to monopolise public opinion, the other actors in the official campaign were now beginning to take up position. Jean-Marie Le Pen was the first to announce his candidacy, on 18 September 1994. Then came the Communist candidate, Robert Hue, on 21 September 1994, followed by Arlette Laguiller, on 27 September 1994, Dominique Voynet (20 October 1994), and Jacques Chirac (4 November 1994). Philippe de Villiers declared on 8 January 1995. Lionel Jospin and Edouard Balladur declared themselves candidates in mid-January and the beginning of February 1995, respectively. The surprise candidate, Jacques Cheminade, spoke out at the last minute. This chronology clearly expressed the strategies and the difficulties of each candidate. Candidates whose political party occupies a peripheral electoral position, as in the case of the Front National or the Communist Party, were the first to declare. Having no real competitor on their own ideological terrain, and exercising no governmental responsibility, it was in their interest to draw media attention as early as possible. Of course, Philippe de Villiers' newly created party gave Jean-Marie Le Pen some worries, and there was some overlap between the electorates of the Communist Party and Lutte Ouvrière, the party of the extreme revolutionary left which supported Arlette Laguiller. As far as Jacques Chirac was concerned, somewhat marginalised after turning down the post of Prime Minister, he was only able to take centre-stage once again on the basis of his candidacy. This allowed the internal dissensions within the RPR and the entire right-wing parliamentary majority to come to light, and the stability of Balladur's role as rallying point for the French began to fragment.

The climate also changed during this intermediate phase. The media put great emphasis upon the theme of corruption in politics during the whole of the campaign. Before we study this point in more detail, let us mention here the scandals which directly affected members of the Balladur government and which had been building up for some time. Alain Carignon, Minister for Communication, was charged for allegedly having the Lyonnaise des Eaux company finance a municipal propaganda paper in his favour, as Mayor of Grenoble, in exchange for the privatisation of the city's waterworks. He resigned on 17 July 1994, was incarcerated on 10 October 1994 and remained in prison for several months in Grenoble. Gérard Longuet, Minister for Industry, was forced to resign in October 1994, accused of asking an entrepreneur to finance his villa in exchange for granting contracts for public works. He was followed by Michel Roussin, Minister for Co-operation, who resigned in November 1994, accused of having participated in the covert financing of the RPR. These affairs culminated in the scandal of the Schuller-Maréchal affair which directly involved the Interior Minister, Charles Pasqua, and which made the headlines for several weeks from February 1995, that is to say just after Edouard Balladur's candidacy announcement. The revelations concerned Pasqua's alleged interference in an investigation into the management of a housing estate in the Ile-de-France region. Pasqua's department allegedly tried to discredit the magistrate in charge of the case, Judge Halphen, by involving the latter's father-in-law in the scandal under investigation. This affair led to Charles Pasqua's progressive withdrawal from the campaign.[29] Most damningly, it was also insinuated that Balladur himself had sought personal enrichment through dubious transactions in the shares of a company he had managed before he became Prime Minister. These stories undermined his pristine image of the uniquely uncorrupt leader, placing him back firmly into the ordinary fold of everyday politicians.

During the long months of the 'Balladurian supremacy', Jacques Chirac entered into what became known, in the Chiraquian legend, as his period in the political wilderness. He had no governmental responsibility, and his party, the RPR, was on the brink of implosion as a result of the tension between two emerging factions: one, opportunistic in nature, was in favour of Edouard Balladur, and led by Charles Pasqua; the other, remaining faithful to Chirac, did not believe that his political career was at an end. But Chirac's marginalisation was also self-imposed. Making himself inconspicuous at the level of the national media, Chirac organised a nationwide tour during which he met literally thousands of people in discussion groups. He prepared his electoral platform with the successful publication of two short books, in mid-1994 and at the beginning of 1995. He also worked on the transformation of his public image, guided by his main communication consultant, his daughter, Claude Chirac. This period in the political desert was to furnish the basis for a remarkably coherent campaign strategy.

The Chiraquian vision, shaped during this difficult period of marginalisation, borrowed more than one idea from the discourse developed publicly by Philippe Séguin since the beginning of the 1990s. The main thrusts of this discourse were a critique of technocratic immobilism, and an emphasis on social issues.[30] This found unexpected favour in various circles and in public opinion. Having found a suitable slogan, 'A France for all', Jacques Chirac and his campaign team repeated the idea that 'another way' of thinking and acting was required, and that France needed a real 'policy for change'.[31] This fervent plea in favour of change was of course accompanied, within the limits of the 'rejection of polemics', by a critique of Balladurian conservatism: Chirac's attacks portrayed Balladur as timid and his initiatives as limited in scope, all entangled in a kind of impotent continuity with '14 years of socialism' which had brought France into decline.

Chirac had suffered from a negative image, on which the press and social satirists were fond of lingering. By choosing a populist discourse orientated chiefly towards social issues, exalting the virtues of contacts with 'real people', of the man in the street, of the 'forces vives' of the nation,[32] criticising the élite, the new Chirac came of age, as the media pointed out, intrigued by the astonishing new maturity of the man, including his body language and his tone of voice.[33]

From February 1995, the press was asking the question: could Chirac win, might Balladur lose? From this point, two phenomena occurred: Edouard Balladur, at a time when he was particularly threatened by attacks against him, became subject to the rule of equal air time. Having been in the foreground during the whole of the first period, he was now reduced to brief appearances at the precise moment when he needed time to justify himself. Balladurians accused Chiraquians of demagogy, Chiraquians accused Balladurians of conservatism. Also, the Chiraquian machinery was set in motion, and the inevitable succession of well rehearsed pro-Chirac jamborees began. Political commentators and Balladur's own supporters complained that his campaign lacked fervour and enthusiasm and he was deemed uninspiring. Hastily readjusting the organisation of his campaign, he organised a large political meeting, christened 'la Fête à Doudou' ('Eddie's Party', on 25 March 1995 at Le Bourget).[34] Political satirists mocked him for having betrayed his true nature, standing on tables in an uncharacteristic display of populism.

The other candidates were fighting to be noticed. Lionel Jospin succeeded quite well, against expectation, in gaining wide support, with a low key yet earnest discourse. Few commentators at the time believed, however, in his ability to rally voters beyond the score of the PS in the 1993 legislative election (19% of the vote in the first round, 30% in the second). Robert Hue made a good impression with his smiling face, his cheerful voice and his measured words. An increase in the score of the Communist Party seemed possible. Jean-Marie Le Pen inexorably repeated nationalistic, xenophobic and anti-European themes, hallmarks of his success, but with a constant effort to demonstrate his respectability, and to portray the Front National as the second biggest party in France (he claimed to have more support than the Socialist Party and than the UDF). Arlette Laguiller was congratulated affectionately by the media for having stayed the same and having retained her deliciously old-fashioned revolutionary fervour.

At the end of 1994 and the beginning of 1995, public discourse thus became less monolithic, escaping the control of the Matignon team, with voters now addressed by a variety of discourses and personalities.

At the time the campaign 'turned', one of the themes which had an enormous impact on public opinion at the expense of Edouard Balladur was that of the corruption of the élite. This one topic attracted the largest share of headlines in this period. Let us consider how the discursive entry of politico-financial scandals, prison sentences and trials altered the political landscape at the moment political alternatives were being given discursive space.

Politico-financial scandals are nothing new in French political life. In recent years, France had witnessed the scandal of the Rainbow Warrior, the Pelat affair which was linked to the Péchiney et Société Générale affairs, and to the affair of the interest-free loan to Pierre Bérégovoy, the affair of contaminated blood stocks, and the Urba affair.[35] But the frequency, the scope and the context of the affairs associated with this campaign gave them a particular significance.[36]

The scandals teemed into the public's perception: France saw the arrest of Didier Pineau Valencienne, Chief Executive of the Schneider Group in Belgium,[37] the charging of Pierre Suard, powerful Chief Executive of Alcatel and a pillar of the French industrial establishment;[38] the charging of the Lyonnaise des Eaux for irregularities in public tenders (the Carignon affair); the Harreckx affair (involving a Senator from the South of France, accused of embezzlement);[39] the opening of the Urba[40] and of the Noir-Botton[41] trials. This last, involving a powerful and once successful politician of the right, a business tycoon, and Patrick Poivre d'Arvor, the most successful French television presenter and star of the 8 o'clock news on TF1, turned into a real-life soap opera complete with widely publicised family break-ups and billionaires' extravagances, as well as the highly-publicised suicide of one of Patrick Poivre d'Arvor's daughters.

All of these matters formed, firstly, the daily background upon which were superimposed charges of impropriety against members of the Balladur government. Secondly, they contributed to the creation of a climate of suspicion and distrust towards the very persons supposed to speak on behalf of the people. To a certain extent, and more so than is usually the case, politicians in the presidential campaign had not only to convince people that they were the best choice, but that it was worth making the choice at all.

Furthermore, the political and institutional context encouraged the emergence of all the *affaires* in the judicial system, and their exploitation by the media. Firstly, at the institutional level, the Chancery, headed by Pierre Méhaignerie, resolved to follow a strict non-interventionist policy from April 1993, which in principle meant that a politician, however powerful, would not be protected in an enquiry, and that an enquiry concerning a politician would not simply be shelved until the dust had settled. This policy left the field open to a group of highly mediatised 'petits juges', young magistrates bent on utilising their full powers and unintimidated by the power of the political authorities.[42] Inevitably, the question of the independence and confidentiality of the judicial enquiry became a major theme, on which the public was invited to focus daily.

Secondly, the curtailing of open debate on the dissensions at the heart of the right-wing majority encouraged the unearthing of new scandals. To preserve the political future of the right, it was in each faction's interest that the confrontation remain latent for as long as possible. However, as ideological differentiation between two candidates of the same party was not possible, supporters of one faction leaked information to the judicial authorities and the media in an attempt to discredit the other. We are close to conjecture here, but such a hypothesis is supported by the important role of denunciation in a number of the aforementioned affairs.[43]

Such sensational revelations were manna to the media. Corruption seemed to have permeated the whole of society, from teachers to doctors, businessmen to politicians. The media developed their campaign emphasising the notion of moral decay, the multiple ramifications of the abuse of power, and the risk of a moralist backlash in the rest of French society (the so-called 'retour de l'ordre moral', a return to morality). The political response to all this coverage took the shape of a series of public initiatives by representatives of the people, led by Philippe Séguin, President of the National

Assembly, and the government, each trying to outdo the other in public attention as the true and indomitable fighter against corruption.

The second closely related topic which attracted an overwhelmingly large share of headlines during the period was that of the decay of republican values and ideals in French society, threatened by the increase in extreme poverty and social inequalities, and the rising number of outcasts. 'Social fracture' served as an apposite counterpoint to corruption. For years, on the basis of statistics and studies of poverty, sociologists had been warning of the risk of a 'société duale', a dual society. The theme of the social fracture became the leitmotiv of the electoral campaign. In a context of economic recession, the discourse of social breakdown operated first as a condemnation of the Socialist record.[44] After the 1993 general election, the rhetorical room for manœuvre was severely constrained by cohabitation and by choices of economic policy. In the campaign theatre of 1995, this discourse, adopted to varying degrees by all the candidates, was allowed to develop fully.

During the campaign, the public was fed a daily diet of the downward spiral and the failures of the social and economic system and of French economic and social policies, all of which was cast against the background of a French society in a state of rebellion. The media, amplifying the apocalyptic discourse of the spokespersons for groupings contesting the status quo (CGT unionists, sociologists commenting on the 'banlieues', extremist parties), quite readily represented France as a country on the verge of revolt, citing the so-called 'explosion sociale', which was in fact to erupt even more visibly in Autumn 1995, several months after the presidential election. In the months preceding the election, the media proffered an almost daily insistence on the record number of high profile strikes and demonstrations motivated by questions about pay and the maintenance of social benefits, established by workers in the course of past disputes and subsequently integrated into the fabric of the Welfare State.[45] This discourse regarding France's decaying Welfare State is not attributable to a single source. Rather, as we explained in our remarks on methodology, it was the product of a range of parallel discourses, issued from administrative sources (studies from INSEE, CERC, l'INED, and consultative commissions set up by the *Commissariat Général au Plan*), from academics, politicians and journalists. This conjunction, treated to wide media coverage, gave rise to a kind of 'vulgate', a commonplace or conventional wisdom, acknowledged by a majority of the election period's protagonists. The catch-all, stereotyped construct of the social fracture allowed for various interpretations. In this respect, it is important to consider for a moment the view of Alain Minc.[46] Minc was asked by Edouard Balladur in June 1994 to lead a Commission of experts to prepare a report on 'France in the year 2000', in order to meet the challenges posed by the budgetary deficits of the social programmes, to substitute for the *equality* ideal, that of *equity*. The report dwelt on the alleged 'collective guilt' of the French regarding unemployment, as if the French nation, at some stage, had made the collective choice of accepting a high level of unemployment in exchange for the preservation of 'acquis sociaux', a piece of French jargon describing the high level of collectively financed social benefits and rights. Jacques Chirac's own campaign themes reaffirmed the principle of equality, and the value of the ideal which once inspired the founding of the French Welfare state. Chirac's campaign exploited with great skill the sentiment of social anguish which affected possibly more than half the voters[47] and which was reflected in tales of poverty told by the media.[48] All the components of the 'social malaise', in the jargon of journalists – unemployment, homelessness, unrest in the 'banlieues', youth problems (which were evaluated afresh at that time,[49]) and Aids – were presented so as to demonstrate that these images were becoming part of daily life in France, the true social reality of the country.

Whether in studies carried out by the official organisations on the increasingly precarious economic situation of many households[50] or in works such as that edited by Pierre Bourdieu, which noticeably influenced a section of the intelligentsia,[51] the picture was the same: France was falling into the abyss, the foundations of the values that made republican France – education, meritocracy, public services, the family, solidarity between generations, traditional urban life – were collapsing. With over three million unemployed, and twice as many, plus their families, living on the poverty line, with a good proportion of jobs threatened by the predictable evolution of French industrial and tertiary production, the opportunity for social progression – particularly through work – was being destroyed.

Conclusion

The pre-campaign and campaign were dominated by several themes: the disappearance of the European issue at a time when there was a question mark over the future of European integration; the theme of depoliticisation and of the irrelevance of the ideological left/right divide; the disillusionment of the electorate as to the capacity of politicians to fight against unemployment; the supposedly increasing volatility of public opinion and its fragmentation into irreconcilable groups; the social fracture; personal factors such as the revelations regarding François Mitterrand's past and Jacques Chirac's so obviously new personality; the calling into question of the élite, especially the political élite. All these themes converged upon the single theme of disillusionment: voters' expectations regarding the political classes were palpably low, and the response of the campaign had to take this into account.

The equilibrium between parliamentarian, governmental and presidential powers can in theory be threatened by two complementary tendencies in public opinion: the temptation for strong leadership, and the discredit of all political leadership. What conclusions can we draw from our analysis about the degree of acceptance by the French voters of current institutions, from a study of the period and of the election results?

The first is that although not all the voters chose Jacques Chirac, it is worth evoking the Chiraquian 'reading' of the presidential myth within the context of parallel discourses we have been describing. To a certain extent, Jacques Chirac offered the image of a suffering and betrayed man,[52] the image of a man whose wisdom was gained from being with simple people, the 'forces vives' of the nation.[53] The image was of course constructed in part by Jacques Chirac's own propaganda, in part by circumstances, in part by public perceptions. Chirac the outsider, Chirac the betrayed, addressed the expectations shaped in public opinion during the months preceding the election. For a country faced by the scandal of corruption amongst its élites, he appeared both as the heir to a glorious past and as the 'renewed' man required successfully to lead this great mission of social regeneration. For a country worried by the imminence of economic and social decay, and by a loss of its original republican social pact, he was the candidate of compassion that the French listened to. Not only had this man met with his time, the time of social distress and the end of the scandal-ridden Mitterrand era,[54] but in pleading for the renunciation of old politics, in calling *all* French people to take part with him in a new collective experience, the candidate Chirac succeeded in associating himself with all of the people while being the only person properly to do so. One of the most striking visual images of the campaign was a picture of the candidate Chirac, immersed in a book, on a rainy day, sitting alone but for a couple of young black women in the foreground, on a dreary, deserted suburban train.[55] This image of Chirac the man sharing in and accepting to learn from suburban life and ordinary people, was widely publicised at the time, and informed the principal strand of the narrative of Jacques Chirac's campaign and media representation.

The image can also be seen as emblematic in a more general way. In an electoral process in which the individual voter is bombarded by the highly-polished public discourses broadcast by the candidates' campaigns, by commentators, by lobby groups and – most importantly and perhaps most misleadingly of all – by the various media and by the polls, it is of particular political importance to the candidate that s/he be seen to make direct contact of some sort with the 'ordinary' elector (evoked in the Chirac picture by the two 'ordinary' women and the train). The cynic might suggest that the political public space is an arena in which one set of synthetic constructs (the candidates) addresses another (the candidates' idea of the voter); and to be sure, some part of the public's disaffection with politics in general is undoubtedly linked to a view of politics and politicians as lacking in sincerity, integrity and concern for the common good. And yet, judging from the seriousness of the numerous opinion polls[56] and the media coverage of the event, and from the electoral turnout rate, it seems evident that – notwithstanding the significance of the Le Pen vote which suggests that part of the electorate was ready for a different kind of practice and perhaps for a different kind of institution – the Fifth Republic has become the accepted framework for the exercise of legitimate power in France.

And yet it is reasonable to ask how far an institutional framework, even a flexible one, can really accommodate variation not only in institutional practices but in a changing society and a changing relationship between politicians and the public. Two pointers indicate the importance of change as perceived by the electorate. The first is that the victor in the presidential contest was a candidate who promised to reinstate those social ideals which emerged at the time of the Liberation and were consolidated during the twenty years before the oil crisis. The second is the remarkable number of voters who supported candidates favouring a radical break with the system in place. These two phenomena would seem to signal a feeling among the electorate that they were approaching the end of the era of ever-evolving social benefits. Such benefits have been coming under increasing threat as the difficult choices occasioned by European integration place constant pressure on the nationalistic element of French people's support for the presidential regime.

From our study of the 1995 campaign, it would seem that, in order to continue to assess the future chances of the Fifth Republic and of the Republican regime in France, particular attention should be focused on three specific areas: a) the role of the media in politics, not only as commentators and as a forum for communication but also in terms of active intervention (for example in effectively 'policing' the public sphere) and taking into account the media's transition from state control to control by commercial imperatives; b) the legal and constitutional aspects of the two cohabitations, and the introduction (or not) of the use of referendums on social questions such as the death penalty or immigration. This would profoundly alter the nature of power held by the state and based on the notion of the Republic, as well as the means by which the President in office sways the nationalist sentiments of the electorate (for example by playing on the ambiguity of his European policies, or by raising his profile in international affairs); c) the outcome of general discussions about the role of public services, the unions and collective financing of social benefits, including pensions.

Jacques Chirac's campaign succeeded, as we have seen, in representing his view of the state of the nation in terms of a coherent political and historical analysis: we may conclude therefore that his campaign was based more on a particular political diagnosis than on an individual personality. We may conclude, too, that the campaign did not arise out of a clash of ideologies as in 1965, 1974 and 1981, nor from a clash of personalities as in 1988, but that it in fact acted much more as a catalyst for updating the social, political and economic structures on which the French nation bases both its sense of identity and its vision of its own future.

Notes

[1] Before joining the European Commission, Jacques Delors was Minister for the Economy and for Finance from 1981 to 1984, at the beginning of Mitterrand's first period of presidential office.

[2] Lionel Jospin succeeded François Mitterrand as First Secretary of the Parti Socialiste from 1981 to 1988, then was Minister for Education from 1988 to 1992, in Mitterrand's second term of presidential office.

[3] This election was marked, in France, by the unexpected and impressive scores obtained by the group led by Philippe de Villiers, traditionalist anti-European candidate emanating from the UDF (PR), who received 12.33% of the votes; and the group led by Bernard Tapie, in the name of Radical, which won 12.03% of the votes. See J. Gaffney, 'France' in J. Lodge (ed.) *The 1994 Elections to the European Parliament* (London, Pinter, 1996), pp. 84-106.

[4] It was Edouard Balladur who, in playing down the potential drama of the cohabitation, then in refusing, during the whole of 1994, to acknowledge his intention to run for the presidency, launched the theme of the depoliticisation of the electorate. See 'L'intervention du Premier Ministre sur France 2: M. Balladur estime que "les Français sont excédés du spectacle que leur a donné le milieu politique"'(Mr Balladur thinks that 'the French are exasperated by the spectacle that the political class has made of itself'), *Le Monde*, 29 June 1994, p. 7; and the CSA opinion poll on the late candidacy declarations published by *Le Parisien*, 5 September 1994. See also Alain Duhamel, 'Le mythe de la dépolitisation', *Le Point*, 1120, 5 March 1994, p. 41 ('Pourquoi ce dégoût de la politique?' on the cover page); and François Brune, 'La dépolitisation par le langage: ces mots qui font accepter l'inacceptable', *Le Monde diplomatique*, May 1995, p. 28.
Although Edouard Balladur himself rejected the idea that the left-right split had disappeared (see in particular the interview with Denis Jeambar and Catherine Pégard in *Le Point*, 1146, 3 September 1994, p. 45), he constantly emphasised the need to reconcile the French with themselves, and to 'réformer sans fractures ni ruptures' (official candidacy announcement, televised declaration of 18 January 1995, see *Le Monde*, 19 January 1995). Jacques Chirac radicalised this approach, proclaiming the end of the relevance of the left-right split, substituting instead such binary oppositions as the 'exclus' vs. the speculators, the 'forces vives' vs. the technocrats, the 'idéal républicain' vs. conservatism, political voluntarism vs. abandonment (See Jacques Chirac, *La France pour tous* (Paris, Nil, 1995), and 'La France pour tous', *Le Monde*, 10 January 1995). The introduction to the manifesto booklet that Chirac sent to the voters, reads: 'Les succès de la France tenaient aux valeurs de la République [...]. Ces valeurs ne sont ni de droite ni de gauche. Elles font de la République un modèle social, une référence morale' ('France's successes have had to do with republican values [...]. These values belong neither to the right nor to the left. They make the Republic a social model, a moral benchmark'). On this theme and its influence in the academic community, see Etienne Schweisguth (ed.), *Problèmes politiques et sociaux, Droite-gauche: un clivage dépassé?*, special issue 719, 14 January 1994; for a more topical

work, see Claude Imbert and Jacques Julliard, *La Droite et la Gauche* (Paris, Robert Laffont/Grasset, 1995).

5   For details of the rivalry and relationship between Balladur and Chirac, see later in this chapter, and John Gaffney's chapter. Of the many manifestations of media interest in the Balladur-Chirac duel, see, inter alia, Nicolas Domenach and Maurice Szafran, *De si bons amis* (Paris, Plon, 1994); and Catherine Nay, *Le Prince et le Régent* (Paris, Grasset, 1994). For a few markers on the media coverage see Olivier Duhamel, 'Balladur-Chirac: la différence', *L'Express*, 2206, 21 October 1993, p. 8; 'Course à l'Elysée: un fauteuil pour deux, plus que jamais', *L'Express*, 2217, 6 January 1994, p. 4; 'Balladur-Chirac: les vraies raisons d'un duel', *L'Express*, 2220, 27 January 1994, p. 18; 'Balladur-Chirac: poker d'enfer', *Le Point*, 1116, 5 February 1994, p. 8; Valérie Lecasble, 'Chirac-Balladur: la guerre des réseaux économiques', *L'Evénement du Jeudi*, 485, 17-23 February 1994, p. 18; 'Plus rien désormais ne pourra réconcilier Jacques Chirac et Edouard Balladur', *Le Point*, 1119, 26 February 1994, p. 32; 'Chirac-Balladur: combien de divisions?', *Le Nouvel Economiste*, 936, 11 March 1994, p. 56; Nicolas Domenach and Maurice Szafran, 'Edouard contre Jacques, Jacques contre Edouard', *L'Evénement du Jeudi*, 489, 17-23 March 1994, p. 12; N. Domenach and M. Szafran, 'Balladur-Chirac: ils préparent l'affrontement final', *L'Evénement du Jeudi,* 502, 16-22 June 1994, p. 10; 'Chirac-Balladur: Journal de guerre et phrases assassines', *VSD*, 896, 3-9 November 1994, pp. 48-53; 'Ces nouveaux scandales qui peuvent faire imploser la droite: Chirac-Balladur, leur stratégie de mise à mort', *L'Evénement du Jeudi*, 524, 17-23 November 1994; 'Chirac-Balladur: les dessous d'une guerre dégueulasse', *Le Nouvel Observateur,* 1588, 13-19 April 1995; Stéphane Denis, 'Balladur-Chirac: la grande rupture', *Paris-Match*, 2394, 13 April 1995, pp. 44-48.

6   Charles Pasqua, Interior Minister of the Chirac Government between 1986 and 1988, and who occupied the same post between March 1993 and May 1995, was presented until February 1995 as the strong man of the presidential majority. He was renowned for his stance on security and anti-immigration policies, which made him, in the eyes of the moderate right, a shield against Le Pen. He finally spoke out in favour of Edouard Balladur on 15 January 1995 (interview in the *Journal du Dimanche*). *Le Monde*'s headline of 31 January 1995 reads 'François Léotard et Charles Pasqua se disputent l'hôtel Matignon'. But he was involved, from the end of 1994, in the so called 'Halphen' and 'Maréchal-Schuller' affairs (for details, see later in this chapter) and subsequently faded from the foreground.

Alain Juppé, long term associate of Jacques Chirac at the Paris Town Hall, Minister for Foreign Affairs in Balladur's Government, took over the presidency of the RPR after the official start of Jacques Chirac's campaign, and became the first Prime Minister of Jacques Chirac's presidency in May 1995 (and the successor of Jacques Chaban-Delmas as mayor of Bordeaux in June 1995).

7   See, for example, Patrick Jarreau, 'MM. Balladur et Delors placent l'Europe au cœur de la campagne présidentielle', *Le Monde*, 30 August 1994, and Edouard Balladur, 'Pour un deuxième traité de l'Elysée', *Le Monde*, 30 November 1994. See also 'La chronique de Jacques Julliard: le demi-tour de Jacques Chirac', *Le Nouvel Observateur*, 10-16 November 1994, p. 49, on the idea that 'the European question is becoming a substitute for the left-right split'. The European question virtually disappeared from the public debate, after causing Jacques Chirac to make a tactical error (*7 sur 7*, TF1, Sunday 6 November 1994): he proposed, in the first instance, to abolish the Maastricht Treaty and announced a new referendum on Europe, then made

a U-turn in an interview with *Le Point* on 3 December 1994, proposing a referendum on education instead. Questions relative to Europe and to international politics were constantly pushed to last place in the order of priority of people interviewed in the various opinion polls listed: see Claire Tréan, 'L'Europe n'est pas un enjeu majeur de la campagne présidentielle', *Le Monde*, 22 March 1995. The question was almost left aside during the televised debate of 2 May 1995.

8 Since the oil crisis of 1973, unemployment had soared from a mere 2% of the working population to above 9% at the beginning of the 1980s, above 10% in 1992, 11% in 1993, 12% in 1994, which amounts to around 3.5 million people officially out of work. Although most of the polls showed that fear of unemployment ran high among the French (see *Sondoscope*), they were quite disillusioned about the ability of politicians to tackle the issue. To quote but one of many similar polls (BVA for Paris-Match, Europe 1 and France 2 on the 17 to 20 February 1995), 36% of interviewees thought that none of the main three candidates, Balladur, Jospin and Chirac, was able to reduce unemployment. This was the highest score for people sharing the same opinion in all the 65 possible answers of that poll.

9 See Olivier Biffaud, 'M. Chirac se présente comme le candidat d'une 'véritable politique du changement'', and Eric Le Boucher, 'La rhétorique du changement', *Le Monde*, 5 November 1994.

10 See Jacques Antoine, 'Le sondage en accusation', *Sondoscope*, 108, May 1995, pp. 3-10; Jean-Marc Lech (co-president of the IPSOS institute), 'Pourquoi nous avons sous-estimé Jospin', *Le Point* (international edition), 1180, 29 April 1995, p. 48; and Laurent Joffrin, 'Quand les experts ont tout faux', *Le Nouvel Observateur* (international edition), 1589, 20-26 April 1995, pp. 31-32.

11 23.2% for Jospin instead of 19-21% predicted, 20.6% for Jacques Chirac, instead of 25-27.5% forecast.

12 From his nomination as François Mitterrand's Prime Minister on 30 March 1993, after the victory of the right in the legislative election in March 1993, to February 1995, Edouard Balladur enjoyed a level of popularity in the opinion polls which may be qualified as without precedent (see for example 'Pour l'opinion, l'élection présidentielle est déjà jouée', *Le Monde*, 12 January 1995). Before his nomination by François Mitterrand, see for example, Catherine Pégard, 'Balladur, le Premier ministre favori des Français' (cover page), *Le Point*, 1066, 20-26 February 1993, pp. 27-30; and Elizabeth Dupoirier and Gérard Grunberg, 'L'année Balladur', *Pouvoirs*, 69, pp. 143-145. For an assessment of 1994, see 'Balladur: [...] un plébiscite sceptique', *Le Nouvel Economiste*, 980, 20 January 1995 and *Le Nouvel Economiste*, 982, 3 February 1995; 'Sept ans! Les Français en veulent-ils vraiment?' *Le Nouvel Observateur*, 1577, 26 January-1 February 1995; and 'Enquête sur Edouard B.', *Le Point*, 1166, 21 January 1995.
For the state of mind of commentators before the change of heart in public opinion, see for example Alain Touraine, 'Le seul candidat', *L'Express*, international edition, 2274, 9 February 1995, p. 14. The U-turn in the opinion polls occurred abruptly towards the end of February 1995, in a context which we shall discuss below.

13 The French ecologist movement, although very divided, obtained (on the basis of a different voting procedure) 10.59% in the European election of 1989 (François Chirot, 'Les écologistes divisés ne sont plus représentés', *Le Monde*, 14 June 1994); and 14.7% in the regional election of 1992 (Pierre Brechon, *La France aux urnes* [Paris, La Documentation française, 1993], p. 155). The trend was reversed in the legislative election of March 1993 when, credited with 19% of voting intentions, the ecologists

finally obtained 10.79% of the votes (Hugues Portelli, 'Les élections législatives de mars 1993', *Regards sur l'actualité*, 190, April 1993, pp. 23-31). There was a further significant fall in the electoral support for the ecologists at the presidential election (slightly more than 3% of votes in the first round for Dominique Voynet). Arlette Laguiller, extreme left candidate (Lutte Ouvrière), obtained more than 5% of votes (5.32%), which put her just behind the Communist candidate, and ahead of Philippe de Villiers. This 5% result must be compared with 2.3% in 1974 and 1981, and 1.99% in 1988. This was the fourth presidential election in which Arlette Laguiller had taken part: see Jean-Marc Requin and Joël Girard, *Le Guide de l'élection présidentielle* (Paris, Editions Deletraz, 1995).

[14] As quoted in Denis Jeambar, 'Pourquoi ce dégoût de la politique?', *Le Point*, 1120, 5 March 1994, p. 30. On the increase in the use of pre-electoral simulations and political barometers, see *Sondoscope*, 73 (February 1992), 84 (February 1993), 95 (February 1994) and 105 (February 1995): these issues are dedicated to trends in the opinion polls of the preceding year.

[15] On this theme as dealt with by current political scientists, see for example Philippe Braud, *Le Jardin des Délices démocratiques* (Paris, Presses de la Fondation Nationale des Sciences Politiques, 1991), and Patrick Champagne, *Faire l'opinion: le nouveau jeu politique* (Paris, Les Editions de Minuit, 1990). In the context of the Fifth Republic, see Jean Charlot, *La Politique en France* (Paris, Fallois, 1994), chapter 4 'Les médias et les sondages', pp. 61-78 and in chapter 8 'De la démocratie des partis à une démocratie d'opinion', p. 171. For a study which puts the debate back into a historical context, see Eric Dupin, 'Les sondages se trompent-ils?', in E. Dupin (ed.), *Oui, Non, Sans Opinion – 50 ans de sondages IFOP* (Paris, InterEditions, 1989). On the significance of opinion polls in the campaign, see Anne Tézenas du Montcel, 'Pour quel sondeur allez-vous voter?', *Le Nouvel Economiste*, Le Cahier du Samedi, 985, 24 February 1995, pp. 79-81; 'Sondages: les électeurs manipulés?' *Le Monde des Débats*, special issue, March 1995, pp. 3-7; Emmanuël Souchier and Yves Jeanneret, 'Le triomphe de la politique virtuelle: tyrannie des sondages', *Le Monde diplomatique*, March 1995, p. 32. Denis Jeambar, 'Pourquoi ce dégoût de la politique – La démocratie 'sondagère' vit au rythme de deux sondages politiques par jour', *Le Point*, 1120, 5 March 1995, pp. 30-31; Jean-Gabriel Fredet, 'Les sondages sont-ils manipulés?', *Le Nouvel Observateur*, 1587, 6-12 April 1995, pp. 46-47; 'Les électeurs sont-ils influencés par les sondages politiques?', Louis Harris opinion poll, *Valeurs actuelles*, 15 April 1995.

[16] See 'Les Français et l'élection présidentielle – Un dialogue entre Pascal Perrineau et Emmanuel Todd', *Le Monde*, 19-20 February 1995. In the few months preceding the election, opinion polls highlighted a large proportion of undecided voters (more than one voter out of three: 55% of the electorate by end of February (SCP-Info-Matin; Louis Harris-VSD). See also 'A 60 jours du premier tour, encore 49% d'indécis' *Paris-Match*, 2388, 2 March 1995, pp. 50-51; and 'Encore 37% d'indécis' *Paris Match*, 2394, 13 April 1995, pp. 62-63.

[17] François Mitterrand suffered from cancer of the prostate during his second term in power, which led observers to think that he would not be able to finish his term of office; this illness forced a dramatic reduction in his official engagements. See Chapter 4.

[18] Jean-Jacques Chevallier, *Histoire des institutions et des régimes politiques de la France de 1789 à nos jours* (Paris, Dalloz, 7th edition updated by Gérard Conac 1985).; Maurice Duverger, *La VIe République et le régime présidentiel* (Paris, Fayard,

1961); Jean-Louis Quermonne and Dominique Chagnollaud, *Le Gouvernement de la France sous la Cinquième République* (Paris, Dalloz, 4th edition 1991); Vincent Wright, *The Government and Politics of France* (London, Hutchinson, 1983); John Gaffney, *The French Left and the Fifth Republic* (London, MacMillan, 1989); and John Gaffney, 'Introduction: Presidentialism and the Fifth Republic', in John Gaffney (ed.), *The French Presidential Elections of 1988* (Aldershot, Dartmouth, 1989), pp. 2-36. For the text of the controversial press conference of 31 January 1964 in which General de Gaulle defines the role of the President, along with significant declarations about the role of the President of the Republic by successors of de Gaulle, see Didier Mauss, *Les grands textes de la pratique institutionnelle de la Ve République, Notes et Etudes documentaires* (Paris, La Documentation Française, 1995).

[19] See John Gaffney, The French Left and the Fifth Republic, pp. 12-30.

[20] There is no consensus on this notion in the scientific community, not even on the definition of the term. See, for example, Pierre Bourdieu, *La Distinction – Critique sociale du jugement* (Paris, Les Editions de Minuit, 1979), especially Chapter 8 'Culture et politique', pp. 463-541. Hélène Meynaud and Denis Duclos, in *Les Sondages d'opinion* (Paris, La Découverte, 1989), pp. 24-41, offer a critical synthesis of the relation between public opinion and opinion polls, quoting in particular the provocative definition by George H. Gallup, 'public opinion [...] is what opinion polls measure'. The basic reference publication on opinion polls is by Jacques Desabie, *Théorie et Pratique des sondages* (Paris, Dunod, 1966): it is now out of print, but was again made topical by Pascal Ardilly's publication, *Les Techniques de sondage* (Paris, Editions Technip, 1994). See also *Mots/ Les Langages du politique*, 23 (June 1990), issue on *Discours des sondages d'opinion*; and the monthly releases of the French journal *Le Sondoscope – La Revue française des sondages*, published by the C.E.S.E.M. (Centre d'Etudes Socio-Economique et de Management) nos. 95-108 covering 1994 and 1995. Issue 100, July/September 1994, a special issue presenting the journal's new format, offers, in its introductory text on 'Veille opinion et société', in section II: 'Du bon usage des sondages d'opinion – Les trois horizons temporels', an interesting distinction between *opinion* (short term), *attitude* (medium term, socio-cultural trend) and *value* (long term), pp. 11-12.

[21] See Hughes Portelli, 'La crise de la représentation politique', *Regards sur l'actualité*, 209-210, March-April 1995.

[22] See, for example, the following media items: 'Emploi, déficit, police, Sécurité sociale, échec scolaire, immigration: mais comment font les autres? La crise française confrontée aux solutions imaginées par nos partenaires', *L'Evénement du Jeudi*, 525, 24-30 November 1994; 'Retraite, santé, famille: ce qui doit changer – *Enjeux* ouvre les dossiers de la présidentielle: premier volet, la protection sociale', *Enjeux-Les Echos*, 98, December 1994; 'La Sécu, c'est fini...', *L'Express*, 2266, 15 December 1994; 'Les inégalités en 1995 – patrimoine, salaires, héritage, fiscalité, richesse et pauvreté: pourquoi ça ne peut plus durer', *L'Evénement du Jeudi*, 530, 29 December 1994-4 January 1995; 'Les enjeux de 1995: Social – répétition générale pour une année chaude', *Enjeux-Les Echos*, 99, January 1995; Georges Valance, 'La revanche du social', *L'Express*, 2269, 5 January 1995; 'Dossier Présidentielle: 5. La santé', *Le Nouvel Economiste*, 985, 24 February 1995; François Bonnet and Franck Nouchi, 'Six enjeux pour la France: 3 l'élargissement de la fracture sociale', *Le Monde*, 30 March 1995; Thomas Ferenczi, 'Six enjeux pour la France: 4. Les troubles de l'identité nationale', *Le Monde*, 31 March 1995.

On the question of the role of the state and its reform as an institution, see 'France: faut-il réformer la Ve République?', *Le Point*, 1164, 7 January 1995; 'Dossier Présidentielle: 3. L'Etat', *Le Nouvel Economiste*, 980, 20 January 1995; 'Etat: un rôle à redéfinir – Deuxième dossier de la présidentielle: ce que les entreprises attendent des pouvoirs publics', *Enjeux-Les Echos*, 100, February 1995; Patrick Jarreau, 'Six enjeux pour la France: 1. Le déséquilibre des pouvoirs – La construction européenne a contribué à accroître la présidentialisation du régime', *Le Monde*, 28 March 1995; Laurent Greilsamer, 'Six enjeux pour la France: 2. La démocratie des juges et des médias', 29 March 1995.

Finally, on the question of Europe and international politics, see: 'France – Présidentielle: les ambiguïtés sur l'écu', *Le Point*, 1172, 4 March 1995; 'Dossiers Présidentielle: 5. L'Europe', *Le Nouvel Economiste*, 989, 24 March 1995; 'Six enjeux pour la France: 5. Un modèle économique affaibli', *Le Monde*, 1 April 1995.

Le Figaro, which, on 16 January 1995 and in association with SOFRES, launched a far-reaching study of 'les vraies questions que se posent les Français', offers an almost exhaustive list of all topical subjects: 'Faut-il supprimer l'ENA' (16 January 1995); le SMIC (17 January 1995); la Contribution Sociale Généralisée (21-22 January 1995); l'ANPE (30 January 1995); le RMI (31 January 1995); l'impôt sur le revenu (2 February 1995); le service militaire (3 February 1995); le juge d'instruction (21 February 1995); le Bac (10 March 1995); les cabinets ministériels (4 April 1995); les limitations de vitesse (6 April 1995); le CNRS (25 April 1995); 'Faut-il privatiser France 2?' (20 January 1995); la Sécurité sociale (23 January 1995); les universités (14 March 1995); 'Faut-il subventionner les partis politiques?' (26 January 1995); 'Faut-il plus de policiers?' (28-29 January 1995); 'Faut-il interdire la violence à la télévision?' (7 February 1995); 'Faut-il réglementer davantage les sondages?' (8 February 1995); 'Faut-il construire de nouveaux supermarchés?' (13 February 1995); 'A quoi servent les syndicats?' (15 February 1995); 'Faut-il restreindre le droit de grève?' (27 February 1995); 'Faut-il un régime présidentiel?' (1 March 1995); 'Faut-il recruter de nouveaux fonctionnaires?' (11-12 March 1995); 'Faut-il reprendre les essais nucléaires?' (11-12 March 1995); 'Faut-il autoriser l'ouverture des magasins le dimanche?' (15 March 1995); 'Faut-il élargir l'Union Européenne?' (20 March 1995); 'Faut-il partager le temps de travail?' (21 March 1995); 'Faut-il fermer les petits hôpitaux?' (28 March 1995); 'Faut-il construire de nouvelles centrales nucléaires?' (5 April 1995); 'Comment défendre le français?' (7 April 1995); 'Faut-il combattre l'intégrisme islamique?' (11 April 1995); 'Faut-il enseigner la physique-chimie aux jeunes enfants?' (12 April 1995); la bioéthique (15 April 1995); 'Faut-il dépénaliser les drogues douces?' (27 April 1995); 'Faut-il maintenir un franc fort?' (28 April 1995).

However, if one compares the list of these questions to voters' priorities as determined by many opinion polls on critical issues for the electorate, there are differences of priority, and in particular of emphasis on domestic social issues. By order of priority, the people interviewed held the following views: tax firms which cause pollution, fight against the sluggishness of justice, reform education, lighten tax and bureaucracy burdens ('Les urgences pour la France', *Le Point*-IPSOS, 25 June 1994); get the economy started again ('Les attentes des Français en matière économique et sociale', *La Tribune Desfossés*-CSA, 5 September 1994); fight in particular for employment, education and social protection ('Les enjeux de l'élection présidentielle', *La Tribune Desfossés*-CSA, 9 December 1994 and 13 March 1995); reform, as a matter of priority, the social security system, education, pensions, justice and taxes. People considered that the 'burning' issues which must be debated during the campaign were pensions, social security, unemployment, education, exclusion, corruption, immigration (Jean d'Ormesson, 'Ce que veulent les Français', *Le Figaro Magazine*-SOFRES, international edition of the *Figaro Magazine*, 743, Saturday 21 January 1995, pp. 25-27); unemployment, law and order, social security, the future of the younger generation, immigration ('Les priorités du futur président', *Pélerin Magazine*-SOFRES, 3 March 1995); unemployment, social inequalities, holding on to social advantages ('Les Français intéressés par la campagne présidentielle', SOFRES opinion poll published by several provincial dailies, 5 April 1995, quoted in *Sondoscope*, 108); unemployment, social inequalities, purchasing power (Opinion poll at the polling stations carried out by IFOP-*Libération* on 23 April 1995 during the first round, published on 25 April 1995). As can be seen from the above, the favourite themes are the fight against unemployment, the maintenance of social advantages and the fight against inequalities. The only theme approached with the same insistence by all candidates during the campaign is that of the all encompassing fight against unemployment and marginalisation.

[23] This law, put forward by the Minister of Employment, Michel Giraud, was passed on 5 October 1993. On Wednesday 25 August 1993, in his end-of-recess press conference, Edouard Balladur reminded listeners that in order to fulfil its ambitions of reform, his government had 'adopted a time horizon of 5 years of legislature' (Jean-Pierre Piotet, *Edouard Balladur ou la réputation à l'épreuve du pouvoir* (Paris, Eska, 1994), p. 102.

[24] See Edouard Balladur's televised interventions on 18 April 1993, 17 October 1993 (*7 sur 7*; TF1); 14 February 1994 (*Heure de Vérité*, France 2), 21 April 1994 (special broadcast *Balladur face aux Français*).

[25] After the vote of the so-called Pasqua laws on immigration (passed on 13 July 1993 after some animated debates), the Conseil Constitutionnel overruled certain measures of these laws regarding the right of Asylum. The government, which can overcome this difficulty by changing the constitution, had two methods at its disposal: a referendum or a parliamentary congress. To avoid open confrontation with the President of the Republic, François Mitterrand, who had declared his opposition to a referendum, Edouard Balladur, in agreement with the President and against the hard core of the Majority, opted for a congress (1 September 1993), and the laws were finally adopted on 26 November 1993.

[26] The same sequence of events as for the Pasqua laws occurred when the Government decided to review a 150 year old law limiting the financing of schools by local authorities (called the 'Loi Falloux'). Withdrawn for a first time in view of François Mitterrand's opposition, then passed just before Christmas 1993, overruled on 14 January 1994 by the Conseil Constitutionnel, this law was finally withdrawn for good. Similarly, in February 1994, governmental decrees on the quinquennial employment law met with staunch opposition in the street: these decrees concerned a so-called Professional Integration Contract which would allow young people, including some graduates, to receive a salary below the minimum wage in exchange for training paid for by the firm. Student demonstrations abounded in Paris and elsewhere (February and March 1994), eventually forcing the government to retreat. In respect of this U-turn, the Opposition was quick to remind the public of the withdrawal, on 24 October 1993, after a very tough strike, of the re-structuring plan for the nationalised air transport company, Air France.

[27] Jacques Chirac insisted on this 'refusal of polemics' right from the announcement of his candidacy in November 1994. The expression became a set feature of all his televised appearances, derided by *Les Guignols de l'info*. This so-called refusal of polemics meant that in the attacks between the Balladurian and Chiraquian clans during the campaign, one (Chirac) denounced immobilism and conservatism, the other (Balladur) denounced demagogy, but no names were named.

[28] The government thus intended to launch a major debate on the reform of the length of the working week, and on the reform of social security. In claiming this debate as his own inspiration, Jacques Chirac justified his early candidacy. In the conclusion of *La France pour tous*, he writes : 'I hope that [the] debate will not be spirited way, that our fellow citizens will have the time to reflect, to make comparisons [...]. One does not have the right to cheat the citizens, or to disguise what is at stake in a presidential election'.

[29] See 'Les dessous de l'affaire Pasqua', *L'Evénement du Jeudi*, 539 (2 to 8 March 1995); 'Pasqua, l'homme qui peut faire perdre Balladur', *Le Nouvel Observateur*, 1580, 16-22 February 1995; *Le Point*, 1170 and 1171, 18 and 25 February 1995, dedicated to Balladur's 'Watergate'.

[30] See Alain Lebaube, 'Philippe Séguin dénonce 'un véritable Munich social',' *Le Monde*, 18 June 1993; and the debate on 'alternative politics', *Le Monde*, 30 June 1993.

[31] '[...] we have come to think that we do not have a grip on anything. The power of governments would be limited to managing, prudently, the constraints imposed by the globalisation of the economies. Thus, the rule of [...] the 'pensée unique' imposed itself upon us. [But] nothing is inevitable [...]. [politics] is also about the art of making possible what is necessary [...]. In the name of the values of the Republic as in the name of economic common sense, I propose [...] a change in the order of our priorities'. Jacques Chirac, *La France pour tous*, electoral manifesto, pp. 6-7.

[32] The expression 'forces vives' is apparently intended to designate the individual men and women who participate at the most humble, day to day levels in the creation of wealth and in the organistaion of daily working life: workers and small business owners, union representatives in larger businesses, local association officials, local elected office bearers....the men and women 'on the ground', to use another expression ('hommes et femmes de terrain') which belongs to the same discourse. The expression 'forces vives' is all the more effective because it conjures up a tacit reference to its symmetrical opposite, 'forces de déclin', ou 'poids morts' ('forces of decline' or 'dead weights'), and also because the line between these two opposites is not clearly defined. The voter is deliberately left free to attribute whatever specific meaning s/he wishes to the expression 'poids morts': politicians, media, intellectuals (of the left, probably, and perhaps even Jewish ones such as Bernard-Henri Lévi or Alain Finkielkraut), immigrants, high financiers, bureaucrats. The populist and demagogic – even xenophobic – dimension of the expression is clear; the term, moreover, had been used by the left for a long time.

[33] Jacques Chirac insisted on many occasions on his 'solitary journey', going out to meet the French people, which he imposed upon himself from 1993 to 1995; and also on his newly found serenity. In this regard, see his two books from June 1994 and January 1995: 'My relationship with time has altered. For a long time, I acted quickly, because there was no time to lose and because I could not accept the inertia of people and of things around me. Nowadays, I measure the weightiness of things, and I take it into consideration, I differentiate between what is urgent, and what belongs to the long

term. This is the prerogative of age and experience'. See 'Introduction', *Une France pour tous*; see also the reviews in *Le Monde* and *Libération*, 10 January 1995. The media echoed this metamorphosis, of course. See: 'Le vrai Chirac a-t-il changé?', *L'Evénement du Jeudi*, 543, 30 March-5 April 1995; 'Jacques Chirac a-t-il vraiment changé?', *Le Nouvel Observateur*, 1582, 2-8 March 1995. *Le Nouvel Observateur*, which openly supported Lionel Jospin's candidacy, never missed an opportunity to deride this alleged change: '[...] in a presidential election, one must take into account the personality of the candidates. [...] Jacques Chirac has changed. Of course he has changed! As far as I can remember, it is the only thing I have seen him do' (Jacques Julliard, 'L'homme aux cent virages', 13-19 April 1995, p. 43); another article in the same issue, by Alain Chouffan, is entitled 'Les promesses de Caméléon Bonaparte'.

34 See for example 'La 'nouvelle image' de M. Balladur', *Le Monde*, 28 March 1995.

35 On 10 July 1985, at the time when Laurent Fabius was Prime Minister, the French secret services blew up a ship belonging to Greenpeace, which was opposing the nuclear tests in the Pacific. The explosion killed a photographer. The discovery that the French secret services were implicated prompted the resignation of the Defence Minister, Charles Hernu, in September 1985.

Patrice Pelat was a close friend of François Mitterrand. The business he founded was purchased at the top of the market by a nationalised group. In addition, Patrice Pelat was alleged to have made unlawful gains at the time when Péchiney, a nationalised firm, bought an American business. He died abruptly at the time when the enquiry opened (February 1989).

Pelat was also alleged to have agreed to a loan without interest in favour of Pierre Bérégovoy, then Minister of Economics and Finance (1984-1993) and in charge of the supervision of Péchiney. The legislative election campaign marked the starting point of a smear campaign against Pierre Bérégovoy, Prime Minister since April 1992. Pierre Bérégovoy committed suicide on 1 May 1993.

The slowness of the people in charge of blood transfusion in France, between March and October 1985, to impose a systematic tracing process for the Aids virus on blood donations, caused the infection of many haemophiliacs and other blood transfusion patients. Those responsible were charged in October 1991 and a first trial took place in October 1992. Political leaders were implicated (Laurent Fabius, Prime Minister at the time of the scandal, and Georgina Dufoix, then Minister for Social Affairs and Health).

Urba is the name of a consultancy which was alleged to have been used as a front for the funding of the Socialist Party. The first indictment in this affair occurred in June 1989.

36 The study of media headlines is in this respect very revealing. To quote only the headlines appearing on cover pages during this period: 'Affaires: Jérôme Monod entre deux eaux', *Enjeux-Les Echos*, 98, December 1994; 'Affaires 1994, ou les infortunes de la vertu', *Enjeux-Les Echos*, 99, January 1995; 'Le scandale de la distribution de l'eau', *L'Evénement du Jeudi*, 517, 29 September-5 October 1994; 'Affaires: le scandale qui recouvre tous les autres', *L'Evénement du Jeudi*, 520, 20-26 October 1994; 'Racket généralisé dans la région parisienne: l'affaire qui panique le RPR', *L'Evénement du Jeudi*, 522, 3-9 November 1994; 'Ces nouveaux scandales qui peuvent faire imploser la droite', *L'Evénement du Jeudi*, 524, 24-30 November 1994; 'Santé, le cancer de l'argent: pourquoi et comment la corruption a envahi un secteur aussi noble', *L'Evénement du Jeudi*, 528, 15-21 December 1994; 'Affaire Halphen: révélations sur la manipulation', *L'Evénement du Jeudi*, 530, 29 December-4 January

1995; 'Financements occultes du RPR', *L'Evénement du Jeudi*, 534, 26 January-1 February 1995; 'Les dessous de l'affaire Pasqua', *L'Evénement du Jeudi*, 539, 2-8 March 1995; 'Révélations sur l'affaire OM-VA', *L'Evénement du Jeudi*, 542, 23-29 March 1995; 'Corruption: 'mains propres' dans la santé', *L'Expansion*, 489-490, 5 December 1994; 'Pourquoi Alcatel vacille', *L'Expansion*, 492, 9 January 1995; 'Le Tour de France de la corruption – Sondage: la réaction stupéfiante des Français', *L'Express*, 2265, 8 December 1994; 'Argent, politique, télé: le procès – Pierre Botton, Michel Noir, Patrick Poivre d'Arvor', *L'Express*, 2275, 16 February 1995; 'Corruption: les juges iront jusqu'au bout', *Le Nouvel Economiste*, 969, 21 October 1994; 'Carignon, un maire tombé du nid', *Le Nouvel Economiste*, 970, 4 November 1994; 'Enquête: GSI – Les mystères d'une entreprise ordinaire', *Le Nouvel Economiste*, 983, 10 February 1995; 'Enquête: les tabous du Lyonnais – Quand l'élite française s'autoprotège au nom de la raison d'Etat', *Le Nouvel Economiste*, 989, 24 March 1995; 'Les vies secrètes de Bernard Tapie', *Le Nouvel Observateur*, 1564, 27 October-2 November 1994; 'Tapie: pourquoi il ne tombera pas seul', *Le Nouvel Observateur*, 1572, 22-28 December 1994; 'Banques: le scandale caché', *Le Nouvel Observateur*, 1579, 9-15 February 1995; 'Ecoutes: le watergate de Balladur', *Le Nouvel Observateur*, 1581, 23 February-1 March 1995; 'Les candidats et l'argent: ce qu'ils n'ont pas dit', *Le Nouvel Observateur*, 1585, 23-29 March 1995; 'Séisme: Carignon en prison', *Le Point*, 1152, 15 October 1994; 'Corruption: tout va exploser', *Le Point*, 1153, 22 October 1994; 'Les juges font sauter les caisses noires', *Le Point*, 1155, 5 November 1994; 'Mais qui protège Tapie?', *Le Point*, 1159, 3 December 1994; 'A quoi joue M. Pasqua', *Le Point*, 1160, 10 December 1994; 'Tapie, c'est fini', *Le Point*, 1161, 17 December 1994.

[37] June 1994, fraud and forgery. The French group was alleged to have a hidden network of Panama registered companies which managed secret funds.

[38] Pierre Suard was placed in police custody on 4 July 1994, alleged to have billed his company for works carried out in his own home, and for over-invoicing the sale of equipment to France Telecom, Alcatel's main nationalised customer. He was forced to step down on 10 March 1995.

[39] Senator of the Var region indicted on 15 July 1994, accused of racketeering in association with the local underworld.

[40] On 3 March 1995.

[41] On 13 February 1995. The trial involved the Mayor of Lyon, Michel Noir, and his son-in-law, Pierre Botton, the latter being accused of embezzling funds from companies he led in order to finance the political career of his father-in-law, bribing on occasions some well-known media personalities.

[42] The best known were Jean-Pierre Thierry, Jean-Louis Bruguière, Renaud Van Ruymbeke and Edith Boizette. See for example: 'Ces hommes qui font trembler le pouvoir', *L'Express*, 2255, 29 September 1994; and 'Les trois juges qui font trembler la droite', *Le Point*, 1170, 18 February 1995.

[43] See 'La délation', *Le Nouvel Observateur*, 1571, 15-21 December 1994; and Olivier Biffaud and Laurent Mauduit, 'La campagne présidentielle et les coups tordus', *Le Monde*, 1 April 1995.

[44] See in particular the interview in *Le Figaro*, 7 October 1992, in which Edouard Balladur criticises the 'four errors' in the economic policy of the Bérégovoy Government.

[45] From the Alsthom strike to the public service strikes. See 'La Mulitiplication des conflits sociaux perturbe la campagne présidentielle', *Le Monde*, 15 March 1995. On

the subject of the political interpretation of these conflicts, see for example 'Les Urnes et la rue', *Le Monde*, 11 April 1995.

[46] See A. Minc *La France de l'an 2000* (Paris, Odile Jacob, 1994).

[47] '[T]he French are worried because inequalities are growing', *La France pour tous*. In 'Nouvelles priorités pour la santé publique', *Sondoscope*, 103 (December 1994), Sophie Banos-Trégan observes on the basis of the numerous polls carried out during the period that 'the phenomenon of unemployment and lack of job security engenders a generalised anxiety-provoking climate'.

[48] See for example 'La maison des sans-abris', broadcast by France 2 on 23 October 1994. This excellent documentary on the Nanterre drop-in centre by Joël Calmettes and Pierre Guitton addressed the questions of poverty, of homelessness, of 'banlieues difficiles', abundantly dealt with in the media, and brought to the fore by some very active organisations. See also Véziane de Vezins, 'Les suites du rapport "Banlieuescopies": les banlieues contre la loi de la jungle', *Le Figaro*, 4-5 March 1995; 'Une centaine d'associations veulent placer l'exclusion au coeur du débat présidentiel', *Le Monde*, 9-10 April 1995; 'MM. Balladur, Chirac et Jospin sont d'accord pour proposer une loi-cadre contre l'exclusion (à l'occasion d'un colloque organisé par 'La Croix' et France-Inter)', *Le Monde*, 29 March 1995. See also the saga of the so-called 'rue du Dragon affair' involving an association called DAL (Droit au Logement): Gérard Petitjean, 'Opération Dragon', *Le Nouvel Observateur*, 1572, 22-28 December 1994; Patrice de Plunkett, 'Les mal-logés et les sans-logis', *Le Figaro Magazine*, 8 April 1995; and Michel Castaing, 'Droits devant. L'Association de la rue du Dragon installe ses "échanges de savoirs"', *Le Monde*, 7 February 1995.

[49] Following the anti-CIP demonstrations and the withdrawal of this project, Edouard Balladur launched the 'National consultation of 15 to 25 year olds' project. 30 million questionnaires were put at the disposal of the public, 1.6 million answers were received. This questionnaire covered all aspects of the life of the younger generation.

[50] See the CERC study published in *Le Monde*, 25 February 1994 and the study of 'Les Français face au chômage' published by the Ministry of Employment in *Les Echos*, 10 June 1994, on the basis of the CREDOC studies.

[51] Pierre Bourdieu (ed.), *La Misère du monde* (Paris, Seuil, 1993).

[52] We agree with Emmanuel Todd's analysis, as expressed in the above-mentioned interview with P. Perrineau (*Le Monde*, 19-20 February 1995): 'I wonder if Chirac's victimisation by the system, his transformation into the suffering Christ of French political society will not end up having the same effect in his favour [as that produced on Tapie]'. It was suggested here and there that Emmanuel Todd was himself the inspiration behind the themes of the Chiraquian campaign. Todd denied this, but if it is true, one could only conclude from the closeness of Todd's analysis here and Chirac's campaign strategy that Chirac's campaign was even more carefully controlled and manipulative than has been openly acknowledged. See the flattering biography in *Paris-Match*, 2399, 18 May 1995: 'Seul contre tous'.

[53] There was not one single Jacques Chirac interview or appearance where his experience, his willingness to listen and enter into a dialogue, and his knowledge of the terrain were not emphasised. In the television debate opposite Lionel Jospin on 2 May 1995, and which was almost the final opportunity for expounding those themes he had hammered out and refined throughout the campaign, Chirac, more than Jospin, was able to play the card of a relationship to simple people. The following quotations from that debate are exemplary:

'I have been out in the field a lot, myself [...] especially in the last two years when I dedicated myself to visiting our cities, our countryside [...] and I am becoming aware of the difficulty that politicians have in understanding what really happens....'
'Stepping back, reflecting, the way I distanced myself from power, and a certain solitude, on occasion, allowed me to think back about my experience, and to tell myself that all of us, one way or another, more or less, were wrong'.
So as not to insult the 'ordinary people' Chirac repeatedly describes them as 'modestes' rather than 'simple' or 'ordinary'. His message was very well received by voters since, in the opinion polls before the election, as in those carried out at polling stations, Chirac came top of the list as the candidate who is the 'closest to people like you and me' (SCP-*Info-Matin*, 7 March 1995; Barometer IPSOS-*Le Point*, 25 March 1995; Presidential Barometer IFOP-*L'Express*, 6 April 1995; and see 'Le plus proche des préoccupations des Français', *Le Monde*, 25 April 1995).

54 See his attacks on speculation and technocracy. The theme of attacking the technocratic élite which failed in their mission is constantly repeated, as it cut itself off from reality and gave in to the charms of the 'pensée unique': 'This single-track attitude, which seeks to control everything, rests on the superiority of technocracy [...]. A technocracy to which government surrendered, for lack of willpower [...] the bulk of its authority' (*La France pour tous*). See also Patrick Jarreau, 'Jacques Chirac contre les élites', *Le Monde*, 18-19 December 1994; Catherine Nay, 'L'élite parisienne est déconnectée de la réalité', *Le Figaro Magazine*, Cahier 3, 8 April 1995; Laurent Joffrin and Robert Schneider, 'Chirac: 'Le danger, c'est le politiquement correct!', *Le Nouvel Observateur*, 1575, 12-18 January 1995; Denis Jeambar and Catherine Pégard, 'Chirac: 'la *manière* de gouverner est en cause'(my italics), *Le Point*, 1159, 3 December 1994. See also Philippe Cohen, 'Radiographie croisée de la crise des élites par Minc et Crozier', *Info-Matin*, 13 April 1995.

55 This photograph was published in many magazines. See for example *Paris-Match*, 2399, 18 May 1995.

56 'Les valeurs idéologiques des Français', SOFRES opinion poll for *Le Figaro*, 21 July 1994; 'Le régime présidentiel fait peu d'adeptes', SOFRES opinion poll, *Le Figaro*, 1 March 1995; 'Les qualités nécessaires et les pouvoirs du président', SOFRES opinion poll for the *Reader's Digest*, April 1995; 'Les Français intéressés par la campagne présidentielle', SOFRES, 5 April 1995.

Indicative Bibliography

Ardilly, Pascal, *Les Techniques de sondage* (Paris, Editions Technip, 1994).

Bourdieu, Pierre, *La Distinction – Critique sociale du jugement* (Paris, Les Editions de Minuit, 1979).

Bourdieu, Pierre (ed.), *La Misère du monde* (Paris, Seuil, 1993).

Chevallier, Jean-Jacques, *Histoire des institutions et des régimes politiques de la France de 1789 à nos jours* (Paris, Dalloz, 7th edition 1985).

Desabie, Jacques, *Théorie et Pratique des sondages* (Paris, Dunod, 1966).

Domenach, Nicolas and Maurice Szafran, *De si bons amis* (Paris, Plon, 1994).

Duverger, Maurice, *La VIe République et le régime présidentiel* (Paris, Fayard, 1961).

Gaffney, John, *The French Left and the Fifth Republic* (London, MacMillan, 1989).

Gaffney, John (ed.), *The French Presidential Elections of 1988* (Aldershot, Dartmouth, 1989).

Imbert, Claude and Jacques Julliard, *La Droite et la Gauche* (Paris, Robert Laffont/Grasset, 1995).

Meynaud, Hélène and Denis Duclos, *Les Sondages d'opinion* (Paris, La Découverte, 1989).

Minc, Alain, *La France de l'an 2000* (Paris, Odile Jacob, 1994).

Mots/ Les Langages du politique, 23 (June 1990), issue on *Discours des sondages d'opinion*.

Nay, Catherine, *Le Prince et le Régent* (Paris, Grasset, 1994).

Portelli, Hughes, 'La crise de la représentation politique', *Regards sur l'actualité*, 209-210, March-April 1995.

Problèmes politiques et sociaux, special issue *Droite-gauche: un clivage dépassé?*, 719, 14 January 1994.

Quermonne, Jean-Louis and Dominique Chagnollaud, *Le Gouvernement de la France sous la Cinquième République* (4th edition, Paris, Dalloz, 1991).

Requin, Jean-Marc and Joël Girard, *Le Guide de l'élection présidentielle* (Paris, Editions Deletraz, 1995).

Wright, Vincent, *The Government and Politics of France* (London, Hutchinson, 1983).

Le Sondoscope – La Revue française des sondages, Paris, Centre d'Etudes Socio-Economique et de Management, nos. 95-108, 1994-1995.

15. FOREIGN POLICY ISSUES AND THE ELECTION

Douglas Johnson

Introduction

Once the elections were over, it was easy for commentators to point out that external affairs had hardly been present in the electoral debate. This, it was said, was nothing new in French elections. The risks of world war had not unduly troubled French opinion, and Europe had appeared as something which was too abstract, too much the subject of debates which were either ideological or categorical. International problems were secondary to the problems of growing unemployment, poverty and exclusion. Therefore they were not important.[1] The former German chancellor, Helmut Schmidt, noted in 1995 that foreign policy questions had been absent from the electoral debate in France. The question of the European Union was seldom mentioned, Germany even less.[2]

For many observers this was not surprising. In French electoral history, although it has sometimes been possible for a political party in government to use a successful foreign policy as a means of distracting public attention away from failures in domestic affairs, it was rare for foreign affairs to be the determining factor in an election. One has to go back a long way, to Guizot and the July Monarchy, for example, to find a statesman whose political standing has been undermined by apparent failure in his conduct of foreign affairs. Conversely, it is true that with de Gaulle, in 1965, there were those who voted for him because he was a world figure (although one can point out that he failed to get a majority on the first ballot) and that with Mitterrand in 1988 the question of France's future in Europe played an important role (although the divisions amongst his opponents did most to ensure his victory). In general, the electoral preoccupations of the French were nearer home, often near to local traditions and interests. As de Gaulle scornfully put it, the French could become most concerned by the price of smoked herring. Expressed theoretically it is said that when voting on matters of domestic policy one is concerned with actions which the government takes or which it promises to pursue, whereas were one to vote on matters of foreign policy then one would be taking decisions about the actions of other states which cannot be foreseen.[3]

More philosophically, it has been argued that the nature of international politics is such that there is a necessary continuity within the system, and that this continuity comes from a structural relationship between states. Although emphasis can be placed differently, a number of authors have used systemic theory in order to discover the nature of the interplay between different powers. This type of analysis would explain how, in spite of major personality differences between de Gaulle, Pompidou, Giscard d'Estaing and

Mitterrand, and in spite of processing a presidential system of government that maximises the opportunities for personal direction, there has been a high degree of continuity in French foreign and defence policies throughout the Fifth Republic.[4]

Put more simply, there was little chance of a new departure in foreign policy for any candidate who appeared to be a serious challenger before the first ballot in 1995. The scope for prescribed change was narrow and the freedom for innovation limited. Theoretically, France could withdraw from the European Union and from the Atlantic Alliance, but to do so would be to reduce France to the level of Salazar's Portugal, of Enver Hodja's Albania, or of a Switzerland without its prosperity. Dossier by dossier, the difficulties of adopting a policy different from that which has been followed are clearly apparent, in, for example, Bosnia or Algeria. 'L'autre politique' is difficult to envisage.[5] As to Europe, the French Communist Party put it even more simply still when it said that the three main contenders in 1994, Chirac, Balladur and Delors, were agreed on the question of Europe.[6]

There were also other reasons of detail why foreign policy questions had to be treated with extreme caution. The uncertainties arising from President Mitterrand's bad health had meant that over many months foreign policy initiatives had come sometimes from the President, sometimes from the Prime Minister, and sometimes from the Foreign Minister, Alain Juppé, and the Quai d'Orsay. But in April and May 1995, Mitterrand was still President, undertaking official journeys outside France and receiving important visitors. It was not known whether or not he would intervene in the debates. It was therefore difficult for the Socialist candidate, Lionel Jospin, to propose a policy which would be radically different from that of his fellow Socialist; equally, as Balladur had worked in relative harmony with the Elysée since becoming Prime Minister in 1993, it was embarrassing for him to attack the foreign policy of the President: such attacks had to be reserved for special occasions. It was not thought that there would be any serious break in foreign policy when President Mitterrand left the scene.[7] Balladur's embarrassment was even greater vis-à-vis his very active Foreign Minister, the Gaullist, Alain Juppé. When the latter became Chirac's most prominent supporter, the threat of a damaging split on government policy was very real, although, in fact, it only occurred when Juppé announced substantial financial cuts in the diplomatic establishment, a statement that was rectified by the Prime Minister. Chirac too suffered embarrassment from having Balladur's Foreign Minister as chief spokesperson, but the greatest obstacle to his discussing matters of foreign policy was the presence amongst his most important supporters of Philippe Séguin, the President of the National Assembly who had been an opponent of the Maastricht Treaty, and whose substantial domestic policy differences with Juppé were surpassed by those in foreign policy. Thus, considerations of a particular and personal nature were additional factors in causing the question of international affairs to be treated with caution in the electoral campaign.

Expectations

There was widespread realisation that the new President would be obliged to play a particularly important role on the international scene. The election coincided with the French presidency of the European Union, which lasted until the end of June 1995. This was particularly important because it was this presidency which was obliged to begin preparations for the Intergovernmental Conference (IGC) of 1996, which would discuss a series of vital issues such as the enlargement of the Union, its institutions, procedure, budgetary provisions, common foreign and security policies, as well as being concerned with the establishment of a common currency and the powers of the European Parliament. The new President would immediately have to prepare for the reports of the

IGC Reflection Group (set up at the Corfu Council in June 1994) which was due to convene for the first time at Messina on 2 June 1995, and the European summit to be held at Cannes on 26 and 27 June. In a list of what the new President was expected to do, these European questions were important, especially those which concerned the future membership of the Union and the possible persistence of some degree of national independence in the probable existence of a federal and supranational organisation. But the European Union was not the only subject about which the new President would have to take decisions. There was the future of the remnants of the dislocated Soviet Union: should they exist as independent entities or should they seek to reconstitute some sort of ensemble around Russia? There was the attitude to adopt towards the conflict that was taking place in the Moslem world, between modernists and fundamentalists. Above all, there was the attitude to be taken towards the preponderance of the United States in world affairs. Having listed these topics, one observer asked if the presidential election campaign might enlighten the nation about the options that were open to them.[8]

It was clear that the circumstances in which these decisions had to be taken were particularly difficult. The downfall of communism had not marked the end of history, nor seen the triumph of political democracy, the rights of man and the market economy. Balladur's Minister for Defence, François Léotard, described the situation as being one where a war had ended but a peace had yet to be achieved.[9] It was said that there was no problem which was not, in fact, international, whether it was concerned with economics, atomic, biological or chemical weapons, the over-heating of the atmosphere, fishing, radioactivity, Aids or migration; whether it was the disasters which were threatening countries such as Pakistan, Nigeria, Mexico and Algeria, or those where catastrophe was already in place: Yugoslavia, Somalia, Liberia, Rwanda. It was therefore to be hoped that the presidential candidates in France would accept the interdependence, the quasi-identity in some cases, that existed between domestic and foreign policies.[10]

Retired diplomats enjoyed the paradox of saying how everything was simpler in the good old days of the Cold War, or of looking back to de Gaulle with a wistful cynicism. 'De Gaulle', wrote Gabriel Robin, 'thought of changing the world but only succeeded in changing France; Federal Germany only thought of changing Germany, but succeeded in changing the world'.[11] In all this there was the question of the place France occupied in the world, what de Gaulle had called 'le rang'. Was Europe to be the instrument of France's strength and position, or was it to be the means of France's decline?[12] And there were dangers too. There might be alliances, but to quote the Minister of Defence, François Léotard, again: 'At the moment of truth a nation has no friends'.[13]

1995

At the beginning of 1995, there were three incidents which took place in France, each of which was connected with overseas countries, and had an effect on the course of the election campaign. The first concerned allegations about a number of Americans, said to be CIA agents, who were accused of political, economic and industrial espionage. The Minister of the Interior, Charles Pasqua, informed the President of the Republic of these facts on 18 February, after having interviewed the American ambassador in Paris on two occasions. Contrary to diplomatic procedure, these facts were made public by the Minister of the Interior and were reported in the press.[14] Later revelations claimed that an attempt had been made to bribe a member of the Prime Minister's staff working at Matignon.[15] It was doubtless hoped that the well-established anti-Americanism of the French would cause them to become indignant at this news and that this would assist the Minister of the Interior in overcoming damaging criticisms that had been levelled at him over other issues. But the revelations caused a certain hilarity ('Pasqua has declared war against America', wrote one newspaper)[16]; more seriously, the question was raised as to how the matter had been made public and why the Minister of the Interior had on this occasion, as on many others, interfered in the conduct of foreign affairs. Pasqua protested that what was remarkable was that American spies had been present in France, not that there should have been a leak of information about their expulsion; at the Quai d'Orsay, however, there was a general exasperation at these '*histoires de basse police*', and the Prime Minister told ministers and officials that they should avoid commenting on this matter.[17]

It was probably no accident that in the second incident Pasqua was the target of an allegation concerning the sale of arms to Iran when such a sale would have been illegal. It was claimed that shortly before the Paris trial of the assassins of Chapour Bakhtiar, the former Prime Minister of the Shah of Iran, in November 1994, the Minister of the Interior had delivered missiles to the Iranian government, sending them via Algeria and Cyprus. In this way, the Iranian government had been persuaded not to protest about the trial by means of the sort of terrorism that had occurred in Paris in 1986. These allegations were officially denied and they had little effect other than again discrediting Pasqua and again pointing to his interference in foreign affairs.[18]

The third incident was the invitation that the President of the Republic issued to the Cuban leader, Fidel Castro, who arrived in Paris on 13 March 1995. Madame Mitterrand claimed that he was in no way a dictator, and although officials pointed out that no Cuban flags would be flown in Paris and that the costs of his journey would not be met from official funds, there were many protests. The invitation was seen as an anti-American gesture by Mitterrand, but it was appreciated rather as an example of how, in foreign affairs, the President of the Republic could do whatever he wanted (like General de Gaulle in Montreal or Giscard d'Estaing in Warsaw).[19] The reaction to these three incidents shows a certain sophistication in French political circles and in the public as a whole. Public excitement would have been inappropriate over minor matters when the electorate was faced by more serious issues.

During the course of the campaign, there was a paradox. It was continually said that questions of foreign policy were being ignored. But this was said so frequently that questions of foreign policy were clearly not being ignored. In the same way, there were those who thought that the campaign was dull, although it possessed many dramatic moments, such as the withdrawal of Jacques Delors from the campaign; the renunciation of a former Prime Minister, Raymond Barre, and a former President, Giscard; the choice of the little known Jospin as the Socialist candidate; the sudden decline of Balladur in the opinion polls. The belief that foreign affairs were being ignored, like the impression that the campaign was dull, sprang from highly particular points of view. Thus a certain type of viewer might have been stimulated by a television debate between Jacques Delors and Edouard Balladur and was frustrated that it did not take place. A certain type of socialist might have found the campaign more interesting had the class struggle and anti-clericalism been mentioned more frequently, and a certain type of Gaullist might have welcomed more sweeping statements about French grandeur and power. In the same way, some of those who complained about the absence of foreign policy discussion were disappointed that their questions about Bosnia, Croatia, Rwanda, Algeria and Iran had not been adequately answered.[20] The intellectual Alain Finkielkraut did not only complain that foreign policy was absent from the discussions. He claimed that the world was absent. Although he admitted that those whom Hannah Arendt had described as 'specialists for solving problems' would think that he was not intelligent because he was emotional, he could not accept that politicians and parties were asking for his vote whilst they washed their hands of what was happening in the world and, like Neville Chamberlain in Munich, treated what was happening in the Balkans as events taking place in a far off country of which we knew nothing.[21] André Glucksman was another intellectual who asked what the candidates would reply about the grave problems affecting different parts of the world, and if they could not promise to conjure away evil, would they at least say who they supported in Algiers, Sarajevo, Moscow....[22]

Otherwise, the question was asked, exactly what were the options and the positions which each candidate would adopt in 1996, and the complaint was made that where a candidate had answered the question the response had been so vague as to make it impossible to judge what the candidate's intentions really were.[23] The candidates were asked about whether they wished to give up the European Union, or whether they wished to take Europe forward, whether they wanted less or more Europe.[24] They were asked what they thought about corruption in the European Union, what their views were about the Schengen agreements and immigration, if they thought it wise to have negotiations between the Algerian government and the Islamic Front, and how they would protect French troops fighting with the United Nation forces in ex-Yugoslavia.[25] Giscard d'Estaing warned that France was faced with the biggest problem it had encountered since the unification of Germany, that of the future of Europe. Raymond Barre warned the French nation that they were in danger of forgetting the two most important factors in their national life, the large government deficit and the Franco-German alliance. After the televised debate between Chirac and Jospin before the second round of the election, in which foreign affairs occupied a relatively small place, Alain Juppé said that it was necessary to talk about them, declaring 'j'ai faim de la politique étrangère'.[26] A writer associated with Edouard Balladur wrote that whilst other countries could be governed by realities and constraints, France, given its universalism and its past, needed to dream. France wanted, from its new President, a grand design for the world, now that the Cold War was over.[27] In many ways, then, the candidates were made aware of the public's concern and curiosity about French attitudes towards the world that lay beyond France.

Balladur

It was relatively easy to understand what were Balladur's principles in foreign policy. Without reviving the statements of some of his collaborators, made in the summer of 1994, that the foreign policy of France was conducted at Matignon, it was certain that Balladur played a more important role in foreign affairs than any other of President Mitterrand's six Prime Ministers. Quite understandably, he presented to the press the successes which were attributed to him, such as the successful negotiations on the General Agreement on Tariffs and Trade, keeping his nerve in the international financial crises of 1993, normalising diplomatic relations with China and therefore benefiting French industrialists, devaluing the French African franc. All these were part of his 'politique étrangère économiste' to which he attached the greatest importance. But he had been active also in European negotiations and had established good relations with Chancellor Kohl (who had stayed at Balladur's home in Chamonix during January 1995), he had devoted a good deal of time to ex-Yugoslavia and to Rwanda, and he had visited French troops in Bosnia and Rwanda. Rumour had it that had he had greater personal responsibility, the French 'casques bleues' would have been withdrawn from Bosnia, and 'Opération Turquoise' would never have come into being in Rwanda. He had, however, allowed himself to be persuaded by the Elysée, and by others (including Pasqua) and this affected his reputation, suggesting that he was weak. In the same way, he disapproved of President Mitterrand's ban on nuclear testing and was in favour of the French resuming their tests (as he was to say in the electoral campaign) but he did not think that it was worth having an open quarrel with the Elysée on this issue. He took responsibility for ordering the attack on the Algerian terrorist hi-jackers of the Air France plane at

Marseilles just after Christmas 1994, but he did not wish France to be drawn into the Algerian conflict, and whilst having supported the allocation of considerable financial aid to the Algerian government so that it could recover economically, he was not in favour of this continuing endlessly.

One can see how in foreign as in domestic affairs, Balladur stressed continuity. There were, however, innovations which he had made and other innovations which he intended to make. There was the 'Pact of Security and Stability in Europe'. Afterwards, it was widely suggested that in making this proposal in April 1993, Balladur not only wished to emphasise his role in European diplomacy, but also had in mind the elections of 1995 and the likelihood that the process which was approved at the Copenhagen summit of June 1993 would lead to a great gathering of states in Paris which would be timed to take place just before the elections of 1995. This in fact was what happened. Balladur mobilised the diplomacy of Europe in order to bring together some forty-three Ministers of Foreign Affairs on 26 and 27 May 1994, and then an even larger gathering was held on 20 and 21 March 1995. The logic of the situation was that since all the countries of Europe had achieved a democratic system of government and had adopted a market economy, then the one remaining problem of principle was that of their frontiers and of minority populations. The most striking example was that of the Hungarians, since some 3 million Hungarians live within the frontiers of Romania, Slovakia and ex-Yugoslavia. The pact of stability wished to organise the settlement of these minority and frontier problems, and encourage all the countries concerned to establish agreements of 'good neighbourliness' amongst themselves (and by March 1995 nearly 100 such agreements had been signed). At the meeting, Balladur was far more aggressive than was usually the case. He condemned states which were turned in on themselves and he said that force should be part of the service of what was right. The point of it all was to prevent another Yugoslavia from developing. It was also to prepare certain states for entry into the European Union or the North Atlantic Treaty Organisation.

There were many who thought this important. When one of Balladur's advisers wrote that because of internal quarrels and ideological struggles, the old nations of Europe had lost their liberty and their place in the world, it was clear that this pact of security envisaged a Europe which went beyond the confines of Franco-German agreement or the ideology of the European Union.[28] There were those who saw many shortcomings in the pact itself or in its supposed internal political preoccupations.[29] More significantly, however, it failed to capture the imagination of politicians or of the public. And for those whose first interest was the European Union, its wider-ranging preoccupations were seen as a distraction.

The determined partisans of European unification were disappointed by the way in which matters had been handled in France during the last years of the Mitterrand presidency. Possibly because of the large percentage of the population that had voted against the Treaty of Maastricht in the referendum of September 1992 (48.95%), because of the increasing power of Germany ('must we make Europe in order to please the Germans?' was a cry that was heard from time to time in public debate), because of the continuing dilemma about whether the institutions of the Union should be given more power and depth or whether priority should be given to its enlargement, little progress had been made by successive governments. It was understood that the new President would change this and would have a programme which would take France and its partners into a new era. Balladur proposed solving this problem by two essential methods. The first was the rapid adoption of a unified European currency in 1997. The second was to revise the institutions of the Union so that they would function efficiently and democratically in an enlarged Europe. The first method was chosen to demonstrate how France contrived to be pro-European. At home it would attract the Euro-enthusiasts of the centre parties; and abroad, by forcing Germany to accept this rapid development, it would assert the leadership of France. The second was designed to increase the power of national parliaments and would preserve national identities. This would appeal to a certain Euro-cynicism.

Into these arguments Balladur introduced a degree of pragmatism. There were some countries which would not be ready for the European monetary union in 1997 and others which would. There were some countries which would be able to play a prominent role in the defence of Europe. There were governments which looked to the East; there were governments which had a particular preoccupation with the Mediterranean. It was these arrangements which became known as the Europe of concentric circles. There would be no federalism; there would be no hard core of advanced European states. Balladur saw a Franco-British agreement on defence; a Franco-Spanish agreement on North Africa. As to Franco-German relations, they were the essential motor of Europe. Without a Franco-German agreement there would be no Europe, but the Franco-German alliance of 1963 would have to be re-negotiated in order to bring it into line with the situation in 1995. This did not mean that France and Germany should impose their will on the remaining powers of the Union.[30]

These proposals were seen by many observers as vague, and in particular it was thought unlikely that France would be ready to meet the Maastricht conditions for the adoption of a European currency.[31] Chirac's spokesperson on defence matters accused Balladur of not giving enough time to important matters of foreign affairs.[32] Those who lamented the absence of important French contributions to the future of Europe claimed that they were unable to see any possible progress coming from Balladur.[33] But above all, Balladur was perceived as correct, moderate, almost impersonal in his attitudes. When he was asked, if elected President, would he go to Algiers, he was surprised and answered in the negative. When he explained his fears that the USA might not fully implement the GATT, and he was asked if he had contacted President Clinton, he replied by saying that he had written to the President of the European Commission. When he was asked if the election of a new President would create a shock in France, he replied that the election of Mitterrand in 1981 had created a shock, but that the effects were regrettable. Although he always stated his belief that France, with its history, culture and language, must always be most important in world affairs, his conviction was not aggressive. One can compare his generalities to the more pointed approach of Alain Juppé. Looking at a future which would be, he said, one of 'transitions, troubles and convolutions', France could obtain results which bore no relation to the simple arithmetic of power.[34] And Juppé was Chirac's chief lieutenant.

Chirac

Chirac's electoral campaign took place in different stages. The British correspondent, Mary Dejevsky, saw it as beginning with Chirac courting his traditional constituencies, the farmers and small business people. He spoke in Gaullist terms about France being a great country and having to keep its Frenchness, and he spoke of the legacy of de Gaulle. It was some time after this that he discovered young, first-time voters, and a mass of the population who believed that France was suffering from deep and dangerous social divisions. His campaign then changed and became more radical and more populist.[35] It was in the first phase of his campaign, in November 1994, as he proclaimed his candidacy (a proclamation that was hurried because of rumours that President Mitterrand's health had worsened) that he stated that before France adopted a single currency, the matter would have to be put to a referendum. This 'gaullien' method which would almost certainly have ended the prospects of such a currency was proposed without consulting Juppé and on the advice, it is said, of an old Gaullist baron, Maurice Schumann. The centre parties shied away from Chirac, the stock exchange slumped, and the Socialist former Prime Minister Rocard accused him of weakening the franc. Chirac withdrew his statement, although the idea persisted that he would hold a referendum before approving any change in the institutions of the Union. From then onwards, Chirac was extremely cautious about foreign policy. The political commentator, Alain Duhamel, asserted that it was on foreign policy that Chirac could be beaten.[36] There was a complaint that when he made a speech at Meaux on 13 March, he spoke for an hour before touching on questions of foreign policy. Apart from his own uncertainties, it was evident that Chirac was embarrassed by the differences between Juppé and Séguin, the latter having written a newspaper article suggesting that the Treaty of Maastricht could be modified.[37] But on 16 March Chirac made a long speech (the text ran to 82 pages) entirely devoted to foreign affairs.

The two main themes of this speech were concerned with Europe and with defence. He was dismissive of many ideas. He was against federalism and proposed 'l'Europe des Etats'; he did not agree with the suggestion that there should be a European Ministry of Foreign Affairs; he had little to say about the European Parliament; he wanted to reduce the powers of the Commission. He was in favour of many principles that were particularly French: the alliance with Germany, the common agricultural policy, French privileges in cultural matters, and an increase in the role of national parliaments. Most specifically he believed that a common European currency would be introduced. He was not specific about dates and he made no mention of a referendum, only saying that it should be introduced after 'un vrai débat national'. He believed that France and Germany should produce a joint memorandum, outlining their agreed policies to the Intergovernmental Conference of 1996. He suggested that a President of the European Council should be nominated for three years and that s/he should act as spokesperson for Europe. He was critical of the Schengen agreements (which were due to come into force). His task was to make a European Union that would win the support of the French people because it responded to their real preoccupations.

On defence, he stressed that the defence of Europe should be given priority, that the methods of French defence (including national service) should be scrutinised, and that France should resume nuclear testing on condition that at the same time France should announce when these tests were to come to an end.

Naturally, reactions to this considerable speech varied. The current affairs weekly, *Le Point*, thought that it had approached the essential problem of how France's national identity would be preserved whilst pointing out that interdependence was both inevitable and indispensable. *Libération* thought that Chirac's speech was too hesitant towards Europe, whilst *Le Figaro* thought it practical.[38] But elsewhere it was clear that Chirac was in a different category from 'les grands absents' of the election, Giscard d'Estaing, Raymond Barre and Jacques Delors. It was not that he was less flamboyant. Although he considered that the Treaty of Maastricht was not the great 'rendez-vous de l'histoire' that it claimed to be, he did not propose to change the architecture of Europe that it had established. He accepted enlargement of the Union and he accepted the single currency. Whilst insisting on the increased role of national parliaments and on the importance of defence and of France's nuclear economy, he accepted the importance of future dialogue with Germany. Giscard d'Estaing supposedly approved of Chirac's policy (and rumour had it that he saw himself as the first President of the European Council). Barre was preoccupied with gaining Chiraquian support for his election as Mayor of Lyon. It was left to Jospin to take up the cause of Europe. He did so diffidently, however (especially given that Jacques Delors was his adviser). This was no longer the voice of French Socialism in Europe as it had been heard in the heyday of President Mitterrand's rule.

Jospin

It was natural that Jospin should, in the course of his televised 'face-à-face' with Chirac, insist upon two points. First was his opposition to the resumption of nuclear testing. For Jospin, this was not necessary because there existed methods of simulation which permitted accurate observation of nuclear weapons in the laboratory. For France to resume testing would be particularly inappropriate at a time when an international non-proliferation treaty was being negotiated. This would provide those states which wished to avoid signing the treaty with a pretext for abstention. Secondly, he was opposed to abolishing national service and to creating a professional army. If the call-up provided more men than were wanted, then those who were not required for military service should undertake civil duties. On these two principles Jospin was faithful firstly to Mitterrand, and secondly to long-established Socialist principles. In addition to these two main points, whilst disapproving of Russian action in Chechnya, Jospin thought that it could not obliterate everything that Russia had achieved in the last war. On Bosnia, he envisaged either joint international action, or a French withdrawal. On Algeria he was in favour of the negotiations which had taken place in Rome between government and islamists whilst rejecting terrorism and the excesses of governmental reactions. Otherwise he concentrated on the contradictions which he perceived in the programme of Chirac.[39]

For Jospin, there were two essential contradictions in Chirac's position and he attacked these both in the televised debate and elsewhere. Before the ballot there was the dramatic weakening of the franc, and Chirac had been obliged to say that he had the support of the Governor of the Bank of France and that he believed in the 'franc fort'.[40] The second was his return to the idea that he would ask for a referendum before proceeding to a major change in European institutions, such as the establishment of a single currency. Although this gave Euro-sceptics some hope, it was followed by reassurances from Raymond Barre that Chirac would not call the Treaty of Maastricht into question.[41] It was this last change which was the major theme of Jospin's final attack on Chirac at his rally in Toulouse.[42]

Conclusion

It can be argued, when one considers the presidential elections as a whole, that although more time was spent on questions such as unemployment, social welfare, education, justice, institutions and the future of French society, there was very little choice open to the electorate in these matters. The margin was narrow, the number of options limited, the detail technical. It was true that Chirac, more than any other, was able to give the impression of making a fresh start, of reconciling the French to their government and of healing social divisions. In this way he had an advantage over his chief competitors, both caught up – albeit in very different ways – in the process of continuity; Jospin to fourteen years of presidential Socialism, Balladur to himself. But over Europe and over foreign policy, the electorate had a real choice, or certainly the illusion of choice.

Firstly, candidates opposed the European Union because it was international, because it was not in France's interests, because it allowed Germany to dominate France, because it encouraged foreign immigration into France and reduced French frontier control (Le Pen); because it hampered French diplomacy and prevented France playing its national role in the world (Philippe de Villiers); because it was capitalist (Robert Hue, Arlette Laguiller); and because its preoccupation with economic progress meant that it created pollution and other ills (Dominique Voynet). If one opposed Europe, one could vote for almost any one of the candidates.

Secondly, there were those who were European in the full sense of the word. They wanted a Europe of social progress, with equality and rights for all. They wanted a federation which would move Europe away from out-of-date national states towards a new future. This Europe, of Jacques Delors and François Mitterrand, was best represented by Lionel Jospin (though with all the diffidence we have already mentioned).

Thirdly, there were those who accepted Europe and a common European currency as inevitable and desirable. But this Europe was hedged with precautions. In the case of Balladur it was more pragmatic; in the case of Chirac it was aggressive: it was a Europe of 'yes, of course, but....'

With Chirac's victory what also triumphed was a Gaullism preoccupied by the situation or, as the General would have put it, 'le rang' of France in the world. On the evening of his election, Chirac promised that France would be a beacon for all the peoples of the world and that France would be the motor-power of the European Union.

There could be no doubt: questions of foreign policy would be decided at the Elysée. The days when, in the first 'cohabitation' of 1986, Chirac as Prime Minister bickered with President Mitterrand over French attitudes in foreign affairs; or when, in the second 'cohabitation' from 1993, Balladur and Juppé, Matignon and the Quai d'Orsay, took initiatives when the President was ill... these days were over. Chirac, if he was to follow his electoral promises, would be a vigorous spokesperson for France in world affairs. It was noticed, as if to emphasise this, that the new governmental organisation was very much a Foreign Ministry, Quai d'Orsay set-up. The Prime Minister, Alain Juppé, had been Minister for Foreign Affairs in the Balladur government. His then 'directeur de cabinet' was Dominique de Villepin, who became Secretary General of the Elysée. The Prime Minister's 'directeur de cabinet' was Maurice Gourdault-Montagne, also from the Quai d'Orsay, as was Catherine Colonna, who became the spokesperson for the Elysée. With this network in place, the new Minister for Foreign Affairs, Hervé de Charrette, was of less importance, and his nomination was a Chirac gesture of thanks to Charrette's close friend, Giscard d'Estaing, for his support during the campaign.

President Chirac's actions rapidly revealed the nature of his policy. His meeting with Chancellor Kohl the day after he had assumed office was more than a polite gesture. It was the affirmation that the privileged Franco-German relationship still existed. On Friday 9 June, the new President entertained the fifteen Heads of the European Union and the President of the Commission to an informal dinner. This meeting was both preceded and followed by a worsening of the situation in Bosnia as the Serbs advanced, eventually capturing Srebrenica and advancing on Bihac. President Chirac fulminated against the Serbs and proposed direct military action by the British and French troops in the 'Force d'action rapide'.[43] He suspended the Schengen agreements for the French frontiers, thus maintaining controls when these agreements would have abolished them for seven member states of the European Union. On 13 June he announced that France would be resuming nuclear tests. Between 19 and 22 July he visited four African states and met some fifteen African leaders. He was accompanied by the octogenarian Jacques Foccart who had been General de Gaulle's special adviser on African affairs and the organiser of much secret activity.

In these ways, President Chirac established himself as a force in world affairs, and as a resuscitation of Gaullism, adopting policies which were important for France and bidding to make France the leader of the European Union. It was noticeable, however, that he supported European Monetary Union, even if he at first left the full statement of this to his Prime Minister. He accepted to reduce the number of nuclear tests and promised to sign the international treaty which would outlaw such tests. He accepted that the United States would play a vital role in Bosnia, although this was a purely European matter. De Gaulle would never have accepted these gestures. Doubts remained also about the nature of Chirac's attachment to the German alliance. He clearly did not view it as the General did, that is, as essential and exclusive.

Thus, if Chirac represents Gaullism, he is often not very Gaullist.[44] The pragmatism and hesitations of the electoral period, together with a personal boldness and determination, indicate the highly personalised rather than truly Gaullist characteristics of President Chirac's view of foreign affairs once he was in power.

Notes

[1] Michel Tatu, 'Précis de politique étrangère à l'usage du nouveau Président', *Politique Internationale*, 67, Spring 1965, p.205.

[2] Helmut Schmidt, 'Les roues changent, l'essieu reste', *Le Monde*, 19 May 1995.

[3] These matters are addressed in the discussions between Claude Imbert and Jacques Julliard, *La Droite et la gauche: qu'est-ce qui les distingue encore?* (Paris, Laffont-Grasset, 1995).

[4] See N. H. Waites, 'French foreign policy: external influences on the quest for independence', *Review of International Studies*, 9, 1983, pp.251-264; Jean Klein, a review of K. N. Waltz's 'Theory of International Politics', *Défense nationale*, June 1982, pp. 97-101; J. D. Singer, 'The Level of Analysis Problem in International Relations', *World Politics*, XIV, 1981, pp.77-92; David S. Yost, 'Political Philosophy and the Theory of International Relations', *International Affairs*, 70, 1994, pp.263-290; and Martin Gabriel Jung, *Worldviews and Theories of International Relations* (London, Macmillan, 1994).

[5] See 'Les limites de "l'autre politique" étrangère de la France', *Le Monde*, 3 May 1995.

[6] *L'Humanité*, 5 November 1994.

[7] See Claire Tréan, 'France du repli, France d'ouverture', *Le Monde*, 21 April 1995.

[8] Pierre de la Gorce, 'Les occasions manquées de la politique étrangère française', *Le Monde diplomatique*, November 1994, pp.8-9.

[9] François Léotard, 'La France et le nouveau monde', *Politique Internationale*, 62, 1993-1994, p. 9.

[10] Jean-François Revel, 'Le désordre mondial', *Le Point*, 22 April 1994.

[11] Gabriel Robin, *Un monde sans maître: ordre ou désordre entre les nations* (Paris, Odile Jacob, 1995). See also François de Rose, *La Troisième Guerre mondiale n'a pas eu lieu* (Paris, Desclée de Brouwer, 1995); and François Gutmann, *Le Nouveau Décor International* (Paris, Fayard, 1994).

[12] Jean-François Deniau, 'Le rang de la France', *Le Monde*, 7 September 1994.

[13] *Le Quotidien*, 6 March 1994.

[14] *Le Monde*, 23 February 1995.

[15] *Le Figaro*, 5 March 1995.

[16] *Libération*, 25 February 1995.

[17] *Le Monde*, 25 February, 26-27 February, 28 February, 2 March 1995.

[18] *L'Express*, 23 and 30 March 1995; *Le Figaro* 24 March 1995; *Le Monde* 26-27 March 1995.

[19] *Le Figaro*, 13 March 1995; *Le Monde*, 14, 16, 18 March 1995.

[20] Annie Kriegel, 'Carnet de campagne', *Le Figaro*, 28 March 1995.

[21] Alain Finkielkraut, 'L'Inutilité du XXe siècle', *Le Monde*, 15 December 1994; 'L'Oubli du monde', *Le Monde*, 15 April 1995.

[22] André Glucksman, 'Avoir le courage de sa question', *Le Monde*, 15 April 1995.

[23] Pierre Lefranc, 'L'Europe sans équivoque', *Le Monde*, 13 April 1995.

[24] Jean-Claude Casanova, 'Europe: le piège électoral', *Le Point*, 24 November 1994.

[25] Personal knowledge of electoral meetings in the Paris region.

[26] Campaign broadcasts on France-Inter.

[27] Alain Minc, *L'Ivresse démocratique* (Paris, Gallimard, 1995), p. 249.

[28] Bernard de Montferrand, 'Stabilité européenne: le pacte Balladur', *Politique Internationale*, 67, Spring 1995, pp.237-247.

[29] Victor-Yves Ghebali, 'La question des minorités nationales à la lumière du pacte de stabilité en Europe', *Le Trimestre du Monde*, 4, 1994, pp.107-136; 'Diplomatie et électoralisme', *Le Monde*, 21 March 1995; 'La leçon de l'affaire yougoslave', *Le Point*, 25 March 1995. See also Michel Foucher, *Fragments d'Europe* (Paris, Fayard, 1993); Jacques Rupnick, *Le déchirement des nations* (Paris, Odile Jacob, 1995).

[30] For Balladur's proposals on foreign policy, see *Le Monde*, 30 November 1994, 19 January 1995, 14 February 1995 and 19 April 1995; *Le Figaro*, 17 March 1995.

[31] Balladur was always prudent, and the French spokesperson in Brussels, De Silguy, had assured him that it was possible.

[32] Pierre Lellouche speaking on the radio station France-Inter, 24 February 1995. Lellouche also attacked Balladur's choice of weapons for the defence of France. *Libération*, 20 April 1995.

[33] Laurent Cohen-Tanugi, 'Europe: la vacance française', *Le Débat*, 83, January-February 1995, pp.40-41.

[34] Alain Juppé, 'Quel avenir pour la politique étrangère de la France?' *Politique étrangère*, 1, 1995, pp.245-259. The text was originally delivered as a lecture to the *Centre d'analyse et de précision*, which is attached to the Ministry of Foreign Affairs, on 30 January 1995.

[35] Mary Dejevsky, 'A New Image for a New Century', *The Independent*, 9 May 1995.

[36] France-Inter, 12 March 1994.

[37] *Le Figaro*, 3 December 1994.

[38] *Le Point*, 18 March 1995; *Libération*, 17 March 1995; *Le Figaro*, 17 March 1995.

[39] For the televised debate as it concerned international affairs, see *Le Monde*, 4 May 1995.

[40] 'Le franc frôle son record de faiblesse face au mark', *La Tribune des Fossés*, 5 May 1995.

[41] *La Croix*, 5 May 1995; *Libération*, 6-7 May 1995.

[42] *Le Monde*, 6 May 1995.

[43] Claire Tréan, 'Sursaut français en Bosnie', *Le Monde*, 9 June 1995; Anne-Marie Gloannec, 'La Stratégie du coup de gueule', *Le Figaro*, 17 July 1995.

[44] André Fontaine, 'Hors des chemins gaullistes', *Le Monde*, 5 September 1995.

Indicative Bibliography

Chirac, Jacques, *Une Nouvelle France: réflexions 1* (Paris, Nil éditions, 1994).

Chirac, Jacques, *La France pour tous* (Paris, Nil éditions, 1995).

Duff, Andrew, John Pinder and Roy Price, *Maastricht and Beyond: Building the European Union* (London, Routledge, 1995).

Duval, Marcel and Yves le Baut, *L'Arme nucléaire française* (Paris, SPM & Kronos, 1992).

Gaffney, John, 'So what difference will Chirac make?', *European Brief*, June 1995, pp.18-19.

Juppé, Alain, 'La Diplomatie française à l'ONU', *Le Trimestre du Monde*, 4 trimestre 1994.

Raimond, Jean-Bernard, *Le Quai d'Orsay à l'épreuve de la cohabitation* (Paris, Flammarion, 1989).

Rémond, René, 'La Politique étrangère dans les élections présidentielles', *Le Trimestre du Monde*, 5 trimestre 1995.

Sutton, Michael, 'Chirac's Foreign Policy: Conformity with Adjustment', *The World Today*, 51, 7, July 1995, pp.135-138.

16. CONCLUSION: FRENCH PRESIDENTIALISM AND THE PARTY SYSTEM

John Gaffney

In conclusion let us examine three aspects of presidential politics: 1) the effects of the Fifth Republican presidency upon the party system; 2) what the 1995 campaign reveals about the dynamics of French presidentialism; and 3) how analysis of the mythology and symbolism of presidentialism offers an understanding of French political institutions and of the wider political culture.

The Fifth Republic: the one and indivisible multi-party system

Systemic effects of presidentialism

The political families of the Fourth Republic (1946-1958) were encouraged by the proportional electoral system to distinguish themselves from one another and to reflect and assert the multiplicity of traditions and constituencies in French political life. From such diversity, they needed to create stable governing majorities if the regime were to survive unchallenged over time, which, of course, they did not. The Fifth Republic (1958-), through its new presidential character and new system for elections to the National Assembly, was an attempt to offer institutional stability in the context of minoritarian political diversity. What we might call the Gaullist settlement was an institutional response to an unstable party system. By drawing upon crisis authority between 1958 and 1962, de Gaulle drew political legitimacy away from the parties, and by extension the National Assembly, and towards himself and the new presidency. The 1962 Reform, whereby the President would henceforth be elected by universal adult suffrage, anchored this legitimacy in the wider political culture. From the early 1960s onwards, the Fifth Republic began a long-term process of partisan bi-polarisation.

The parties grouped around poles of attraction on the political right and left in alliances, albeit shifting ones, in order to produce two rival but stable blocs, each capable of forming governing majorities. The focus of such groupings, although partisan, quickly became highly personalised, since the parties within each alliance became the support networks for presidential candidacies which themselves purported to transcend the party political. The parties therefore encouraged policy-oriented agreement within alliances as well as the personalisation of leadership. In order that the two blocs be distinguishable from one another, the ideological divide between right and left was accentuated, the respective leaders and candidates being encouraged by the system to 'represent' their political families ideologically and rhetorically, while distinguishing themselves clearly from one another. Paradoxically, however, the two blocs had also to become *similar* to one another, because in presidential elections they must attempt to capture the same middle ground in both partisan and electoral terms – hence the courting of small centre-left and centre-right parties and groupings on the one hand, and the appeal to floating voters on the other. The two opposing blocs in French politics, therefore, often share policy preferences as well as styles, images and discursive registers. For reasons similar to those influencing relations between the two blocs, the same processes are taking place *within* the two alliances: personalisation, policy alliance, and rhetorical and ideological differentiation, diffuseness and conflation of policy choices and styles are features both within and between parties and between alliances.

The result of all of these factors is that parties, leaders, candidates, and potential candidates all need to be simultaneously like and unlike one another. These dynamics result in an increased dependency of politics upon the individual, not simply in terms of the projection of a political image but in order to reconcile a whole series of strategic and organisational contradictions.

From 1958, French party politics became an institutional confederation of political families competing essentially for the presidency in order to bring stability to the party system. However, the way in which such stability was pursued inevitably created intense and often longstanding rivalries (again both within and between alliances), and pushed the regime into constant and organisationally debilitating leadership struggles. Such struggles, some of epic proportions, invariably intertwined with petty jealousies and vindictiveness, often masked or were masked by, ideological and policy differences. The system too became subject to surges of opinion – often surges of indifference – in an electorate sometimes sympathetic to, sometimes weary of the rhetoric of crisis and calls for dramatic change generated by leadership rivalries.

Systemically, therefore, and almost in logical sequence, the Fifth Republic:
i) forces the parties into bi-polar alliances;
ii) contributes to the acute personalisation of the system in spite of the partisan emphasis of bi-polarisation;
iii) intensifies the ideological divide between left and right; while
iv) simultaneously diminishing the divide because presidential candidates must represent more than their own party and capture the political centre;
v) encourages partisan differences but displaces them on to the personalities of leaders; and
vi) encourages both leadership control of and leadership rivalry within the political system.

Contingent effects of presidentialism

a) Asymmetrical political cycles

In this context, one aspect of a strengthened presidentialism in a strengthened party system has been of major significance: the asymmetry of the parliamentary and presidential cycles. The fact that the cycles are, respectively, five and seven years is an accident (the weak President of the Third Republic served for seven years, and the tradition was not changed in the Fourth or Fifth). The consequences of aligning the two cycles along the lines of the American system are unpredictable, but their not being aligned has created a system in which contingency is often very influential. For example, it matters a great deal not only who is the Prime Minister and who the President, at any given time, but at what stage of their term of office they are (that is, what stage of each cycle they are at in relation to the other). Even this asymmetrical authority is unpredictable. The first two Presidents did not finish their terms: de Gaulle resigned and Pompidou died in office. Mitterrand called new National Assembly elections, thus twice breaking the five-year cycle. These relationships will also be affected by the contingent political configuration: the relative strength of the parties in both the majority and opposition alliances, and the relationship of each to the government, to the President, and to opinion. It should also be remembered that each of these developments takes place in the context of a semi-permanent flow of regional, municipal, senatorial and European elections, as well as by-elections, which affect alliances in both major camps, and that the overall complexity is made even greater when the government and President are from rival blocs.

This asymmetrical movement of two political cycles, moreover, means that it is extremely difficult for parties to plan either their policy strategies or electoral strategies. They are, therefore, quite severely constrained by the behavioural and programmatic imperatives of the presidentialism that they themselves sustain. Let us look briefly at two examples to illustrate this.

The Socialist Party watched almost helplessly during the Mitterrand years of the 1980s and 1990s as its own support, particularly working class support, deserted it. Locked into a logic which made it the 'President's party', the Socialists had little alternative but to obey a set of political imperatives which had little to do with the standard role of parties, that of aggregating interests and expressing them. By the mid-1990s, half the unemployed in France were voting not for the PS but for the National Front, itself in great part the creation of the presidential Republic with its discourse of crisis and encouragement of personalised leadership. The other and traditional recourse for the working class had of course been the French Communist Party, but it too had, by the mid-1990s, been ground almost out of existence by the logic of presidentialism and the dominance of its Socialist partner, not to mention events in Eastern Europe.

The logic that undermined the left did not spare the right. The presidential rivalries within the right have dominated the life of both the UDF and the RPR since the early 1970s onwards. For most of the fourteen years between 1981 and 1995, the divisions of the right effectively allowed the left to govern (and provided political opportunity to the FN). Because, by the early 1990s, the electorate had moved decisively to the right, the political right could in fact tolerate a fight between two rivals for the presidency, even from within one political party. A certain amount of voter dissatisfaction, and disillusion at such rivalry, was perhaps a small price for such an indulgence. In fact, according to polls, by 1995 a majority of the electorate wanted a Chirac-Balladur confrontation, perhaps simply to 'get it over with'. Hence the futility of a formal UDF candidacy in 1995 by Charles Millon, Valéry Giscard d'Estaing or Raymond Barre, who each hoped to, then decided not to, stand. Nevertheless, for what was arguably a majoritarian constituency to have lost the elections of 1981 and 1988, and conceivably have endangered its grip on the 1995 election, demonstrates the extent to which the right too has been the victim of the contingencies of presidentialism.

b) Adventurers and personality types

The vulnerability or openness of the system to individual undertakings brings a further factor to the fore, namely, the role of other individuals. Given the vulnerability of the system to personal 'adventures' such as Balladur's candidacy, the role of adventurers' supporters takes on inordinate significance: in the case of Balladur as we have seen, the counsel of Nicolas Sarkozy and Nicolas Bazire, and the eventual support of Charles Pasqua were significant factors in the creation of challenges to Chirac's authority. In the same way as this process creates opportunity, it also adds further uncertainty to the political process – not least to those who would play the role of king-maker. Pasqua went from being one of the most powerful men in French politics to being politically inconsequential overnight. Sarkozy's promising career faced total eclipse as a result of his having backed Balladur (perhaps, however, the better to return one day in more propitious circumstances, thus adding further unpredictability to relationships within the overall system).

The major effect of the personalising of political activity is that it increases still further not only the role of individuals, but also the belief in the view that individual viewpoints do not simply represent but *embody* political traditions and ideologies. This has significant effects upon the political system in that some traditions lend themselves more easily than others to personalisation. The Gaullist right is the essence of a personalised tradition. The UDF depends less on a 'heroic' typology, but also encourages a range of second-rank leaders each with their own supporters. For the extreme right, the personalisation of leadership is unbridled. For the non-communist left, highly complex and fragile adaptations of doctrine to personalised leadership have taken place. For the Communists, its traditional leadership cult proved to be clumsy and ineffective in the context of the personalisation of the whole system. For groups such as the ecologists, personalisation is an extremely difficult organising principle to cope with, leading to fragmentation and often to ineffective campaigning.

An ironic twist to the relationship between personality and political tradition was that in spite of Edouard Balladur's not being a UDF member, he – and only he – represented the centre-right tradition against the 'Gaullist' Chirac. It should be remembered, moreover, that Balladur was considered an appropriate rival in that he represented a 'type' antithetical to Chirac. That Balladur could become a rival was essentially because Chirac himself had been seen in many quarters as personally inadequate, not having quite the 'weight' of those he had opposed from the mid-1970s onwards. It is not, therefore, simply a question of the political party or the tradition or ideology being represented by a person, but also of the effects of this transfer of political identity, in particular the fact that personalities can themselves then move between and influence parties and traditions. The fact that the RPR did create two major presidential candidates, however, also demonstrates that a party system designed to create dominant leaders, and even one of the most authoritarian parties within that system, could not stop the phenomenon of personal rivalry and individual ambition escaping partisan control and upsetting the painstaking alignment of parties and presidential candidates.

In both institutional and electoral terms, however, strong parties are as necessary to the proper working of the system as are strong leaders. The strong party is necessary to create and support leaders, if necessary through difficult times too, to offer ideas and policies, and to maintain a national presence over time. In spite of the personal antagonisms within the right before round one of the 1995 election campaign, the party discipline of the RPR and UDF in round two was striking. But the amount of manœuvring and then sustaining of the leadership, in order that a particular individual should become the candidate, and, once this is attained, in order to help position the leader/candidate for the election itself (all this for one post, and which once won – or lost – lasts at least seven years) is phenomenally expensive for parties in terms of effort and time. It is hardly surprising then that the political parties – over and above the complexity of, on the one hand, their internal, factional, relationships, their relationships with their alliance partners and potential partners (themselves subject to similar internal forces), and their antagonistic, personalised relationship to their opponents, and on the other their nurturing, personalised relationship to their constituencies and potential constituencies – are in a state of perpetual organisational activity, constant change, and near-permanent campaigning for the presidency.

In maintaining two organising cycles of activity – essentially the five-year parliamentary cycle involving the parties in their traditional role, and the seven-year cycle of party activity around presidential candidates – the Fifth Republic therefore has certain contingent effects. Notably, it:

i) enhances the role of individuals – candidates and others – as compared with a non-presidential party system, thereby increasing the dependency of parties upon them;

ii) increases the range of effects upon the relationship between 'personalities' and parties; the former can express the latter, may sometimes be their only expression, and may act as a 'currency', exchanged within the political spectrum between different political families;

iii) creates a state of permanent campaigning at multiple levels within the overall personality-vectored factionalism within the system;

iv) paradoxically, increases the need for strong parties in order that such a system function effectively;

v) creates the conditions, for all those involved – individuals and parties – in which the system becomes extremely expensive in terms of time and energy, and is strategically very complex.

The campaign

Happenstance and long waves: the election as the organising moment of French politics

In 1995, contingency played a significant role even given the 'over determination' of politics in the mid-1990s by an overwhelmingly strong right. This was in large part due to the latitude and initiative of individuals positioned in key areas at key moments. We mentioned the decisions and comportment of certain of these such as Charles Pasqua and Nicolas Sarkozy. To these one would need to add a much longer list of the names and activities of people like Alain Madelin (a major UDF figure who supported Chirac from the beginning of his campaign), Alain Juppé, Simone Veil and François Léotard. There were also 'passive' actors, i.e. actors whose fortunes and misfortunes were influenced by or whose inaction influenced developments: on the right, these included government ministers – in particular Gérard Longuet, a potentially leading figure in the Balladur campaign – who by late 1994 were publicly embroiled in corruption scandals; on the left, figures such as Martine Aubry who was set to become the symbolic leader/candidate of a reborn PS after the crushing defeat of the Socialist Party in 1995 (the defeat came but it was not crushing), and who went on to become a strong supporter of Jospin's leadership, gaining in integrity and respect what she was losing in political opportunity (and also perhaps in influence upon gender politics in France). The two most significant contributions or non-contributions of individuals outside the mainstream were of course those of Balladur himself whose decision to run for the presidency overturned the received view that each political party should have only one major candidate; and Jacques Delors whose decision not to run removed the possibility of a left win in 1995, thus creating the conditions for a Chirac victory (it was assumed only Balladur could beat Delors). Conversely, Delors' action provided the opportunity for the candidacy of Lionel Jospin and, subsequently therefore, the revival of the PS under his leadership. The withdrawal of Delors also allowed for the unimpeded reassertion of the party political (Chirac and Jospin) over the chimera of non-party-based executive power and leadership (Delors and Balladur).

In terms of gathering support from various sections of the national constituency during the campaign, the timing and organisation of candidates' appeals were also crucial. Each candidate's speeches – Chirac's offer the best example – demonstrate that support was appealed to in discrete groups: an appeal to the farmers, the pharmacists, the business community, an appeal to the right, to the centre left, the modernisers, the traditionalists, and so on. These appeals usually involved separate speeches. The most difficult subject, whatever the audience, was Europe which did involve the problematic mediation of contradictory (pro- and anti-European) themes. The example of Europe also reminds us that this mediation of ideas in speeches and discourse is done essentially through the mass media itself (even the total number of people directly addressed by all of the candidates in the whole of the campaign is but a fraction of those reached through the media). It was often, moreover, the analysis of speeches or events by media journalists which determined the public's reception and therefore the success of a speech. Chirac's speeches on Europe, for example, were usually well received by the media for their expert reconciliation of European views held within the party and wider constituency. Good media reception therefore played a part in the overall success of a campaign.

The opposite was true for Balladur, as we have seen: the darling of the media and the opinion polls throughout 1993 and 1994, the media, in part, brought about Balladur's downfall. From the beginning of his 'official' campaign in February, the Prime Minister's tactics and image, and his campaign speeches (what they said and how they said it, and what they failed to say) were badly received by the press. Mediated in this way his campaign became, for many, a bad campaign. Seeing it in this light helps us understand that the manner in which images of leadership are mediated is crucial in political exchange, especially at this exalted presidential level.

Examples such as these show that *individual* decisions, tactics, and timing take on an inordinate significance in the contemporary politics of France. Even the actors' tactical relationship to the capricious polls was of bewildering complexity: should Edouard Balladur, for example, have declared his candidacy in January, considered by many to be too early, or February, considered by others as being too late? In order for Jospin to overtake Balladur in the polls, the point at which he started to attack Chirac and ignore Balladur was of great tactical importance. In order to achieve the same, i.e. go into the second round against Jospin, Chirac's tactics needed to be similar to Jospin's, that is to say that for some time he needed to behave as if the opposition were Balladur, not Jospin (in order that the true opposition in round two be, in fact, Jospin). And in terms of the wider configuration of the hundreds of strategic actors involved, the decisions of one would – to greater or lesser effect – alter the significance of all the others.

It is worth mentioning in parenthesis that this vast network of individual influence was itself constructed not only from ideological choices, political trajectories and the opportunities and challenges provided by strategic and tactical advantages and setbacks but also, and inevitably, from personal vanities, allegiances and, more particularly, hatreds. And these too were often dependent upon circumstances, some of which are almost lost in time: Balladur and Giscard's mutually disdainful relationship goes back to the 1960s; Madelin's positive attitude to Chirac was in part determined by Balladur's negative attitude to Madelin during the 1986-88 government; Léotard, in fact, had reason to dislike both Balladur and Chirac in terms of the lack of respect shown to him by them in the mid and late 1980s. In the French case overall (where, moreover, many of the major actors have known one another for decades; Balladur, Chirac, Jospin, Giscard, Rocard, Fabius, Séguin, Juppé, Chevènement, de Villiers and Léotard, among others, all having been educated at ENA), the institutions and their relationship to élites are framed by and in their turn frame the many individual political relationships that exist.

All of these personal decisions were taken, however, in the context of long term influences, or 'long waves': shifts in the economy, in the party alliances, the relative stability of the élite class itself, and the gradual but by 1995 overwhelming ascendancy of the right, in terms of both the political parties and the overall electoral geography. The long-term influences upon political change are structural, and as regards political opportunities provided to actors, are institutional in nature. We said earlier that individuals occupying key sites and at key moments had significant influence upon the political system. The same observation can be made from a different perspective, namely, that *unless* individuals are 'in position' at 'the right moment', the chance to influence passes; unless they have access to an institutional position, they cannot influence events. And the sites of influence, although not always easily identifiable, are themselves created by shifts in the long-term political configurations: the role and influence of the various political parties over time, the nature of change within electorates, and perhaps most of all, the changing influence and scope for the presidency itself in an evolving economy and political culture. Politics is, of course, always the combination of contingency, agency and structure, that is to say is the result of the interweaving of Machiavellian 'fortune', Aristotelian individual 'practical wisdom', and the contemporary institutional and constitutional framework of a given polity: but in French politics political action operates to a particularly high degree at the nodal point between contingency and structural processes, a situation which confers upon individual 'practical wisdom' (i.e. the ability to perceive, to judge and to act) a role normally unexploited in contemporary democratic politics.

The French political system, through its institutional mythologising and constitutional sustaining of individual political attributes, has allowed an unprecedented situation to arise whereby agency and personal capacity continuously influence the political process. The dynamics of contemporary French politics are created by individuals acting and thereby fashioning the relationship between contingency and structural processes. This means two things. Firstly, these dynamics of individual initiative affect not just politicians' successes but also their failures (resulting either from their inability to act at a crucial point or as a result of miscalculation of the forces at play at a particular time – i.e. a misinterpretation of the relationship between contingency and structure at a given time). Secondly, although the possibility of influencing politics in France is perhaps greater than in other comparable political systems, this contingency is itself, ironically, more 'predictable' – if no less powerful – than in other political systems: opportunities to influence outcomes can be reliably expected to present themselves constantly.

The interplay within this set of institutions, structures, processes and individual undertakings of course culminates in the election. In its turn, the election and its aftermath become the founding moment of a new wave of activity. Following the campaign in 1995, the left set about rebuilding; the hard right reassessed its opportunities for influence; President Chirac addressed the immediate policy issues of government spending and the European single currency, and so on: each of these new developments which would form the context of future political activity built on and was shaped by the experience of the election. As regards the activity of individuals, we need only say that it was from the morning of 8 May 1995 that the planning, manœuvring and decisions regarding the following presidential election, scheduled for 2002, began.

The 1995 Election as an end and a beginning

In this volume we have considered the extent to which systemic and contingent conditions and variables must be taken into account when trying properly to assess the presidential election and its role in the French polity, as well as the extent to which they are formative, predictable and explanatory. We have observed that there was a series of long-term social, electoral, party political and economic trends and tendencies as well as countless influential acts, each moment of which affected other moments. In terms of short-term decisions with long-term consequences, the final line up of candidates was itself not without significance for the French political scene: the consequences for the party and for the campaign would have been profound if the Socialists had failed, as sometimes threatened to be the case, to field a credible candidate; ecology, as an election issue, might have received a quite different focus if the Greens had fielded a different candidate, or a second candidate, or achieved a greater unity of purpose as a movement; the theme of Europe would most certainly have been given a different spin across the campaign if Delors had stood; the 'loose canon' effect of Bernard Tapie, if his luck had not finally run out and he had been a candidate as articulate as he had been during the 1994 European elections, can only be guessed at.

Further to such speculation, in terms of who the candidates were and their effects within the system, two remarks concerning the extremes of politics are appropriate. First, the Le Pen candidacy, gaining 15% of the national electorate, contested (once again) the received view that the FN was still marginal or secondary to 'the mainstream' in electoral terms. The Le Pen vote can be expected to have a series of long-term and contradictory consequences upon the right and upon politics more generally. On the one hand, although it is not clear whether the Front is near the limits of its expansion, with such a strong, heterogeneous, and loyal vote, it has become a major feature of French politics; and aspects of both its policies and its discourse have spread across the political spectrum. In this way, the effect will have been the opposite of that intended by Mitterrand in the mid-1980s when (through the momentary adoption of proportional representation) he helped the Front gain national prominence (in order, he hoped, to divide the right). On the other hand, there is also the question of Le Pen as a 'charismatic' personality, *personally* rivalling, challenging, luring support away from, and appealing to the traditional right's constituency (it is now commonplace in political analysis to note that his presidential score is consistently higher than his party's national vote in other elections). In this way, it is clear that one of the main vehicles of the hard right's relative success has been the institutional framework and the cultural mores of the Republic itself.

Second, on the far left, similar developments have not taken place. For many complex reasons, the Communists have rarely rivalled the PS at this level of campaigning. Of great advantage to the Socialists was the PCF's inability to cope with the exigencies of presidentialism at the level of leadership and leadership image. (In many ways, the personalisation of left-wing politics has profited the even more marginal left, the Trotskyists led by the tireless Arlette Laguiller). The consequences of the 'successful' PS campaign in 1995 (the PCF were left as speechless as everyone else by Jospin's first-round score) also had effects upon the longer-term relations between the two parties, locking the PCF further into a subordinate role. The ironic corollary to this is that in a bipolar system the weakening of the PCF has threatened the PS' own viability, making it curiously dependent upon its junior partner for the purposes of maintaining the left's overall vote, especially at the local level. The 1995 presidential campaign, which seemed to offer the possibility of a Communist revival and the chance for a renewed PCF to rise from the ashes of a poor Socialist score saw Jospin go forward into the post-1995 period, the new and uncontested leader of a revived non-Communist left and the symbolic leader of the left as a whole.

The politics of virtual reality: images and myths of leadership

Let us conclude with some remarks on the symbolic aspects of the 1995 election, especially those which pertain to the personalisation of politics, and more specifically to the winner of the contest, Jacques Chirac.

Our volume has led us to focus on the role and fortunes of individuals in the French electoral process. In the case of Jacques Chirac, had he really changed? Once the elections were over, such questions perhaps became meaningless. And yet during the campaign, this was the kind of question being constantly asked by the media, doubtless by much of the electorate too. In fact, responses to such a question arguably influenced the outcome of the election. This brings us not to the issue of whether or how Chirac might have changed, but to the significance of the question itself: what is the political effect of a changed person in the context of a claim for the presidency of the Republic? This is perhaps the least researched and yet most fascinating aspect of French presidential politics: what mythical world, and what 'virtual reality' refracted through the media is being created by the presidential system, and how do these express or respond to the wider, or deeper, French political culture?

De Gaulle encouraged the idea that France needed saviours. The Fifth Republican presidential system has maintained this idea at the symbolic, ceremonial, and institutionally-structured levels. This 'saviour' aspect to French politics became doubly potent because, from 1965 onwards, after the revision of the constitution in 1962 to elect the President by direct adult suffrage, it was deployed throughout the political system with the approval and participation of the people (and a developing and evermore sophisticated media). The saviour that France waits upon now is also the expression of the 'general will', the 'nation' personified. The personality, the 'type' that a presidential candidate corresponds to and the virtues and vices he or she portrays or displays inscribe themselves in a complex mythical structure.

From this perspective, Chirac's success takes on new significance. He won because he came from behind, an eternal loser who became a potential winner. Balladur lost because he seemed to have become assured of winning. Jospin did well because he had, until receiving the 'calling', almost abandoned politics. In the chivalric and epic narratives of the mass media and campaign rhetoric, archetypal patterns are imposed on political events, organising and structuring them, effacing their 'contingent' aspect to a large extent, and manipulating them into stories whose shape broadly corresponds to that of the major myths and legends which are a central part of our culture. Thus Chirac won because he had been a loser; Balladur lost because he had been a winner; Jospin was famous because he was unknown; and Le Pen became mainstream because he had been marginalised. The fact of such parable-like narrative structuring of political events is not a complete explanation for the events themselves, and the media that portrays French politics exclusively in this near-biblical way is usually trivial, largely the result of journalistic imaginations and the overuse of metaphors: it is clear from many of the analyses in this study, however, that these 'mythical' resources are there in the system and play an extremely important role.

As we have said, such mythologising of the individual requires (and the media encourages) the creation of 'types' or archetypes: as we saw with Chirac, he was the young (impetuous) warrior who went out beyond the pale to reflect and prepare, returning to claim the crown, now older and wiser. Variants of such types are repeated across the political spectrum. We should stress again, however, that this mythical France and its heroic struggles are enacted in conjunction with the everyday politics of the parties, their policy elaboration, and backroom dealings. In the case of Chirac, for example, it was necessary that he be 'down' but not of course 'out'. Whatever the mythical or chivalric requirements of tasks, trials and dragons to slay, these are illusions which, if realised in foolhardy gestures, would probably lead to the rapid eclipse of a political career. It was imperative, for example, that at all costs Chirac maintain his grip on the RPR. The same is true for other aspects of activity: to characterise discussion in archetypal terms as bad counsel, treachery, wise counsel, constancy and so on is a simple enough rhetorical device exploiting the reserve of mythical images and structures which we have called the realm of 'virtual reality': but it can only be used effectively in the context of a strong institutional and party political system. That allusions are rhetorical or mythical, however, makes them no less consequential for that.

Related to this question of mythical traces informing the polity on the one hand, and archetypes fashioning political comportment on the other, is that of the role of memory in French politics. The French have a sense of their past and its pertinence to contemporary attitudes, allegiances and behaviour that is significantly more acute than in many comparable countries. This is not to say that such memory will be accurate or sensitive; in fact, its inaccuracy is one of the reasons it is exploited by politicians. Given all their claims, it is truly ironic that *both* Chirac and Balladur were, in spite of their filial devotion to de Gaulle in public, perhaps the least 'Gaullist' of the 1960s Gaullists (and probably did not even like him very much). But both Balladur and Chirac were obliged, in their campaigns, to cite de Gaulle as their chief point of reference. Laying personal claim to a particular heritage is the significant point here. In terms of widening electoral support, candidates can, much more dextrously than parties, slide between and exploit elements of the collective memory. For some, in 1995, after his period of reflection and communion with 'la France profonde', Chirac *became* a true republican, at last perceiving the value of the old 'république sociale' and at last, therefore, bringing together the left and right in the old Gaullist tradition. For others, of course, Chirac remained a dangerous Bonapartist, careless of the republic and of its profound value; or else simply a Radical of the Third Republic with the media trappings of modernity. Such epithets and labels can only be deployed to any effect in a culture that recognises the cultural referents they invoke.

Presidentialism and its place in politics

In the 1995 election, following a deep and established trend in all French elections, more people abstained, spoiled their ballot papers, or voted for non-mainstream candidates than ever before. It is also the case, however, that of all elections, the presidential remains the most popular. Moreover, apart from one or two small movements on the extreme left of politics, there is today no anti-presidential culture, and this despite presidentialism having been seen for so long as antithetical to republicanism. And apart from the anti-republicanism of the two extremes of politics, the republican tradition itself remains generally robust and uncontested. It is clear, as we have demonstrated in this book, that in elections – and especially the presidential one – the French do more than (as de Gaulle feared) pass judgement on the price of artichokes. It is ample evidence of the tendency to political disillusionment in the French, however, to cite the almost immediate fall in Chirac's popularity once he was elected President. There is a 'mythical' and a 'real' element to this. Our discussion of the mythical issues suggests that the 'fall', seen but not explained by the opinion polls, is like a fall from grace. In real terms, however, it is clear from our study that the claims made by candidates and the expectations of them go far beyond the institutional capacities of the presidency. It is a cliché, though no less true for that, to say that the President cannot solve all of France's problems; in fact he can solve very few of them. The sense of crisis which pervades French politics, however, is, in part, created by the lack of correspondence between expectations and outcomes, and once the election is over, the rational aspects of daily life and routine politics – the price of artichokes – ensure that the French realise this. The fact that candidates comport themselves for the duration of the campaign as if they can solve all of France's problems (and if they do not, like Balladur, they lose), and that the French seem almost to believe them, is evidence of how the myth of leadership still invigorates France's political culture.

The chapters in this volume demonstrate the complexity of French presidential politics. One of the characteristic features we have emphasised is their highly symbolic nature, a symbolism which points to the strength of the myth of leadership in French political culture. In the 'real' world, however, as we have also seen in this volume, the internationalisation and globalisation of economies now mean that all national executives are constrained by events, to the point where – on reducing unemployment, for example – their ability to intervene decisively is severely restricted. In the French case, the relative protection afforded by a strong state sector has also disappeared as, from the mid-1980s onwards, France followed the example of other countries and privatised and deregulated many of its industries. This overall situation has created in the presidency, and in presidentialism and the personalisation of politics more generally, a strange phenomenon: a strong, vigorous, highly personalised form of politics in which, in order to achieve power, promises by would-be heroic leaders and images of a new France must be deployed almost in inverse proportion to their realisation once the office is won, power has been achieved, and 'governing the country' becomes the political imperative. For the moment the Gaullist settlement prevails: an uncontested presidency in an uncontested republic. The nature of this relationship, however, is one of great historical, political and cultural complexity and dynamism. We hope that our volume contributes to a greater understanding of it.

CHRONOLOGY OF THE CAMPAIGN[1]

CHRISTOPHE TEXIER

1993

28 March: The right-wing RPR-UDF coalition wins a landslide victory in the legislative elections translating into a large majority of seats in Parliament (484 out of 577).

29 March: Edouard Balladur (RPR) is nominated Prime Minister.

2 April: Philippe Séguin, Mayor and MP (RPR) for Epinal, is elected President of the National Assembly.

3 April: Michel Rocard replaces Laurent Fabius as leader of the PS.

27-28 April: National Conference of the RPR. Jacques Chirac invites delegates to prepare for the next great victory, in two years time (i.e. the presidential election).

1 May: Pierre Bérégovoy (PS), ex-Prime Minister, commits suicide in his hometown of Nevers.

18 May: Philippe Séguin declares that Jacques Chirac is the 'natural candidate' of the Right.

16 June: Philippe Séguin warns of social unrest in France by referring to a potential 'Munich social', created by the Balladur government because of its social policy.

1 July: Charles Pasqua (RPR), Interior Minister, declares that Jacques Chirac is the only suitable presidential candidate in the RPR.

2-4 July: National Conference of the PS. Michel Rocard announces the 'come-back' of the Left.

19 September: Valéry Giscard d'Estaing (UDF), former French President, declares that a movement such as the UDF needs to have a candidate for the next presidential elections.

26 September: Conference of the RPR in La Rochelle. Jacques Chirac reassures members of the party about his good relationship with Edouard Balladur.

23-24 October: PS Conference in Le Bourget. With 80.9% of the votes, Michel Rocard is confirmed as First Secretary of the party.

12-14 November: General Assembly of the Green Party in Lille. Dominique Voynet is elected, with 62.3% of the votes, as new leader of the party.

20 November: General Assembly of the MRG. Merging of Bernard Tapie's movement, *Energie Sud*, with the MRG run by Jean-François Hory.

19 December: François Léotard (PR), Minister of Defence in Edouard Balladur's government, comes out in favour of the latter's candidacy in the presidential elections. Simone Veil (UDF), Minister of Social Affairs, states that Edouard Balladur would make a great President.

20 December: Edouard Balladur, in an interview with *Le Figaro*, declares that he will not stay in office at Matignon for more than two years.

1994

23 January: Martine Aubry (PS) declares that Michel Rocard would be her preferred candidate for the presidency.

29 January: Robert Hue is elected National Secretary of the PCF, replacing Georges Marchais who had held the position since 1972.

3 March: Students demonstrate in Paris against the creation of the 'Contrat d'Insertion Professionnel' (CIP), equivalent to a special minimum wage for young people.

20 March: Cantonal elections, first round:

RPR, UDF and various independent parties	44.60%
PS	22.45%
PC	11.50%
MRG and various independent parties	6.45%
FN	9.80%
Greens	3.50%

27 March: Cantonal elections, second round:

RPR, UDF and various independent parties	51.50%
PS	30.20%
PC	7.57%
MRG and various independent parties	6.97%
FN	2.63%

28 March: The Prime Minister's office in Matignon announces the suspension of the CIP.

30 March: The PS presents its candidates for the European elections, under the leadership of Michel Rocard.

5 April: Dominique Baudis (UDF), Mayor and MP for Toulouse, is nominated to lead the RPR-UDF alliance list at the European elections.

29 April: Michel Rocard, in an interview given to the *Journal du Dimanche*, declares that nothing will stop him from standing in the presidential elections.

12 June: European elections:

RPR-UDF	25.58%
PS	14.49%
de Villiers	12.33%
MRG	12.03%
FN	10.51%
PC	6.88%
CPNT[2]	3.95%
Verts	2.95%
Chevènement	2.54%
Lutte Ouvrière	2.27%
Génération Ecologie	2.01%
Sarajevo	1.56%
Various	2.82%

19 June: Michel Rocard resigns as leader of the PS and is replaced by Henri Emmanuelli.

1 July: *Le Figaro* publishes the results of an opinion poll financed by Charles Pasqua's movement, *Primaires à la française*, according to which 61% of right-wing supporters would be in favour of primary elections in order to nominate a single candidate of the Right for the presidential elections.

1 September: Publication of Pierre Péan's book, *Une Jeunesse française*, containing revelations about François Mitterrand's early friendship with the Vichy collaborator, René Bousquet.

12 September: During an interview on *France 2*, François Mitterrand talks openly about the revelations in Péan's book and reassures the public of his ability to stay in office until the end of his term in spite of his illness.

16 September: Philippe de Villiers, founder of the movement *Combat pour les Valeurs* announces his official resignation from the PR.

17 September: Jean-Marie Le Pen, leader of the FN, officially declares that he will run for the presidency.

21 September: Robert Hue, National Secretary of the PCF, officially declares that he will run for the presidency.

27 September: Arlette Laguiller, leader of Lutte Ouvrière, officially declares that she will run for the presidency.

11 October: Jacques Chirac organises a presidential campaign committee including Alain Juppé (RPR) and Philippe Séguin (RPR).

23 October: The Green coalition (La Convention de l'Ecologie Politique) nominates Dominique Voynet as its presidential candidate.

24 October: Edouard Balladur criticises Jacques Chirac for taking refuge in his party 'as in a citadel' and thus 'not obeying the ideal of the Fifth Republic'.

27 October: Charles Pasqua (RPR), Interior Minister, publishes a list of 224 Members of Parliament who have signed a document in favour of primary elections.

3 November: A picture of François Mitterrand's illegitimate daughter, Mazarine, appears on the cover of *Paris-Match*. Inside, an interview with Philippe Alexandre, the author of a book containing revelations on the private life of the President, gives additional details.

4 November: In an interview given to the regional newspaper *La Voix du Nord*, Jacques Chirac announces his candidacy for the presidency.

7 November: Edouard Balladur raises the question of organising primary elections in order to designate a common candidate for the right-wing majority in the presidential elections.

12 November: RPR conference in Paris without Edouard Balladur who is on holiday in Chamonix. Jacques Chirac officially resigns as leader of the party. Alain Juppé is nominated as acting chairman.

18-20 November: Special conference of the PS in Liévin. Henri Emmanuelli is re-elected as the head of the party with 87.57% of the votes. He urges retiring President of the European Union, Jacques Delors, to stand for the presidency, 'in the name of all Socialists'.

20 November: Philippe de Villiers launches his Mouvement pour la France.

4 December: Nicolas Sarkozy (RPR), Budget Minister, considers that Edouard Balladur is the only candidate of the majority able to unify the right and beat Jacques Delors in the presidential elections.

11 December: In the course of an interview on TF1, Jacques Delors declares that he will not stand for the presidential elections.

13 December: Bernard Tapie and Michel Rocard, followed on 15 and 21 December respectively by Jack Lang (PS), former Minister of Culture, and Pierre Mauroy (PS), ex-Prime Minister, announce that they will not stand for the presidency.

21 December: Raymond Barre (UDF), former Prime Minister, announces that he still does not rule out the possibility of running in the presidential elections.

1995

4 January: Lionel Jospin, former head of the PS and former Minister of Education, announces that he is 'available' as a candidate for the presidential elections.

8 January: Philippe de Villiers, MEP and founder of the *Mouvement pour la France*, officially announces his candidacy.

12 January: Charles Pasqua, Interior Minister in the Balladur government, informs Jacques Chirac of his support for Edouard Balladur.

14-15 January: During a meeting in support of his campaign in Tours, Jean-Marie Le Pen presents his programme based on 'simple ideas' and a project for a 'Sixth Republic'.

18 January: Edouard Balladur, Prime Minister, announces his candidacy for the presidency, with 'no particular allegiance to any party'.

28 January: During their national conference, members of the PR confirm their full support for Edouard Balladur.

2 February: Robert Hue, candidate of the PCF, presents his programme entitled: 'Transforming society and creating a new future'.

3 February: Lionel Jospin is elected as the candidate of the PS for the presidential elections following a vote in which party delegates give him 65.83% of the vote against Henri Emmanuelli.

13 February: Edouard Balladur presents his programme based on the idea of a new 'engagement français'. Charles Millon, chairman of the UDF in the National Assembly, abandons the idea of standing for the presidency.

17 February: Jacques Chirac presents his programme, 'La France pour tous', based on the idea of a 'deep' but 'calm' transformation of politics.

21 February: Ibrahim Ali, a young French citizen of Comorian origin, is killed by FN billposters in Marseilles. Interviewed on the matter a few days later, Jean-Marie Le Pen describes the incident as only an 'unfortunate accident arising out of self defence'.

23 February: Jean-François Hory, leader of *Radical* (formely MRG), announces his candidacy for the presidency.

6 March: Raymond Barre (UDF) abandons the idea of standing in the presidential elections.

7 March: Lionel Jospin, candidate of the PS, presents his programme entitled: 'Propositions pour la France'. Valéry Giscard d'Estaing declares that he will not be standing in the presidential elections.

8 March: Antoine Waechter, chair of the *Mouvement Ecologiste Indépendant*, presents his programme including a 'nine priorities project' for a 'gentler France'.

10 March: Jean-François Hory unveils his programme, claiming to be 'at odds with the traditional Left'.

15 March: Brice Lalonde, chair of *Génération Écologie* and former Environment Minister, abandons the idea of standing in the presidential elections.

16 March: Dominque Voynet, candidate for the Green coalition, presents her programme in a document entitled: 'Pour l'écologie d'aujourd'hui'.

31 March: Jean-François Hory abandons the idea of standing in the presidential elections.

2 April: In an interview with the *Journal du Dimanche*, Lionel Jospin declares that, in the event of his election, he will offer ministerial posts to Communist representatives.

4 April: Jean-Marie Le Pen presents his 'Contrat pour la France avec les Français'. Having failed to obtain the required support of 500 elected representatives, Antoîne Waechter is forced to abandon the idea of standing in the presidential elections.

7 April: The *Journal Officiel* publishes a list of the nine candidates entitled to run for the presidency: Philippe de Villiers (*Mouvement pour la France*), Jean-Marie Le Pen (*Front National*), Jacques Chirac (RPR), Arlette Laguillier (*Lutte Ouvrière*), Jacques Cheminade (*Fédération pour une nouvelle solidarité*), Lionel Jospin (PS), Dominique Voynet (*Les Verts*), Edouard Balladur (RPR) and Robert Hue (PCF).

23 April: Presidential elections, first round:

Lionel Jospin	23.30%
Jacques Chirac	20.84%
Edouard Balladur	18.58%
Jean-Marie Le Pen	15.00%
Robert Hue	8.64%
Arlette Laguillier	5.30%
Philippe de Villiers	4.74%
Dominique Voynet	3.32%
Jacques Cheminade	0.28%
Abstentions	21.62%

24 April: Raymond Barre and the UDF confirm their support for Jacques Chirac.

29 April: Edouard Balladur and the leaders of the right unite behind Jacques Chirac during a public meeting in Paris.

1 May: At the traditional May-day meeting of his party in Paris, Jean-Marie Le Pen refuses to give any voting instructions for the second round and declares that 'Chirac is just like Jospin, only worse'. During the same rally, a young Moroccan, Brahim Bouraam, is killed in Paris by skinheads, apparently supporters of the Front National.

2 May: 'Courteous' two-hour television debate between the two candidates for the second round.

7 May: With 52.64% of the vote, Jacques Chirac is elected as the fifth President of the Fifth Republic. (Abstentions: 20.33%. Spoilt papers: 5.97%)

10 May: Edouard Balladur resigns from the office of Prime Minister.

17 May: Jacques Chirac officially takes up his duties as President and nominates Alain Juppé as Prime Minister.

18 May: Nomination of the new government with 42 ministers, including 12 women.

Notes

[1]   Sources: *Le Monde, Le Journal des Présidentielles, Esprit, Agence France Presse* (online).
[2]   Chasse, Pêche, Nature, Tradition.

NOTES ON CONTRIBUTORS

David S. Bell is Professor of Politics at the University of Leeds and the author and editor of numerous books and articles on French and Spanish politics, including (with Byron Criddle) *The French Socialist Party* (O.U.P., 1988), and *The French Communist Party in the Fifth Republic* (O.U.P., 1994). He is Head of the Department of Political Studies at the University of Leeds.

Jean Charlot was Professor of Political Science at the Institut d'Etudes Politiques, Paris. He also worked as an official adviser on public opinion. His many books on political parties include publications on the Gaullist party, and on French politics, most recently *La Politique en France* (Livre de poche, 1993) and *Pourquoi Jacques Chirac? Comprendre la présidentielle 95* (Fallois, 1995).

Monica Charlot is Professor of English Civilisation at Paris III, Sorbonne. She was Director of the Maison Française in Oxford from 1984 to 1991. She is the author of several books on British politics, especially on election campaigns and political persuasion. Most recently she has written *Le Parti travailliste britannique* (Montchrestien, 1992) and *Institutions et forces politiques du Royaume-Uni* (Masson/Armand Colin, 1995).

Alistair Cole works in the Department of European Studies, University of Bradford. He has published widely in the sphere of French politics, notably *François Mitterrand: a Study in Political Leadership* (Routledge, 2nd edition 1997). He recently completed an ESRC-funded project on 'Local Policy Networks in Britain and France'.

Byron Criddle is Senior Lecturer in Politics at the University of Aberdeen, and co-author, with David Bell, of *The French Socialist Party: the Emergence of a Party in Government* (O.U.P., 1988); *The French Communist Party in the Fifth Republic* (O.U.P., 1994); and, with Robert Waller, *The Almanac of British Politics* (Routledge, 1996).

Catherine Fieschi is a doctoral candidate in the Department of Political Science at McGill University and Lecturer in the Department of Languages and European Studies at Aston University. Her work is in the field of comparative politics of industrialised nations, particularly on patterns of political mobilisation and collective action. Her doctoral research focuses on the evolution of the extreme right and of New Social Movements in France and Italy since the Second World War.

John Gaffney is Professor of French and European Politics at Keele University. He has published widely on European politics, most recently editing *Political Parties and the European Union* (Routledge, 1996) and *The Language of Leadership in Contemporary France* (co-editor with Helen Drake, Dartmouth, 1996).

David Goldey is Fellow and Tutor in Politics, Lincoln College, Oxford He has been observing and writing about French politics and elections since 1962. He has been a Visiting Professor at the Sorbonne-Paris III, a Visiting Fellow of the Western Societies Program, Cornell University, and one of the two foreign members of the Conseil Scientifique du Centre pour l'Etude de la Vie Politique Française (CEVIPOF) of the Fondation Nationale des Sciences Politiques and the Centre National de la Recherche Scientifique (CNRS).

Irène Hill is Senior Lecturer in French Contemporary Studies at Oxford Brookes University. Her current research interests include the circulation of élites and European integration.

Douglas Johnson is Emeritus Professor of French History, University College London, Visiting Professor in the French Department of King's College, London, and British Representative to the Fondation Charles de Gaulle, Paris. He was formerly Professor of Modern History at the University of Birmingham and Professor of French History, University College London. He is the author of numerous books and articles on French history and politics, including *Guizot: Aspects of French History 1787-1874* (Routledge & K. Paul, 1963); *France and the Dreyfus Affair* (Blandford, 1966); *An Idea of Europe* (with Richard Hoggart, Chatto & Windus, 1987); and *The Age of Illusion* (with Madeleine Johnson, Thames & Hudson, 1987).

Mairi Maclean is Senior Lecturer in European Business in the School of Management, Royal Holloway, University of London. Her research interests centre on French business and the French political economy. Her publications include *Europeans on Europe: Transnational Visions of a New Continent* (Macmillan, 1992), *French Enterprise and the Challenge of the British Water Industry: Water without Frontiers* (Avebury, 1991), and numerous articles on the French economy.

Lorna Milne is Lecturer in French at the University of St Andrews. Her research interests include the study of myth in modern and contemporary French literature and within the socio-political sphere. Her publications include *L'Evangile selon Michel: la Trinité initiatique dans l'œuvre de Tournier* (Rodopi, 1994) and book contributions on political discourse in France.

Susan Milner is Senior Lecturer in European Studies at the University of Bath. She is the author of *The Dilemmas of Internationalism: French Syndicalism and the International Labour Movement* (Berg, 1990) and has written numerous articles and book contributions on the French labour movement in the twentieth century.

Pamela M. Moores is Lecturer in French in the Department of Languages and European Studies at Aston University. She has researched and published on the nineteenth century novelist, journalist and Communard, Jules Vallès, and on the contemporary French media. Her current research and publications focus on regional and national newspapers, press agencies, media personalities in politics, and the street press.

Peter Morris was Professor of French Politics and History in the Department of Languages and European Studies at Aston University, and Visiting Professor at the Paris Institut d'Etudes Politiques. His many publications include *French Politics Today* (Manchester University Press, 1994).

Catherine Pradeilles is a graduate of the Ecole Normale Supérieure (Ulm) and of the Institut d'Etudes Politiques, Paris, and holds the title of professeur agrégé de Lettres. She has taught in the Universities of Aix-en-Provence and Aston, and has also worked on financial markets for a major French Bank. Her research interests include Renaissance and Classical literature as well as the study of discourse in French politics.

Christophe Texier has taught in universities in Leeds, Warwick and Birmingham on French media and French cinema. He is completing a PhD on the social responsibility of the press in France and Great Britain.

INDEX